God's Magnum Opus?

Searching for a Person, not a Process

Book 1

Apologetics not Apologies

Timothy J Waters

Thank You and Contact Details

- -

My thanks to family members who helped me with this book –
especially my mother Christine Waters, who has proof read the book
with me.

Contact me using the following address:
Email: authortimwaters@gmail.com

This book is available in a variety of formats. You can find all
purchasing and any other details on Amazon.

- - - - - - - - - - - - -

If after reading this book you have found it helpful then please
could you consider doing two things for me?

1) It would be a great help if you could please leave a review of
   this book on Amazon where you purchased it.
2) Would you please consider either passing on this book or
   purchasing another copy for someone else who you think will
   also benefit from reading it?

Note from the author

- -

I once listened to a mathematician give a talk as to why he had been put in charge of a language project. He said that it was his skillset that he had obtained in his area of expertise that was being used by the team that he fronted, not his personal knowledge of language. There were enough professionals around him to keep the integrity of the work at the excellent standard of 'English' that was required in order for the project to succeed. The language experts, however, were in need of his mathematical mind. He could think logically through each step that had to be taken in order to bring about the final 'shape' that the information needed to be presented in at the end of the project; so two disciplines were working together, maths and language, to provide an excellent outcome.

You might say the same about me and the writing of this book. Why is an I.T. person writing about science? Well simply because I have an analytical mind that can clearly present the book's information and arguments, all based on the work of PhD scientists, in a very straightforward manner and in such a format for everyone to be able to understand. I can also use my I.T. background to present arguments when biology crosses over with that of I.T. – that is when I begin to talk in the book about the 'code' of life, which is called DNA. It is here that I can show insights that a biologist will not be able to see; to show that information **cannot** arise all by itself from within the natural world. I will also be able to show what really is happening when DNA mix takes place (the creating of offspring when animals mate). Evolutionary biologists make bold claims that 'new information' is being created when observing various biological mechanisms. Even a basic I.T. programmer, however, will be able to clarify this statement and show that all we're observing is mere '**data expression change**' and not 'new information' at all. So I will bring to the table clarity about evidence, observations and arguments that a biologist will misinterpret or overlook.

I have worked hard to make sure that most of this book is easy for every person to understand. There might be the odd phrase here and there that sounds very alien to you, but if you come across them then don't be put you off reading the rest of the book. At times I will have to dip into 'science terminology' to convey an argument or talk about a process. If at any point you become a little lost amongst the concepts or the rhetoric, don't worry about it. *Just keep on reading* and you'll soon be able to pick up again the threads of thought as the book continues. You don't have to understand the fine details in every part of the book in order for the book to be of great benefit to you.

There's one last thing to say. Throughout this book I reference YouTube videos as sources of information and encourage you to watch them to help you understand the information that I'm talking about. If you've purchased this book as a Kindle digital download then you'll be able to click on each YouTube reference link and it will take you to the video. If you've purchased this book as a paperback, and you still wish to watch the videos, rather than painstakingly typing in the YouTube video addresses into your web browser you can visit my website www.authortimwaters.co.uk and find links to all of the videos there.

- -

Message from the author – the main problem that we face!

- -

I've heard it often said that,

> *"It's hard to know what you're seeing if you don't know what you're looking at."*

That's one of the foundational problems that this book outlines. We're all 'seeing things' as we observe life around us – but what are we actually 'looking at'. If we were to observe two people side by side, one rubbing the left side of his chest and the other slightly bent over and holding his left arm, then what are we looking at? Many would say that both were in some kind of discomfort but wouldn't know what the problem really was. It would take a doctor, however, to properly diagnose what we were all seeing. He could then inform us as to what we were *actually looking at*. He might say that the person rubbing their chest had simple heartburn. He might also say that the person leaning over and holding their left arm was having a heart attack. Heartburn and heart attack are *very different things*. So we're *all seeing the same things*, but **do we know what we're actually looking at**? Making a correct diagnosis is so important; it can be the difference between life and death.

This is one of the essential problems within the science world today. Biologists are really good at biology. They are not so good at 'Information Technology'. This causes us potentially great problems in interpreting the evidence correctly that we observe in the natural world. Let me make a couple of foundational statements that the latter half of the book will demonstrate.

Biology *is subject* to information theory.

Information theory *is not subject* to biology.

This is so important. Information is at the heart of life. It runs the cell – this is something that Darwin had no idea about in his day. This 'living' information (DNA) is at the centre of everything that literally drives the processes that makes life possible. Without information, biology does not work. All life has DNA at its heart. We human beings are the apex of life and we are the most sophisticated information carriers and processors in the known universe. The information storage and information flow through us is too difficult for us to comprehend. Biologists don't know how to handle this. This is because they don't know what they're looking at when they observe information for…

- what it is
- what it reveals when it is at work

…therefore so many of them still think that it's sensible to believe that information can 'evolve' from a dead cosmos all by itself. Such notions are profoundly mistaken, especially when you take into account the **structure** of information, the context of information and the **nature** of information.

The structure of information can only be properly understood when you know the difference between data, code and information. All three are linked but they are not the same. The nature of information is that information has no mass and no mathematical relationship to energy. All of the above dictates to us that information cannot arise by itself from a dead cosmos. So this book, after outlining the theory of evolution and pointing out its flaws, then goes on to tell you **what we are looking at** when we see and observe information at work within the cell. Once this is clarified, we see that evolution is not only improbable, it is absolutely impossible. Many biologists still want to tell us that life evolved. An I.T. person who understands information theory and the limitations of biology will tell you that, as information coding cannot evolve, so therefore the rest of biological life cannot evolve either. One cannot happen without the other. Once we know what we're looking at, then we can clearly understand what we're seeing. Then we can make a proper diagnosis of the activities and behaviours of the biological world that we observe all around us in this amazing thing called 'nature' or 'life'.

- -

Foundational Statement

---

*It is not possible to bring about order,
complexity, interdependent design
and purposeful coding
out of chaos via **random** and
unguided processes.*

Secondary Statement

---

*The forces of raw energy in the natural world
only produce by-products. Within the cell
we see the continuous creation of
precision machines (proteins); crafted,
shaped and **fashioned for purpose** in order to be
living answers to provide solutions to problems
within the body to facilitate its survival.*

Final Statement

---

*Code, that facilitates the **accomplishing of work**,
is the result of **questions asked** and an
answer imaged in the light of a **problem**
that needs to be solved!*

Book Conclusions

1. You cannot evolve information from a dead cosmos.
2. You cannot evolve new information via hereditary exchange (DNA mix), mutation and natural selection.
3. The universe cannot auto-organise and calibrate itself in order to enable life to exist within the confines of a hostile environment.
4. Life is meaningless and contradictory outside the framework of a deity driven universe.

Contents

Preface to the Book

This book started out as a group of connected chapters in a science section within another book. The purpose of that book was to show/illustrate that the movement of secular spirituality that we currently see across Western culture is, in fact, not the all-unifying, all-inclusive philosophy it presents itself to be, to make everyone and everything in society equal, but just another religion that is as narrow in its thinking as any other religion that exists in the world today and, at the same time, is highly exclusive in nature. Once the book has clearly defined secular spirituality as a religion, it then challenges the credibility of secular spirituality ideologically, philosophically and scientifically. To do this a whole section of the book needed to be dedicated to science to prove that the secularist's creation story is false. That is, a series of chapters that together challenged the naturalistic world view that we are all here because of a random 'Big Bang' explosion that just accidently happened without the help and guidance of deity and consequentially was responsible for bringing about the known universe and all that we see around us today.

So that section of the book was written to illustrate that it is **not sensible** to believe that the random and unguided movements of raw energy that we see in the cosmos today, being the results of an unplanned and random 'Big Bang' explosion, could be responsible for and have the ability over time to,

- create
- construct
- organise
- assemble
- and attune

...the materials in the cosmos in such a way so as to,

1) Calibrate the universe for life to exist.
2) Bring life from non-life materials via chemical and then biological evolutionary processes in such a way that would...
   a. Create a cell.

      i.   Auto-organise a cellular environment where purposeful resources are constructed, housed and made ready to interact with each other.

  b. Create and store code.

      i.   Randomly generate data strings, coming together in a precision sequential order, that would together form sensible and intelligent code (DNA) with intent written within the code for work that needed to be done in the body to be achieved.

     ii. Construct and calibrate the environment of the inner cell for the code to be safely housed, stored and accessed.

  c. Match the cell's environment to the code.

      i.   Organise and order the movements of the resources within the cell so as to enable the coding at the heart of the cell to be read, copied, transported and then processed.

     ii. Using the processed code to enable the selection of available resources from within the cell to assemble and construct new machines (proteins) that will complete the work that's needed to be done within the body in order for the body to function properly.

...and so that science section of the book argued that these random and unguided movements of raw energy, that are the direct results of a 'Big Bang' explosion, were **not able** to bring about the order, complexity and interdependent design that we see all around us today in both the calibration of the universe and the microbiological structures in the cell that makes life possible. Life, therefore, cannot just emerge from a dead cosmos on its own.

As I wrote that science section, I found that I had to give more and more time to that area of the book than to any other, simply because I had to clearly and logically undo well over 150 years of wrong information and uninformed thinking. When such 'false news' has been actively poured into a culture over a long period of time, and accepted as fact for much of that time, then it is hard to even start a conversation on the subject without people being highly sceptical and even scornful from the moment they begin to read your arguments. Also, on this particular subject, there are so many historic academic reputations at stake, that even though it is clear that 'the emperor has no clothes', the ill-informed and loyally devoted followers of evolution theory in society still imagine those clothes to be firmly in place and prefers the emperor's stark-nudity to the stark-facts. It would not be the emperor, however, who would do the blushing if our eyes were truly opened. The blushers would be all of those people who had, over the decades, talked and lectured about the amazing clothes that the emperor is said to wear, how fantastic his garments are and how much we can learn from observing them. So to spend your life and career as an evolutionist and then to find out that it is not true after all, well that would be something that's very hard to face and to come to terms with. It would be the equivalent of not just having egg on your face, but a giant sized omelette. It's a very brave person, however, who has the humility and integrity to face the facts, admit that they've been wrong, and then to build their career on truth and not that which they've leaned on for perhaps most of their life.

As the science section in my book grew larger and larger, it was pointed out to me by my father, Rowland Waters, that this body of work was probably a book in its own right. He suggested to me that, after writing it as a separate book, I could just summarise its contents within one chapter of the original book that I was writing and so succinctly make all of the points that I needed to make on the subject. This would also protect those book readers from getting bogged down with lots of new scientific information that they might not be familiar with and potentially cloud their minds with information overload; which might also prevent them from understanding the main arguments of the book about secular spirituality.

Information overload is a bad thing in any book and it is important to remember the initial reasons and goals that caused you to write your book in the first place. So this is the reason why I am writing this science material as a new and separate book in its own right, which has now also become book 1 in this 'Apologetics not Apologies' series. As a book in its own right it serves as a deeper reference point to any who may read my other work on secular spirituality (which will now become book 2 in the series) and who, as a result want to delve more deeply into this particular science subject. It also meets the needs of any readers who also just want to get to grips with seeing how secularists within society today have unwittingly propagated an old and out of date theory that should have been binned decades ago; being kept in place due to either ignorance or a blind commitment to the religious creed that the theory underpins. Whatever your reasons for reading this book, I have written it so that you can see through the secularist's thinking that is presented to society today. So you can clearly see that we cannot be here without God, that science clearly makes the case for this, not just as a theory, but overwhelmingly so when we look at the facts.

Introduction

Does the Humanist's creation story stand up to scientific Investigation? This is the question that drives this book. Throughout much of it I am standing on the shoulders of different PhD scientists who have dared to ask this question. Is evolution theory really true or have we had the wool pulled over our eyes by a clever but deceptive rhetoric that makes unscientific assumptions sound reasonable? Each of the people that I quote in this book has gone on their own journey of discovery and come to the realisation that the foundational assumptions that they'd been given from childhood by Western education institutions was fundamentally wrong. In the book I have often either summarised parts of their work or taken the main insights that they've presented in their work and used them to create specific arguments. Then, due to spending nearly 25 years in the I.T. industry, I've taken my knowledge of programming and the I.T. world and looked at the hereditary DNA exchange argument, along with mutation and natural selection, and illustrated that all we see as the result of this process is *data expression change* within the code itself (which causes sideways adaptation movements within a species) and not the generation of new information that evolutionists believe, by faith, causes an upwards evolutionary development – by which all creatures are said to have evolved over millions of years from a lower life form into a higher one; which eventually led to all creatures existing in the form that they are in today.

To achieve the above I have laid out the information as clearly as I can from chapter to chapter, defining and developing the concepts in the most straightforward and simplest way possible. In order to keep the information flowing from page to page and so that we don't get stuck in too many examples that illustrate what I'm trying to say, I will sometimes put the fuller details of the examples that I mention into the appendix and just reference them from within the main body of text. If I'm covering something that is of great interest to you, therefore, you can quickly visit the appendix to find out more. Otherwise you can keep on reading at a good pace through the rest of the book.

SECTION 1

General Objections to the Humanist Creation Story

The misuse of terminology.
The misinterpretation of the evidence.

Chapters 1-5

- starting off on the wrong foot...
- criticisms of evolutionary theory
- false arguments from a false perspective
- how the cell works and how it is impossibly complex
- the impossibility of life starting by itself

Chapter 1 – Getting Started

Who Owns Science?

Science is Secular?

For a long time now humanism has laid claim to science. It has made the claim that science affirms and supports the secularist's world view. Secularists claim that the cosmos randomly appeared, all by itself, by chance via a 'Big Bang' explosion. Then, after appearing via this 'Big Bang' explosion, it then slowly evolved into its current state by the *natural observable processes* that we see around us in the cosmos today – and all this without the help of deity. So if you were to ask the following questions,

Why is everything in the universe here today?
Why is it all in the form and shape that it is in today?
What accounts for the intricate complexities of life that we see around us in the universe today?

The answer will always be that everything we see and observe around us is here because of a set of *natural processes*. These processes are *natural events* that take place within the cosmos itself. They happen as the cosmos continues to expand from an original 'Big Bang' explosion that kick-started everything.

So here's a quick summary of the secularists scientific world view,

- the cosmos started itself off via a random 'Big Bang' explosion
- from this explosion all physical matter came into existence
- as the cosmos expanded, the repercussions of the 'Big Bang' explosion continually expressed themselves as random and unguided movements of raw energy moving throughout the universe
- these random and unguided movements of energy within the universe caused all non-living matter to interact with itself – continually 'bumping into itself' over billions of years

3

- these 'bumps' and 'collisions' of non-living matter (called natural processes/chemical reactions) caused **actions** and **reactions** within the universe that...
  - provided the circumstances for life to exist
  - enabled life to come from non-life
- all of this took place over billions of years
- we can see and observe these same forces and processes at work within the universe today
- by observing these same forces within the universe we can...
  - see/illustrate/show how these natural processes caused everything to be in its current form
  - trace back, by recording a step-by-step process, the self-assembly of each item in the universe...
    - showing how each part, each component, came together as a result of the 'bumps' and 'collisions' of non-living matter
    - showing how each component within the universe, created by these random and unguided movements of energy, can be traced back to a single 'Big Bang' explosion

Initial Conclusions

So secularists confidently conclude,

1. We can explain all of our existence by using science and reduce all we see around us to natural processes.
2. We don't need deity to explain our existence.
3. Explosions can create things of incredible complexity.

Another statement we could make is this,

If it exists within the universe, then it got here by itself, via self-assembly – energised by the raw energy in the universe that caused non-living matter to 'bump' into itself, via the actions of motion and chemical reaction.

So the cosmos started itself off and, by natural processes within itself, evolved everything within it into its current state. Everything is accountable for and is explainable by a set of processes that we can still see at work today within the cosmos and natural world. All we have to do is to trace them backwards to the random 'Big Bang' that started it all off; if it's here then we can show you **how it got here** via a process of energy movements, caused by a 'Big Bang' explosion.

The Only Viable Theory?

Secularists also argue that this is also the only viable world view that has scientific plausibility when compared to the other creation stories of theism - Christianity, Judaism, Islam, Hinduism, etc. These latter creation stories are meant to be immature and 'out of date' in their understanding of the universe in the light of 'modern science'. The theistic 'revelatory world outlook' that makes sense of life and the world in which we live (God being the creator) is declared to be at odds with scientific investigation and the laws of the universe. We no longer 'need God' to help us explain where everything came from and how we all 'got here'.

Sadly most people in the Western world today still currently hold to this mistaken viewpoint. It is again, just one example, of modern mass misinformation. You wouldn't think it by watching our TV screens, but in the last half century science has swung greatly in favour of the theistic world outlook and away from the world view of the humanist. Most people today are not aware of this because the decision makers, those who have the power and influence to decide what goes on our TV screens or what is taught in our schools, are humanist in their allegiances. You won't see today, for example on the BBC, any programmes that systematically undermine and overtly highlight the weaknesses of the secular world view. The BBC would not do that because it has a very strong humanist emphasis. It might still show *religious programmes of interest*, but it would not broadcast any programme that systematically undermined the theory of evolution or that challenged the basic spiritual assumptions of secular spirituality.

Ideologically, philosophically, scientifically and theologically, however, there are fires breaking out all over the secular camp that reveal the holes in their thinking and assertions. It is also very

5

interesting to observe on the internet how the secularists are responding to them. Each of these individual fires is a witness in science that there is a God and that without this God we cannot be here. What the humanists are doing in response to this is focussing on one problem at a time, as if it was an 'isolated incident' or as if that particular fire is the 'only fire out there' that needs dealing with. The reality is, however, that they are surrounded by fires, which they are desperately trying to put out, and when you put all the fires together, then you get one great big burning blaze.

So in this book is I'm going to show that science does not belong to the humanist but to the theist by listing just some of the fires that the humanists are now trying to extinguish. I'm going to pull together those few fires that I mention and therefore give you a taster, a glimpse of the inferno that's really there. That inferno is now so hot and established that, no matter how much water you have and try to pour on it, you will never be able to douse and snuff it out. I cannot even begin to do justice in this book to the evidence for God that is now in the science world, because there is too much information to cover on the subject; that is on the intricate, multi-complex and interdependent processes contained within life that all fit together and only come together by the intervention and work of a person who is a designer, not by a random and unguided process which is the result of raw energy moving within the cosmos.

Life's Interdependency

Life in all its multi-complex interdependency has to suddenly 'be here' via a non-evolutionary route, in order for its interdependency to work. A car has to be assembled over a short period of time in a factory because its parts are interdependent. You cannot start off with a car seat or a single wheel and expect it to take you from A to B on a map. It comes as a single package, all together, preassembled and in its final state. You could fill books and books and more with the interdependent technological relationships within life. For example, if I were to pick out a random illustration, I could mention the way in which a baby in the womb makes its own blood – being dependent on a single protein called transthyretin to make the process possible. Without this protein in place, life is over for everyone. Here is a short overview of the problem (I will revisit this example again in greater detail later on in this book).

6

A baby has to make its own blood and cannot use the mother's blood for its own, or it will die. To make its own blood it needs iron. The source of iron that it uses to make its own blood comes from its mother's blood. The placenta is a natural barrier that supplies the baby with all that it needs to feed and grow and it also protects the baby from the mother's blood. The placenta, however, is also a problem to the baby. Iron does not pass through the placenta. It has to fetch iron from the mother's blood and this placenta is a natural barrier to it. The only way in which this can happen is by a protein, created by the DNA with the human body, called transthyretin. Transthyretin has the ability to go across the placenta, grab haemoglobin, which contains iron, and take it back to the baby to enable it to create its own blood.

So for a baby to safely make its own blood it needs the following in place,

- a placenta to keep it safe from the mother's blood
- the programming in DNA to create the transthyretin protein
- a working transthyretin protein that is programmed to fetch and retrieve the haemoglobin which contains iron

This 'baby making its own blood' illustration is just one example of integrated dependency. There is a high cost if the whole process is not all in place **at the same time**, i.e. the baby dies. There is no future life for the next generation.

The above simplified list is incredible. The placenta feeds and sustains the baby, but the mother's blood must not mix with the baby's blood or the baby can die, so the baby is kept safe via the placental barrier. The protein transthyretin comes to the rescue, but this protein has to be in place and ready for use along with the rest of the life sustaining package that the growing baby finds itself in. It is an amazing interdependent relationship that cannot be evolved via a step-by-step process over millions of years.

The Gap and Unanswered Questions

This is just one of the many problems that humanists skip over and pretend is not there (or is completely unaware of because these issues are not generally broadcast or taught). This 'gap' in the general populace's knowledge allows humanists to still maintain that the interdependent, precision-designed machines that we all are, came about via a random and unguided step-by-step self-assembly process. Theory upon theory is put forward as humanists imagine and reimagine this bit and that bit of 'the evolutionary process' and somehow the multitude of imagined theories, along with the general acceptance of the word 'mutation' or the phrase 'it evolved', means that we can accept it all as if it were an almost given fact. The evolutionary theories do not, however, look at the whole machine in front of us and say, "If this multi-complex organism came about by chance then…"

1. Which component came first?
2. Why was this first component retained so that **in itself** and **of itself** it *worked* *in some way* and gave an advantage for the creature/organism to survive?
3. What caused the second component to be made?
4. Why was the second component added to the first?
5. Why was this second component retained so that **in itself** and **of itself** (alongside the first component) it *worked* *in some way* and so gave an advantage for the creature/organism to survive?
6. How were all the other bits created and how was each one *guided by a random process* to **fit** into the equation so that the machine was beneficially working in some way before it was completely finished?
7. How did random and unguided 'copy errors' in DNA produce the fine-tuned code to create each component – when observable copy errors are always neutral or not beneficiary in nature?
8. From where did the other bits of code that joined together the other components within the organism come?
9. How did 'copy error' in the DNA know when to stop evolving so that there was a complete and sensible final

set of instructions for the machine's assembly, so that the code's final state is in the refined form that we see now?

10. Who fine-tuned these precision commands to form such perfectly engineered technology? Like flight in insects and birds for example, where the technology for getting up into the air and staying up there requires precision coding and calculation to,

- o form the correct wing structure
- o supply energy to the wing
- o provide the right type of movement in the wing to get the creature off the ground, etc.

In fact there are so many unanswered and unanswerable questions that it's amazing to see how far evolution has come without the general populace seeing through it.

We Just Don't Go There

The continued solution to these problems has been very simple, we just *don't go there* in our TV programmes, in our books and in the school classrooms. We don't talk about intricate relationships that are non-reducible and just focus on the bits that we can talk about, from which we **choose to interpret life** in a certain way. For example, when we do talk about what is called 'cooperation' (two parts of life being dependent on each other) then we'll do it at a very simple microbiological level and we'll keep our explanation at that level. This is done so that the explanation is kept in an overtly simplified form, like throwing two pieces of a jigsaw puzzle together (where the whole jigsaw is only made up of two pieces) and saying "Look, here's an example of evolutionary cooperation taking place. We can see how two microbes have collided with each other, one has gone inside the other, and now both work together as a unit." It's all very well seeing how something so *'simple'* can collide and still work, like a child blowing bubbles and seeing them hit each other to form a larger bubble. It's a completely different matter, however, when you take a 5,000 piece jigsaw puzzle and say, let's randomly throw these onto the table and see how they auto-organise into a recognisable multi-dependent picture where each piece complements the other to form a beautiful countryside scene. Each living cell in the body (or the human body as a whole) is complex beyond our imagination and no-one can even begin to find a sensible route for its development. The question has to be put, therefore, as to why this obvious problem (the problem of multiple components forming interdependent relationships to make the body work) *is not highlighted and seen by more people?*

- -
The World View Question
- -

Your Agenda

In order to answer the above question we have to understand that when we look at any scientific enquiry that specifically asks about our origins, how the universe (and all that is in it) got here, then it is specifically **a world view** that *drives* and *guides* our thinking, not the neutral scientific method as is often cited. A humanist may well not agree with this statement at all. It is true, however, and is a fact from which we must not hide. World views drive science, not the other way round. The boast of science is that the **scientific method** is *neutral*; you look, you observe, you hypothesise, you test, you record results and from those results you bring about logical conclusions, but this is not the point. It is *your* approach and *your* assumptions behind the approach that **colours everything**.

What are you looking for and *why* are you looking for it?

This is the question! Here are some more.

1. What bias do you bring to the table when looking for evidence in the first place?
2. What are you setting out to prove?
3. What assumptions have you already made in your decision to set up the experiment in the first place?

These should be the real questions that we ask. No-one just sits and looks with nothing but a blank space in their minds to guide their 'looking' and thinking. You look at something for a purpose, for a reason. You look because you've already **asked a question** that will cause you to look and to seek specific answers. Those answers will specifically be related to the question that you have already asked.

*If the question or the reason for asking the question **carries a bias at its heart**, then the answer will also **contain that bias**.*

The question asked is the *motivation* behind the looking. That motivation is everything. You will **want** to prove something; therefore you look down a certain line of enquiry to see if you can find evidence for that which…

…*you **want** to prove!*

This doesn't mean that your results will always be predictable or that you cannot be surprised by your experiment's results. On many occasions unpredictable data has opened doors for new scientific discoveries. However, when it comes to the origins of the universe it is the motivation, which you unwittingly carry with you at all times, that ensures that there is always a **world view** question behind life that drives and guides you in your thinking and in the conclusions that you reach. It **colours** how you interpret all that is happening in the natural world, whether you're using the scientific process or not. Your **world view** assumptions tell you 'how to go about looking' and 'what to lookout for' in order for you to find the '**true evidence**' that *proves your world view* i.e. answers your bias. So what is that world view that you and I continually adhere to? Well, here I'm going to very briefly outline the clash that exists between the basic foundational assumptions of theists and of atheists. I'm not going to spend too much time on this, as it will all be outlined in book 2 in this series that I'm currently writing in 2019, but here's a snapshot of the disagreement.

The basic foundational assumptions of theism are that,
- the spiritual world has substance of its own
- the spiritual world existed before the physical world
- the spiritual world is the cause of the physical world
- all things in the physical world ***point back to the divine***

The basic foundational assumptions of atheism (humanism) are that,
- the spiritual world has no substance of its own

- the spiritual world is just 'personal belief' originating from the physical world (humans choosing to believe)
- the physical world has no spiritual cause
- all things in the physical world point back to **just a process** without the divine

So a theist or an atheist will propose theories according to their world view convictions. The world view conviction of an atheist is that there is **just a mere process** by which everything came into being and therefore...

...all we need to look for...

...is **a process** to describe the **existence of everything**. To look only for a process to be the only reason for us to be here, not taking in to account anything else, is seen as genuine science. So the initial question of enquiry asked by an atheist, which contains the bias that an atheist therefore brings to the table, is this:

What are the natural *processes* that caused that which I am currently observing to be in the form that it is currently in?

These 'process seeking' theories (which form the basis of an atheist's thinking) will direct their line of scientific enquiry and the conclusions reached. This line of enquiry is always to seek to verify that *a process* is **the only possible solution** to the problem of our existence. To an atheist true science is only done when 'God is not included' as an option in the scientific process. This is because of the basic 'gut conviction' that the atheist has that 'there is no God!' It is sensible, to the atheist, to believe that we can be here without God. All things come from random processes which in turn came from a random and unplanned 'Big Bang'. By seeking to verify any theory formed by this type of thinking the scientist is, therefore, adhering to his/her world view that caused him/her to ask the question in the first place. This is most often done without anyone being aware of it. Not understanding that you have already, unwittingly, answered the foundational questions of life by the world view you follow, and that these questions bias you in your thinking and observations, means that you have not understood yourself and the exclusive context...

...*that you carry with you* at all times.

So we're all seeing the same evidence before our eyes. However, the diagnosis of *what we are looking at* is always influenced by a world view.

World View Illustration – the meaning of common DNA

Here's an example of this world view influence. Later on in this book we'll look at DNA – which is the code of life. DNA is the storing of genetic information inside the cell. It is a fact that there is a lot of shared information between the different life forms on earth. We humans share over 50% of our DNA with the plant world. We share over 80% of DNA with cows. We share over 60% DNA with bananas. These facts need interpreting! So all of life on this planet is 'linked together' via DNA – we all have it. **What are we looking at** when we observe this? What is the nature of that link? That's the question.

What does this linkage mean?

How are we to interpret this shared DNA code? To an **atheist** it will be the following,

- we all share the same code
- this **compels** us to assume that **we are all linked** via **shared ancestry**
- the code of life evolved over billions of years
- life began as a single cell organism and now we are as we are due to a **growth in the information** in that cell which has developed and changed over time

Richard Dawkins expresses this assumption in a short YouTube video https://www.youtube.com/watch?v=A0ZLJP9Zc9U where he says, "The DNA code of all creatures that have ever been looked at is all but identical and surely that means that they're all related, doesn't it?" As an atheist, his world view is that we don't need God to justify our existence and therefore the sensible conclusion, from the given evidence, is to say that we share this DNA code from an evolutionary process.

> **NOTE:** By the way, when he says that DNA is all but identical, that statement is an over-simplification of DNA. It is an example of the many **careless statements** often made by scientists within their world view framework. In what way are they 'all but identical'? Is he talking about the structure of the DNA or the code within the DNA? Such **sloppy statements** can be very misleading, as we will see later on in this book.

To a **theist** the **same evidence** will mean the following,

- information (precision data that is constructed into meaningful code) cannot arise by itself from a dead cosmos via random and unguided movements of energy
- a designer (deity) therefore used a sophisticated and complicated code to construct and hold life together
- a designer will not need to reinvent a totally new code for each creature type but will use the same *operating system* for each device/creature type that will hold the code
- a designer knows that for a human to eat a banana, or a cow, that the object that a human eats has to share a strong DNA similarity to ourselves in order for us to digest and absorb the food into ourselves, make it a part of ourselves – (humans don't eat rocks for sustenance)
- seeing that such a complex code is in everything (the DNA in a bacteria cell is too complicated for a human being to write) and that **complex code cannot randomly evolve**, this tells us that there is a super intelligence behind all life in the universe

The world view of the theist enables a very different interpretation from that of the atheist when **looking at the same facts**. *The world view dictates not only the initial question but also the conclusion.*

It sets the framework for the interpretation of the evidence that makes up life.

So an atheist, for example, will **not** set out to find the *fingerprints of God* on the cosmos as a theist will. His/her whole thinking will be focussed on *natural mechanisms* that do not require a creator. If evidence for the creator is found, ***that evidence will be reinterpreted*** to fit a naturalistic belief. That is…

*…a **process** that explains the facts rather than a **person** who explains the facts.*

To even begin to think in a direction that interprets the evidence that sits before us from a theistic framework would be anathema to an atheist. All the thinking and the theorising of an atheist will be towards a non-theistic process of events. You will see in this book that I show that some atheists will entertain almost anything in science, except that there is a God behind it all. This is what it is to be part of the,

"Anything but God Society"

…and this reasoning colours and taints the scientific method.

So there are no theistic assumptions behind the type of questions that an atheist will ask when searching for scientific evidence. If you're looking for *evidence*, then you're looking for the *evidence* that supports your *world view*. Why would you even begin to look for evidence for something that you don't believe in and you're not looking for? This is how the human mind works.

*So any evidence that points to God's handiwork in the cosmos would be unwittingly overlooked or reinterpreted in a different way because it **does not even begin to form part of the framework of enquiry** that the atheist is using by which to interpret the facts via the scientific method.*

Everyone has a world view **agenda** and we need to recognise this every time we pick up a book or read a paper or watch a video. This agenda is carried into all aspects of life, including science. It is also expressed in the questions that are asked, even before the scientific process is begun. If you want to read more on this subject of how a world view affects our thinking then visit the Appendix A at the back of the book.

> **NOTE:** This world view agenda dictates that a theist will always be more broad minded than an atheist. The theist looks for two things, a process and a person. An atheist looks for one thing, a process. A theist will not miss a process (as s/he is already looking for one) but an atheist will miss a person (because s/he is not looking for one). The atheist has fewer options to work with and is therefore narrow minded in his/her interpretations from the outset. The most important question, the most important reference point in life, has **already been left out** – that of, "Is there a God?"

- -
My Focus
- -

Witnesses for Evolution, Information Creation and Universe Calibration

So, in the light of the above, there are three things that I'm going to concentrate on.

- the mechanisms by which evolution is said to have happened and the evidences that are presented to support those mechanisms
- the mechanisms that the secularists provide as evidence for
    - the spontaneous beginning of life
    - and the so called self-powered auto-arranging processes via which life is supposed to have developed into a complex cellular structure with **information** at its heart
- the notion that the universe could calibrate itself so that life can exist via a haphazard 'Big Bang'

In order to do this sensibly and carefully, I'm going to make reference to the writings and works of many qualified and educated scientists, who have presented their materials over the decades. References will be made to books, lectures and interviews. You can find all kinds of lectures and short teachings about science and evolution in the book world, on DVDs and now finally on the internet, especially on YouTube; in fact YouTube has opened up the academic world and put the knowledge 'out there' for anyone to access, that is anyone who puts in the time to dig it out and process it themselves.

> **NOTE:** Where I have summarised or quoted an online interview or lecture, I shall give the web address that links to it for your reference so that you can watch it too, and any other videos that are associated with it. That way you can further your own education by seeing the large variety of voices that are out there, all of them often saying the same things or touching on the same subject matter, even if it is from different perspectives.

The Witnesses for God

From these many sources I'm going to show how the whole variety and complexity of life together form one corporate witness that there is a God. I'm going to show how it is impossible for us to be here without the workings of the divine. I'm going to use different aspects of science to do this, from looking at calibration in the physical world so that we can physically survive in the cosmos to looking at the irreducible technology that runs life. I shall look at information theory and the way in which information is created in the computer world to show how information needs to be processed. This is because we humans are the most complicated information carriers and processors in the universe, not just in the cell but in the brain, and our technology is stunning, though we have to look first into the computer world to see this clearly.

I'm going to systematically dismantle the theory of evolution, first by looking at it as it currently stands, but mainly from the perspective of information. Information cannot arise from the natural world via chemical or biological evolution. Most evolutionists think it can. That's because they're biologists and not informed by the I.T. industry. Through their extreme naivety they confuse data with information.

17

Data is not information and thinking that it is, is a huge mistake. So one of the questions that I will later ask is,

What's the difference between data, code and information?

This is just one of the questions that will change everything once you understand the answer to it and it's far reaching implications. Evolutionists may attempt at forming data by chance within the cosmos (which is still actually impossible) but you cannot create information. It's not that the odds are against information arising by chance naturally from the cosmos; it's that it is simply impossible. This will be one of the climaxes of my arguments against the evolutionary theory.

One last thing to say on my focus is that I will quote from a variety of scientists and commentators, many of whom may not agree with each other on some aspects of science, **especially the age of the universe**. My interest is <u>not how old the universe is</u>, my focus is on presenting evidence that shows that it is impossible for the universe to auto-organise itself into its current complex form. You may agree or disagree, therefore, with some of the work of some of the scientists that I quote from, *that's not my interest*. My interest is to gather evidence from any source that I can, where the facts have been presented in a clear manner, to show that we cannot be in our current complex state without the divine. This sums up both the focus and the limitations that I have placed on this book.

- -
Four Specific Language Problems
- -

The next things to briefly highlight are four specific, interconnected language problems that are often expressed in the science world today. The confusion lies in the incorrect categorisations that are applied to events and objects within the theoretical talk on the subject of our origins and the subsequent careless labelling that takes place. This in turn hides the problems within evolutionary theory. These categorisation problems are expressed in,

1) The difference between **UPWARDS** evolution and **sideways** adaptation.
2) The difference between data expression **change** and **new** information.
3) The difference between **data** and **information**.
4) The word 'evolution' being applied to real processes of evolutionary change (where there are real mechanisms for UPWARDS change) and also to non-evolutionary change (without the correct mechanisms) as if they are the same thing.

1st Language Problem:
UPWARDS evolution and sideways adaptation

When talking to evolutionists one of the most difficult things to deal with is their refusal to make a distinction between sideways adaptation and UPWARDS evolution. Sideways adaptive changes take place within the DNA coding of a creature all the time. When any offspring are produced in the plant, insect or animal kingdoms there is a mixing of the parent's DNA. This DNA mix will cause variants within the bodies of the offspring. Over time this will lead to finely tuned family traits which are always **expressed within the confines** of the original plant's / insect's / animal's body parts from which the offspring came. Eventually, due to isolation within the environment, these separated sets of offspring move sideways so that, when their communities meet each other again, they can no-longer mate and produce generational offspring outside of their immediate group. When this happens evolutionists call this sideways progression a *new species*. It only happens, as I have said, once these creatures have moved far enough apart that they can no longer mate and produce multi-generational offspring. We see this process happening all around us today. This sideways adaptation is a proven fact that has been noted for thousands of years. Our problem is that this classification of a '*new species*' is presented also as **direct evidence** for the **totally unproven** UPWARDS evolutionary movements that the evolutionists imagine has taken place in the past where one creature is meant to have **moved** UPWARDS **into another type of creature** – to change its flesh type, its body parts, its body temperature, its technology that makes it work and its mentality and inbuilt behaviours (birds go 'cheap, cheap' in the morning and frogs go 'croak, croak, at night). There is no distinction in the evolutionist's

19

vocabulary about these two separate events. So a proven event, a sideways change, is labelled as a *new species* and this same term is used to convey something is that is only theoretical, the evolutionary **UPWARDS** movement from a frog to a lizard to a bird. The language used to talk about these separate events, however, references them both as *new species* as if one is just as true as the other; more on this subject later on in the book.

2nd Language Problem:
No Distinction between Data Expression Change and New Information

This 2nd language problem is about how to define the changes that we've just been describing (sideways adaptation rather than UPWARDS evolution) but expressed at the microbiological level. It's amazing to see how proven DNA adaptation changes that take place by DNA mix (creatures mating and having offspring) which can change the length of dog hair in the dog family for example, are presented as direct evidences for **new information** within the DNA code. New information would be needed for UPWARDS evolutionary change to happen. A dog's offspring changing its hair length via breeding, however, is a sideways change that takes place by **tinkering with the DNA coding** that is *already in the animal*. Tinkering with current code is not evidence for the development of new coded information. However, this code tinkering that we see happening all of the time is talked about **as if it was new information** and is used as direct proof to show that new information can be added to a creature. However, the notion of a frog evolving over millions of years firstly into a lizard and then into a bird represents, at the microbiological level, not a data expression change (a tinkering with current code) but a complete re-writing of the DNA code. There are no mechanisms, however, within the bodies of any creature to do this level of work. We will look more at this later on in the book.

3rd Language Problem:
No Distinction between Data and Information

Information *is* made up from data but **data is certainly not information**! Data is useless but coded information is useful. If this doesn't make any sense to you then you'll have to wait to get to that part of the book. It is essential, however, that we understand this because life is driven by coded information, not by mere data. When talking about the origins of life and the development of life, all evolutionists can do is an attempt at data creation when:

1) Trying to create life from non-life via unguided random processes.

2) Trying to generate new information to evolve a creature UPWARDS from one kind of creature into another.

The raw energy movements found within the natural world, however, do not produce data, let alone information; in fact they do nothing except remove information. Information produces products that are created and crafted for purpose; the forces of raw energy found in the natural world only produce by-products which are not fashioned for purpose. Evolutionists, however, talk about information creation when in fact they're attempting to describe data creation. We'll pick up on this topic in a later chapter.

4th Language Problem:
Confusion via the Misapplication of the word Evolution

The original word 'evolution' is only true when it is applied to processes that have specific mechanisms and drivers in place that **enable complexity increase** to happen. If the correct mechanisms are there, then UPWARDS evolutionary technological change will take place. It can used, for example, to describe persistent mechanical advances where humanity works hard to evolve a product over time, such as a car or jet engine. The mechanisms for this type of evolutionary advancement are the human minds who are continually working to push the product forward with their ideas and ingenuity. As the engineers develop their thoughts, translating them into sketches and blueprints, so slowly the product evolves over time. Newly designed components are purposefully added and the product becomes equipped with extra advanced technology. This usage of the term '*it evolved*', therefore, is a correct application of the word evolution.

However, the word 'evolution' is now being applied in our general conversations to many different aspects of life that do not show technological increase. For example it is often used to describe the slow change that takes place within a culture's belief system or its moral base; we are evolving as a culture. It can now also be used to describe the development of a musician's composition style over the course of their career or the changes in an artist's work as their artistic expression grows with the passing of each decade. In fact the word 'evolution' is now readily applied left, right and centre to any situation in the world where **change of some kind** is observable. So we have true and false applications of the word and this continual correct and incorrect usage gives it general credibility where it is not due. The problem is that most people assume that, just because some of the ways in which it is used are correct, that all misuses of the word to describe change are also correct.

There are consequences to this. The first is that when the word 'evolve' is used people no longer automatically **look for the correct mechanisms and drivers for change** to be in place in order to ensure that the word is being applied accurately in the conversation. The follow on from this is that the meaning of the word 'evolution', has changed from not only meaning **complexity advancement** but to mean 'simple change' – whether that change is real technological advancement or devolutionary in nature or static, i.e. changes that happen that just look slightly different from the original but do not contain any technological advancement. So today all a person means by the word 'evolution' is that something is changing in some way. If change can be observed then that change is said to be evolution in action. To change, therefore, automatically means to evolve. Its usage has, therefore, become sloppy and clumsy and the frequency of its use means that people no longer recognise this misapplication.

The next consequence is that evolution in the mind of the average person 'happens all the time'. Evolution is all around us. Everything evolves and therefore evolution has **become a fact** that we can all see. Therefore biological evolution, along with everything else that *evolves*, is just assumed to be **a proven fact** – as one person tried to tell me years ago.

The final consequence is that biological evolution is given credibility where it is not due. Biological evolution can only be real if the mechanisms and drivers for change within it have the capacity for UPWARDS technological increase at a cellular level. If there is no increase in information within the DNA code that will cause a new technological body part to be produced then any change that can be observed within the biological world is **only adaptation**, rather than evolution. So when change is observed within the body of any living creature the phrase 'it is evolving' is slapped onto that observable change without any thought as to whether it is true or not.

> **NOTE:** You will see for example that today many people are talking about the 'evolution of the elephant'. It is said to be taking place right in front of our eyes. This is due to the fact that, even though only one third of female elephants are born without tusks (and therefore the majority of elephants are born with tusks and still have 'tusk DNA' within them) poachers specifically target and kill female elephants that have tusks. So the minority of females who are born without tusks now have a greater chance of having more offspring over their lifetime than those with tusks. As a result of this we are therefore **seeing an increase** in elephants without tusks. This change is now branded as 'evolution'. In fact, it is actually **devolution**. We are observing *a systematic loss of information* from within the elephant population. In the long run we may end up with a devolved creature without tusks, leading, for example, to the loss of the ability for the elephants to effectively defend themselves against predators such as lions.

We are surrounded by continuous change, some of which is technological and some is not. All change, however, is now being labelled as 'evolution'. This has brought about a false meaning of the original word – which should mean technological increase. We do see change in the biological world. To simply label that biological change as 'evolution' just because we talk about the 'evolution of society' or the 'evolution of the music or fashion industries' or any other part of life, is a misapplication of the word.

> *Labelling biological change 'evolution' mixes fact and theory together as if they were equally the same.*

The theory of biological evolution is not about change, like the evolution of an artist's colour pallet as the person goes through their 'blue phase' or their 'green phase' etc. Biological evolution is all about **technological advancement**, in the same way that a car engine has evolved over the decades under the guidance of intelligent and qualified engineers – as Hyundai's latest advert says, "Progress doesn't happen by chance." Biological evolution, however, **is still an unproven theory**. To group biological evolution together with every other usage of the word and to talk about them as if they are just as true as the other *just because* **'change happens'** is a misrepresentation of reality. To say that '*everything changes therefore everything evolves*' is a mistake.

The fact that a car engine can evolve over time due to intelligent engineers developing it and the theory that all life has evolved from one single cell, all by itself without intelligence to drive it forward, are two completely different things. The car engine evolving over time is a fact, the idea that biological life can evolve over millions of years from one species of creature into a completely different one via random and unguided processes is still just a theory. They are not the same, yet they are talked about as if they are the same. We will look at this in more detail towards the end of the book.

These four language problems hinder our ability to understand and weigh up the theory of evolution. So each of these will have to be tackled again as I present the general evidence against evolution throughout the rest of this book. Without a correct understanding of these errors, it is very difficult to see how the theory misleads those who still adhere to it today.

- -
Mechanism and Evidence
- -

The Two Drivers towards a Fact
The next thing to say before we dive into science is that true science itself is driven by fact and not theory. A theory may come first, and a theory is something to consider, but unless it becomes a fact it will not, or should not, stand. A theory has to point towards a fact, and must in some way move towards fact over time with gathering evidence, or it is not viable. We must also remember, however, that all sensible science is driven by two things, a mechanism and evidence.

The normal way of doing things is to observe something, or that which can be envisioned based on observed evidence, and then we look for the **mechanism** which **brought about** that which can be seen. This is so that we can,

- find out how that which we are observing got into its current state
- make sure that we have properly understood the current state of that which we're observing and not misinterpreted it in some way

So, for example, if I observe a magnet pulling a piece of metal towards it, I have observable evidence in front of my eyes that something has happened. A piece of metal has moved and attached itself to another piece of metal. Now I need to find out the **mechanism** by which that **happened**. If I then think that the mechanism is that magnets have an invisible vacuum around them, then the mechanism I have created in my head (a theory) is wrong. I could test this theory by putting lots of other small *non-metal* objects within close proximity to a magnet and they would remain stationary. Therefore the theory and its invisible vacuum **mechanism** is proved to be wrong. If, however, I discover that a magnet is internally north/south aligned at the atomic level and this produces around the magnet invisible lines of force which attract other metals, then the **mechanism** by which metal objects are **pulled** towards the magnet is discovered. You can see those lines of force by simply putting a piece of paper on top of the magnet, scattering iron filings on top of the paper and then tapping the edge of the paper with your finger a couple of times. The tapping on the paper will cause all the iron filings to jump into the air, land on the lines of force and reveal their location. You can repeat this experiment over and over again and it will always come up with the same results. Why? Well, simply because the **mechanism**, that is the lines of force that drag a metal object onto the side of a magnet, is a testable and proven fact.

If the mechanism cannot be established as true, then we are forced to reinterpret the evidence in a different light and we need to reassess our conclusions about that which we are observing. This works at all levels in the world and the universe, from that which can be observed through a telescope or a microscope.

Mechanism Example – Sockets in a Skyscraper

A.E. Wilder Smith says very much the same thing in his book, "The Natural Sciences Know Nothing of Evolution." Here he gives the illustration of a skyscraper. He says that you can check to see if each of the plug sockets in each room has an electric supply to it by going to each socket and testing it or you can go down into the basement where the mains power supply comes into the building and see if the power supply is dead or not. If the mains power supply to the building is dead, then all the plug sockets in all the rooms will also be dead. All of the sockets are completely dependent on the power supply, which is the **mechanism** to supply electricity to the building. Turn it off and everything else follows. This way of looking at the viability of a mechanism works too with the theory of evolution, the idea that life spontaneously came about from non-living matter; so too with the theory that everything came from a haphazard 'Big Bang' at the start of the universe. If the basic **mechanisms** that are meant to bring about valid change and evolutionary development do not work, then the whole theory falls over. The mechanism is all about the **'how'** question. "If we're here by accident then **how** did that which I am looking at come about by a step-by-step traceable process?"

*If the mechanism that you initially imagine in your head (the theory of **how** it happened) is incorrect, then you have to drop it and begin again.*

So let me say that again. A sensible question to ask would be to say,

"How do all these plug-sockets in a skyscraper get electricity to them?"

The answer is,

"They get their electricity from the mains supply which centrally feeds them all."

If the mains supply is proved to be faulty, then you will not get anything from the sockets no matter how many sockets you test. You can test socket upon socket upon socket. You can talk about this socket and that socket as much as you like. You can photograph the sockets, sketch them, lecture on them and write books about them.

None of those things will make any difference; if the mechanism is dead, so too are all things that come from that mechanism. The mechanism, therefore, **is everything**.

You cannot fudge your way through a theory by saying, "Well I can see **some things** that *suggest* that my theory is true," if in fact your mechanism, that is meant to make the theory workable, is proved to be false.

'Other evidences' that complement the theory do not compensate for a faulty mechanism.

If the mechanism is false then your interpretation of that which you're seeing is also false too. So you will have to change your interpretation on what you are seeing and how it got there. A new mechanism is needed and new tests need to be done to validate whether the newly imagined mechanism is true or not.

For example, if evolution does not work at the microbiological level, i.e. if there is no **mechanism** via a combination of DNA mix, mutation and natural selection that will produce new information within the creature in order to produce an **UPWARDS** evolutionary movement (and in time therefore to create a new type of creature – a bird from a lizard from a frog for example) then the whole thing falls over. It doesn't matter how many creatures you compare with each other to say, "Well this creature looks like us," or "This creature looks like that creature" or "Well these creatures share a similar technology within their limbs,"; none of those observed things will be relevant.

Where there is no mechanism for real change, change cannot occur and your interpretation of that which you are looking at is wrong.

So if the power supply is switched off, it does not matter how many 'sockets' there are out there to look at, they will all be dead too. So you can say, "We have similar hands to an ape or a monkey," or "Many creatures have teeth to use to eat with," these statements become meaningless without a viable evolutionary **microbiological**

mechanism to make them work, that is to create an UPWARDS evolutionary chain of events (where new sophisticated coded information is actively written within the creature's DNA) to move one creature into another; a cold blooded, densely-boned frog into a lizard and then into a warm blooded hollow-boned bird, for example. You also have to look at the problem from an engineer's point of view. Just saying, "It mutated" or "it evolved" does not get around the fact that a half formed wing will not cause a creature to fly and will inhibit its movement and therefore its ability to survive. Who, in their right mind, would give up their front legs to turn them into wings if, during the *evolutionary process over millions of years*, they could no longer 'hop away' properly from their enemy who wants to eat them for tea? Or who would want to have a half formed wing flapping around on their back (if they wanted to keep their front feet to hop with) and retain it for millions of years when it does nothing but hinder their hopping through the air as they jumped. Extra weight does not do anything to help when you want to hop away from a snake! Engineering in the real world is a real problem to evolutionists who tend to live in their imaginations, which often become a fantasy world, where they imagine the finished products only, and forget all of the impossible in-between stages along the way that do not work.

The Consequences of No Naturalistic Mechanism

If there is no **mechanism** for naturalism that will also conform to **practical engineering design**, then you have to look towards a creator and a designer instead who simply used similar technologies in the different things that were created, as they shared the same environment, so that they could survive on this planet alongside each other. That would also be a perfectly logical conclusion to arrive at. Humanists do not want to go there, however, as they don't want 'God' in science. That would get in the way of the 'scientific method' according to their God-replacement world view convictions.

"God is not scientific," they ***religiously*** say.

This notion, however, is just an expression of the world view agenda of secularists who insist that the divine was not the main reason for why we are here. Secularists will argue that we are **definitely here by chance** and that any thoughts or movements towards the divine, though absolutely true, are labelled as pseudo-science. The real fact of the matter is, however, that this world view agenda of humanism gets in the way of us doing proper science today. It closes the door on a multi-disciplined enquiry whereby science and information theory and philosophy and theology all work together to create an more informed and rounded understanding of the world – which is what real life is really made up of (more of this in book 2 in this series).

Part of the true calling of science is to
find evidence for the divine,
not to direct our thinking away from God.

NOTE: Many a person today and throughout history, even Einstein, has noted that the fact that the universe which we see all around us is logical and understandable. This fact is seen as a most amazing thing. The universe fits purposefully together. It has logic at its heart. We human beings also think logically. This fact that we are also programmed to think and reason in a logical way will cause us to naturally ask questions that will bring us an understanding of our environment. When you truly think about it, it is quite astounding. This is not the work of a haphazard 'Big Bang' explosion whereby everything would be haphazard and meaningless. As Einstein commented this strongly suggests to us that there is a logical mind behind the universe that wants us to understand and to come to terms with the environment in which we find ourselves alive.

Life from Non-Life Mechanism Questions

This same method that I've mentioned above extends to the mechanism for life coming from non-life. The question is, "Is there a *viable mechanism* that demonstrates to us **not only** how the first protein or RNA strand appeared, but how it then continued step-by-step along that journey to **auto-organise** itself into the first cell?" After we've asked that question we then need to ask,

By what mechanism *did it then organise and calibrate the cell so that the irreducible and*

29

*interdependent processes that we now find within it
had a step-by-step evolution into their current state?*

DNA, for example, resides in the nerve centre of the cell. Later on we'll see how DNA has to be read, copied, transported and processed in order for new machines, called proteins, to be assembled for the purpose of fulfilling tasks in the human body – vital jobs that need doing to keep us alive and well. The question we will need to ask about the cell is,

What is the mechanism by which the
natural world **auto-organised** *a
single protein into such a complex factory?*

Then we will ask,

What were the **mechanisms** *by which,
as the cell developed, the engineering within cell
all worked properly during its time of evolution
without it breaking down?*

Don't tell me that this process just appeared via an evolutionary 'leap' – that phrase is just an **excuse to re-label the divine's touching of the cosmos**. The process by which this complex environment works today must be step-by-step reducible back to its basic components and along that ever reducing path the cell must still be **empowered to survive**, reproduce itself and still have purpose and meaning in order for the evolutionary model to be viable.

This line of questioning also extends to the so called **mechanism of chance** that secularists say accounts for our existence, that is the quadruple level calibration of the universe that we see around us in order for life to not only exist on this planet but also for it to be sustained. So, as we look at the observable evidence, the universe and all that is around us, we ask...

*"**What** is it that we are looking at and **how** did it journey over time so that it arrived at it's the final state that we see it in today?"*

We then develop ideas and theories from what we can see, each of those ideas and theories will have a **mechanism** that drives them and at the same time an output of real testable evidence from that mechanism that is an example of sensible engineering in the real world. Then we test those theories to see if the mechanisms we have chosen to use are true or not and if the biological engineering of the creature is still viable along its so called evolutionary path.

The Mechanism vs Other Evidence
If the mechanism is incorrect, however, then either,

- our interpretation of what we are observing is incorrect
- our theory of what the mechanism is, i.e. the driving force that caused the universe to exist and everything in it to come about, is incorrect

If this is so then we have to **change the mechanism**. This is probably the most important point that I need to make about science in this book. That is this,

*You cannot put **supposed extra evidence and imaginary ideas** above the mechanism and the practical engineering!*

As I have just said, evolutionists are so in love with their theories that they don't give much thought to engineering and how it would work if it was only half-made. Don't forget that the mechanism is also the measureable and **repeatable** process by which something happens. Where there is no mechanism for **valid, provable and observable change that works in the real world** then there is no validity to the theory. If we still hold onto the theory after it has been proven to not work in the real world then we are just living out of the imaginings and fantasies in our heads. These imagined theories become, as I've heard it said, "Fairy tales for adults." If the mechanism

31

you have chosen is proved to be false, then all of your other theorising that follows, along with complementary evidences to prop up the theory, are also false. Refusing to change a false mechanism is not science but most probably a conviction attached to a **religious worldview** that the person does not wish to give up! Continuing to present your disproved science as a valid option for the populace to listen to is then classed as 'false news'. True science is then put to one side for the purpose of giving precedence to a worldview religious conviction!

- -
Where Science and Religion Meet
- -

Choosing a Mechanism based on World View

As we have already said in this chapter, the problem we have is that if the science we're engaging in is about our origins then the mechanism that we **choose to test out our theories** will always come from a religious world view conviction. If we 'believe' that there is no God and we're all here by chance then we will choose "**chance encounters within the cosmos**" to be the **mechanisms** that we will observe and focus upon to continually test for the reason why we are all here. We will ask,

"Which chance encounters are responsible for us being alive in the cosmos today?"

We will focus upon those bumps and chemical reactions that take place between lifeless materials in the cosmos as they collide with each other. The reason why we turn our attention towards them is because we are **already convinced** that their random interactions are **the only viable reason** for us being here. They are solely responsible and nothing or no-one else is or can be. So we will **choose them as mechanisms** to observe in order to gather our evidence to prove our religious world view conviction. We choose to imagine in our minds as many different ways as possible that 'this' or 'that' process could possibly have taken place in order to cause the right effect to fit into our world view. Every fantasy idea has **the possibility of being 'plausible'** because it is an opportunity to reinforce the religious world view that we *already know to be true*.

32

After a while we get so used to hearing so many different theories that we begin to says to ourselves,

"So many people are thinking in this direction, we can't all be wrong. These theories are as good as a fact – almost."

This type of thinking then gains momentum and before you know it the general consensus is set in a certain direction and at the same time everyone gets the general feeling that we're **just a short way away from proving it to be a fact**, so we might as well talk about it in our day-to-day conversations as if it already is a fact – even when it isn't!

So if random collisions are the mechanism that we have chosen, then we have already opted for a non-God evidence route by which we conduct our experiments. If we can prove that those chance chemical reactions can indeed create life, then we don't need a designer to create the universe for us. However, if it is impossible for chance encounters of non-living matter to be responsible for,

- the calibration of the universe
- the starting of life
- the growth and development of the code of life (DNA)
- the design of the cell, enabling its components to process the DNA within it to create machines to keep us alive
- the engineering examples of complex life that we see around us today

…then our conclusion has to be that we can only come from something or someone who has intelligence. Then we suddenly find ourselves in the presence of someone who is greater than us to whom we may well be accountable. That is a completely different matter! So this is where science and religion meet. The fundamental question is not, "What is the process by which we got here?" but,

"Can we be here without God?"

If the answer is a clear, "No, we can't be here without God," then the implications from this are that you and I need to find out who this God is and what this God's mind is on matters such as,

- who we are
- what our state of being is (morally good, neutral or fallen)
- what we're here for
- how we should be relating to Him
- where history has come from and where/what it is moving towards (open ended living or judgement day!)

Anyone with any basic common sense would seek to find out the answers to the above. Science would take on a new role of supporting the other disciplines of philosophy, theology etc. as general 'talk about God' is beyond the remit of science – except that the handiwork of the divine within the cosmos points to extreme intelligence.

Holding onto a Non-Viable World View Mechanism

There's one last thing to say on this matter. Due to the world view implications involved in rejecting a mechanism that upholds the humanist creation story (and so by default letting God back into science) we will find that many people still try to hang onto a non-God mechanism, even when it is already dead in the water. This is because they do not want to change their religious world view and they would rather keep a disproved theory, **propped up by other evidences that are not central to the argument**, rather than have no theory (or mechanism) at all. Rejecting the humanist's mechanism for creation and having nothing in its place opens the door wide to let God take centre stage again in the world of science. This would also lead to total religious change in Western culture and the problem is that a person can often strongly resist this as a person's inner loyalties to their own personal self-worshipping religion can be exceedingly strong. When this happens we can see that it is not the facts, therefore, that often drive science, but the behind the scenes religious worldview conviction that the person carries within them.

We saw an example of this four hundred years ago when Galileo Galilei was first warned by the Catholic Church to stop teaching a heliocentric solar system, which is that the earth orbits the sun. This eventually led to his trial for heresy in 1633.

> **NOTE:** This stand of the Catholic Church was actually due to a false understanding of the Bible and brought about the subsequent wrong doctrine that the sun orbited the Earth, something that the Bible does not teach.

The problem is, however, that we are seeing the very same thing happen today, but this time from the side of humanism. Secular spirituality's foundational assumptions about life and the universe are being proven to be scientifically false right under our noses. Despite this being the case, we see an unwillingness to 'let the truth out' as...

...those who control the creation story of a culture have the **central ideological power** in the culture.

The above is a most important statement. Every culture has a central religious drive to it, whether the culture recognises it or not. That cultural drive satisfies our conscience. There is a huge difference between a 'God-conscience' and a 'humanistic-conscience'. One looks to divine law and the other to humanity who will make up their own rules. This clash is central to that which is taking place in our Western culture right now. The creation story of the culture will free some up to fulfil their conscience and give restrictions to others who find they can't fulfil that conscience in the light of the dominant creation story – which sets precedence for living. From that perspective there is no such thing as 'equality' because there is a conscience clash at the heart of each religious group's bias, especially between humanism and theism. My next book, book 2, in this 'Apologetics not Apologies' series is all about this issue.

> **NOTE:** This then means that the truth about our origins as a human race ceases to be a matter of pure science; it becomes religious **and political** in nature. When this happens, when people supress the knowledge of the truth for their own advantage, history tells us that society becomes closed and

controlling, even when the rhetoric within the culture says the opposite.

So in these next chapters I'm going to look at the scientific evidence that is in front of us, that is the observable, measureable, testable evidence from which we can formulate strong and solid conclusions. From those conclusions I'm going to use deductive logic to show that there is a super intelligence behind life (DNA is a programming language far too complicated for a human being to write). Once we've established that there is a God, then we will also have to come to the conclusion that the spiritual was in existence **before the physical**. This then tells us that the spiritual world has a **life of its own** outside of human 'belief', that spirituality is preeminent in the universe (not physical matter). The consequences of this will be that the whole of Western secular thinking has to change and we have to look elsewhere for our reasons for,

- being alive
- who we are
- what our purpose is
- where we are going

Everything changes and the whole underpinning assumptions of our education system about spirituality and morality, the reasoning within our judiciary and the preaching of our politicians, will have to change with it.

*Spirituality ceases to be just 'personal belief' that totally originates from within humanity, but true spirituality is now 'within a divine person' who is **outside us** (God).*

As I said a few paragraphs ago, these latter implications that I have just outlined, however, will not be covered in this book. In this book we're just looking at the initial science evidence that proves that there is deity behind life.

Chapter 2 – To Evolve or not to Evolve? That is the Question!

Biogenesis from Many Sources

No Common Biological Tree

A.E. Wilder Smith wrote in the preface to open up his book "The Natural Sciences Know Nothing of Evolution" the following paragraph,

"On January 14, 1975, in Zürich, Nobel Prize laureate Jacques Monod stated that today no one any longer harbours doubts regarding evolution. Everybody admits that it took place. If Monod thus wished to express the idea that every single form of life (plant, animal, human) developed ontogenetically from nonliving matter, then he may have been entirely correct. But if, as was probably the case, he meant that man shares common ancestors with all animals and plants - that is, that transformism, the changing of one species into another higher one, took place - then many highly qualified biologists will protest. For in the course of the last few years, a number of mostly young experts have become convinced that biogenesis, the origin of life, is to be understood polyphylogenetically (from many sources) rather than monophylogenetically (all life stemming from one primeval cell). So today well-informed experts exist who no longer believe that all species originated from one primeval cell by means of transformism. They believe in no common biological family tree for all species, possessing a single root for all forms of life. Rather, they hold the opinion that life resembles a field in which many organisms flourish side by side without necessarily being connected phylogenetically."

The thrust of this paragraph basically says that, since we've discovered so much more of the complexity of life, many biologists now cannot believe in a one single cell origin theory from which all life came. The general tree of evolutionary life is rejected. Life is not connected in this way and each 'kind' of creature stands by itself and did not come from another one lower down the evolutionary tree. The rest of this chapter will show how that conclusion is arrived at.

The Theory of Evolution – how we got here

Introduction

Here's an outline of an online video called, "How evolution works." It is one of the best quick summaries that I've personally come across of what evolution is on the web. The video was created by humanists and I've deliberately chosen this video therefore so that I can't be accused of twisting anything. If you want to watch it for yourself then it is located at this address:

https://www.youtube.com/watch?v=hOfRN0KihOU

This video clearly shows and demonstrates the mechanisms of evolution. It is an accurate and down to earth representation of the evolutionary model as it is taught today. I'm going to summarise this video *in my own words* in the next paragraphs. Also please note that any of the following paragraphs which are totally *in italics* are **my interjections** and not part of the original video text. So let's get down to it. To start off we have to say that there are three things that drive the theory of evolution. They are DNA mix, mutation and natural selection. Here's an outline of each.

The Mechanisms of Evolution – DNA Mix

To the humanist evolution is the reason why life developed on planet Earth. This process is said to have taken billions of years to happen, where small changes have taken place over a long period of time. Evolutionists claim that it is still continuing today. They say that it is the reason why there is such a huge diversity of life. If you look down the family tree of any ancestral line you'll see that the descendants all look slightly different from each other. Not only do they look slightly different from each other but they develop, over time, into totally different species. How can this happen?

Well, the first thing to get established is the answer to the following question, "What is the definition of a 'new species' of animal?" To put it simply, a species is a group of animals that live in community with each other, that are able to breed and have offspring and those offspring are also able to breed and have offspring too.

I will disagree with this definition later on as I think that, though valid in its initial claims, the way the definition is used by secularists today is misleading.

*So according to humanists a pride of lions is a species and they are a different species from the cheetah or the leopard or the tiger. Even though they are all part of the **cat family**, they are each classed as being a different species, which means that we have a minimum of 36 species of cats on the earth today. This is because even though it is possible, for example, for a lion and a tiger to have offspring, their offspring are always infertile and cannot pass on their genes. They have moved too far away from each other in their DNA mix for reproduction to function anymore.*

The first thing to note on this subject of DNA mix is uniqueness. Every creature in existence is unique and this uniqueness is cited by secularists as a **mechanistic driver** that **makes evolution work**. You will see amongst any animal group, traits and characteristics that are slightly different from everyone else's. The reason for this is as follows,

- all creatures are made up of cells
- every cell has a nucleus
- within each nucleus are chromosomes
- each chromosome contains DNA
- DNA is made up of genes and these are the information carriers within the animal
- the information in the genes contains the instructions for the cell and determines the characteristics and traits that each creature has

So it is the DNA in every creature that makes it unique. Whenever creatures mate they are presenting a double shuffle of their DNA. The first DNA shuffle is when parents produce sperm and eggs. Each sperm and egg contains 50% of the DNA of the sperm creator or egg producer. The selection of the particular DNA that goes into each sperm or egg is done by a random process, so each sperm and each egg will have a unique set of DNA selected by chance. This is the first shuffle. The second shuffle takes place when the sperm and egg come together and the randomly chosen DNA that's already in them recombines into one new code. The combination of the two gives the offspring their unique DNA mix and therefore unique genes which display the new individual's unique traits and characteristics. As animals in nature often have lots of offspring (so that those who do survive the dangers of the wild have a good chance to continue the family line of the community) then we get as a result a lot of DNA variations amongst the many new babies within the group. This type of recombination DNA change is called **heredity exchange** (DNA mix) which, as we have just said, is the passing on of part of your DNA (genes) and the joint combining of each set found in every individual sperm and egg. When they come together, they form a new creature. Even though there will be similarities between them, they will all be slightly different as they will each inherit different combinations of their parent's DNA.

The Mechanisms of Evolution – Mutation

The next thing that evolutionists throw into the mix is mutation. Mutations are accidental changes that happen by random chance within the DNA, normally during the cell copying process.

> **Note:** These *mutations* are also often described as **copy errors**, which is exactly what they are, **errors** within the DNA code.

There are different things that can trigger these changes, such as toxins, chemical substances or radiation. So a mutation happens when the DNA is altered in some way. It is admitted that most of these changes are negative and may result in illnesses, such as cancer. Most have a neutral effect and some...

...are said by humanists,

...to have positive effects, such as human beings having blue eyes. One thing to remember on this subject is that the mutation will **only be effective if it gets into the DNA that is in the sperm or the egg**, which is in the 50% that the parent passes on. If it does not get into the sperm or the egg, then the mutation stays with the parent and is not found in the child. All of this mutation change also happens by random chance.

The Mechanisms of Evolution – Natural Selection

The last thing that evolutionists throw into the mix is what is called natural selection. This is because, even though the change that takes place within animals is random, for some reason each species seems completely adapted to its environment. Evolutionists say that natural selection plays its part in the evolution of any species. Every creature is subject to this process. That is, all creatures live within an environment which includes predators, parasites, and toxins. There is competition amongst the creatures within the community to survive and the habitat itself may change and/or the climate may change. All these factors are continually at work. The unique traits and characteristics of each creature will either help or hinder survival.

If a creature, such as a rodent, has really great eyesight or hearing then it may well avoid being caught by an eagle when compared with another one of its own kind that doesn't see or hear too well. Thus it has a better chance of surviving and passing on its genes and giving the next generation good eyesight or hearing. If an insect looks like a leaf in shape and colour then it stands a better chance of not getting eaten, so over time future generations of insects will look more leaf-like.

The most famous example of natural selection at work is on the Galapagos Islands, which are located in the middle of the Pacific Ocean. There a group of finches were once stranded, often thought to have arrived there by a storm that blew them onto the land. The islands were a finch paradise. There were lots of food sources and no predators. The finches thrived and had many offspring. Soon, however, there were so many of them that they were in competition with each other and food became short. Some finches had beaks that were longer and thinner than others and they took to a diet of worms. These finches naturally fed on the muddy areas where the worms were available and they tended to mate with finches that ate the same diet. Other finches had broader and stronger beaks and these were experts at cracking open seeds. They ate in the parts of the island where seed was plentiful and tended to mate with each other. Over many generations those groups of birds changed their shape.

41

This was brought about by limited DNA being passed on by birds that had similar diets and therefore similar traits and characteristics. As they moved apart, evolved, the distinct groups could no longer mate and produce offspring. This meant that new species of finch appeared as time went by and this has continued to this day. Now on the Galapagos Islands there are over fourteen different species of finch, all of which are descended from the same original group.

Conclusion

The final conclusions, therefore, from the makers of this short video is as follows.

"This is how new species are made by evolution; through the interaction of unique individuals, the excess production of offspring, recombination and mutation in hereditary, and finally, through selection."

"This tells us where the variety of life comes from and why living creatures are so perfectly adapted to their habitat."

Criticisms of Darwin's Basic Mechanism

Trying to Maintain the Original Theory

The above information is not the original theory of evolution that Darwin put forward because it contains references to DNA, which forms the information that is found at the heart of the cell (which we today call our genes). We have to remember that when Darwin first made popular his grandfather's theory it was not possible for him or anyone at that time to look inside a cell. The technology available during the 19th Century simply allowed the people of the day to look through a microscope that was limited in strength. Through this they could observe a cell that seemed like a blob which sometimes moved in an unpredictable way. So the fact that all of life is driven by precision data (DNA coding) was completely alien to Darwin and the rest of the science world. Ever since we've become aware of the complexity of the cell, its multiple parts and the multiple interdependent processes that take place within it for it to function, evolutionists have been trying to maintain the original theory that

Darwin proposed. This is often done by leaps of the imagination, trying to 'imagine this' or 'imagine that' or simply by using the word 'mutation' or the phrase, 'it evolved' as a verbal excuse to steer us away from the nitty gritty problem of data and complexity. We'll look at this more in a later chapter.

Additionally we must also say that a theory cannot remain a theory forever. At some point it has either to move towards a fact, via the route of proof, or be rejected as nonsense. For evolution to move from theory to fact it has to be proved **by the rules of science** and those rules have to be strictly adhered to. Proof is not only established by observable repeatable experiments that deliver the same observable and measureable results (every time the experiment is repeated) but also by the witnesses of the laws of science that accompany them. Basic logic has to be applied to ensure that the person interpreting the results has not brought any assumptions to the table when explaining those results from which they made their final conclusions.

So let's begin to tackle the above theory of evolution that suggests that tiny mutations, along with a mixing of DNA, when combined with natural selection has produced all the creatures on this planet in all their variety from one small cellular life form.

The Mechanisms of Evolutionary Theory
The first question to ask is,

What is truly *achieved* by the *mechanisms* of evolutionary theory?

Remember that if the mechanism is incorrect, then everything that follows is incorrect too. Here's an overview of what each mechanism does in reality.

1) **Hereditary Exchange** – Producing Offspring (babies)
   a. Shuffles the DNA code by taking roughly 50% from each parent and then joins them together giving the baby a unique set of genes.

b. This brings about a unique shape change where each of the body parts will have a slightly different expression from its parents and its siblings.

    i. **NOTE:** This shape change is **NOT new information** – just a different expression of the same information that is within the parents.

    ii. **NOTE:** Shape change is sideways **adaptation** not UPWARDS evolution. The humanist video used the word 'evolution' when talking about how new species are made. This is in fact not true. New species, that is new types of the same creature within its own family group, are made by sideways adaptation.

2) **Mutation** – copy errors within the code

    a. The errors are at best neutral or not beneficial to the creature.

        i. **NOTE:** The humanist video I've summarised above gave 'blue eyes' as an example of a 'beneficial' mutation **which is wrong**. Blue eyes do not represent new useful code that will lead to **a higher technology** within the creature. Blue eyes are a sideways data expression change and **NOT new information**. We will see more of why this is so later on.

        ii. **NOTE:** Copy errors within the DNA code do not produce sensible new code that can be used to create new UPWARDS technology within a creature.

3) **Natural Selection** – the environment's influence

    a. Natural selection only serves to **remove DNA** from the gene pool.

    b. Creatures that do not fit the environment as well as others are often taken out of the gene pool by being eaten by predators and so do not get the opportunity to pass on their genes via hereditary exchange.

i. **NOTE:** The removal of DNA from the gene pool by natural selection **does NOT create new DNA information**. There is no new code being written by a creature dying and failing to pass on its genes.

ii. **NOTE:** A surviving creature that does pass on its genes, because it is well fitted to the environment, does **NOT mean new DNA information** is being added to the gene pool as all they are doing is initiating the hereditary exchange DNA shuffle which, along with neutral or unhelpful mutations, does **NOT** write new code. **So no new code for new body parts is being written**.

So let me summarise the above. When two creatures mate their DNA shuffle will create offspring that look very similar to them. *If all goes well* with the DNA exchange when mating occurs then they will have,

- the same number of limbs
- the same internal organs
- the same flesh type
- the same species mannerisms

...as their parents. This is because the DNA shuffle is a 'limited code cycle" that, once initiated, is programmed to keep all of the essentials of the creature in place; whilst providing room for **DNA expressions** to be *slightly different*.

The 'shuffle' when DNA is mixed (mating takes place) is programmed to keep the 'structure of the creature' intact but allows for the expressions within that structure to move slightly.

The length of your arms may be slightly longer or shorter than those of your parents. The colour of your hair or your skin may be a different shade. These differences are '**DNA expression**' differences that produce a sideways movement within the species – which we call

adaptation. However, the mechanism, when observed under a microscope, provides no evidence of any new sophisticated code that will generate an UPWARDS evolutionary movement that will cause a creature to increase in complexity and move, over time, from one creature into another.

Sideways movements are NOT evidence for UPWARDS change.

Evolutionists *choose to believe*, **by faith**, that sideways change (adaptation) is direct evidence for UPWARDS evolution. This is where the foundational problem is in the theory of evolution. I'm now going to take a few more pages to unpack this and look at it in more detail.

What really is a new species?

As we have said, when an evolutionist talks about a new species, what they mean is simply that a set of creatures has moved in its internal DNA so that they (or their offspring) can no longer produce, by mating with other family members, an ongoing family line – as my previous example with a lion and a tiger. The problem we have with the evolutionist's use of this term is that these examples of 'new species' are still within the origins of the creature's wider family group. What do I mean by that? Well simply put, a tiger, a lion, a cheetah, a leopard, a jaguar and a pussy cat (that you may have as a pet in your home) are all part of what we call the **cat family**. Yes, they may not be able to inter-breed anymore and some may be faster than others and have markings that others don't have etc. but they are all still essentially *cats*.

All of the DNA coding that is in them is 'cat' code.

This cat code produces cat characteristics and cat mannerisms and cat behaviour and cat diet; all that goes into making a cat a cat. A cat, for example, does not go 'Woof" when it comes to greet you. It doesn't even go "MeeoWoof" in any way, as if there is any connection (no matter how distant up the ancestral line) with the dog family or any other kind of animal. It's "Meow" may be a quiet one, if the cat is small, or a little more terrifying if the cat is the size of a leopard or jaguar and a little more deafening if the cat is the size of a lion or a tiger. It is, however, the same essential "cat call" if I can label it that. Two pussy cats scrapping in an alleyway over territory in a city will have a 'sound' attached to the fight as the cats howl at each other. Two lions scrapping with each other on the grass plains of Africa over the rights to a pride of lionesses will also have a 'sound' that accompanies the fight. Both sounds, though distinct, will be recognisable as being part of the **cat family**. None of those sounds will sound like dogs or elephants or apes or bears when they are in territorial disputes with others **of their own kind**.

So what I am initially saying is that there is a certain amount of code in a cat that makes a cat a cat and we can recognise the results of that coding in the body shape, the retractable claws, the cat's movements, sounds and behaviours etc. The code in the cat family can be shifted around by hereditary breeding and the influence of diet and climate i.e. the environment. Over time those separated groups will take on their own unique shapes and characteristics as the DNA code is mixed up and they continue to move/shift sideways in their development and adaptation to their environment. The DNA within them will still essentially, however, **be the same foundational cat code** that came from the first two cats. The programming within the sperm and the egg coming together dictates this to be the case. There is a 'framework' that makes the creature what it is – that the code is programmed to stick to (we'll see more of this later in the book). The hereditary exchange code within the DNA is set up to do the following:

- create a creature of the same 'kind' as the parents
- maintain the same number of body parts
- maintain the same internal organs
- give a slightly unique body shape expression to those body parts, a sideways adaptation shift

This is the case too, on the Galapagos Islands, that we've already mentioned where there are now fourteen different types of finches. They all come from the original group that landed there a long time ago. However, all of them are still 100% **bird** in their genetic makeup. All that has happened is this *sideways shift* in the DNA which we've been talking about that causes beaks to change shape, heads to change shape and plumage to alter etc. with the result that, over generations, they can no longer mate with other finches because they've not interacted with them over many generations. Each of these 'new species' however, are still all made up of 100% bird code! So even though evolutionists label them as a *new species*, they are simply…

…an expression of a creature within its own family type

…that is a type of finch within the bird family, just as a tiger is a type of cat within the cat family.

The 'New Species' Inference Problem

So why am I working hard at unpacking this usage of the phrase 'new species'? Well, it is what is inferred by the phrase that's important. The inference that an evolutionist will put onto the phrase it this,

Every 'new species' represents a movement away from the creature's family group towards a potentially new creature!

This is where the point of contention is. **Does a sideways movement really mean that an UPWARDS process has begun?** Is a new species just a sideways shift or can it be used as evidence to say that an UPWARDS evolutionary movement has also taken place? An evolutionist will say the following. A new species is,

- **a new expression**
- of an *ever moving creature*
- *away from its own kind*

In reality, however, a 'new species' is nothing more than,

- **a new expression**
- of an *established creature*
- *within its own kind*

NOTE: These two sets of statements arise from religious conviction. For the atheist life HAS TO BE continually on the move. Every species of creature HAS TO BE part of an ever moving process... **because random processes created all things in the first place**. So, as we are the result of random and unguided movements within the cosmos that trace themselves back to a 'Big Bang' accident, all creatures have to be in a state of flux and change when we look at them within the context of 'deep time' i.e. billions of years. For theists this is an assumption that is not acceptable. To assume that all creatures are 'on the move' is to deny that God created creatures 'within their own kinds' and this denial is without foundation – and the evidence we see around us of sideways only adaptations is extra proof of that!

The evolutionist, however, insists that life is 'on the move'. S/he insists that *sideways* = UPWARDS. So the phrase, 'a new species' will carry with it the **inference of an ever present movement** as the underlying and unproven assumption is that...

...nothing ever stays within its own kind/family group...

...over billions of years. To the evolutionist, there are no 'kinds' of creature in the long run. All will change over time. We categorise creatures into their 'kinds' as this is a convenient way to describe them 'as they currently are' at this moment in time. Without this temporary categorisation we would not be able to make sense of the ever moving life that surrounds us. So we categorise life, give it names according to that which we...

...currently see.

The humanist will argue that what we will see in the future, however, is a totally different thing. Over billions of years all these creatures that we currently name and label today may change into totally new and different creatures/family groups. This is the foundational assumption behind the thinking of evolutionists *as they use the term 'new species'*.

*Creatures are not **established** within their family groups, they are **moving** UPWARDS towards new creatures and new families of creatures.*

Here's another way of putting it. An evolutionist will say that,

A new species is
an expression of continuous change
that continually shifts over time
to create something with its
own distinct appearance
that enables it to evolve UPWARDS
away from its current family group
and into a new creature.

However, the problem is that a lion, a tiger, a leopard, a cheetah, a jaguar etc. are all examples of **sideways identity shifts** that are observable and verifiable today due to DNA mix and groups of animals living in isolation. They are, however, all **in the cat family** and have the same foundational 'cat code' within them. New information is **NOT** being generated via DNA mix when each species is created, just variants in the code to express that same data in different ways. This is the correct usage of the phrase, *new species* – a sideways movement from within a creature's 'family group' or within its own 'kind'. So here's a more accurate statement about 'new species'.

A new species is
an expression of an established family identity
that has shifted over time into its
own distinct appearance
that prevents it from mating with
others within its original family group.

So here is the foundational assumption clash between evolutionist scientists and those scientists who have a theistic world outlook.

Evolutionists – there are **no ultimate family groups**, all of life is moving/evolving into something new.

Theists – family groups are **set into place** by deity and we see continuous new expressions of these family groups as creatures adapt within their environment.

This argument may go on for some time. The issue is, however, that the actual movements that we see before our eyes through hereditary exchange, mutation and natural selection have only given us viewable evidence for sideways shifts. **On no occasion has new information for new technology and new body parts been observed by these processes!** So we see that evolutionists verbally tag onto this term something that is not proved, UPWARDS evolutionary change, but talk about it...

...as if it was actually proved,

...as if adaptation and evolution are both one and the same thing. Their kind of talk is a misuse of the phrase, 'new species'.

The Misuse of the Phrase, New Species
So when evolutionists talk about adaptation and UPWARDS evolution they will use the same phrase, 'new species' for both examples when talking and writing about our origins and they make **no distinction** between the two.

*They talk as if one (adaptation) is **just as true** as the other (UPWARDS evolution).*

The problem is that one is proved and the other is not. The proved mechanism shows a slight change in the DNA code (**data expression sideways change**) and the un-proved change requires nothing less than a complete set of extra new code to make the new body parts work (**totally new sophisticated information**).

So the example of sideways adaptation, something that we can see all around us, is talked about as if it is just as real as UPWARDS change.

*Sideways adaptation is casually presented as **direct** and **real** evidence for UPWARDS change.*

The two are presented as being just as real as each other, just as acceptable as each other. The evolutionist does not clarify this in their talk on the subject. The link between the two is totally assumed. They,
- believe it to be true

...and
- talk about it **as if it were true**

This is a misuse of language and it is not scientific. True science identifies weaknesses in a theory, evolutionists do not do this; they presume in their thinking and their discussions and communications that UPWARDS evolution naturally follows on from viewable *sideways* DNA change.

Sideways shifts in DNA code are easily possible – we see it all the time. UPWARDS development in DNA code to create new body parts and behaviours has never been observed!

So let me say it again. No **new information** in any shape or form will be added to any creature via,

- the route of hereditary exchange, that is of parents breeding, mixing their DNA, and passing it on to their offspring
- mutation, which are small copy errors and can't bring into being new sophisticated code
- natural selection, which simply removes code from the gene pool

...as there is **nothing contained within those mechanisms** that have the ability to write new complicated and sophisticated code for the creation of new technological body parts or to change the 'flesh type' of a creature as well as its behaviours and mannerisms.

Examples of Misuse – Fish turn into Lizards

So let's look at how the misuse of the phrase, 'new species' works when applied in the field of science. There is plenty of evidence that fish, like cats, birds and insects, will separate from each other via hereditary DNA mixes and produce different kinds of fish. There is absolutely zero evidence that DNA mixes have ever...

...turned a fish into a lizard.

A fish through generational DNA hereditary shuffles (breeding) cannot leave behind its 'fishiness' and take on the form of a lizard and adopt a lizard's flesh type, body parts and behaviours. The DNA between the creatures is too different. The flesh of the creature is different, the skin is different, its movements are different and its whole programming and mentality is different. The language of an evolutionist, however, when talking about both of these, is to simply say, 'it evolved' and 'new species'. What in fact they are saying is,

- sideways DNA shift takes place
- this sideways shift is labelled as the creature evolving – not just adapting
- whole sections of new sophisticated and intricate information is created within the DNA of the creature through these sideways shifts
- sideways DNA shifts cause a completely new identity to appear
- we see 'new species' all of the time within nature (expressions within a family)
- DNA sideways shifts, therefore, cause new creatures to evolve and appear

So we are told that...

*... sideways shifts in the DNA code **are enough** to create new sophisticated body parts.*

> **NOTE:** New body parts require the most complex code. Sideways shifts (adaptation) only produce variants within the current code.

Some might say,
"Aren't there fish that can come out of the water?"
Answer – "Yes."
"Aren't there fish that can move across the land?"
Answer – "Yes."
"Isn't this evidence of UPWARDS evolution?"
Answer – "No."

There is no new code within these fish. Its fins are not in the process of being turned into legs. There is no new code within the fish to do so, **nor is there any new viewable code appearing within the fish as it continues these activities**. This is an example of 'other evidences' being put alongside a faulty mechanism. We will look at this later on.

One Final Statement about Hereditary Exchange

Let me run the risk of repeating myself and work this point just a little more. The hereditary mix, caused by breeding, is just the same data rejigged over and over again. You can see this most clearly in dogs. Dogs are the easiest creatures to breed as far as changing the DNA mix. There are more types of dogs than there are of any other creature. Here's a list of the current known breeds that we have created, and by the way, I don't expect you to actually read all the way through the list in the next paragraph. It's just there to show you the extent of the breeds. Just cast your eye over it. The different dog breeds from DNA mixing to produce their current stand out traits and characteristics are:

Affenpinscher, Afghan Hound, Airedale Terrier, Akita, Alaskan Klee Kai, Alaskan Malamute, American Bulldog, American English Coonhound, American Eskimo Dog, American Foxhound, American Pit Bull Terrier, American Staffordshire Terrier, American Water Spaniel,

Anatolian Shepherd Dog, Appenzeller Sennenhunde, Australian Cattle Dog, Australian Shepherd, Australian Terrier, Azawakh, Barbet, Basenji, Basset Hound, Beagle, Bearded Collie, Bedlington Terrier, Belgian Malinois, Belgian Sheepdog, Belgian Tervuren, Berger Picard, Bernedoodle, Bernese Mountain Dog, Bichon Frise,Black and Tan Coonhound, Black Mouth Cur, Black Russian Terrier, Bloodhound, Bluetick Coonhound, Boerboel, Bolognese, Border Collie, Border Terrier, Borzoi, Boston Terrier, Bouvier des Flandres, Boxer, Boykin Spaniel, Bracco Italiano, Briard, Brittany, Brussels Griffon, Bull Terrier, Bulldog, Bullmastiff, Cairn Terrier, Canaan Dog, Cane Corso, Cardigan Welsh Corgi, Catahoula Leopard Dog, Caucasian Shepherd Dog, Cavalier King Charles Spaniel, Cesky Terrier, Chesapeake Bay Retriever, Chihuahua, Chinese Crested, Chinese Shar-Pei, Chinook, Chow Chow, Clumber Spaniel, Cockapoo, Cocker Spaniel, Collie, Coton de Tulear, Curly-Coated Retriever, Dachshund, Dalmatian, Dandie Dinmont Terrier, Doberman Pinscher, Dogo Argentino, Dogue de Bordeaux, Dutch Shepherd, English Cocker Spaniel, English Foxhound, English Setter, English Springer Spaniel, English Toy Spaniel, Entlebucher Mountain Dog, Field Spaniel, Finnish Lapphund, Finnish Spitz, Flat-Coated Retriever, Fox Terrier, French Bulldog, German Pinscher, German Shepherd Dog, German Shorthaired Pointer, German Wirehaired Pointer, Giant Schnauzer, Glen of Imaal Terrier, Goldador, Golden Retriever, Goldendoodle, Gordon Setter, Great Dane, Great Pyrenees, Greater Swiss Mountain Dog, Greyhound, Harrier, Havanese, Ibizan Hound, Icelandic Sheepdog, Irish Red and White Setter, Irish Setter, Irish Terrier, Irish Water Spaniel, Irish Wolfhound, Italian Greyhound, Jack Russell Terrier, Japanese Chin, Keeshond, Kerry Blue Terrier, Komondor, Kooikerhondje, Korean Jindo Dog, Kuvasz, Labradoodle, Labrador Retriever, Lakeland Terrier, Lancashire Heeler, Leonberger, Lhasa Apso, Lowchen, Maltese, Maltese Shih Tzu, Maltipoo, Manchester Terrier, Mastiff, Miniature Pinscher, Miniature Schnauzer, Mutt, Neapolitan Mastiff, Newfoundland, Norfolk Terrier, Norwegian Buhund, Norwegian Elkhound, Norwegian Lundehund, Norwich Terrier, Nova Scotia Duck Tolling Retriever, Old English Sheepdog, Otterhound, Papillon, Peekapoo, Pekingese, Pembroke Welsh Corgi, Petit Basset Griffon Vendeen, Pharaoh Hound, Plott, Pocket Beagle, Pointer, Polish Lowland Sheepdog, Pomeranian, Pomsky, Poodle, Portuguese Water Dog, Pug, Puggle, Puli, Pyrenean Shepherd, Rat Terrier, Redbone Coonhound, Rhodesian Ridgeback, Rottweiler, Saint Bernard, Saluki,

Samoyed, Schipperke, Schnoodle, Scottish Deerhound, Scottish Terrier, Sealyham Terrier, Shetland Sheepdog, Shiba Inu, Shih Tzu, Siberian Husky, Silky Terrier, Skye Terrier, Sloughi, Small Munsterlander Pointer, Soft Coated Wheaten Terrier, Stabyhoun, Staffordshire Bull Terrier, Standard Schnauzer, Sussex Spaniel, Swedish Vallhund, Tibetan Mastiff, Tibetan Spaniel, Tibetan Terrier, Toy Fox Terrier, Treeing Tennessee Brindle, Treeing Walker Coonhound, Vizsla, Weimaraner, Welsh Springer Spaniel, Welsh Terrier, West Highland White Terrier, Whippet, Wirehaired Pointing Griffon, Xoloitzcuintli, Yorkipoo, Yorkshire Terrier.

http://dogtime.com/dog-breeds/profiles - is where I obtained this list.

The reason why I've included the list is to show that DNA does really mix up in some creatures when you simply breed two sets of animals that are made up of very different characteristics. The amazing thing, however, is that **all of them at the end of the day are fully dog**. None of them have any cat in them and none of them have any extra information in them that makes them somehow more than a dog. Why is this? Well, simply because the shifting around of the same essential data doesn't create something new, just variants of what is already there. Evolutionists would label each of these dog breeds as **a movement away** from the original dogs and a movement towards a new species, if they were left long enough that is to continue breeding in isolation from each other. They are not classed as a new species as they can still all breed with each other and have offspring of their own who can also still have offspring too, to carry on the family line. However, in reality...

...there is no movement towards a new species at all ***if you define new species from the perspective of leaving behind the family group to create a new kind of creature.***

You'll see that all the dogs mentioned are simply variants within a kind, i.e. they still all belong to the 'dog' family.

The Fox, the dog and the wolf

Let's take this a little further, however. It is now known that the fox and the dog and the wolf all have one common ancestor. Looking at these three types of animal we can see that they are, as defined by evolutionists, separate species – just like those in the cat family. They cannot breed with each other to produce multiple generations of offspring and they would see each other as threats to their communities. However, I have to say again, none of them have taken an UPWARDS step in their DNA changes. They have not gone higher up the imagined evolutionary tree.

The whole push of evolution is that animals not only change within their kind, but that they produce **new types of creatures** that are more technically advanced than the closed family community that they **leave behind**. So when a fish is meant to have evolved into a reptile it...

...leaves behind

...the enclosure of the fish family and becomes something higher and more advanced and well adapted to living on land. It is meant to develop new breathing apparatus, not using gills but lungs to receive air gasped in through the mouth and nostrils, and to develop legs and feet and claws etc. All of these require new DNA information and we have seen that this is not achievable by simply mixing your parent's shared DNA at conception.

Even natural selection won't get this job done. The role of natural selection, in the past called 'The Survival of the Fittest', is just the **removal** of a number of creatures from the DNA pool that, for various reasons, don't manage to leave behind any offspring. This removal mechanism takes data out of the 'DNA pool of life' rather than adding to it. Natural selection does not add new data to a creature, it just simply tries to explain why some creatures survive in a given environment and why others keel over and die or are eaten. No beneficial DNA data is added by this process in any way, shape or form. So the **only mechanism** that you have left that could possibly enable new information to enter into a creature's DNA in order for it to evolve UPWARDS and to become a more complex animal, is **mutation**.

Hindrances to the Mutation Mechanism

The Mutation Mechanism – Mutation Repair

Now here's another major problem for evolutionists. It is all to do with a process that naturally takes place within the body. It is called 'mutation repair' and it happens as part of a continuous running programme within the DNA environment. I'm now going to quote from a lecture given by Dr David Menton which is available on YouTube. You can see the full lecture at this address: https://www.youtube.com/watch?v=Jck4naOUGQo

Dr David Menton – Mutation Repair

"Have you heard of mutation repair? You all ought to hear about it because none of you would be here today if it wasn't for mutation repair. It turns out that in a given day we can have up to a million molecular lesions in our DNA, that is per day. Most of these get corrected by a mutation repair process... The bad strand is snipped out by enzymes and then thrown away. A complimentary copy is made of the good strand and it is spliced in where the bad strand was. Without that we wouldn't be here. It's been estimated that without DNA repair mechanisms, that there is not a single living creature on earth that would survive. Every creature ever studied has these mechanisms, from bacteria to humans. It involves several different enzymes to make it work. Without this repair system cancer runs wild. As a result you will die whether you are a bacterium, a human, a mouse, rat or a dog."

So first we see that there is a mechanism within us that actively works against mutation. It is there, constantly working away, to **prevent the DNA from losing its original integrity**. The activity of mutation repair is continually working against the theory of evolution, therefore, which says that change is driven by small random mutation changes that take place over long periods of time. Yes, small changes do occur within us, but the mutation mechanism that evolutionists continually refer to has an obstacle to overcome, that of mutation repair. This self-correcting activity is an observable in-built programme running inside every living thing that continually fights to...

...and at the same time to keep us alive. Leaving these mutations to just run wild would result in our death, not in an UPWARDS evolutionary progress. As I've just said, some mutations do get through. Yet we have to note that none of them add any new effective information into the creature that will take it, in evolutionary terms, UPWARDS – that is into a new species by bringing new structures and technology into the body of the creature.

Here's a transcript from part of a YouTube video interview with Professor Jonathan Wells of UC Berkeley on this subject of mutations. You can watch the full interview at this address:
https://www.youtube.com/watch?v=xZn7tTdCm6U&t=6s

Professor Jonathan Wells – Mutations
"We've known all along that most mutations are either harmful or neutral, neutral meaning they don't have any noticeable effect, at least not right away. Really beneficial mutations, which would be the only kind evolution could use anyway, are extremely rare. Furthermore they are biochemical in nature, for example in antibiotic resistance. We know mutations can lead to antibiotic resistance and then those bacteria can survive in the presence of say streptomycin, where others could not. But the bacteria that survive are still the same species of bacteria, still tuberculosis for example. So even the rare beneficial mutations we find, do not really transform the organism. They make minor changes within existing species which have never been controversial, and of course the evidence for mutations has already suggested that to us. I can take a fruit fly embryo, and this has been done in fact, and it can be mutated in every possible way, the DNA, and there are only three possible outcomes, a normal fruit fly, a deflective fruit fly or a dead fruit fly. That's it. You can't even change the species; much less get a horsefly or even a horse."

Then he goes on to say,

"Well we've certainly found a lot of evidence but for what? Darwin's theory is that all living things are descended from a common ancestor, modified by unguided natural processes such as natural

59

*selection and variation. Darwin didn't write a book called, "How existing species change over time." That's not even relevant. People have known that for centuries, so minor changes within existing species are not the issue here. Yet when Darwinists say there is overwhelming evidence for Darwin's theory, 90% of what they talk about is minor changes within existing species, that's not the point at all. The point is the origin of new species by the **same process** and no one has ever observed the origin of a new species through variation and selection. They've tried. They've tried many times. That key element in Darwin's theory, the origin of a new species, the title of his book, has **never been solved**."*

Again Dr David Menton in his online lecture…
https://www.youtube.com/watch?v=Jck4naOUGQo

…quotes James Crow, who is an evolutionist and professor and chairman of genetics at the University of Wisconsin 1997, where he says,

*"The typical mutation is very mild. It usually has no effect, it shows up as a **small decrease in viability or fertility**."*

Dr Menton adds to this the comment that, *"this is the wrong way because we are meant to be going **UP** if evolution is true."*

The Difference between Adaptation and Mutation
It is important that we know the difference between adaptation and mutation. If an organism changes **due to an inbuilt mechanism**, and that mechanism is *part of the organisms design*, then the change that occurs is an **adaptation**. Mutation that is meant to lead to UPWARDS evolution is different. Evolution is where something develops **beyond itself**, brings in **new information** that will change the character of the organism. Evolution is the movement from one kind of creature into another. I'm saying this because I want to clarify the quote I used on the previous page from Professor Jonathan Wells on Mutations. He said,

"Really beneficial mutations, which would be the only kind evolution could use anyway, are extremely rare. Furthermore they are biochemical in nature, for example in antibiotic resistance."

60

I want to clarify this statement and say that no *mutations* will provide UPWARDS beneficial change, just as the quote from James Crow states. He puts it succinctly that there will be a *"decrease in viability..."* Here's a quote from an online video called "Evolution And The Fabled Mutations..." which can be found at the following address: https://www.youtube.com/watch?v=_s9oKio-fEU

*"The Evolutionist will ask, "What about the mutation of viruses, for example the flu virus becoming more and more resistant to vaccines?" Bacteria do not become resistant to antibiotics merely by experiencing genetic mutations. In fact there are at least two important **genetic mechanisms** by which resistance may be conferred. First there is the process of conjugation, during which two bacterial cells join and an exchange of genetic material occurs. Certain enzymes exchanged in this process, coincidently, assist in the breakdown of antibiotics, thus making the bacteria resistant to antibiotics. Secondly bacteria can incorporate into their own genetic machinery, foreign pieces of DNA, by either of two types of DNA transposition. In transformation, DNA from the environment, perhaps from the death of another bacterium, is absorbed into the bacterial cell. In transduction, a piece of DNA is transported into the cell via a virus, for example. As a result of incorporating new genetic material, an organism can become resistant to antibiotics. So in other words bacteria and viruses **adapt** rather than purely mutate. This medical scientific fact is now so well known that many evolutionists have dropped this argument for their proof."*

The video then adds this statement concerning mosquitoes.

*"What about the mosquitoes amazing ability to resist each new repellent used against it? The source of the mosquito's ability to resist repellent is found in adaptation ability within its genomes. As it adapts, it is still a mosquito, and no new body parts have been found. This amazing ability is identified as natural selection or **adaptation**, not evolution. No new species or additional body parts are arising from this process."*

So we see from these different sources that mutation does not bring about any viable change within any creature that will add new constructive information for **UPWARDS** evolutionary change. The only influence on a creature's development is the DNA change that comes from the parents, which is then influenced by the diet and the environment that takes out DNA via natural selection.

Some will still argue, however, that creatures (especially insects) change according to their diet and their immediate environment. Some evolutionists will argue that dietary change can be seen to actually *trigger* change within a creature. They say that changes occur within a creature as the food sources change and that this change is not just due to hereditary exchange happening within that environment. In order to explain this we'll have to very briefly mention the option of dormant code.

Dietary Change and Dormant Code!

One thing that evolutionists miss when they argue that creatures such as insects react quickly to dietary changes is the understanding that there is code with the DNA of the creature that will activate when the environment changes. DNA is an amazing thing. **No-one has ever observed new code being written**, but we're discovering all the time just how complex and flexible DNA is. Later on in this book we'll see that DNA can be read forwards and some of it backwards and it can also communicate information in a variety of other ways too. We have not even begun to understand the true complexities of DNA, there is still so much to learn. The activation of dormant code, for example, is something that evolutionists do not take into account. A deity designer, who understood that his creatures would have to live in a variety of environments, would naturally create an 'all terrain code' that could react to change. This would be a sensible thing to do. This idea, however, doesn't even register on the evolutionist's radar as their world view prohibits that kind of thinking. It is, however, something to take into account – especially as we move through this book to see the many other evidences that tell us we can't be here without deity.

An Example of Evolutionary Propaganda

John Cleese and Lemur 'Sideways' Evolution?
https://www.youtube.com/watch?v=7rdSF0CV-Qo

Now let's examine what the mechanisms of hereditary DNA exchange, mutation and natural selection really do by looking at a documentary about some isolated lemurs. Many years ago John Cleese, a firm supporter of evolutionary theory, hosted a documentary about lemurs – you can still find the programme on YouTube today via the address above. On the programme Mr Cleese made the case for evolution saying that we and the lemurs have a *"common ancestor"*. He used physical similarities between us and them as evidence for this, for example the hands of a lemur and our hands are similar, even though they're not quite the same – we'll look in more detail at this type of 'evidence' later on. He then went on to talk about the differences between us and lemurs. There are a couple of things from what he said that I want to highlight and focus upon in the next few paragraphs. Here's a transcript of some of the text from the documentary.

> *"It's interesting to note that there is one glaring difference (between us and the lemurs) and that is that these are, compared with us, a little bit dim. Which raises the question, "Why is it that on the island of Madagascar our common ancestor developed into these little fellows whereas on the mainland of Africa they developed into a species that has put one of its own on the moon?" The answer, in a word, is* **competition**. *Sixty million years ago, we were all tiny primitive lemur-like creatures living together on the mainland of Africa.* **But as time went on competition from other mammals in Africa forced us to do develop bigger and bigger brains**. *However, a lucky few of those original primitive lemurs managed to escape the evolutionary rat race and found asylum on this paradise island across the sea. But how did they get there?"*

In the film he then puts together a quick theory of how the local lemur population got onto the island of Madagascar and that theory also included extra ideas as to why larger and heavier animals could not follow them. Then he said...

*"...with the result that when the lemur ancestor finally arrived, it found that there were no predators and no competitors for food either, as there were no apes and no monkeys. So they were able to sit back, relax and evolve; not perhaps **UPWARDS** so much as **sideways** producing many different species of lemur, big ones, small ones, nocturnal ones, diurnal ones, tree hoppers, ground dwellers, solitary ones, social ones, some with a marked interest in phenomenology..."* etc. and then he went off into one of his rambling jokes, which was very funny.

Initial Criticisms

First, I have to make a minor point about his statement that we had ancestors who were *'forced'* to develop bigger and bigger brains due to **competition**. Such a statement is completely unscientific. Just because there is competition or predators, does not mean that new DNA information is **automatically added** into the creature's code in order for it to become more intelligent and so better survive by evolving UPWARDS. Yes, we see sideways adaptation movements amongst Darwin's finches due to food competition; longer beaks for birds feeding on worms, shorter and broader beaks for birds feeding on seeds. As breeding in closed communities continued over generations then a slight change in body shape expression took place but they are all 100% finch. However, just because I have competitors or predators to interact with within my environment does not automatically mean that I am **getting more intelligent** and evolving UPWARDS. I, as a human being, may become more educated by thinking, discussing, reading and reasoning but that is not the same as intelligence increase or DNA change.

Being very sarcastic I would say that a zebra, for example, has a lot more problems than a horse. Zebras are often chased by lions and other meat eaters. They are in competition for a 'safe space to live'. When they're having a break from being chased, and are munching away on grass, they're not going to have a little internal mental chat with themselves about, "those bothersome lions," and "what on earth can we do to either make ourselves faster or defend ourselves, when they start chasing us again tomorrow?" If intelligence and UPWARDS evolutionary change was produced by the pressures within the environment (predators and competitors) then the zebra would be more intelligent than the horse by now.

As illustrated by Mr Cleese in his lemur example, the horse should be getting more *chilled* and stayed in its ways whilst the zebra should be on a one-way trip to genius in order to defeat the oversized pussy-cats that continually pursue them. However, as I said at the start of this paragraph, competition **or any other kind of environmental pressure** does not add new DNA information into any creature. It is a strange idea that we gain new DNA information that increases intelligence just by us having predators or competition. Competition for food sources or from environmental pressures from predators does not, in itself, generate new DNA code for UPWARDS change that will increase intelligence. It simply moves creatures towards particular food sources and those creatures that can survive the best with the new food source in that isolated environment have the opportunity to leave behind offspring with their family traits.

My main point, however, on John Cleese's comments are to do with the phrase,

> "So they were able to sit back, relax and evolve; not perhaps **UPWARDS** so much as **sideways** producing many different species of lemur, big ones, small ones, nocturnal ones, diurnal ones, tree hoppers…"

It is so interesting that these isolated creatures did not evolve into anything but more types of lemur. The reasons for this are due to all that we've already stated in this chapter:

- hereditary DNA remixes do not add new DNA information into offspring
- mutations are only small and most commonly corrected and replaced by the body's DNA repair process, with those that are not fixed either being mainly neutral or bad for the animal

- natural selection is a process that **only** takes DNA **out** of the creature community, it does not add totally new and sophisticated DNA code to those who are part of the creature group

These are the reasons why the lemurs did not evolve 'UPWARDS' as John Cleese put it, but **sideways** instead. Sideways shifts in DNA *cannot* evolve anything upwards. There is **no mechanism** for them to do so, which we'll look at in more detail later on.

*In fact John Cleese's lemurs and Darwin's finches that are stranded on their islands and separate from everything else are living proof that 'evolution' **only goes sideways**.*

Just as the finches produced different types of finch so too the lemurs produced different types of lemur; different shapes, different sizes, different strengths and weaknesses, but all of them either 100% finch or lemur. None of them dog, cat, cow or any other kind of creature, but all of **the same family type**, that is of the same set of creatures **within their own kind**. They are, at best, described as different expressions of their own kind, (kinds within a kind) that is within their own enclosed family species. So John Cleese has really helped us with his insight and statement that the lemur population on the isolated island of Madagascar has 'evolved'...

*"...not perhaps **UPWARDS** so much as **sideways** producing many different species of lemur, big ones, small ones, nocturnal ones, diurnal ones, tree hoppers..."*

In that one statement he has...

...hit the nail on the head!

So in that statement we have encapsulated yet another living example that creatures **only move sideways** and not UPWARDS. This now takes us nicely on to the next chapter where we look at how evolutionists conveniently ignore this problem and **take the conversation to the wrong place**, that is, away from the microbiological level (which is where the real driver /mechanisms for life and real change exist) to that which can be seen by the human eye. Why do they do this? Simply to bring alongside their theories 'other evidences' that they can choose to interpret within the context of evolution. This they can do without reference to the faulty microbiological **mechanism** that does not work. Despite this shift in the conversation, however, we will still see that these 'other evidences' which evolutionists refer to as proof for evolution can equally be interpreted as the work of an intelligent designer.

Chapter 3 – Taking the Conversation Elsewhere

Common Ancestry

Sharing the same Technology as other Creatures

So, ignoring this very big problem that DNA mix only takes evolution **sideways**, evolutionists persist with their theory and choose to focus on the next bit of 'evidence' that they say proves that,

- we (humans) evolved from animals
- all creatures evolved from other creatures lower down the evolutionary family tree
- everything is connected on the tree of life

The argument states that we share the same technology as other creatures and this proves that we have come from them. Before I dive into this subject let me first use a phrase that I have already touched upon and shall continue to use over and over again in this and my next book. That is that...

...the conversation is taking place at the wrong level.

What do I mean by this? Simply that we should still be talking about the microbiological world when considering the theory of evolution. Whenever any so called evidence is given in favour of a theory the question should be asked,

1. How did this happen at the microbiological level?
2. What **mechanism for change existed and was executed** at the microbiological level that caused this change to happen?

If evolution **does not** work at the microbiological level **then it won't work at all**, even if there are observable similarities between creatures that appear at the level of the human eye. You may look like a close relative of mine, but if the DNA tells us otherwise, then you can compare features as much as you like, the DNA truth (the mechanism of change) is where the rubber hits the road and gives us the final conclusion. Let's listen again to Professor Jonathan Wells of UC Berkeley who, in the same interview as already quoted above, says on this subject of common ancestry:

Professor Jonathan Wells – Ancestry
https://www.youtube.com/watch?v=xZn7tTdCm6U&t=6s

*"Now the common ancestry part, the argument for that is usually based on similarities and differences. Why I have certain similarities to this animal or that animal and certain dissimilarities which show this or that. Well those arguments are interesting but they are not conclusive because you can **argue the same way on the basis of common design**. I look like this and not like that because there is a design reason for that. You can do the same with cars, in fact Darwinists have used car models as an illustration of modification, but cars are designed, they are created by engineers. So until you get this one important step, where one species can originate from another species, why should I accept common ancestry at all, because the **mechanism is not there**? The similarities and differences can cut either way but what we're totally lacking at this point is good evidence for Darwin's **basic mechanism**."*

On this point, therefore, Professor Jonathan Wells cuts straight back to DNA and says that there is no **mechanism** at the micro-biological level to bring about new, useful information into any living creature that will cause evolutionary change **UPWARDS** towards a new creature type, a new family type away from the current family.

- -
The Problem of Homology
- -

As I've already said, if the **mechanism** for a theory is proved to be false, then it doesn't matter how many other 'evidences' are available, the theory is still false. Despite this, however, evolutionists still insist on trying to tell us that we evolved by DNA mix, mutation and natural selection because of the similarities that we all see around us, forgetting that they have no viable mechanism to be connected to each other. Let's humour the secular camp for a few more paragraphs, therefore, and see if their assertions, despite their failed mechanism, still ring true or whether even the other 'evidences' that are offered also prove the theory to be false.

The Science of Homology

Homology is the study of shared structure and anatomical position between different organisms. It seems currently to be the driving force for evolutionary argument and is used for justifying common ancestry or the evolutionary origin of species. The main form of evidence for evolution, therefore, ignoring the limitations of the evolutionary microbiological mechanisms that we've already talked about, is the fact that there are similar technologies built into so many creatures right across the animal kingdom. As John Cleese said in his lemur documentary, that our hands are very similar to those of the lemur species, except that our thumbs work differently. Let's look at this for a few moments and see if there are any extra things to say on the subject, to see whether their claims that, just because we can see similarities in technology between different kinds of creatures, that that automatically means that we evolved from them rather than these similarities being the sign of a designer/creator.

Homology - The Frog's Front 'Feet' and the Human Hand

It has been argued, for example, that not only does the lemur, the monkey and the ape have similar hands to us but also the frog does too, when looking at its front feet that is. In fact the bone structures in the arm as well are based on the same technology. Here's a couple of paragraphs from the "How Stuff Works" website.
https://animals.howstuffworks.com/amphibians/frog2.htm

"As anyone who has dissected one in biology class knows, a frog's internal organs look a lot like what you'd find inside a much larger animal. Just like mammals -- including people -- a frog's body has a heart and lungs as well as a stomach, pancreas, liver, gallbladder and intestines."

"Even though frogs don't look much like people on the outside, their skeletons are similar to people's skeletons, especially when it comes to their limbs. Just like in a person's arms, in a frog's front legs are bones called the humerus, the radius and the ulna."

The evolutionist will still shout out that these similarities are here via an evolutionary process and will insist that these similarities are **genuine evidence** that **must** be interpreted in an *evolutionary light*. This is because the frog appears lower down on the evolutionary scale than many other creatures. It is considered an early land animal and that the technology within it, as an early creature, will be reproduced up the evolutionary tree of life. That too is basic logic.

> *If one thing came from another then that*
> *which had been 'established so far'*
> *by the evolutionary process would be*
> ***retained and built upon***
> *to be made more complex.*

You would, however, be able to see the retention of most, if not all, of the foundation stones of change and to trace them back to their logical beginnings. It would be like an archaeologist looking at a modern city that had been built on top of multiple other cities on the same site over time. You'd be able to dig down and see the foundations of each city, clearly laid out and how each foundation 'met the other' as they rested on top of each other. The evidence would present us with...

> *...a single set of sensible and logical biological*
> *'archaeological **connections**'*

...as we clearly would see one biological 'new build' resting directly upon an older one.

The Problem of Ontogenesis
On this matter of connections up the evolutionary family tree, however, there is another stumbling block in the way of the evolutionary theory. It presents itself again at the **microbiological level** and is not talked about too much in the evolutionary classroom. It is called ontogenesis. Ontogenesis is the development of an organism from its earliest stage right through to maturity. So yes, according to the eye, a human hand and a frog's 'hand' (front foot) are similar. The problem, however, lies in ***the way in which they***

71

develop from their embryonic stage to find their final shape. If we had evolved from each other then…

*…the **DNA programming** that makes all living creatures **take their form**, as they develop in the womb or change from a tadpole into a frog, would basically follow the **same pattern of execution**.*

This logical conclusion has already been thought about by evolutionists who have spent a good amount of time trying to find evidence to prove this.

Haeckel's Fraudulent Drawings

Who can't remember, for example, the fraudulent work of Ernst Haeckel? For any who don't know he was an evolutionist who in 1868 published a book called Natürliche Schöpfungsgeschichte (The History of Natural Creation) and in it put together drawings of human, monkey and dog embryos. He sought to show that the different embryos went through identical stages of development. This was to prove that their development was based upon evolutionary processes. If we came from other species, then it was to be expected that our early development was also to be the same. There would be no reason whatsoever for it to change. You may, for example, get different species of butterfly, but they all go through the same basic transformation process either within a cocoon, a chrysalis or by burrowing underground or into leaf waste. The process that each butterfly or moth goes through to leave behind its caterpillar state is always pupation, and this is to be expected as they are all related.

Haeckel's drawings, however, were fraudulent and even though they were proved to be false, they have gained iconic status and have popped up again and again in educational science books for over a hundred years, **as if they were true**. Here's a quote from an online article by Casey Luskin on the subject.

"The notion that Haeckel's drawings were fraudulent or fake did not originate with proponents of intelligent design. Those criticisms originated with evolutionary scientists like embryologist Michael

Richardson, who called them "one of the most famous fakes in biology," or Stephen Jay Gould who said "Haeckel had exaggerated the similarities by idealizations and omissions," and that "in a procedure that can only be called fraudulent," Haeckel "simply copied the same figure over and over again." Likewise, in a 1997 article titled "Haeckel's Embryos: Fraud Rediscovered," the journal 'Science' recognized that "generations of biology students may have been misled by a famous set of drawings of embryos published 123 years ago by the German biologist Ernst Haeckel.""
https://evolutionnews.org/2012/10/darwin_lobbyist_1/

Oops, Different Ontogenesis

So we understand that evolutionists have really wanted to make an ontogenesis connection, the development from *foetal (fetal) status* to full creature, (foetal in the UK is often spelt fetal in the US) between the different species in order to prove their theory. The reason why so much time has been spent on this is because it is very, very important – in fact it is essential to do so. As we've said previously, there has to be biological archaeological connections with the past for the evolutionary tree of life to be viable. Let's pick up, therefore, on the issue that we've begun to talk about, that is the similarities between a frog's 'hand' (front foot) and a human hand. When we look at the development of the human hand and that of the frog's, then we see something very interesting taking place. At the microbiological level the programming that causes them to take shape, that is….

*…the ontogenesis of each, is **totally different**.*

For a human being developing in the womb, the hand starts off looking like a paddle. The babe in the womb initially forms fingerless paddles at the end of each arm and then gaps appear in the paddle and the fingers are revealed. This process is specifically controlled by the DNA programming within human beings. For a frog it is totally different. There is no paddle, there is just a fist and from the fist the fingers grow outwards from points on the fist. To the human eye this difference is interesting. At the microbiological level, however, the difference is astounding. It is a **totally different code** in the DNA that causes something to grow out from a fist than it is for a paddle to

73

separate and to reveal fingers via gaps that appear within it. This throws a spanner in the works for the evolutionist. It is one of the gentle reminders of the sheer genius and complexity of the coding that runs life and how **one set of coding cannot just evolve from the other** (via DNA mix or copy errors) otherwise their programming would be essentially the same.

> **NOTE:** It is also a poke in the eye for anyone who insists that just because we share a common operating system, DNA, that this automatically means that we evolved from each other – as we said earlier when citing Richard Dawkins' assertion of this idea. His sloppy use of language suggests that common DNA proves that evolution is a done deal. He said that it was identical – but the *execution of the code* to create fingers/toes is totally different and not identical at all!

The finger development of a human being and the front toe development of a frog are completely separate. In their coding they are executed very differently but in the end they produce a similar looking technology at the level of the human eye. How amazing is that! There is no naturalistic world view explanation for this. Random changes (copy errors) that are supposed to enable evolutionary **UPWARDS** development do not re-write complex coding in this way.

*If we all stemmed back to one single organism then the **method of ontogenesis** would have the same foundation **in all body parts** of all living creatures.*

Haeckel's drawings moreover, which finally extended to a fish, a salamander, a turtle, a chicken, a rabbit and a human, would all be true. They are, however, grossly wrong. When you see real photos of these embryos you can see that they are remarkably different.

The article from the "How Stuff Works" website, https://animals.howstuffworks.com/amphibians/frog2.htm goes on to say,

"But a frog's skeleton isn't so similar to a human's once you get past the extremities. Frogs have skulls but don't have necks, so they

can't turn, lift or lower their heads like people can. A frog also doesn't have ribs. The rib-like structures you can see in the picture above are part of its spine. A frog's pelvis can slide up and down its spine, which may help it jump. The vertebrae at the bottom end of the spine are fused into one bone called the urostyle."

The more you look at a frog the more you can see that any evolutionary change would not bring about a bird. If you were an alien and had never seen a bird or a human before and you were told that a frog had 'evolved' into something else then the last thing that you would imagine a frog to become would be a bird or a human. Neither is there the fossil evidence to prove this (which we will look at in a few pages time). We would also see a persistent ontogenesis 'footprint' in all of the different body parts as they developed from mere 'dividing cells' into the full creature. Small changes over long periods of time, as the evolutionists say, would provide us with a clear **breadcrumb trail** of biological archaeological connections that demonstrates a path of easy to follow ontogenesis evidence that is straightforward to locate and trace. The evidence would be very clear and conclusive. It is, however, not there.

Homology - Conclusions

So when we look at homology, the study of shared structure within animals, we still see that there is no common route for the development of these structures within each creature up the so-called evolutionary tree of life. Their ontogenesis is quite different both in its features and the programming that determines it. So we can see that just because something looks similar, at first glance, it does not follow that they are the same and have a common root. This is especially evident when we get to the microbiological level where the differences expressed are huge. That which the evolutionist interprets as evidence for evolution, can just as easily be interpreted as the fingerprint of a common designer – and the problem that ontogenesis brings to the table firmly puts the weight of the argument on the side of a designer.

So for me, a theist, the answer is simple. The fact that ontogenesis is so different shows us that we all have a common designer, not a common ancestor, who put together all the creatures on this planet and intelligently used similar designs in them...

75

...knowing that they would all have to share the same spaces as each other.

Certain technologies were used again and again, therefore, so that we could all live effectively in the same environment. That would be obvious. If a group of engineers and I.T. specialists were to create an environment that needed many different types of robots to inhabit it, (like an automated factory shop floor) you can guarantee that the small robots and the big robots would all have similar engineering in them, that is in their 'nuts and bolts' that made them work. Why create a set of designs for one robot and a completely different set for another when they both simply need to 'walk down the same corridor' and do their job? Components within the limbs would be similar and they would all share the same operating system. There would be extra programming within the code to make specialised technologies work but there would also be a good deal of overlap in the programming. All the robots would be connected in some way, yet distinct in their features and function according to how the engineers wanted them to behave and initiate change within the environment. So too a creator/designer for life would obviously use similar technologies when creating creatures to inhabit the earth and use the same basic 'operating system' for all life to live by (DNA). This is a logical and sensible conclusion to arrive at. Biologists, however, are not I.T. experts, nor are they trained in mathematical engineering. This is why secular biologists propagate idealised fantasies about things evolving without any knowledge of their impossibility at the **microbiological *programming* level** or the ***engineering*** level.

- -
Integrated Technologies & Processes
- -

Interdependency within Creature Structure

Now we meet another huge problem for the theory of evolution, which is the engineering that can be seen in all living creatures, called integrated technology. You and I, and all living creatures, are mind-bogglingly integrated in our technological makeup. It is a well-known fact that partially developed or partially assembled engineering does not work. You can only strip down a machine so far before it stops

76

being able to do that which it was designed to do. I can take the bonnet off a car and its doors too and it will still run well, but as soon as I remove one of the wheels it ceases to go. It is the same with any process on a production line. Perhaps I can miss out a cosmetic activity that does not add to the product but as soon as an essential component or an activity that is vital to the final outcome is left out, then the production line process fails in its attempt at making something useful or fit for purpose. So there are two things to note about machines and systems that are made up of many parts,

1. Each machine has essential components that have to be in place to make the machine work – remove the components beyond a certain level and the machine ceases to function.
2. There are processes that take place when creating something and those processes have to happen and be completed in a certain order – if the order is not followed, then the process fails.

A simple example each of the above would be,

1. a mouse trap
2. a cake recipe

A mouse trap has a certain number of components to it so that, if you take one of those components away, it will no longer work and catch the mouse. (We'll look at this more in a moment when examining the work of Michael K. Behe). The cake recipe outlines a process of cake creation. It must be followed in the right order or the cake will not cook properly. You cannot bake the eggs first, for example, and then add the rest of the ingredients and cook later, not unless you're making the kind of cake that I'm capable of creating! These are two examples of integrated technologies or processes.

Integrated Technologies & Processes – Blood Clotting

I'm now, in a very simple format, going to summarise what is called the blood clotting cascade. Blood clotting is a very complex process. I've listened to science programmes and watched online videos that show that there are over forty different actions that have to take place for clotting to happen so that when we humans cut our finger, thumb, knee etc. the blood clotting process will halt the blood flow and eventually stop the bleeding. Not only are there over forty separate actions that need to happen but each action has to happen **in the correct order** or the blood does not clot and we continue to bleed. The following text on this subject, a **simplified version** of blood clotting, comes from a YouTube video at the following address: https://www.youtube.com/watch?v=PjhHQHMnMjI

> **NOTE:** Don't worry if you are not a scientist and can't understand the words used below, just read them to get the idea of the process.

1) Damage to the blood vessel exposes collagen fibres.
2) The platelets are activated by collagen fibres and change shape, forming a temporary 'platelet plug'.
3) Activated platelets and damaged cells produce a protein called Thromboplastin.
4) Thromboplastin then activates a series of enzymes that in the presence of vitamin K and calcium ions convert the protein Prothrombin into the enzyme Thrombin.
5) Thrombin catalyses the conversion of soluble fibrinogen to the insoluble fibrin.
6) When any fibrin molecules have been formed they can polymerise creating a mesh of fibrin that traps more platelets and red blood cells, forming a clot and effectively sealing the wound.

As you can see, even from this very simplified model, there are many different steps to blood clotting correctly and stopping us from bleeding to death when we get a wound. For a more complete overview of the process you can watch a short five minute video at this address:
https://www.youtube.com/watch?v=fa5rbkFpq0w

Here I'd like to make reference to a book called, 'Darwin's Black Box,' where Michael K. Behe talks about reducing machines to their basic components. He gives the example of a traditional mouse trap, which I've mentioned before, and then goes into much greater depth about the clotting of blood when a wound occurs. Only when you read at the level at which he writes, will you understand not only the complexity of what happens when a wound appears but also the different stages that have to take place for the clot to be successful. Behe also goes into great detail to tell us why the attempts by evolutionists to say how the blood clotting process may have evolved are incorrect and inadequate. This is yet another piece of essential technology that the evolutionary theory cannot even begin to account for.

Integrated Technologies & Processes – Babies Making their own Blood

I've already mentioned the YouTube lecture by Dr David Menton where he talks about a baby making its own blood, a process that cannot be evolved via small step-by-step changes, https://www.youtube.com/watch?v=Jck4naOUGQo
Let me just repeat again this illustration as a reminder of integrated technology. Dr Menton says,

"The whole surface of the placenta is one cell, one single cell. In order to get out you have to go through the cell wall. Baby's blood cells are on the inside and the mothers are on the outside. The baby has to make its own blood, that's one thing the placenta cannot do. It supplies most things for the baby to survive but it doesn't give blood. So the baby has to make its own blood. What does a baby need to make its own blood? It needs haemoglobin for one. Haemoglobin contains iron and it's only source of iron is from the mother's blood. Iron does not go across the placental barrier. It's impermeable to iron. Life is over. (Sarcastically he then says...) *By the incredible stroke of dumb luck, one of the hundred thousand different proteins in our body is called transthyretin. Transthyretin goes across this barrier picks up the iron from the mother and is able to go back through the barrier and release it to the baby via which the baby can then create blood. Without this you can't, therefore, have the next generation."*

Fetching haemoglobin for its iron resource to use for blood creation requires the following:

- having the pre-knowledge built within the DNA of the baby that,
  - haemoglobin is needed to create blood

- haemoglobin is available for it to use
- knowing where the haemoglobin is specifically located
- knowing that the protein transthyretin can get it for you
- knowing what order of amino acids will create a transthyretin protein
- knowing what code to have in the DNA that can be copied to RNA for its reading and the exact assembly of those amino acids
- having the ability to send the 'go get it' instruction to the transthyretin to initiate the fetch process
- knowing how the transthyretin can locate and take hold of the haemoglobin

knowing how to bring the haemoglobin back and what to do with it to create the babies' blood. All of this requires pre-knowledge and it cannot be evolved in a step-by-step process.

This intricate relationship between the placenta and transthyretin in order to create haemoglobin isn't something that can be evolved via mutation by a step-by-step process over a long period of time. You cannot break this process down into stages. It all has to come together as one unit, or it doesn't happen at all.

There are thousands of other examples like this that evolution just cannot even begin to account for, from the human eye to the ear to the different parts of the brain to the immune system, to the technology of flight for birds and that of sonar, called echolocation, in the dolphin, to the metamorphosis undertaken by a butterfly.

The more we know about the biological and microbiological world and its complexities, the more the theory of evolution falls apart because life is built upon...

...integrated pre-programmed technology that cannot be reduced to a lower level and still work.

No one builds a half robot and says, "Well it can't walk or talk, but that will do for the moment." If it cannot function then it has no use.

If a robot has to find a plug to recharge itself, but the same robot has no legs to move by, then it will not even self-maintain its internal power source – let alone evolve its internal coding. How much more in the multi-complex microbiological world? The complexity of the code that drives life and the multiple components that all work together to make life work are not reducible. There are no evolutionary half-way houses of change that can keep everything working whilst still under development. It's like trying to live in a multi-story building whilst it is still under construction. There are no stairs, lifts, windows, doors, just a foundation and blocks going upwards and a structure ready to be built upon. It is not habitable, however and the whole thing will not function. Life inside it is impossible. So too with the microbiological world, you cannot evolve the **UPWARD** technological jumps between creatures via DNA mix and mutation (copy error) and expect everything or anything to work. We'll continue looking at this a little later on.

The Fossil Record

The last section on integrated technology brings me on nicely to the fossil record. You would assume that, with the abundance of fossils available to us today, that the story of evolution would be told in full and in detail by the rocks. We'll spend the next few pages of this book looking at that. First of all, however, let me build on an illustration that I came across a few years ago.

An Alien Conversation!
The Fossil Record – Unicycles, Bikes, Trikes, Cars and Motorbikes
I'm going to pick up an illustration that A.E. Wilder Smith proposes in his book, "The Natural Sciences Know Nothing of Evolution," and I'm going to slightly adapt the illustration in order to make my point.

Let's imagine, and I hope this never happens, but let's imagine that there was a terrible war with the following consequences

- all life on this planet was wiped out
- the planet turned into just one big pile of dust and rubbish

81

Then an alien landed on our planet (I don't believe that there are aliens but let me pose that question just for the sake of this illustration). The alien tried to find out what had happened in the past. The sensible thing to do would be to look at the debris. Amongst the debris would be the clues as to what went on in Earth's history. Let's then imagine that the alien came across a few items that it had not seen before and tried to make sense of them.

First it came across a bicycle and had no knowledge of what it was. It would probably think that the bike was the remains of a strange creature. The alien then says to itself, "This is an interesting creature, look it's got two round things (which we call wheels). It's a bit bent and sort of fossilised but I can still clearly make out its shape." Then the alien comes across a motorbike and says, "This also has two round things (wheels), but far more complex." Then the alien come across a car and says, "Wow, look at this!" Then a child's scooter is found and then a three wheeled bike. Then, after much more searching, a single wheeled bike, a unicycle, is found. Then the alien comes across a go-cart, then a child's buggy and then a full sized jeep. Finally, after finding lots of variants of all of these, the alien comes across the remains of a racing car. If after finding all these things the alien said, "Oh look, here is the simplest one, the unicycle, here's the next simplest which is the scooter, then there's the bicycle, then the tricycle, then the go-cart, then the little buggy, then the motorbike, then the car and then finally the racing car. Look at the evolutionary process that has gone from the simple one wheeled item to the two, to the three, to the four, to the different types of four, to the different engines and up to the super racing car. Look how this species has evolved!

You would know, however, that each one of those items was created separately by someone with a mind, who created different levels of technology according to how each one **fits into the environment** according to its **place in life**. The unicycle for entertainment, the bicycle for easy short distance travelling around, a tricycle for a very young child to learn on, a scooter for fun, a motorbike for the biker who wants to dodge traffic queues, a car for the average person to use to get to work and back and the racing car for the extreme minority who will enter the racing arena. All these have different purposes, different reasons why people use them.

Then a second alien arrives on our planet. This alien listens to the first alien's theory of how this 'bike creature' developed over time from the evidence that is before them. The second alien, however, is not convinced and begins to critically examine the theory. The first line of questioning goes something like this.

1. "Which part of the first wheel appeared first?
2. Was it the spokes or the tyre?
3. If it was the spokes then how did they begin?
4. Did they begin as blobs that elongated over time and if so what was the process and **mechanism** by which they elongated and why did they do so?
5. What caused the spokes to become attached to each other and why did they form a perfect circle by themselves?
6. **How can a random process**, left to itself, **create this perfect and flat circle**?
7. What caused the spokes to **be equally set apart by the same distance** around the rim of the wheel?
8. How was the rubber for the tyre originally generated?
9. What caused the rubber tyre to fit so neatly around the metal rim?
10. How did the tyre get its unique shape at the edges so that the tyre could stay attached to the rim?
11. What caused the metal rim to become attached to the metal spokes?
12. How did the wheel move by itself, even with the tyre attached to it?
13. What guided it to grow and change and develop?
14. How did the frame begin and what purpose did it serve whist it was only partially formed?
15. How did the brakes form and again, what purpose did they serve when they were only partially formed?
16. etc.

All these questions, and so many more, would be valid engineering questions. The more questions that were asked, the more difficult it would become for the incorrect theory to be maintained. You would need fantasy theory upon fantasy theory, all stacked on top of each other, to still uphold the initial theory.

Once these questions were answered by the first alien entertaining secondary fantasy theories (in order to justify the initial theory about the origins of the bicycle and its first evolutionary steps) then the second alien would bring up the problem of the huge 'jumps' in technology to account for. Not only are the wheels different from a bicycle to that of a jeep or motorbike but there are no pedals to make the more advanced machines run. Instead we now have an engine to account for. Now the first alien, who put together the initial theory, will say that the bike evolved not into the jeep but firstly into the motorbike, as there are still similar systems between them, such as handlebars and a single seat. The technological jump, however, from bike to motorbike is, as we've said, huge. There is fuel that needs to be contained, transferred and **processed** in order to produce power; that power has to be sensibly used and directed to create motion that will drive the wheels. None of these things can come about via **small and gradual changes**. They come together as 'group parts' that fit together to make a whole.

"You haven't got here any fossils that show any kind of movement from one creature to another with just some of these engineering technological jumps in place. Show me an example of one of these creatures that has a partially evolved fuel system!"

So the first alien starts to talk about 'missing links' in order to justify keeping his theory intact. The second alien, however, mocks this notion by saying,

"Well done, you're calling them 'missing links' because that is exactly what they are, 'missing'!

So the first alien **changes his language** and calls all of the missing link fossils that are in his imagination '**transitional creatures**' because that sounds better. It makes them *sound as if they are not missing* at all. Then he comes up with the idea of *punctuated evolution*, a term that describes the technological 'jumps' that are between the creatures. He says that one species jumped in its technology from one to the other.

"Nature does this," he says to the second alien. "We see microbes collide and then new information merge between them. One swallows another and the DNA in them merges." He points to the unicycle and says, "One swallowed another one and the creature now has two wheels and not one. Simple you see."

The second alien laughs, "Since when does a large object, pointing to the bicycle suddenly jump in its technology by swallowing another, pointing to the motorbike and the car? You might very well convince yourself that one simple single-wheeled creature swallowed another one to become two wheeled but you can't take that simple analogy and use it to move from this," pointing to a motorbike, "to this," pointing to a car."

"It would have four wheels," protests the first alien. "If this," pointing to the motorbike, "swallowed/attached itself to another of its own kind, then it would have four wheels!"

"Look at it!" says the second alien. "Its whole frame is different and the engine is totally different. How on earth can you maintain that one 'jumped technologically' into the other? You can't just use a simple collide theory based on the simplest of these creatures to justify large technological jumps further up your evolutionary tree."

The first alien still clings onto his theory, however. "Well there are similarities between them. They both process fuel. They both steer. There is commonality between them all if you look carefully enough."

"But where are all of the in-between fossils?" protests the second alien. "There should be loads and loads and loads of them, all showing in detail every stage of development, which should extend even to your *jumps* that you say can happen."

"Oh I'll find them," says the first alien. "It's just a matter of time."

"You should have found loads of them by now," says the second alien. "In fact, if your theory is correct that they evolved over a long period of time via small changes and some jumps, then we should see **more half-way-house fossils than the full creatures**. There should be loads of them everywhere! You've got multitudes of missing links!"

"They're called 'transitional creatures' insists the first alien and we'll find one or two soon I'm sure."

"One or two!" shouts the second alien, beginning to lose his patience. "One or two, you need thousands upon thousands to even justify moving from this," (pointing to the bicycle) "to this," (pointing to the motorbike).

"Well," says the first alien, "this is because this type of evolutionary jump happens so quickly, at the drop of a hat in fact, that it is not possible for it to be represented on the geological timescale. It's like trying to record minutes or even seconds using the hour hand of a clock. You just can't do it. That's the reason why we can't find fossils. The fact that we can see different types of handlebars on different types of these creatures shows just how quickly these things move in their evolutionary activities. There are so many different types of handlebars you know. This is direct evidence showing just how quickly they move from one into the other."

"That notion is ridiculous," says the second alien.

"Look at these handlebars," says the first alien. "They're so similar. This type of movement from one to the other," pointing from the bike to the motorbike, "is the next *logical* step."

"*Logical step*?" cries the second alien. "Since when has random and unguided movements of so called evolutionary change ever had anything to do with logic? If something is random and unguided there is no '*next logical step*!' Randomness always brings about chaos, not expert engineering."

"Evolution is hap-hazard," says the first alien, "but over time it always finds the path that is most attractive for its development."

"*Most attractive*," says the second alien, almost pulling his hair out. "You're not trying to give evolution some kind of personality again are you? It doesn't have any rationality behind it. There is no reasoning mind! There is nothing to '*be attracted to*' along its haphazard journey!"

"It's just the luck of random chance," replies the first alien.

"Luck!" shouts the second alien. "Since when has *luck* found its way into engineering and science? Luck doesn't construct anything!"

"Well," says the first alien, "my computer programme shows that it's possible. It shows, in fact, that it's not only possible but that it is more than probable and happens rather quickly."

"Your computer programme is a con!" replies the second alien. "All your programme does is to simulate what's in your head. You've programmed it for success. It's not a simulation of what might happen, it's a film of what you imagine to have happened. It's a fraud! It's just a projection of your imagination!"

"Your problem is that you just *lack the creative thinking* to do proper science."

"**These are precision made machines**," says the second alien. There is a mind behind their existence..."

"Oh you're not going to bring up that religious thinking again are you?" says the first alien in a tired tone. "Science can't be used to test any statement that 'A mind created these creatures.' We're meant to be doing science here, not religion!"

"And you're just using your *religious* imagination to imagine that they evolved one from another just because you *religiously believe* that there is no super intelligence behind the universe," said the second alien. "The notion that they evolved is all pre-set in your head. **All you're doing is picking out different levels of sophisticated technology and choosing to believe that a simpler one evolved into another one**. The religious blind belief is all on your part, not mine!"

> **NOTE:** You'll see how Richard Dawkins does exactly the same thing in a lecture on the supposed evolution of the eye towards the end of this book.

No-one in their right mind, after examining the evidence before them, would say that the technological jumps between the bikes, motorbikes and cars just mutated themselves into existence by haphazard chance events, or would use the phrase 'punctuated evolution', as has been used in the past by evolutionists to explain those technological jumps in the supposed evolutionary tree. If there wasn't any **religious world view reason** why the first alien should keep up the theory, then the theory would be dropped. The inability to account for the technological gaps would be enough to cause a complete rethink. However, if the first alien already believed the following:

- the existence of all aliens in the universe was due to chance
- that there wasn't a creator behind the universe
- that true freedom for aliens is for them to live their lives as they wish without being judged by a 'creator'

...then this particular alien might be very reluctant to give up the evolutionary theory about the wheels and bikes and cars as the theory supports the alien's **world view convictions**. The alien might not be thinking this overtly, but the religious world view of any creature is always in the background of their mind – where it continually sits and influences their reasoning. No-one likes their religious world view to be knocked and the scientific method is always influenced by the motivation of the person *doing the looking* as they look to fulfil that world view.

The above illustration is a little like evolution today. We have theory upon theory upon theory, plus academic reputation, plus theory, plus academic reputation, plus theory, plus theory etc. and somehow, amongst the mix of all the 'talk', the theory still stands despite the huge gaps that are totally unaccounted for and the absent **mechanisms** that would cause it to work. So, in the light of what's just been said, let's look at the fossil record.

The Witness of the General Fossil Record

Darwin said that if the fossil record did not show the intermediate stages of evolution then his theory would be undone. When you think about it, if it took millions of years for creatures to evolve then, for **most of their history**, they would be classed as 'creatures in transition'. This is because we're told that the mutations that brought about all of the complexity of life are **minute** ones and that, **minute changes** over **a long period of time** are supposed to add up to big changes.

> **NOTE:** By the way, as a side point on this issue, evolutionists tell us that the reason why no one has ever observed a cell increasing in complexity in the laboratory is because it only happens every now and then over billions of years. The thought has occurred to me, however, that there are trillions upon trillions of cells within you and me and many different trillions of highly organised and specialised cells within other creatures found around this planet too. So if we've only been evolving for **billions** of years then, to be honest, basic maths and logic tells us that cells **upgrading** themselves with totally new DNA information coding for new body parts via random DNA mix and mutation must actually be quite a common activity. It has to be so in order for internal auto-organisation to take place. Trillions upon trillions upon trillions of changes need to take place in order to get to the final 'me' from a single cell (and that over just billions of years). This frankly suggests quite a frenzied activity in order for it to all happen in such a short space of time. Not only do you have to account for the trillions of successful changes, you also have to account for all of those random changes *that didn't work*, which would be the vast majority of

88

them as copy errors are no more than errors within the code. So don't forget that, if **random chance** is the driver and **mechanism** for change at the microbiological level, then the majority of the imagined evolutionary changes would be false ones and these failed attempts would also appear in the fossil record; chance, however, never built a car let alone a living creature, but let's ignore that for the moment and focus on the fossil record.

These small changes that took place over a long period of time would provide plenty of opportunity for partially developed, half-developed, mostly developed, and almost completely developed animals and insects to die and turn into fossils. Our fossil base is a very rich resource that comments on the past, it tells the story of what happened. So what does it actually tell us? Here's a transcript from part of a YouTube video called "Fossil layers DO NOT support evolution and Darwin's tree of life." The video is found at this address: https://www.youtube.com/watch?v=X28MZbQGjZk&t=175s
Here the commentator says:

*"Perhaps the most damaging blow to Darwin's theory is the fossil record. If all living organisms have descended from the same primitive lifeform, then the rock strata of the Earth should be filled with the fossilised remains of animals that were once part of a great evolutionary chain; a chain of small biological modifications ultimately leading to a spectacular diversity of life. Yet after two centuries of research, highlighted by excavations in southern China, the multitude of transitional experiments, or missing links, that should exist are conspicuous only **by their absence**."*

I will come back to this video in a moment but first I want you to read a short interview with Professor Roberto Fondi who is a specialist in palaeontology at the University of Siena.

Interview with Professor Roberto Fondi
Here's a transcript of the interview with Professor Roberto Fondi who is asked the question, "Does palaeontology prove evolution?"
https://www.youtube.com/watch?v=_3K5Pgu7wkY

Interviewer: Let's turn to the science that studies fossils, the science of palaeontology. Professor Roberto Fondi is a specialist in palaeontology. He teaches at the Department of Earth Sciences in the University of Siena in Italy. Amongst his other activities he acts as scientific adviser for the reconstruction of prehistoric animals.

Professor Roberto Fondi: You may be surprised to know that the fundamental assumptions upon which evolutionary thinking is based are not at all confirmed by palaeontology.

Interviewer: What are those assumptions?

Professor Fondi: Firstly, that living cells arose from non-living matter by spontaneous generation. This means that purely as a result of a chain of chemical reactions in a hypothetical primordial soup a living cell was formed. Secondly that these cells grouped themselves together into colonies to form complex multicellular structures. These structures were then supposed to transform during the course of time into animals and finally man. According to these assumptions the ancestors of all living creatures, including man, can be traced back to a single cell. This ancestry is represented as a gigantic genealogical tree with numerous branches sprouting from a single trunk whose roots sync directly into non-living matter.

Interviewer: Doesn't palaeontology confirm those assumptions?

Professor Fondi: Not at all. All the biological groups from bacteria to man appear abruptly in the fossil record without any links connecting them with each other.

Interviewer: Why is it then that so many people believe that fossils prove evolution?

Professor Fondi: Evolution is presented to grown-ups and taught to the very young as a fact that has been verified and demonstrated for so long, that it is a waste of time and even ridiculous to question it. In my books 'Beyond Darwin' and 'de Oganische Evolutie' I give names of well-known scientists who firmly believe evolution is a proven fact such as George Gaylord Simpson and Steven J Gould of Harvard University. Yet there are also equally well-known scientists who believe evolution and admit that there is no real proof such as E. Guillenot van Genève and G.A. Kerkut of Southampton University.

Interviewer: So what is the truth of the matter?

Professor Fondi: Well, there is a history book of the past and that is the rocks and the fossilised remains in them. So it is up to the palaeontologist to read that book and give the answer.

Interviewer: What do you read in that book professor?

Professor Fondi: The fact is that after nearly two centuries of intense research the palaeontological evidence for evolutionary theory is not only rare but highly questionable. The point is that if evolution had really happened **the evidence would be in great abundance** and incontestable. The museums would be overflowing with the fossils clearly documenting the transitions between the various biological groups. Yet there are none. Moreover there is no indication that the situation will change in the future. Those very few fossils which are *claimed to show* some kind of evolutionary link such as the amphibian Ichtyostica, the reptile Prognognoptocus, the bird Archaeopteryx and the ape called Homo Habilis are very far from conclusive.

Interviewer: What about the supposed evolution of man?

Professor Fondi: The idea of gradual evolution of man from such creatures as apes is totally without foundation and should be firmly rejected. Man is not the most recent link in a long chain of evolution. He represents a type which has existed without any substantial change since his first appearance. The justification of this statement is abundantly clear from my books.

Interviewer: What then is your final conclusion?

Professor Fondi: Quite simply that more progress will be made in biology and other disciplines if they kept away from the dead end roads of evolution mythology and resumed the fruitful approach of Aristotelian, Linnaean, Cuvierian and Goethean Morphology.

Claims for Transitional Fossils

Many evolutionists claim that the fossil record does have lots and lots of transitional forms but again this is due to evolutionists choosing to believe that a **sideways** 'new species' fossil is direct evidence for UPWARDS evolution; a sideways fossil is seen as a transitional fossil just as much as a '**missing link**' is seen as a transitional fossil. This again is the language problem that we have already dealt with in this book. When creationists talk about transitional forms, or missing links, they are talking about fossils which clearly show an UPWARD movement from a fish to a frog / lizard and then from a frog / lizard to a bird. So once we get beyond the initial communication barrier, the language problem, and we begin to talk accurately about all of those fossil transitions that will clearly show the move from one creature within its own kind into that of a completely separate kind (a new family group), then we begin to see that there is, as we have already stated, **a complete absence of these transitional forms in the fossil record** which should be here in numbers almost beyond our counting.

The gradual, minute changes that took place over long periods of time would give you a map of the step-by-step processes that took place for creatures to evolve. The fossil record should be an idiot's guide to evolution. Why are simple step-by-step hand books called idiot guides? Simply because they will take you step-by-step over the process, **missing nothing out**, so that a task can be performed correctly and anyone can follow it. The fossil record should also be an idiot's guide to evolution. It should tell you in minute detail, **not missing anything out**, about all of those things that happened from every single small stage of successful *and unsuccessful* evolutionary attempts. They should all be contained within the hard rock, via fossilisation, for us to clearly see.

One very famous evolutionist is a gentleman called Dr Colin Patterson. He was a palaeontologist at the Natural History Museum in London from 1962 to his official retirement in 1993. He wrote a book simply entitled "Evolution". This book was widely read as an excellent authority on the subject. Below is a link to a creationist YouTube video. In it a creationist says that he wrote to Dr Paterson asking him why, in his book "Evolution" he had not provided one single drawing of a truly transitional fossil to support his theory and to provide the full evidence to show that evolution took place. Thankfully Dr Paterson wrote back and gave the reply that you can see below. Here is an excerpt from the video,
https://www.youtube.com/watch?v=SWDRz5cSziQ

"*I wrote to Dr Colin Patterson and asked him why he didn't put a single picture of an intermediate form on a connecting link in his book on evolution. Dr Paterson, who has **seven million fossils in his museum**, said the following when he answered my letter. "I fully agree with your comments on the lack of direct illustration of evolutionary transitions in my book. If I knew of any, fossil or living, I certainly would have included them". Later he said, "I will lay it on the line there is not one such fossil for which one might make a watertight argument.""*

Dr Colin Patterson later in life complained that creationists had often taken his words out of context. However on this issue there is very little to take out of context. He is very emphatic and very clear in his words on the subject. There is **not one fossil** by which a **watertight argument** could be made to say **that evolution took place**. We will look at claims for so-called transitional fossils in a few paragraphs time.

The above video goes on to point out,

"Since Darwin's time evolutionists have aggressively searched for vital fossil evidence to support the idea that lifeforms evolved. Even Darwin admitted that his own theory was worthless speculation without invaluable fossil proof for transitional forms. In collaboration with evolutionists, oil companies have drilled wells throughout the world examining layers of the Earth to depths in excess of five miles. Of the millions of fossils unearthed, not one sample of a transitional form has been discovered. Over the years the research of geology and archaeology have also failed to produce evidence that supports evolution's claims."

The video goes on to say,

"Reptiles are supposed to have converted their scales into feathers. Now a scale on a reptile is nothing but a fold in the skin. How in the world could a fold in the skin have ever been frayed out into the intricate design of a feather? There has never been anything found intermediate between the fold in the reptile skin and a feather of a bird... In the evolution of flying creatures, an animal's forelimb (good for walking or climbing) must have gradually changed into a wing. We have never found any fossils that show this in-between structure. I suspect such a creature long before he had a wing had a lousy forelimb and it could neither have walked nor have flown. The whole idea is ludicrous."

The fossil record, therefore, is quite the opposite to that which evolutionists claim it to be. It is totally inadequate to support evolutionary theory.

The Cambrian Explosion - A Huge Problem

This next example from the fossil record is not taught in secondary schools from the perspective of undermining evolution. Let me pick up again the video entitled, "Fossil layers DO NOT support evolution and Darwin's tree of life." The video is once again found at this address: https://www.youtube.com/watch?v=X28MZbQGjZk&t=175s

This video says, *"The most graphic example of this void (missing links) in the fossil record is a geological era known as the Cambrian explosion."*

In the same video Professor Jonathan Wells adds,
*"The branching tree pattern of Darwin's theory is actually not seen anywhere in the fossil record, **unless we impose it with our own minds**. So the Cambrian explosion is the most dramatic refutation of the tree of life."*

The video goes on to say,
"The Cambrian explosion of life was a dramatic episode in geological history. Usually dated at around five hundred and thirty million years ago, the exquisitely preserved Cambrian fossils reveal that the body plans for virtually every major animal phylum appeared, not gradually and slowly, as Darwin had speculated, but instead with astonishing suddenness."

"In a geological instant the animal kingdom leapt from small relatively simple organisms to extraordinary creatures with spinal cords, compound eyes and articulated limbs. The record of this explosion of life looks nothing like Darwin's slowly branching tree."

Professor Jonathan Wells adds,
*"Darwin's theory is that there is a tree of life where you have one organism diverging into many other organisms and big differences appearing at the top... This does not exist in the fossil record. If I was using a botanical illustration it would be a lawn, with separate blades of grass sprouting **independently of each other** and this would be the phyla. Now within each phylum there is subsequent diversification, but even there I don't see the branches connecting that would make them a tree of life. As scientists it's not our job to force the evidence into a theory that just doesn't fit it. So I have absolutely no desire or reason to uphold Darwin's theory at this point."*

In this botanical illustration Professor Jonathan Wells links back to A.E. Wilder Smith's book, "The Natural Sciences Know Nothing of Evolution," where he says that life began polyphylogenetically rather than monophylogenetically – which means life started from many sources rather than evolved from one single cell.

The Fossil Record – The Cambrian Explosion – Hugh Ross

Here's a transcription from a lecture given by Hugh Ross who runs the organisation, *Reasons to Believe*. He says about the Cambrian explosion,

"Today on planet Earth we have about thirty five basic different body plans of animals. There was more than double that at the time of the Cambrian explosion. They all show up at once. Now I remember when I was at high school when we were studying this and the belief was that the phylum that we are part of, the chordates, they showed up about forty to fifty million years after the Cambrian explosion began. Today we know they show up right at the beginning of the Cambrian explosion, even including the vertebrates. The vertebrates show up right up at the beginning of the Cambrian explosion. So they all show up at once and over half of the phylum has disappeared. As one evolutionary biologist declared, "This is evolution going the wrong way." They'll suddenly appear and then they begin to disappear. Now let me show you a couple of comments from some of the leading evolutionary biologists who do take a nontheistic perspective."

Huge Ross goes on to say.

"Probably the most famous atheist in the world today is Britain's Richard Dawkins. He is very blunt and aggressive in his attack against God. But back in 1987 he wrote a book called the Blind Watchmaker in which he tried to claim that God was not behind life. This is what he said about the Cambrian explosion. "The Cambrian strata of rocks, vintage about 600 million years ago, are the oldest ones in which we find most of the major invertebrate groups and we find many of them already in an advanced state of evolution the very first time they appear. It is as though they were just planted there without any evolutionary history..." This is recognised as the biggest problem of the fossil record for the nontheistic worldview. The fact that we just had this amazing explosive event that literally comes out of nowhere. And what you've got is a planet with bacteria on it and then suddenly these

95

animals pop up out of nowhere. Kevin Peterson wrote a review a few years back where he said that, "Elucidating the materialistic basis (that is the nontheistic basis) for the Cambrian explosion has become more elusive, not less, the more we know about the event itself." This is kind of the main theme of 'Reasons to Believe'. Namely the more we learn about the record of nature, the greater the evidence accumulates that the God of the Bible is responsible for what we see and the Cambrian explosion is one of the most dramatic examples of that."

So Hugh Ross concludes that the fossil record, especially the Cambrian explosion, demonstrates to us the sudden appearance of fully functioning and multi-complex creatures. There is no gradual evolution towards them, they are just suddenly 'Bing' there, without evolutionary explanation.

> **Note:** I have quoted from different Christian scientists in this book who hold different beliefs about the earth's age, who interpret the time scales in Genesis 1 differently. Some Christians will be disappointed about this, wanting me to keep to one group and excluding the other, but first and foremost my main aim in this book is the bringing together of as many witnesses that I can on the subject of debunking evolution's different assertions. Evolution can be attacked from many different directions so, in order to do this effectively, I will make reference to a variety of Christians who are experts in their field of science.

Famous Missing Links Debunked

Ignoring the Cambrian explosion and the fact that the fossil base should be almost filled to the brim with transitional creatures, every now and again a single fossil will appear that evolutionists initially claim to be a transitional, and get very excited about. There have, in fact, only been a small number of famous fossils held up over the years by evolutionists saying, "We've found it! Here it is," they say, "A missing link! We've finally got the proof we've been looking for!" One of the latest was a discovery in the Canadian Arctic in 2004 of a fossil that was called the Tiktaalik roseae. It was said to have both fish and reptile attributes. Here's a transcription from an online video that talks about this short-lived famous so called missing link between fish and four legged animals. Use the link below if you wish to view the full video on YouTube.

https://www.youtube.com/watch?v=9-v-cmPCaAI

"According to an intriguing article from Creation Ministries International, tracks of footprints found in a quarry in Poland have turned the evolutionary world upside down. For years there has been a neat evolutionary story, CMI says, about how fish evolved four legs and came out of the ocean onto the land. Probably the most famous fossil in this sea-to-land icon of evolution is Tiktaalik roseae, a fish with fins that was claimed to have had features intermediate between fish and tetrapods. Creationists consistently rejected the evolutionary spin put on the fossil and showed that it had nothing to do with the alleged sea-to-land transition. All the same, evolutionists promoted Tiktaalik relentlessly; it even has its own website, as well as features in evolutionary diagrams, stars on the covers of books about evolution and was even the theme of a song to promote evolution. Richard Dawkins in his latest book, "The Greatest Show on Earth", claims Tiktaalik is the perfect missing link. Perfect because it almost exactly splits the difference between fish and amphibian and perfect because it is missing no longer, Dawkins says. But now this footprint evidence from Poland consigns Tiktaalik and all its companion fossils onto the garbage heap. From being stars of the show they have suddenly become an evolutionary dead end. So the creationists, as it seems, were right all along. Creation International claims that it has now been demonstrated in a strong case that the supposed evolutionary links were in reality four-legged animals that resembled large lizards. If four-legged animals existed eighteen million years earlier, then Tiktaalik can't be the transitional fossil it has been claimed to be. Tiktaalik has suddenly been demoted to an evolutionary dead end along with all the other fossils connected with it. In other words, all those neat evolutionary diagrams that vividly display the transition from fish to four footed animal ancestor now need to be disposed of. The evolutionary house of cards, so proudly paraded before the world, collapses with a breeze of evidence from Poland. "And this is not some small correction," CMI says, "or a minor detail." It has turned the evolutionary world upside down. Something of the magnitude of the upset can be gleaned from statements made about the find in Nature Magazine. "This forces a radical reassessment of the timing, ecology and environmental setting of the fish tetrapod transition, as well as

97

the completeness of the body fossil record." And this quote, "It will cause a significant reappraisal of our understanding of tetrapod origins." Those scientists who have dedicated their lives and careers to the standard 'fish-to-beast' story will not be very infused by the implications of the latest find. "They will be reluctant to change, especially since they have nothing to replace it with," CMI says. Curiously there are a few different ways they could rework the evidence and hold on to Tiktaalik at the same time. If that doesn't work, they may simply ignore it. Time will tell. But in the meantime the fairy-tale of the magic mud of evolution continues to unwind and fall apart."

Basic Evolutionary Assumptions

A Summary based on words by Dr Jobe Martin

Here's a summary of a YouTube interview with Dr Jobe Martin who, for the first half of his life, was an evolutionist. He began to look at the assumptions behind evolution when his dental students challenged him on the subject. As he looked at the assumptions and saw that they were not proven, but in fact were more than highly unlikely, he moved from being an evolutionist to being a creationist. You can see the interview at this address.
https://www.youtube.com/watch?v=WWvfypeMEFY

Dr Jobe Martin argues the following five assumptions that underpin the theory of evolution. He says that an assumption is simply a guess, whether it is an educated one or not. The first assumption is the following:

1) Spontaneous Generation Occurred

What this means is that somehow dead chemicals came to life. He says that there wasn't any life and then, in some primordial ooze, something that is alive just appeared. Then he adds that it somehow was able to reproduce itself. He then asks the question, "*Why is it an assumption?*" and the simple answer to that is because no scientist, even with all of our resources, sophisticated laboratory equipment and computers, can make it happen. That is the case still today, even in our modern controlled environment. We have all the different kinds of chemicals needed, we have all of the instrumentation that's needed, but we still can't make life. So his challenge to any evolutionist who argues with him is,

"...mix them up, make it come to life. That's all you have to do, because evolution assumes that happened at one time in the past."

The above, therefore, is the first major assumption, that dead things can come to life all by themselves. Here's the next assumption.

2) Spontaneous Generation Occurred Only Once

The question that he poses is, *"Why would most evolutionary scientists assume that it only happened once?"* This is because the probability of it happening even the first time is zero. It is zero even if we're just aiming at a single protein being formed by the random process of amino acids coming together. If we had a protein that was made of just two hundred amino acids, which would be a simple protein, then the odds against it is something like 1^{141} (that would be a 1 with 141 zeros after it). He reminds us that it is sensible to believe that there are far less electrons in the whole universe than that number, so you don't have enough material to mix things to even equal the odds in order to come up with even a simple protein. On top of that they would all have to be left handed amino acids. If you had any right handed ones in there, then the assembly process from amino acid to protein goes wrong.

We will look at this in greater detail in a later chapter.

Here comes the next assumption.

3) Viruses, Plants, Bacteria and Animals are all Related

It is an assumption that we all came from the first cell. From this comes the evolutionary tree of life. Dr Martin then references those text book drawings where there's a single cell at the bottom and lines are drawn up to the different branches of the evolutionary tree. There are lines drawn from protists to protophytes to seaweed and other types of plant life. There are lines drawn from protists to protozoans or coelenterates or sponges or echinoderms or worms. Then you'll get lines drawn from vertebrates to fish to amphibians or fish to reptiles to birds etc.

They hook all these creatures with lines, to show that they are related. However, Dr Martin points out that there's **nothing on the lines**. They are empty spaces. He poses the question,

"Why is there nothing on those lines?"

He then points out that **they are the missing links**.

*"There's nothing there because there's **nothing there**,"* he says.

He makes the point that the lines serve the purpose to give the impression that these things are all connected, they're all hooked up. However, it is a fraudulent thing to do. There is nothing on those lines because there is nothing to put on them. They represent jumps between the animals, distance that cannot be filled. From this fake diagram come the next two assumptions.

4) **Invertebrates gave rise to vertebrates**
5) **Fish gave rise to Amphibia, the Amphibia to reptiles and reptiles to birds and mammals**

Dr Martin points out that the problem we have with this is that reptiles are cold-blooded and have dense bones. Birds, on the other hand, are warm-blooded and have hollow bones. So Dr Martin asks the following question,

"Is there any such thing as a lukewarm blooded semi-dense boned creature that's in-between reptile and bird? No. You either have a reptile or you have a bird."

Then he poses the question about Archaeopteryx and states that leading evolutionists today now accept that it is a bird and just a bird, not a transitional creature at all, which is what it was claimed and hailed to be for decades. In fact older fossil remains of birds have now been found that existed before Archaeopteryx. Dr Martin then asks the question, *"What is evolution then?"* The answer he gives is this,

*"Well it's a **faith system** because it's based on assumptions that even today, the leading evolutionary thinkers of our day, cannot hook up these vast distances between various types of creatures."*

So the transitional forms are missing. He points out that the new name for the missing link is 'transitional form' because it doesn't sound as if it is missing if you simply call it a transitional form. The promise of evolutionists to us is that we will find these missing links if we only give them enough time. They've had, however, around two hundred years now to prove that those transitional forms exist and they're still not there, despite the abundance of fossils around the world.

Dr Martin completes his argument with one final example, and with this example we again go back to the place where we should have been all along, the **microbiological** realm. He says that Ramapithecus was supposed to be an ancestor of man until an evolutionist, Vincent Sarich – who was Professor Emeritus in anthropology at UC Berkeley, using **molecular biology**, discovered that Ramapithecus is an ancestor of an orangutan. However, Ramapithecus is still in some textbooks listed as an ancestor of humanity, when it has been proved at the **molecular level** that it is nothing to do with us.

He finishes off by saying that evolution is all based on assumptions.

*"So evolution then, in my opinion, and I was an evolutionist for the first half of my life, it is a **faith system** - if we're talking 'Big Bang' to molecules to life to man."*

I could go on and on and on about all of the evidences against evolution. I could choose all kinds of examples to show irreducible technologies or carefully balanced relationships that make life work and that cannot have evolved slowly over time. This chapter, however, has to come to an end at some point; otherwise we'd be reading forever. So I'll finish off by using a summary of the main points in order to bring together the arguments that I have used so far. Hopefully you can see that, as the evidence stacks and the fires that I talked about at the start of this section come together, you can see that a good blaze is already burning. It will get hotter, however, when we go on to look at the cell, data, coding, information, chance, calibration and explosions in the next chapters. Then we'll finally end this book by looking briefly at the calibration of the universe.

Final Dissent

Quite some time ago more than six hundred scientists with Ph.D.'s from major universities throughout the world signed a document entitled, "A Scientific Dissent from Darwinism." It says,

"We are sceptical of the claims for the ability of random mutation and natural selection to account for the complexity of life."

The numbers of people in the scientific community, who are now seeing that we cannot be here except for a creator God, is continually growing as we discover more and more about the intricate nature and irreducible complexity of life.

- -
Chapter Summary
- -

Overview

So let me summarise the different things that have been said in this chapter before we go on to more detailed things in the next. In this chapter we've made the following points.

- hereditary DNA mixes do not create new data but just presents the same essential information that is already there in a slightly different form
- mutations are mainly harmful or negative and the only beneficial ones are biochemical in nature, for example in antibiotic resistance, but the bacteria are still the same species of bacteria
    - biochemical mutations, however, are in fact adaptation and not evolution as there is a mechanism already in place for the antibiotic resistance to take place
- typical mutation is very mild, usually has no effect, and is normally a small decrease in viability or fertility
- mutations are most commonly corrected and replaced by a DNA repair process

- natural selection only takes DNA information out of the gene pool and does not add into it
- the mechanism for evolution to go **UPWARDS** is not found amongst the combinations of hereditary exchange, mutation and natural selection
- **UPWARDS** evolution has never been observed
- examples of animals left in isolation, the finches and the lemurs, show that only sideways adaptation takes place
- common ancestry is easily explained by a designer and since there is no mechanism for **UPWARD** evolution at the microbiological level, logic tells us that a designer is the only viable answer
- common ancestry technology does not explain the problem of ontogenesis, the way in which a creature develops towards its final mature state when the routes of growth are completely different, even when the end result looks similar
- common ancestry should have brought about not only a common method of development within every creature but also its shape during those developing stages, as Ernst Haeckel's attempt at creating a false portrait of embryonic development illustrates for us, but in reality it does not
- the ontogenesis of different creatures is wide and varied in their different developmental expressions
- integrated technologies and processes need to be fully packaged before they work, creating these via the mechanisms of
  - small mutations and errors in DNA
  - hereditary DNA mix
  - natural selection
    - does not work as there are no mechanisms to create multiple components quickly and effectively and to bring them all together at the same time
    - all of the above will not create complicated procedures that have to happen in a specific order, such as blood clotting

- complex machines are needed in living creatures to produce essential products or services in order for us to survive
- today's creatures are jam-packed full of integrated technologies (machine supporting machine or process supporting process) and the existence of these cannot be explained by evolutionary theory
- if we evolved via small mutations the fossil record should be filled with transitional fossils showing the minute steps that were taken over billions of years as one thing moved slowly into another – amongst the vast wealth of fossils that are available to us **all of these missing links** continue to be missing
- the fossil record is direct evidence of the past and does not in any way, shape or form show an evolutionary process and in fact presents evidence for sudden creation by a creator
  - the Cambrian explosion is a very uncomfortable fact in the fossil record where evolutionists cannot account for the sudden appearance of complicated organisms and creatures
  - after the Cambrian explosion we see a decrease in the number of complex creatures rather than an increase, which is the opposite of evolution
- evolution is a faith system as it is based on assumptions
- evolutionists keep this faith system in place by
  - not exploring the areas of life that cannot be explained by their theory
  - using confusing language, labelling a proven **sideways** DNA shift as a 'new species' and then using that same phrase and applying it to a supposed **UPWARDS** movement that is unproven

Main Points Made

So here are the main points made in this chapter,
- there is no mechanism for real UPWARD change in the theory of evolution
- life is **not connected** by a slow step-by-step process

- claims for common ancestry are misinterpretations of design, put there by a designer, and ignore the microbiological ontogenesis evidence that says there is no common development from foetus (fetus) to fully formed creature
- common coding combined with interdependent design show the work of a designer
  - using the same basic 'operating system' to make everything work is a logical thing for a designer to do
  - using excellent unique code expressions to provide different routes to create similar technology
- the fossil record shows a sudden appearance of a multitude of creatures
  - without any evolutionary sequence
  - in a moment of time, not according to the evolutionary timescale
- evolutionary theory is based on many unproven assumptions that
  - are without scientific foundation
  - are imposed upon the evidences we find in life, even when those evidences don't fit

So these are the main points of this chapter telling us why the evolutionary theory is at fault. I'm not going to stop here, however. **I've not made my main points in this book yet**. All of the work so far is an *introduction to the subject* to give us the background information that we need in order to press on to the more detailed issues.; there's so much more to say in science that tells us it is impossible for us to be here without the help of the divine. Science not only disproves evolutionary theory, by deductive logic it directly points to God.

So where do we go from here?

In the next chapter we will build on all of this evidence by looking at the microbiological world. We will specifically start with the cellular environment and see how it is constructed with such complexity and interdependency that it cannot arise via any random or unguided process. Then, over the following chapters, we're going to look firstly at data and see what it is and how it works. We'll see just what data produces inside a creature when it changes in any way, which is always a sideways adaptive change, never an **UPWARDS** evolutionary move. Then we're going to have a good look at coding and information. We'll look at what makes something information, and not data. We'll see the constructed environment that must all **be fully in place first** for information to work.

We'll also see how data change is not information growth!

This is one of the greatest mistakes in the evolutionary theory. Making this distinction changes everything. This is because,

- information is at that heart of all living things
- information cannot arise from the natural world by itself as the natural world cannot **provide the context** via which information is **processed** in order for work to be achieved
- we do not see any new information being added into the universe

...and so when we see a creature adapting to its environment, we see just a movement within the data pool (simple digits of data within the code of life called DNA) we do not see new information being added. Adaptation is only data change. New coded information is required for **UPWARDS** evolution. This producing of new coded information is something that is totally lacking in the natural processes that we see all around us within nature. We'll pick this thread up and continue it over the next few chapters.

Chapter 4 – It's Life Jim...

...and completely beyond our intelligence to compute it!

The Complexity of the Cell

Initial Questions

So in this chapter we're going to look at how life cannot arise from naturalist means due to the sheer complexity of the cell. We're going to visit the heart of the microbiological world. We're going to see that the more we 'zoom in' on what's happening inside the cell, the more complex life becomes. It is not just the complexity of the cell, however, that provides the evolutionist with a great challenge. It is the very **nature** and **structure** of the information that resides at the very heart of the cell. This too is an insurmountable evolutionary problem. Before we do that, let me start again by reminding you of my foundational statement that underpins the whole book. It is this,

*It is not possible to bring order, complexity, interdependent design and purposeful coding out of chaos via **random** and **unguided** processes.*

This general rule-of-thumb law is so important to keep in mind when we look at the DNA information that resides at the heart of the cell. DNA is complex in its make-up, far more complex than the average person even begins to imagine. Even more complex, however, is the cellular environment that processes it and uses that information to enable the work that needs to be achieved in the cell to be realised. So DNA is more complex and mature than our ability to write this level of coding ourselves. The factory workings of the cell that surrounds DNA, however, represents in comparison a quantum leap in complexity.

To guide us in our thinking on this matter we need to pose the following questions about the place of information within the cell and its origins. They are,

1. What type of random and unguided process, found within nature, could possibly generate the intricate and complex precision coded data (DNA) that is at the heart of all life?

2. How is it that, by random chance, information (DNA) *was conveniently placed* and sensibly housed **at the centre** of the cell's control mechanism, in what we call the nucleus?

These questions that we've just asked, however, are still too simplistic if we want to appreciate the size of the problem for anyone wanting to suggest that the cell could 'auto-organise' itself into its current multi-complex mindboggling state. It is not just the DNA programming that exists at the centre of the life of the cell that's the problem. It's the careful construction and calibration of the rest of the cell's environment that's required to **make the DNA information *work*** within it and **perform its tasks** that is just as problematic.

Every part of the cell has purpose. There is no waste of space within the cell. The purpose of each part is expressed by its shape and the resources that it contains and how those resources work with each other in the context of what needs doing to keep the cell working properly. So when we look at each part of the cell, we see that everything within it, every part of it, has been purposefully and thoughtfully crafted in order to facilitate the DNA coding that is contained there. All of the activities in the cell run from or support the DNA code. So here's the next question,

3. How do the unguided and random processes of the natural world build an ordered and carefully constructed microbiological factory for the processing of DNA information to take place within it that will, in turn, create machines to run the cell and keep it alive?

The more you look at the problem, the more complex and insurmountable it becomes when trying to find a naturalistic evolutionary answer. You'll see what I mean after you've read the next few pages. Before we do that, however, let's try and merge all three of the questions that we've asked above into one single set of flowing questions so that we can see what we're driving at in this chapter.

The Problem of the Cell's Complexity

QUESTION: What kind of random and unguided process within nature was able to **auto organise** non-living matter in such a way as to,

- construct DNA - a string of meaningful sequential symbols set into a specific order to produce **a language** of sensible and meaningful 'talk', that behaves like computer code, in order to execute commands to ensure that jobs are done in the cell

and at the same time was able to,

- set up an environment (the cell) that has mutually interdependent resources that rely on each other to work, which all came into existence **at the same time** for the specific purpose of housing, protecting and processing the code

and was able to,

- construct a complex multi-roomed layout that is able to use the *resources* within each room for the processing of the DNA so that, as the DNA is processed, resources can be selected and assembled and machines be made to meet 'known needs' within the cell to help it stay alive and function

and was able to,

- create 'talk' within the cell amidst its multiple, interactions and jobs undertaken by the machines that work within it, so that it is able to move and ship resources around this mind-bogglingly complex environment in such a way as to organise the cells resources efficiently

and all of this being achieved without the support of a reasoning mind?

Chance chemical reactions cannot account for the construction of the cell. Nor can those same random chemical reactions account for the programming that runs the cell (called DNA) to appear in all of its wonder and complexity and **the way in which they** (the DNA and the cell's resources) **relate to each other**. Chance chemical reactions will not be able to create the 'setup' by which DNA can be processed within the cell and so create the machines that run the cell. Neither

109

can chance and randomness account for the way that jobs are purposefully fulfilled in the cell and the way in which the information at the heart of the cell *has pre-programmed knowledge* of what those jobs are, i.e. a knowledge of **what needs doing** in the cell to make it work! Before we go any further, however, we need to have a proper working definition of life in the cell.

- -
The Incredibly Busy Life in the Cell
- -

A Simple Cell?

So let's begin by describing what the cell looks like under a microscope. When I was at school I was taught evolution. This was done on two occasions. Once when I was 10 years old, by what is called in the United Kingdom (UK) a Primary School teacher. Then at the age of 12 I was taught it again at what is called a 'middle school' which teaches 12-14 year olds. I was taught, very clearly, during my time at the middle school how the first amino acids came together in a primordial soup and, via lightning strike, formed the beginnings of potential life which in turn was the first step towards the first *'simple cell'*, as they called it. Strangely enough, you can still find on YouTube today, videos that present this information as if it is something that is a viable explanation of our origins. Well let's first of all look at the complexity of the cell in the form of a general description so that you can get a brief overview in your mind at just how 'busy' a cell is.

The Complexity of the Cell

The average cell in the human body is an interdependent factory/city where there are so many parts, packages and components that you cannot trace and keep track of them. They are also totally dependent on each other, interdependent that is, so that you cannot have a starting point for its logical assembly and then build, step-by-step from a simple format, the complex environment we see before us today. At the heart of the cell (not necessarily at its physical centre) is what's called the nucleus. Within the nucleus resides DNA. DNA is the mind bogglingly complex code that runs the cell. It is the instruction code by which the minute molecular machines (called proteins) which do most of the jobs in the cell are constructed. In order to illustrate just how busy the cell is, I'm now

110

going to quote four paragraphs from a book called, "Does God Believe in Atheists?" It has a really great way of giving an overview of the cell's complexity in a way that I cannot express. I shall put the whole of the quote in italics so that you can easily see that it is all taken from the same document. As a result of reading this you will get a good insight into just how active and complex the cell is in the microbiological world.

"To grasp the reality of life as it has been revealed by molecular biology, we must magnify a cell a thousand million times until it is twenty kilometres in diameter and resembles a giant airship large enough to cover a city like London or New York. What we would then see would be an object of unparalleled complexity and adaptive design. On the surface of the cell we would see millions of openings, like the portholes of a vast spaceship, opening and closing to allow a continual stream of materials to flow in and out. If we were to enter one of those openings we would find ourselves in a world of supreme technology and bewildering complexity. We would see endless highly organised corridors and conduits branching in every direction away from the perimeter of the cell, some leading to the central memory bank in the nucleus and others to assembly plants and processing units. The nucleus in itself would be a vast spherical chamber more than a kilometre in diameter, resembling a geodesic dome inside of which we would see, all neatly stacked together in ordered arrays, the miles of coiled chains of the DNA molecules. A huge range of products and raw materials would shuffle along all the manifold conduits in a highly ordered fashion to and from all the various assembly plants in the outer regions of the cell.

We would wonder at the level of control implicit in the movement of so many objects down to so many seemingly endless conduits, all in perfect unison. We would see all around us, in every direction we looked, all sorts of robot like machines. We would notice that the simplest of the functional components of the cell, the protein molecules, were astonishingly complex pieces of molecular machinery, each one consisting of about 3,000 atoms arranged in a highly organised 3-D spatial conformation. We would wonder even more as we watched the strangely purposeful activities of these weird molecular machines, particularly when we realise that, despite all our accumulated knowledge of physics and chemistry, the task of designing one such molecular machine - that is one functional protein molecule - would-be completely beyond our capacity at present and will probably not be achieved until at least the beginning of the next century. Yet the life of the cell depends on the integrated activities of thousands, certainly tens, and probably hundreds of thousands of different protein molecules.

We would see that nearly every feature of our own advanced machines had its analogue in the cell: artificial languages and their decoding systems, memory banks for information storage and retrieval, elegant control systems regulating the automated assembly of parts and components, error fail-safe and proof-reading devices utilised for quality control, assembly processes involving the principle of prefabrication and modular construction. In fact so deep would be the feeling of déjà vu, so persuasive the analogy, that much of the terminology we would use to describe this fascinating molecular reality would be borrowed from the world of the late 20ᵗʰ century technology.

What we would be witnessing would be an object resembling an immense automated factory, a factory larger than a city and carrying out almost as many unique functions as all the manufacturing activities of man on earth. However, it would be a factory which would have one capacity not equalled in any of our most advanced machines, for it would be capable of replicating its entire structure within a matter of a few hours. To witness such an act at a magnificent magnification of one thousand million times would be an awe-inspiring spectacle."

The previous four paragraphs begin to let us into the life of the cell. They open the door to us understanding its amazing complexity and the amount of traffic that it creates and allows to pass through it. The drawings of the cell that you'll see as illustrations in books are over simplistic. They only show the cell's basic components. All the traffic and frenzied activity, showing what is actually happening in the cell, would cloud your view of those basic components, and so that activity is removed. If you could see close up what was actually happening you would not know where to look because so much is going on.

The Complexity of the Cellular Environment

Over the next few pages I'm going to provide several quotes from the following video.

https://www.youtube.com/watch?v=7Z_oaT1ZxH8

I would personally recommend that you watch the video for yourself. It is an excellent portrayal of the complexity of the human cell and the impossibility of auto organisation by naturalistic means. Let's start off with some quotes from Michael Behe, a man who has spent his career examining the design of cell and how its contents operate. He has recorded for us how the complexity of the cell forms a biochemical challenge to the theory of evolution. Here's what he has to say.

"In the 19th century when Darwin was alive, scientists thought that the basis of life, the cell, was some simple glob of protoplasm like a piece of Jell-O, or something that was not hard to explain at all. But with the hard work of science in the 20th century we've seen that the cell is far from simple, it's got very complicated molecular machines and things that are very resistant to Darwinian explanation."

He goes on to say,

"Most people have no idea of how small and complex cells are. A typical cell from you or me, called a eukaryotic cell, is probably a 10th of the size of the head of a pin. Yet in that single cell there are about three billion units of DNA making out the chromosomes and those three billion units make the molecular machines of the cell, literally machines that make the cell work."

and

"It's like going into an automobile factory. A factory has a large number of machines, the parts have to fit together in very specific ways to do their jobs and if things go wrong then the cell is in big trouble. Just one cell is enormously complex but humans, you and I, are made from trillions of cells and those trillions of cells have to fit together in the right way and do their own job. Darwinism was a lot more plausible when we were thinking about blobs of protoplasm than it is when we're thinking about molecular machines."

113

The Complexity of the Machines within the Cell

Not only do we have a complex cell environment but we also have very complex and well manufactured machines within that environment. Michael Behe is very well known for his study of the flagellum, which is a rotary motor machine in the microbiological world. Again he says,

"I remember the first time I looked into a biochemistry textbook and I saw a drawing of something called a bacterial flagellum with all of its parts in all of its glory. It had a propeller and a hook region and the drive shaft and a motor. I looked at that and I said that's an outboard motor, that's designed, that's no chance assemblage of parts."

Talking on the subject of the flagellum, Scott Minnich - Molecular Biologist - University of Idaho says,

*"Howard Berg at Harvard has labelled it the **most efficient machine in the universe**. These machines, some of them are running at 100,000 rpm and are hardwired into the signal transduction or sensory mechanism so that it's getting feedback from the environment....It's got some tail proteins which act as the propeller when the flagellum rotates, these push against the water and therefore push the bacterium forward, and the motor uses a flow of acid from outside of the cell to the inside of the cell to power the turning."*

Scott Minnich adds,
"The bacterial flagellum has two gears, forward and reverse... It has a starter, it has a rotor, it has u-joint, it has a drive shaft, it has a propeller. It's not convenient that we give them these names, that's truly their function."

"In all, about 40 different protein parts are required to build a flagellar motor. Half of them are constructor proteins, specialised mechanisms that assemble the flagellum's individual components. Since its discovery, biologists have tried to understand how a machine of such superb design could have arisen gradually without foresight or plan through the biological pathway Darwinian envisioned."

Michael Behe has given a name to such complex machines and processes that take place in the microbiological world. It is called 'irreducible complexity'.

Irreducible Complexity

Scott Minnich - Molecular Biologist - University of Idaho says on this subject,

"Irreducible complexity was coined by Michael Behe in describing these molecular machines. Basically what it says is that you have multi-component parts to any given organelle or system within the cell, all of which are necessary for function, that is if you remove one part you lose the function of that system."

The concept of irreducible complexity also applies to biological machines including the bacterial flagellum. The video goes on to say the following that,

*"All told there are about 40 different protein parts which are necessary for this machine to work and if any of those parts are missing, then either you get a flagellum that doesn't work because it's missing the hook or it's missing the drive shaft or whatever, or it doesn't even get built within the cell. **You can't put something like that together gradually** because they need a large number of parts interacting with each other at the same time or they won't work at all."*

The video ends by making the following statements,

*"Without the tools to observe the machinery of the cell and long before the idea of irreducible complexity, Charles Darwin offered a way to test his own theory. In "Origin of Species" he wrote, "If it could be demonstrated that any complex organ existed which could not possibly have been formed by **numerous successive slight modifications** my theory would **absolutely break down**.""*

and

*"Darwin acknowledged that if someone identified a biological system that could not have been **constructed in incremental steps** over long periods of time then his theory would be invalid. And what Michael Behe and others have discovered is the existence of biological machinery that cannot be explained away by Darwinian processes. Darwin's failed predictions have in fact falsified his own theory."*

Now that we've shown that the cell and its resources are incredibly complex in its makeup, let's now focus on the complex and interdependent processes that take place within it.

- -
The Cell – How it works
- -

The Components of the Cell
All cells have,

1. **A cell membrane** - this is the outer shell that houses all the contents of the cell.
2. **Cytoplasm** - a fluid that is a little like jelly that fills the inside of the cell in which the different parts of the cell float around and move through.
3. **DNA** - This is the coded information that is inside the cell that makes the cell work.

There are two basic types of cell. Neither of them is simple as they both contain DNA information. One, however, is more complex than the other.

1) Prokaryotic cells
These are always one celled organisms such as bacteria.
These have genetic material, DNA, inside them but the DNA just floats around in the cell. The DNA is not housed inside anything but the cell itself.

2) Eukaryotic cells
These are more complex cells. They are the cells found in plants and animals. Eukaryotic cells have what are called *Organelles*. An

organelle simply means a *little organ*. These are specialised objects within the cell that play an important role in the life of the cell, just as we have organs in our body (lungs, heart, liver etc.) that work to keep us alive, so too the organelles have jobs to do. There are many organelles in the cell. I'm not going to list them all here, as it would get too complex to describe. Here's an outline of some of the cell's main organelles.

1. **The nucleus**. This is a spherical chamber at the heart of the cell. It is the cell's control centre. DNA is housed in here. DNA is the genetic set of instructions for the cell, telling it what to do and how to behave. DNA lives inside the nucleus as strings of information. At the centre of the nucleus is the nucleolus. This is a rounded structure which creates what are called ribosomes which are used in the creation of proteins.
2. **Endoplasmic reticulum**. These look like connected squashed sacks or tubes. You can get rough and smooth endoplasmic reticulum and they are located just outside the nucleus. The rough endoplasmic reticulum often has lots of ribosomes attached to it, (small round balls) which sit there waiting to be picked up and used in the creation of new proteins.
3. **Mitochondria**. These sausage shaped organelles produce the energy to power the cell.

There are more organelles than those I've listed above but I don't want this book to be too complicated for people without a science background. Those I've listed above are the only ones necessary in order for me to communicate all that I need to say to present the arguments for interdependent complexity within the cell.

> **Note:** When a cell is ready to **copy itself** the strings of DNA condense and form structures called **chromosomes**. The DNA is kept safe in these structures whilst the copying process takes place. Once the chromosomes have been duplicated, then the cell is ready to divide and to make two new cells from the original. It is a most complicated process that is too difficult for us to emulate.

The Role of Proteins

Proteins do the majority of work in the cell. It is their shape that gives them their function. Even though there are about five different categories of proteins, there are thousands of different kinds of proteins that are used in each cell. It is not possible to count them and the estimations of their numbers over the years, based on different methods, have ranged greatly, but the latest calculations put the number at tens of millions. In fact some of the latest research now puts the number at around 42 million proteins per Eukaryotic cell, but I personally have no way of verifying that number. Other cells will have far more proteins. For example a blood cell has haemoglobin in it. Haemoglobin is a red protein that carries oxygen from the lungs and transports it around the body. As haemoglobin is smaller than the wavelength of light, you can get a huge number of them compacted into a small space, the haemoglobin molecule is about 6.5 nanometres in size. Each blood cell, therefore, has typically around 280 million haemoglobin molecules in it. From this number you can begin to see how complex the human body is. So, as there are trillions and trillions of cells within the human body, and each cell is specialised for purpose and has a huge number of specific proteins working in it, it is not possible to accurately count or estimate the final total number of proteins that the human body contains; it is a number beyond our imagination. Yet all the time that we are either awake or asleep, they are all busily working and getting on with their jobs to keep our bodies working.

Proteins are used for all kinds of functions in the body. For example, they are used to create and repair body tissue. Enzymes, hormones and other body chemicals are also made from proteins, so also are skin, muscles, bones, cartilage, and blood. Here's a set of protein functions and descriptions taken from the U.S. National Library of Medicine website https://ghr.nlm.nih.gov/

The specific page address is:
https://ghr.nlm.nih.gov/primer/howgeneswork/protein

> **NOTE:** I have added some words in capital letters and brackets to the following information to give added clarity to the meaning of each protein function.

Protein Function – **Antibody** (DEFENCE)
Description – Antibodies bind to specific foreign particles, such as viruses and bacteria, to help protect the body.

Protein Function – **Enzyme** (ASSISTS & SPEEDS UP CHEMICAL REACTIONS)
Description – Enzymes carry out almost all of the thousands of chemical reactions that take place in cells. They also assist with the formation of new molecules by reading the genetic information stored in DNA.

Protein Function – **Messenger** (C0MMUNICATION)
Description – Messenger proteins, such as some types of hormones, transmit signals to coordinate biological processes between different cells, tissues, and organs.

Protein Function – **Structural component** (BUILDING BLOCKS)
Description – These proteins provide structure and support for cells. On a larger scale, they also allow the body to move.

Protein Function – **Transport/Storage** (CARRIERS)
Description – These proteins bind and carry atoms and small molecules within cells and throughout the body.

Protein Example – the Enzyme

For example, the protein called an 'Enzyme' is critical in all digestion. Without it we could not break down our food and feed our bodies. Digestive enzymes enable your body to use those broken down small units of food to feed itself. Without that initial breaking down process, performed by the enzymes, we could not survive. Enzymes do far more than break food down, however. They are necessary to start off **at least four thousand other chemical reactions** in the body that are essential for its health and function. They kick start processes and speed them up that would otherwise take too long to complete.

Some Enzymes also make essential chemical reactions take place in the human body that would not normally take place at the body temperature.

Proteins are therefore critical to the body. Without them we could not live or survive. One of the best YouTube videos on proteins can be viewed at this address:

https://www.youtube.com/watch?v=wvTv8TqWC48

If you want to see just how crowded the cell is then watch this animated and more complex YouTube video:

https://www.youtube.com/watch?v=VdmbpAo9JR4&t=5s

Here's a quote from an evolutionist called Fred Spier who wrote a pro-evolution book called, "Big History and the Future of Humanity". Even though I profoundly disagree with his stance on evolution, I'm quoting from his book because he describes the role of proteins, specifically enzymes, so well. Here it is from page 128.

*"Within cells, a great many bio-molecules are manufactured, the most important of which are proteins. These are made by using information encoded in DNA or RNA. Proteins act in many different ways. The most important function is **catalysing chemical reactions that would otherwise not take place**. Such proteins are called 'enzymes'. These bio-molecules can speed up chemical reactions by lowering the energy barriers that prevent these reactions from happening at the moderate temperatures and pressures that are characteristic of life. In other words, the most important function of enzymes is to provide Goldilocks circumstances that allow these reactions to take place as well is to regulate them. This is essentially what enzymes do, for instance, in modern detergents, namely break down organic molecules (stains) that are hard to remove with more traditional soaps. But enzymes can not only break down molecules but also synthesise them, while they can also regulate the speed of chemical reactions. Inside cells, long and complicated chains of chemical reactions take place with the aid of a great many different enzymes. In addition to the cell's own production, these reactions include the extraction of matter and energy from outside, the use of matter and energy for manufacturing the molecules needed for survival, the secretion of waste materials and, in more complicated cell structures, the processing of information within neural networks."*

In a nutshell this quotation shows us that we could not survive without these proteins being active within us.

*The DNA programming behind them shows **pre-knowledge** of what needs doing in the body.*

We'll look more at this '**pre-knowledge**' later on in the book but it's important to say now that the human body is so sophisticated that there are machines within us that are pre-programmed so that they are 'living answers' to deal with the body's problems for survival. The activity of proteins is an answer to a question. That question varies according to the job that the protein does. The question starts in the same way, however. It goes something like this, "How on earth can we get around this problem so that life can survive? What machine can we manufacture that will engage with the problem and provide a solution to it?" These solutions, called protein machines, are very complex in their makeup, simply because the problems they have to face and solve are also incredibly complex.

The Creation of Proteins

One of the most important things to understand about the cell is that it **processes** the information (DNA) that is contained with it. This processing of DNA forms the basis for the design and construction of the cell's molecular machines, the proteins. Here's how it happens.

There are two distinct phases of specific activity that are necessary to create a protein. They are called **transcription** and **translation**. Only *after* **both processes** have *completed* will a protein be formed. It is also important to note that these processes take place in **different 'rooms' in the cell**, which tells us that this is a planned activity where the correct resources are made available for the activity to start and then be sensibly completed.

Part 1 - Transcription

Transcription takes place inside a spherical chamber at the centre of the cell called the nucleus. This is where the long strands of DNA are located. DNA looks like a coiled ladder. Just as a ladder has rungs that a person uses to climb up it, so too the DNA has what looks like rungs of material that join its two sides. Each 'rung' of the ladder is made up of two parts that extend from the ladder's sides and meet in the middle. You can see a digital drawing of this illustrated on the front cover of this book. The two sides of each rung are called '**bases**'. Each base is a '**strand**' of material. Their names are,

- adenine (A)
- cytosine (C)
- guanine (G)
- thymine (T)

Together these form the code of life. It is **the order in which they appear** on the ladder that gives us the code's meaning. Just as someone will type a line of code on a computer, which you can read if you know how to interpret the computer language that has been used, so too you can look along the line of the DNA and read the code that's imprinted there. The placement of each base, therefore, is important as it specifically **carries meaning within the context of the other code letters that surround it.**

> **NOTE:** This is most important. Each base is not just a recognisable symbol. It is a symbol **within a language** that carries meaning within the context of the other symbols. So, if I were to write the following letters, 'lloeh', then they would **not** have meaning. If I were to write the same letters in a different order, "hello," then those letters have meaning when they all come together **in the right order** – as long as you can read 'English' that is. If you don't understand the language then, even if you can recognise the letters, the meaning is still foreign to you.

Each string of DNA is a written code. This code is split up into different sections along the DNA ladder. Each section is called a '**gene**' and all of them together make up what science calls your 'genes'. Together they are called the 'genome'. These gene sections are the coded information for life. The 'bases' that make up each line of code can be read, sometimes in both directions. **The order of the bases has meaning, which is the code for life.**

As we've said, the first part of the process for creating a protein is called transcription. This takes place within the nucleus of the cell where the DNA material is located. For transcription to happen a gene has to be activated on the DNA ladder and then it has to be 'read' by a protein and a copy of that gene has to be created. The copy of the gene is called an **RNA strand**. It's not an exact copy, but I won't go into that here as I don't want to complicate things. Here's a **simplified overview** of the process that must be completed for transcription to take place.

1. A section of the DNA chain, called a gene, is switched on.
2. This 'switching on' activity causes a protein called RNA polymerase to attach to the starting part of that particular gene.
3. This RNA polymerase protein then moves down the strand of DNA, unzipping it as it goes, and reading the different bases of information that are on one side of the DNA ladder.
4. As it reads the bases on the DNA ladder it takes into itself new building blocks of material and assembles them in an order dictated by its reading of the DNA code.
5. This new code of information is all fitted together onto a new platform.
6. This new platform, which now holds the newly assembled code based on the DNA that it has just read, is called the **Messenger RNA** strand.
7. This Messenger RNA strand is now a coded template, based on the DNA that has just been read, from which the new protein will eventually be created.
8. This Messenger RNA strand is then briefly spliced open by some proteins, who take bits out and put other bits in, and then stitch it back together again so that it is **ready for use**.
   a. This process of splicing, opening, removing, adding and then stitching back together activity is classed as a **preparation** of the Messenger RNA strand because the strand is being prepared, being 'made fit for purpose' so that it is ready for use later on.
9. Now the transcription is complete and the RNA strand is ready for phase two, which is called translation.

Part 2 - Translation

For translation to take place the Messenger RNA strand has to **travel out** of the nucleus. This movement is important. It is like taking a half made object from one room in a factory into another. In the next room are the **resources needed to finish the job** of constructing the new machine. This clearly shows a sensible and intelligently put together two stage process for the creation of a protein. Here's what happens at the second stage.

1. The Messenger RNA strand (carrying a copy of the DNA code) leaves the nucleus where it was originally made.
2. Proteins, called **Ribosomes**, grab the Messenger RNA strand at one end of the platform.
3. The Ribosomes then join together to form a mini-factory at the end of the RNA platform.
4. The Ribosome factory then pulls the full RNA strand through itself.
5. As the Messenger RNA strand passes through the Ribosome factory it reads the RNA bases in sets of three – this **reading** of the bases is the **processing of the code**.
6. Each group of three bases on the RNA platform is a code that matches the identity of what is called an amino acid.
   a. There are twenty different types of amino acid for the Ribosome factory to choose from.
7. As each group of 3 RNA bases are read, the corresponding amino acid type is selected from the environment of the cell and they are all joined together into a long string.
8. This string comes out of the Ribosome factory at the same time as the RNA platform is read.
9. A 'stop' command at the end of the Messenger RNA platform prevents any more amino acids being attached after the RNA strand has been fully read – if more amino acids were to be attached to the amino acid string at this point then the whole process would fail.
10. After the new chain of amino acids has been created by the RNA strand being read, the amino acid chain leaves the Ribosome factory.
11. The amino acid chain briefly enters a chamber.

12. Then the amino acid chain, according to the number and order of the amino acids that make up the chain, folds into a specific shape that becomes the new protein.
13. The shape of the protein determines its job in the cell.
14. The protein then leaves the chamber and goes off to 'do its duties' within the cell to ensure that work is done.

Wow, that is an amazing process (and you may be surprised to find out that I've simplified the number of components that are involved so that the above instruction list is easy to follow). So we can see that there is a two stage process for a protein to be created. The chain of amino acids that makes the protein finds its genesis in the cell's DNA. It is the DNA that has the coding to say what the amino acid string should finally become. So here is the full process again in short.

1. A section of the DNA, a gene, switches on.
2. That gene is unzipped and the information in it copied.
3. That copy strand, called Messenger RNA, is snipped open, bits taken out, bits added and then stitched back together again.
4. That strand of RNA then travels out of the nucleus.
5. The strand is grabbed by a couple of Ribosomes to form a factory.
6. The RNA strand is read by the Ribosome factory and a new string of amino acids is created as a result.
7. The amino acid string folds to create the new protein.

NOTE: It is very important to note that the final processing of the code to make a protein has a 'start' and 'stop' command built into the code. Without this programming in place the protein machine could not be built. Amino acids are selected from the environment in response to the code being read. The **start command** starts the process but the formation of the protein would fail if there wasn't a **stop command** at the end of the code, as too many amino acids would potentially be selected. These 'start' and 'stop' mechanisms ensure the correct assembly of the product. Any computer programmer will also understand that 'start' and 'stop' commands are put into code by an intelligent mind that wants to **control** how the code is implemented.

NOTE: Once the amino acid chain has been created it is moved from the ribosome factory to a barrel shaped machine. This machine helps to fold the chain into its exact final shape. This shape fold is critical to determine the protein's job in the body, which is its function. The way in which each fold takes place is due to the shape of each amino acid link in the chain, how they 'touch' each other determines how they will 'bend' and the final shape of the protein comes into view. Once the folding process is complete and the protein has taken its final shape, then it exits the barrel shaped chamber and it is then escorted by another molecular machine to its exact location, the place in the cell where it is required to do its job. See the video https://www.youtube.com/watch?v=O6d8aI07mzY for more information on this.

So there are two preparation activities and one processing activity that need to take place in order for the protein to be made.

1. The section of DNA called a gene is **copied** (*prepared*) to create the Messenger RNA strand.
2. The newly created Messenger RNA strand is **spliced, altered**, (*prepared*) and then put back together again.
3. The Messenger RNA strand is **read** (*processed*) in order for the assembly of the new amino acid string.

Note: The process of protein creation is irreducible. If you miss out any part of the process then it will not work. You cannot, therefore, evolve this process within the cell.

The Role of the Ribosome Factory
THIS IS SO IMPORTANT – The Messenger RNA platform does NOT make the new protein. It is the Ribosome factory **reading** the Messenger RNA template (and the Ribosomes adding the amino acids together into a string as they **read** the RNA template) that makes the new protein. By itself, and of itself, the Messenger RNA strand **is useless**. It does **not have the power** to do or achieve anything. There is nothing built into the RNA Messenger strand that has the capacity to initiate change, it cannot read itself and do something with that

code. The RNA strand is a docile object; it is totally dependent on the Ribosome factory to do the work. Without the Ribosome factory, RNA strands are useless and pointless. Life cannot originate, therefore, from a single RNA strand!

This passing of the Messenger RNA strand **through** the Ribosome factory (**its reading** of the template and the resulting **assembly** of the amino acids) **is the processing** that turns the Messenger RNA strand from simply **dead data** into **effective** and functional **information**.

If the Messenger RNA strand was not encountered by the Ribosome factory then the whole process would fail.

NOTE: We will look very soon at how data and information are different from each other. However, I'll let the cat out of the bag at this point and tell you that information is precision data, **processed** through a constructed and calibrated **environment** in order to ensure a job done. It is the Ribosome factory that provides the last part of this **environment**. It is the Ribosome factory that does the job of processing and construction. **Only at this point** does the Messenger RNA strand *become information*. Until that time it is useless code that will do nothing by itself! As I've just said, in itself and of itself, the data that makes up the Messenger RNA strand is useless. It is processed information, therefore, that drives plant and animal life, not code and not mere data! We'll look into this very soon.

Animation Examples
This construction of proteins is an amazing process and it is happening all the time in every cell in your body. All of the tens of millions of proteins in each of your cells are created in this way. To help you understand this even more, here are some YouTube video addresses that you can use to watch some excellent animated explanations of this process. They clearly show how proteins are created by the processing of the DNA information, the movement of that data from one place to another as the Messenger RNA travels out

of the nucleus and then the turning of the RNA strand into information as it is processed by the Ribosome assembled factory.

1. This is a good graphical depiction of the process from DNA to protein and will give you a basic foundation.
https://www.youtube.com/watch?v=1lou4jSP0DY

2. This is an excellent animation that shows the process from DNA to protein in real time (the actual speed in which it happens in our bodies) and it shows a more accurate animation of the shapes of the molecules involved.
https://www.youtube.com/watch?v=D3fOXt4MrOM

3. To see an animated video with even more details on it have a look at the video at the address below.
https://www.youtube.com/watch?v=fOl7lrNuOnk

Products not By-Products
One of the things to say at this point is that the forces within nature only produce by-products, not products! A protein is a precision made product (not a by-product) that comes about from sophisticated programming in a carefully constructed and calibrated environment.

*The forces of the natural world do not create products because **products** are **fashioned for purpose** inside a constructed and calibrated environment.*

A volcano, for example, will only produce by-products from its spewing of lava onto the earth's surface. The ash from a volcanic eruption too, is a by-product of the process. Hot gasses escaping through the Earth's crust form by-products. No force of nature can in any way shape or form create a fashioned and crafted product! Random and unguided processes do not create products. Chemical reactions do not create products. Products come from processes put together by a thinking mind. We will return to this point and develop it in much greater detail later on in the following chapters.

Questions on the Cell

Now I could spend the rest of this chapter looking at the cell and talking about its complexity. It would also be natural to ask the following questions,

- Which came first, DNA or the cell?
  - The cell does not work without DNA and DNA is useless outside the cell! They both, in their amazing complexity, have to appear together at the same time to work.
- How was the first protein created?
  - You use DNA to create proteins, but you need pre-existing proteins to unzip DNA in order to copy it and then use more proteins to grab that RNA copy platform to read and assemble amino acids in order to create a new protein. It is a circular and interdependent process that has no evolutionary beginning. You cannot create proteins without proteins helping in the process.

The evolutionists say that they have some sort of an answer to this. So, in the next chapter, we'll examine the evolutionist's claims about the origins of the cell. They side step the issue of the irreducible complexity of the **current processes that we see already in place** to create proteins – they provide no route in their theories for the full step-by-step assembly manual where the emerging cell 'all works' at every stage of its supposed evolution. So despite the fact that there is no viable route for the auto-assembly of the cell and the processes we see in it, we still have *theories* from secularists who again choose to imagine how it all began, but their theories have no empirical evidence to support them.

There are two main theories out there. One of an accidental assembly of amino acids as the result of lightning hitting a primordial soup which contained amino acids and the other that an RNA strand came together and somehow learnt how to reproduce itself (though no actual description is given of this process – how convenient!)

So the first longer standing theory says that a single line of amino acids came together by chance and either formed the first protein or became a part of the first DNA string. This chain of amino acids is said to be the beginnings of the cell and that somehow this chain found its way inside the protective boundaries of an environment that worked like a cellular wall whereby it was kept safe. The second theory states that a single RNA strand formed all by itself, also as a random action of pure chance. Then, somehow, this strand became self-replicating. So this RNA strand is said to be the beginning of the code for the cell. So, it is important to point out that *some* **evolutionists speculate** that,

RNA came into being before DNA.

The platform is then said to have copied itself and developed its code over time.

> **NOTE:** The RNA platform, as we've said, is the means by which a string of amino acids are formed together by the **Ribosome factory reading** the Messenger RNA strand. Today we see that the Messenger RNA is totally dependent upon the Ribosome factory to get this job done. In the imaginings of this video we're told that the creation of the first protein is said to have happened without the help of the Ribosome factory! The RNA Messenger strand is pictured as having powers beyond that which we see it has now!

Some evolutionists argue therefore that RNA came first and that DNA comes directly from RNA – though they are yet to outline how that process of growth from a simple RNA strand to mindboggling DNA code happened because they can't explain how that level of coding comes together by chance or how all of the resources that run the cell came together by chance. There is no auto-organisational route from one to the other because DNA and the environment that runs it is so precision complex and DNA is specifically written from the standpoint of 'knowing what needs to be done' out there in the rest of the body for the living organism to live, survive and grow! So evolutionists say that it is possible and sensible to suggest that those amino acids that make up a protein can somehow come together by chance to form the beginnings of DNA or RNA. Let's now have a look at these two theories.

Chapter 5 – The Theories of Cell Creation

THEORY 1 - A Single Protein Forming by Chance

A Single String of Amino Acids

Let's first see if it is logical and sensible, and indeed possible, to believe that a string of amino acids can randomly come together by themselves in some primordial soup to form the first set of DNA or the first protein. This DNA string or first protein, we are told, then somehow managed to auto-organise itself into the first cell, which evolutionists call the first 'simple cell' – as I was taught at school. If we can clearly show that it is not possible for the first amino acid string to have come together by chance, then we can forget the rest of the incredible theory that also tries to tell us that the first DNA string or protein somehow miraculously auto-organised itself into a cell with its intricate processes, its precision use of coding and its carefully placed resources.

The Impossible Odds of this Unguided Process

If the above facts of science that we've shared so far about the cell's irreducible complexity have not already moved you to understand the impossibility of the cell auto-organising itself into its own existence, then let's look at pure chance to see if amino acids can indeed come together to form a protein without the help of DNA paving the way. I'm going to quote from the film "Chance of Life Appearing Randomly" put together by the Vatican, which itself makes reference to a book by Stephen C. Meyer called "Signature in the Cell" from which it quotes throughout the film. Here's what just a small part of the film has to say about amino acids coming together to form a single protein by chance.

"Now if we were to consider, for the sake of argument, the chance that an amino acid compound could have formed into a protein by itself on the early earth, what would the chance of that happening be? Let's pretend that a prebiotic soup existed and that this soup contained the necessary conditions and components required for an

amino acid chain to form randomly on its own. Of course this is not realistic or scientific, for to say that something came into existence out of nothing violates the law of causality, moreover the assumed early condition of the earth would not have been conducive to the constituent parts of the cell arising and surviving on their own. The assumed condition of the earth would have been hostile to it. Nevertheless, for the sake of argument, let's suppose that a chain of amino acids could have formed by chance into a protein. Let's assume this could happen in order to analyse the chance that it would happen. The one hundred thousand kinds of proteins in the body are comprised of twenty different kinds of amino acids in various combinations. Since only twenty kinds of amino acids form proteins, the probability of a small chain of amino acids forming randomly into a protein can be calculated. A short protein is about one hundred and fifty amino acids long but for the sake of understanding this point let's first consider a hypothetical chain that is two amino acids long. If you had a two amino acid chain the number of possible combinations in the chain would be twenty to the second power (20^2) or twenty times twenty, for a total of four hundred possible combinations. That's because there would be twenty possible amino acids in the first spot of the chain and twenty possible amino acids in the second spot, resulting in twenty times twenty or four hundred. In a three amino acid chain the number of possible combinations would be twenty to the third power (20^3) for a total of eight thousand because you would have twenty possibilities in each spot of the chain. In a four amino acid chain it will be twenty to the fourth power (20^4) for a total of one hundred and sixty thousand possibilities. Now there is no such thing as a protein with two or four amino acids. A short protein has around one hundred and fifty amino acids. The number of possible combinations in a one hundred and fifty amino acid chain would be twenty to the one hundred and fiftieth power, (20^{150}) that is twenty different possibilities in every spot of the chain. That number is roughly equivalent to 10^{195}. To get an idea to just how large a number this is consider that the total number of atoms in the viewable universe is believed to be about ten to the power of eighty, (10^{80})."

The film then goes on to remind us that there are millions of atoms in a single grain of sand. If you were asked to blindly, by a random choice, pinpoint a designated atom in that grain of sand, then you would say it was almost impossible. The odds against it happening would be too great. If we were to gather all the sand in the Sahara desert and ask someone to find the correct grain of sand and then, within that grain of sand, locate the designated atom, they'd say that that really was impossible. However, the film tells us that the number 10^{80} represents **all** of the atoms in the viewable universe, that is all matter out there for us to see. The human mind cannot even begin to comprehend the size of the physical matter that is scattered across the universe, even if it was all gathered to one place, let alone get its head around the number of atoms that make it up. Yet the odds against a single chain of amino acids correctly coming together in a short chain to form a single short protein, which is just one hundred and fifty amino acids in length, is 10^{195}. This number of 10^{195} is so much bigger than 10^{80} and I cannot even begin to express how much bigger it is. However, these impossible odds are not the end of the story. It gets worse. Here's some more quoted text from the film.

*"Many proteins are far longer than one hundred and fifty amino acids long and therefore more complex. Let's also remember that **only left-handed amino acids** can be used in the construction of proteins, so if a right handed amino acid strayed in there, it would ruin the whole process. The chance that all of the amino acids in a randomly built chain would be only left handed is 10^{45} and this set of odds also needs adding into the final calculation that we've made earlier. Along with this add into the mix the information that peptide bonds (the joining blocks between the amino acids) do not always form when amino acids come together in this random way, making the situation even more unstable. By the time we've taken into account all of these factors, the odds against just one amino acid chain randomly coming together to form a protein is beyond our imagination; even then we have to remember that, that which we've described so far, it is only representative of a moderate length chain. One single chain does not in any way shape or form represent the workings of a living cell which requires, for it to be minimally complex, **at least 250 proteins**. The only honest answer to this statement is that it is impossible for life to begin by chance."*

So we can see that this theory is a dead end. Even if a miracle had happened and one amino acid string had formed in the past, then we don't even have the beginning of the 250 proteins needed for the cell to begin to function. However, the situation is more complex than that which I've described. If you really want to dig deep into this particular subject, how amino acids in the oceans cannot form, then please get a copy of Stephen C. Meyer's book called "Signature in the Cell" or A.E. Wilder Smith's book, "The Natural Sciences Know Nothing of Evolution". Both of them build complementary arguments showing how the random coming together of amino acids cannot begin the life of the cell.

THEORY 2 - The RNA World Hypothesis

RNA – the Beginning of Life?

Here's a very brief outline of the evolutionist's theory to suggest how a single string of RNA can turn into a living cell. Once again I've chosen a humanist YouTube video on this subject so that I can't be accused of bias. The web address for this video is, https://www.youtube.com/watch?v=VYQQD0KNOis

The video is called "The RNA Origin of Life"

Let's first of all remember that the RNA strand is that which is created when a gene in the DNA is turned on, then the DNA is unzipped by a protein called a RNA polymerase, and as this protein reads the DNA and makes a copy, a representation of the DNA code, by assembling blocks onto a platform. This platform is called the Messenger RNA. Remember that this platform then leaves the nucleus to travel to another part of the cell and is then read by a couple of Ribosomes which form a factory at the end of the RNA platform. By reading the RNA template the Ribosome factory uses amino acids to create a new protein.

The video begins by posing the question of where does life come from. It says that it is probably the most important question that anyone can ask. It says that the cracking of DNA's genetic code has been really helpful and this evolutionary video then goes on to *claim* that understanding the DNA code now enables them to trace back the history of evolution to the first single cell. The video goes on to say that it is at this point that they are stuck. It then says,

*"The problem is DNA is a great way to store information but it **doesn't do much else**. Cells rely on other molecules like proteins to replicate, grow and survive. Proteins on the other hand work great as molecular machines to keep cells alive and healthy but they can't store information **or copy themselves**, they need DNA for that. So we have a chicken and egg problem. DNA needs proteins to function and proteins need DNA to exist. So **which came first**? Which molecule made life possible?"*

> **Note:** The question that is asked in the video is, "**Which came first**?" If you remember I have already told you that *religious world view drives science*. Humanists don't want God in science, so they ALWAYS look for a step-by-step process as being the answer to how we got here. They don't say, "This is irreducible. Wow, we've stumbled over the fingerprints of God, the very place where the divine touched the cosmos!"

The video then goes on to suggest that RNA is the answer because it claims that RNA can do the two things that are needed for a cell to survive. It can,

- store information
- perform various functions so that the cell is kept alive

> **NOTE:** Both of the above statements are in fact **not true**, but we'll pick up on this later on.

The theory states that in some primordial soup a **self-replicating** RNA strand just **appeared**. Three suggestions were put forward as to its location.

- volcanic vents on the deep ocean floor
- clay clumps may have enabled the building blocks to self-assemble
- some scientists say RNAs could have formed on Mars and been brought here by via an asteroid strike

The video then goes on to say that these self-replicating RNAs (there is no such thing as a self-replicating RNA) did 3 things. They,

- 'emerged'
- 'multiplied'
- 'evolved'

...and then these RNA strands are suddenly relabelled by the video's narrative as *microscopic proto-lifeforms.* The film goes on to tell us that they 'blossomed' and 'competed' and this competition caused the best code to 'live on' whilst the not so good code died out. (This is all based on the survival of the fittest theory). The subsequent battle for survival, due to there being 'competition' amongst the RNA strands, led to...

- RNAs evolving in order to produce excellent proteins which were
    - strong and stable
    - able to carry out complex biological processes
- RNA strands then evolved by turning themselves into DNA
- DNA then became a stable archive for the best and most successful information

The film finally finishes by saying,

*"Life became more complex over trillions of tiny steps and **happy accidents**. And all the while the RNA line-up grew, alongside lengthening genomes of DNA and complex proteins. **And it's all still happening inside your body**. RNAs have adapted to become the 'Swiss Army knives' of our cells. Today they can slice, dice, catalyse, build, destroy, code, replicate and transform; a remarkable diversity from the simplest of beginnings, a single self-replicating RNA molecule."*

> **NOTE:** This video is the perfect example of the, '**If we can imagine it, then we can believe it,**' fantasy theorising that so many evolutionists engage in. We can 'see it in our mind's eye, like a cartoon animation, and therefore its *imagined possibility* becomes a viable *theoretic probability* in our thinking. Amazing, isn't it!

So there you have it in a nutshell, the RNA World View Hypothesis. It all sounds very grand. However, the above is all a load of self-imagined, verbal 'codswallop' (that's polite slang for nonsense) on the part of the evolutionists. Never in my life have I come across such a bizarre, fantastical and self-imagined fairy story to justify evolutionary theory. As I said earlier, some evolutionists will think up and imagine anything in order to justify their theory and to keep God out of science. Now let's criticise the theory, just as we did when we examined Darwin's overall theory in a previous chapter.

- -
Criticisms of the RNA Hypothesis
- -

Initial Criticisms

First the video claims that we can now trace back the history of evolution right back to the first cell because of DNA. This is a very bold statement. We have already said that all living cells contain DNA. Just because they contain DNA does not follow that DNA is therefore a marker by which we can trace evolution. Yes, all living creatures have DNA in them and therefore there is a 'common operating system' that runs all life. It is an assumption on the part of those people who hold to a naturalistic world view, however, to say that DNA has therefore evolved from the lower level life forms to upper level life forms; **we will see later on why information in the cell does not, cannot and has not evolved.**

> **NOTE:** We have also already seen that the mechanisms of evolution do not work and that you can just as easily interpret everything we see around us in the context of a designer. A common operating system and multi-complex components that **need to come together** to enable life to work are evidences for a programmer, designer and engineer.

Saying that we can trace life backwards simply assumes that a creator/designer was not involved in implanting DNA into His creation. It is just another expression of the 'Anything but God Society'. A creator/designer would naturally use the same type of programming language when putting all life together. As I've already

137

said, it's just what a group of I.T. technicians would do if they needed to create an environment in which robots did most of the work. Small robots, tall robots, etc. would all have a similar operating system to run them, they would all have the same computer language to use to run the code that makes them work. The coding to perform their particular specialist jobs, however, would be unique and complex. So some basic code would be the same, then there would be specialist complex coding to make the different body parts work that only certain robots would have depending on their jobs. That would be quite logical.

We then come to what the film called the 'chicken and the egg' problem. Which came first, DNA or a protein? Well the answer for the evolutionist is that...

"...something has to come first,"

...because the film makers are not looking for evidence for a creator, they are religiously looking for a **process** because their **religious world view** dictates that there must be a **process** to find, *not a person*. I mentioned this a few paragraphs ago. So, due to the assumed 'fact' that all the components in the cell **cannot arise at the same time** because there was no creator involved in its assembly and because the film makers are not looking for the fingerprints of a creator, they look to the RNA strand to do the work instead.

So here they say that the reason for looking at RNA is because it can do two things, as we've already mentioned,

- store information
- perform various functions so that the cell is kept alive

Here's where I begin to get annoyed with evolutionists as both of those statements are not just inaccurate and misleading, they are without foundation and totally wrong.

A Store of Information?
An RNA strand does not store information. It may **temporarily hold data** as it travels through a safe and constructed environment within

the cell, but it does not store it. If something is stored it is put somewhere for **safe keeping**. DNA is kept safe by first being inside a cell membrane. That membrane is specifically designed to keep the DNA safe from outside interference that would possibly damage it – the forces of raw energy in the natural world will do nothing but remove information from any environment if they collide with it, so information needs protecting / shielding from those forces. In Eukaryotic cells the DNA is also placed within the nucleus, which again works as a 'safe house' for the information to be stored and kept safe. To store something is to keep it safe for future use. The environment around that which is being stored is created, crafted and calibrated for that purpose. The RNA Messenger is called what it is, simply because it is a **messenger**, not a **store**. It doesn't have any natural barrier around it to keep it safe from the elements. It is only there to temporarily transport information. It cannot keep information safe. An RNA Messenger strand floating around in the oceans is not a store. It will be destroyed.

RNA has no Proactive Abilities

So RNA cannot keep information safe nor does it have the **energy or mechanism to develop genes** *along its own line of code*. There is no facility for it to develop in that way or any other way. What on earth would enable and cause a single strand of RNA to examine itself and say, "Well, this is where one gene starts and ends and this is the beginning of another gene! I've now ended one part of my code and now I'm going to start a new section." Who says so? An RNA strand cannot,

- assemble itself
- think about itself
- organise itself
- process itself

Who or what is doing the thinking to develop an RNA strand into a DNA store? Who or what is doing the thinking to write new and sensible code? The concept is quite ridiculous. Just as importantly where does the energy come from to do such things? If you invented a miraculous theory that somehow RNA became empowered in some way then the next question would be,

*How is that energy being **sensibly guided** in order to build something as delicate a code? Raw energy within the cosmos **always produces chaos**, not order!*

Another thing to note is that for the RNA platform, with all its coding blocks on it, to come together in a sensible order by itself with the coding blocks in the correct order, well that has the same odds against it happening correctly as the string of amino acids faces that we saw in the first theory. Self-assembling these blocks into a meaningful and correct order is impossible. Note also that there has to be an intelligent language in place beforehand for those blocks to mean anything. So the bigger problem that we have with a self-developing RNA Messenger platform is that,

....language comes before code,

...we will look at this later in this book.

The rest of the arguments that I have to criticise this theory are put into the appendix as I can go on for pages and pages on this particular subject but I don't want this book to get bogged down in detail over one issue. So to read a fuller criticism of this video, please go to Appendix B and the section that is entitled 'Criticisms of the RNA World Hypothesis Theory'. Here are some bullet point notes, however, to summarise what is said in the appendix.

RNA...
- cannot perform tasks
- cannot process itself
- is passive and lets other molecular machines work on it in order for proteins to be made
- has no way of using energy to perform tasks

RNA therefore is given a host of abilities in the video that it does not have even now! Anyone **not knowing** the actual role that RNA has within the cell would be deceived by this video, being led to believe that RNA can do things that it simple cannot achieve.

Here are some more quick criticisms of the video,

- the word 'evolve' is used in the film without any explanation of 'how'
- saying that it can do multiple things, such as replicate, slide, dice, etc. gives it super abilities that it cannot now do
- there is nothing purpose built about an RNA strand that enables it to replicate or process itself or to develop in complexity
- just because the cell self-replicates does not mean that RNA can do the same, it has no mechanism to do so
- saying that 'competition' is a cause of the evolution of the code is a nonsense as lifeless code does not have an awareness of 'itself' or have a concept of scarcity of space in the environment or of food
- how did the RNA 'feed' itself so that it was sustained?
- how did is replenish its bits of code when they wore out and got old?
- code is deliberately written with 'intent' within it for 'work to be done' and this cannot be evolved randomly
- data change within DNA is not new code being written but simply a data expression change and this activity should not be used as a model to say that RNA could write 'new code'
- evolving/bad/incomplete code does not work
- we're told that the code becomes 'stable' – unstable code does not work and does not become stable – it has to be corrected via an intelligent mind
- the words 'proto-life' and 'blossom' are added to the mix without any foundation – this is sheer wilful belief on the part of the evolutionist expressed as a blind leap of faith in the dark
- billions of years is 'added to the pot' of evolutionary rhetoric because if we clothe the 'impossible' (evolving code) with the 'unimaginable' (billions of years) then somehow we can believe the theory
- we're told that 'little steps' and '**happy accidents**' are responsible for the code – but these are verbal excuses to get around imagining something that is impossible

NOTE: The biggest problem is, however, that bad code or inaccurate code does not work. Any computer programmer knows that. So to even talk about 'evolving code' is ridiculous. We'll look more at this in the following chapters.

A Misrepresentation of the Facts

Then we come to the 'first lie' that is slipped in at the end! Once you've been mind-boggled by the graphics that display throughout the film, showing what supposedly happened and the rhetoric that washes over your thinking, then we're told that this same process that has been described **is still going on in your body today –**

as if it is something that can be observed!

That is, that you and I are still developing our genetic code! Let me make it very, very clear.

It has never, ever been observed at any time in the history of science for any cell to increase in complexity or to add brand new code for the creation of newly engineered body parts.

No new code being written has ever been observed. We see copy errors all the time. Copy errors, along with hereditary exchange, are not the writing of brand new code. Copy errors are changes in the current code that are either neutral (blue eyes rather than brown, long hair rather than short) or negative. No new body parts have ever been constructed or created via copy error and DNA hereditary mix. So for this video to say that we are still going through the same process of development, well its blatantly not science but just sheer imagination based on a desire for its 'RNA World Hypothesis' to be declared as true. It is taking what is essentially data change and describing it as new information. These are totally different things. You'll understand what I mean by this after reading the next couple of chapters.

The second lie is in the ending phrase where it says that the RNAs that are in the cell today can, "slice, dice, catalyse, build, destroy, code, replicate and transform". Again, this is not true. They cannot do any of these things. The RNA stand platform is just a **passive template** that is **worked on** by the busy and active proteins in the cell. The RNA strand platform is just a messenger template that floats out of the nucleus, away from the DNA from which it was originally constructed, and then it is the Ribosome factory, made up of two proteins assembling together at the end of the platform, that puts together the new protein. All of the work is done by the proteins. It is the proteins that are created in the cell who, "slice, dice, catalyse, build, etc." not the RNA strand! The RNA strand is useless by itself. By itself it is a floating piece of dead code. **It is powerless to effect change**!

Now that I've spent a little time criticising the video perhaps you can see for yourself how many fantastical assumptions there are behind its thinking. All this video is based upon pure fantasy; none of its assumptions are grounded in the true science based on what the cell is and how it works today. It is all a reimagining of current processes to make them do something in the past that they cannot do now. The RNA strand is not a route to a cell. In a moment I'm going to go onto a real world illustration comparison to show how impossible the RNA strand World Hypothesis is. Before I do that I want to make one more reference to another humanist video on the same subject. Its YouTube address is here:
https://www.youtube.com/watch?v=1WS712DHfmg

This video also puts together a hypothesis of how RNA strands could be the source for all life. I'm not going to go into the contents of the video except to say that it starts off by defining life and shows how life is different from the inanimate universe. After briefly tracing the history of how scientists found out that life is not some 'force in the air' they then look at the work of a chemist called Friedrich Wohler who was able to use inorganic chemicals in an experiment to synthesise an organic chemical. This one experiment seems to be enough evidence for the rest of the film to suggest that life is just the **process** of chemical reactions and nothing more.

The video then goes on to talk briefly about the two different kinds of cells, those that we've already mentioned, the prokaryotes and the eukaryotes. If you remember the prokaryotes have DNA floating around in them whereas the eukaryotes have organelles and the DNA lives in the nucleus. The prokaryotes are said to have evolved first, because they are the 'simpler' of the two and then the eukaryotes are said to have evolved as a result of the prokaryotes continuous evolution over time. The film makers, however, made a couple of brief statements that are very telling. They say of these so called 'simple' prokaryotes,

"But the thing is, even in its earliest stages, single cell life was **massively complex** *compared to the inanimate universe."*

Then they add,

"But how did an object **as ridiculously complex** *as a prokaryotes first emerge?"*

Then we get the normal blurb and rhetoric when we're told that,

"...some prokaryotes floated near to the top of the ocean and started using sunlight, water and the carbon dioxide that was abundant in the Earth's atmosphere to sustain their own complexity using this sweet chemical process that **they'd come up with** *called photosynthesis."*

We're not told how these prokaryotes were able to **invent** photosynthesis, they just did. Again they just 'evolved' the process themselves. Then this film continues the theme that these *"primitive organic chemicals eventually came together into balls with protective membranes,"* and that they, *"would have* **reproduced** *and proliferated much as life does today."*

> **NOTE:** It is amazing how no explanation of '**how**' this might have happened is given.

At the same time this primitive life is admitted to have had **faults**, that the code would have been '**clumsy**' and '**inaccurate**' and '**badly programed**' but somehow it all survived.

*The films strongly suggests, however, that despite the **flaws** in its code, that this 'earlier' RNA strand could **code itself** and **replicate itself** (something which is cannot do today).*

It then continues by saying that the copy error that sometimes takes place in a cell is the main driving force for evolution. It says,

*"On the scale of millions of years, these **copying errors** are the **engine of evolution** and the origin of new species."*

Let me repeat a couple of things about code, you'll learn about this in the next chapters.

1) Language comes before code. Code is the expression of a **known language**. If there is no sensible language developed, then there is no code and **no meaning** to the code.
2) Code has to be accurate. Bad or inaccurate code simple does one thing only, **it does not work**.
3) Code cannot, therefore, develop step-by-step over time and remain meaningful, purposeful and useful.
4) Code has to be purposefully processed by its environment in order to effect change.
5) For an environment to process code it has to be,
   a. Constructed with purpose in the light of what the code will do,
   b. Powered by something so that the resources that work together to process the code can do their job and make the code's programming effective.

Copy errors do not provide or facilitate any of the points above. If copy errors are meant to be the 'engine of evolution' then you've just proved the theory of evolution to be wrong.

Multiple copy errors in biological code produce cancer, not higher forms of life.

Over the next couple of chapters I'm going to continue to tear this whole idea apart by looking at the difference between data, code and information; a single RNA strand, or even loads of them all swimming around together in a primordial soup, are not information, they are simply dead bits of data! Data does nothing and can do nothing. Before we look at this, however, here's one last illustration about the possibility of an RNA strand auto-organising itself into a cell. The RNA strand is not built to do that, not fit for purpose, just as a robotic arm in a factory is not fit to create the factory itself.

A Robotic Arm Comparison

So far we have looked at a fantastical, imagined theory of how evolutionists say a protein is meant to have been created or how an RNA strand was responsible for the cell. We've looked at how it is impossible for either of these to actually happen. Even if by some miracle beyond our imagination we had a single protein come into existence by chance and retain its shape or somehow an RNA strand came together with its blocks of information in the correct order, how did it then auto-organise itself into a cell and at the same time resist the different forces of nature that naturally remove information from the Earth's environment? You can see the point that I'm making here. The movement from protein or RNA strand to cell is like moving from a single robotic arm (that you might find on a factory assembly line) to the factory itself by an unguided and random process whereby the robotic arm simply interacts with its environment.

A robotic arm is something that you can find as a common component of some factories, such as in car assembly plants. The robotic arm has no consciousness of its own. It is not 'self-aware' and does not seek to understand its own environment. It does a job because it has been fashioned and programmed to do so. Its shape, its components and its programming have been added to it by the 'hands of others' who were involved in its making. It is powered by the car assembly plant itself and there is an 'on/off' switch that supplies the power to the robotic arm so that it can perform its duties. Everything in its immediate environment has been designed and calibrated for the arm to work smoothly and perform its tasks. To suggest that a robotic arm, if put in just the right conditions, could create a factory would be a preposterous idea. The basic questions asked would be,

What does the robotic arm 'do to itself' and its environment in order to change itself into a factory and how does it 'do this'?

Then we would ask the following questions.

1. From where does it get the energy to perform this amazing task?
2. How is it able to move within its environment?
3. How does it locate and assemble the different factory parts?
4. How does it keep all of the parts together during this assembly process whilst they all float around together in this 'primordial soup' of an environment?
5. How does it prepare each part of the environment so that its contents have a comfortable home in which to fit and work?
6. How does it figure out the relationship between each part so that processing can take place?
7. How does it even 'get its head' round how these different components of the factory will relate to each other in order for them to complete their work?
8. How does it create products that are fit for purpose to not only make the factory run, but also create products (like the car) that will run outside of the factory?
9. How does it have knowledge of what happens outside the factory walls and what must be done inside the factory to meet those various needs that are on the outside, such as car brakes, lights and windscreen wipers so that the car can work in different environments?
10. How does it invent 'self-consciousness' so that it can think about any of the above questions?

Let's remember that a robotic arm is a single item that is purposefully built to sit on an assembly line and to interact with the products that pass by on a conveyer belt. It cannot think for itself. It is created and purposed for one thing only, to do a single job. To say that a robotic arm can somehow auto-organise itself into a factory is ridiculous.

*Don't forget, a car factory is very simple
compared with a cell.*

That, however, is exactly what the evolutionist is asking you to believe about the movement from a single protein or RNA strand that will auto-organise its environment and itself into a living cell.

*A single protein or an RNA strand is made
for a purpose within the cell, **neither of them are
the reason for the cell**.*

The cell, and everything in it, gets its energy and power to do its work from the organelle called mitochondria. Without mitochondria there is no energy to **do** anything; it powers the cell for its multiple activities. The so called 'first protein' or 'first RNA strand' would just simply be a piece of dead data, floating around in a pool of chemicals and nothing more. That pool of chemicals would eventually split up and tear the RNA strand apart, according to the forces of nature which are subject to the second law of thermodynamics.

The only reason why this kind of fantasy is entertained by humanists is simply because they've got nowhere else to go. The '**Anything but God Society**' will imagine any kind of scenario it can in order to put together some kind of theoretical process of development in order to justify us being here without the divine touching the cosmos. It is amazing to see to what lengths evolutionists will go in their imaginations (without any scientific basis) in order to make a so called theoretical excuse to avoid God. At all costs they must keep God out of science. So at all costs, even at the cost of exchanging basic common sense for fantastical stupidity, they imagine a route for evolution to happen and believe it to be the case, until they are proved wrong and then they can reimagine something else just as fantastical in its place, anything but God!

If you think that everything that I've said so far is highly problematic for the evolutionist, however, let me say that the problem is far greater than that which I've already outlined. The problem is not just that it is impossible for the natural world to create

148

a cell wall and a nucleus and all of the components and behaviours that make to be what it is today. The problem is far worse than that.

The problem is that **information,** (DNA) is at the heart of the cell. Without DNA the cell does not work. The movements and forces that we can observe in the natural world around us only do one thing, **they remove information**.

In order for us to understand this, however, we need to look at what information is. So we're going to take a break from the cell for the moment and we're going to look at information and see its relationship to coding and data and its relationship to the infrastructure that it needs to surround it in order for it to **do its job**. We're going to do this by going into the computer world because the data flow in the computer world shows us very clearly

- what data is
- what code is
- what information is
- how they are different
- the environment that is needed to make them work

...and from there we can then come back to, and understand in a new way, the life that is within the cell and see that it is impossible for the cell to be here without the divine. Let me, however, let the cat out of the bag even before I've started. Here's some of the main thrust of the next chapters that will unpick the theory of evolution.

1) **Data** is recognisable characters ordered in a sequential way, set within the context of a **known language**.
2) **Code** is *purposefully written* data, *carefully constructed*, **written with intent**, in order to communicate or to facilitate a process, a job to be done.
3) **Information** is precision code **processed** by its *environment* in order to ensure a job done.

All of the above is only created by the workings of an intelligent mind and cannot come about by random chance and unguided processes. When we understand the true nature of these three things, data, code and information, we see that random and unguided processes are dead in the water. The activities of raw energy within the cosmos cannot even begin to be used as a route to produce any of them. Life is impossible without the intervention of the divine.

SECTION 2

The World of Data, Code & Information

Wrong definitions of data, code and information.
Wrong applications of information change.

Chapters 6-10

- correct definitions of data and its uses inside and outside the cell
- a correct definition of code and its uses
- a correct definition of information and the environment it works in
- the contextual questions of information and code
- the workings of data expression within DNA
- the hostile environment to data, code and information
- how the evolutionary deception is kept in place

Chapter 6 – It's Data Jim...

...and only understandable in the context of language!

Introduction

Right, I'm just about to start this book! Everything that I've said so far is just background information that I needed to communicate. In around ten pages time I'm going to go into *'my world'* – that is the world of information technology (I.T.) and away from the world of biologists. As biologists are not I.T. people they don't understand information properly – and due to this severe lack of knowledge they make huge mistakes when trying to maintain the theory of evolution. As information is at the heart of life and it is information that makes life work, biology is subject to information theory, not the other way round. Get information wrong and everything else, your deductions, theories and conclusions are, by default, wrong!

Data is the Glue of Life

In order for us to get a final proper perspective on the complexity of life we now need to look at data. This is because data is the basis for all of life. Without this foundation stone in place there is no life at all. Data, however, is not just a foundation stone to make life possible, it is also a **stepping stone** to true knowledge about what makes life work. Once we've understood data, it then becomes essential that we look beyond data at things far more complex. Those 'things' are what we call 'code' and 'information'. Unless we know what code and information really are, how they behave or what they communicate (and have this understanding clearly laid out in our minds) we will not know what we're looking at when we examine the contents of the cell and the processes that happen within it, nor will we be able to come to proper conclusions about it. So let me start off by making a quick distinction between data, code and information.

Data is foundational for all life. Code and information, however, act as facilitators of life, they make life work.

A Car Analogy

Information is greater than code and code is greater than data, just as a car is greater than any of its individual components, such as the engine or the wires or cables that are within it. This is because a car can hold/contain an engine and the cabling within itself but the engine and the cabling (and wires that are used in a car) cannot hold/contain the car. The engine and the cabling may be essential to the car, they are necessary to make it work, but the engine and cabling are simply **part of the story** that makes a car what it is. The car is much more, much greater, than any of its components, no matter how essential they are. The car houses the driving experience of the people in the car. The car houses and facilitates the needs of the people who use the car. So too information will have code and data within it, but coding and data are only **part of the story** of information, information is so much more than coding and data.

Definition: Data, Code and Information – part 1

Here are three very important statements which we'll unpack over the next couple of chapters.

1. Data acts as **the basis** for life in the cell.
2. Code is the **expression of intent** for life in the cell.
3. Information flow **actively facilitates** the life of the cell.

A House Analogy

Using another analogy, a house is made up of bricks and mortar. Without the bricks and mortar there is no house. The bricks are the building blocks that make the house; they are like data that is foundational to life. The mortar **surrounds** the bricks to **bring them together** to make the house stable and workable as a unit; the mortar is like code that pulls the data together and makes it work. The frame of the house is the end result of the bricks and the mortar 'being together'. That end result of that 'togetherness', where the bricks and mortar are joined **as one**, is the shape of the house. The house, however, contains the bricks and mortar, the bricks and mortar do not contain the house. The mortar is that which brings it all together and makes it stable but when people look at their home, they don't see a collection of bricks and mortar, they see a house that is **home** for them to 'live life' inside. The house's function, therefore, is greater than its shape from the joining of bricks and mortar. So much more happens in the house. The house **facilitates** all kinds of activities where people just 'live life' inside it. The house is **home** to the lives of the people who live there. So too, information is that which houses and **enables life** in the cell.

Definition: Data, Code and Information – part 2
Putting it simply,

*Information **facilitates** life,*
information <u>is made up from</u> code,
*code **expresses** intent for life,*
code <u>is made up from</u> data,
*and data is **foundational** for life.*

NOTE: If the above definitions don't make immediate sense to you then don't worry. It will become clear as you continue to read.

This understanding will also render all of the evolutionist's attempts at auto-organising information into existence via a naturalistic process as useless. All of their attempts are actually attempts at *creating* **data** (bad and inaccurate code) not **information**. Those attempts at data creation will always fail – the reasons for which we'll look at in a little while. You cannot, however, auto-organise mere data into code and then code into information via a random and unguided process; the jump between them is too great for the natural world to accomplish. Code is that which exists between data and information and code has to be constructed within,

- the context of the **language** of data
- the **rules** of coding
- the **intent** of coding

Coding requires **intent** to communicate/achieve work (we'll look at this in a bit) and then the environment has to be **prepared to process the code** in order for it to *become* information *by which the intent for work to be done is finally achieved.* In fact there are no mechanisms within the natural world to accomplish this movement from data to

154

code to information. Before I get too far ahead of myself, however, let's start off by looking at data.

A Definition of Data

Data – Quite a Particular Thing

When Darwin first made popular his grandfather's theory of evolution, he had no idea that all life is made up of precision data that has been turned into useful information in order for the cell to work. He did not know that it is information (processed code made up from sensibly ordered data) that drives everything. He did not have the instrumentation to look inside a cell, as we do today, to find out what it is made from. If he has known this, then he wouldn't have been able to put together his theory. Before we dive into that, however, here's a simple but profound question that still needs asking,

"What is data?"

NOTE: There is a difference between data imprinted onto the cosmos and taking data readings from within the cosmos. I can take data readings about the temperature of an object as it cools down within space, perhaps it once was a burning sun, like ours in our solar system, which will one day cool down and die - becoming what is called a white dwarf. These temperature data readings that I can measure and write down are different from data within the cell. Data that I record, that tells me what is happening in the universe, is a human way of telling the story about the behaviour of the physical matter that is around us. That data, however, is not contained within the context of the physical matter itself; it is me watching and observing the cosmos and finding a way of translating those actions and activities into a format that is meaningful to reveal what is 'going on out there'. Data in the cell forms part of what we call 'imprinted information' where the cosmos is shaped in such a way that it can be 'read' and processed by something or someone.

Data in the cell are the strands of material that make up the bases on the ladder of DNA. As we said earlier in this book DNA is like a coiled ladder. Each rung on the ladder is split in the middle. Each half

155

of the rung is a base, a strand, of material that is fastened to the ladder. These strands(bases) are known as,

- adenine (A)
- cytosine (C)
- guanine (G)
- thymine (T)

Together these form the code of life.

*Each **strand**, therefore, is a **single digit** of **data** on the DNA ladder.*

When you understand biological data (DNA) properly you'll see that biological data is actually a quite particular thing. What I mean by that is that biological data (the strands/bases on the double helix that make up DNA) may be very common wherever you look at life within nature on this planet but it is **not common** to find data expressed in a variety of circumstances in the universe itself. In fact biological data within the cosmos is only found within one area, which is life on Earth. There may be an abundance of biological data in nature to suggest that it is very common, but outside that one area where it can be observed, data cannot be seen at all. It's as if data has been 'stuffed into the fabric of life' on this planet but outside that one context where it's found in abundance, it's not found anywhere else. So here's a short definition of data that we can begin to look at and unpack.

A Working Definition

Data is a set of **recognisable** characters or symbols which appear in a particular **sequential order**, one after the other, that is **stored** in some way within the context of a known language.

Let's unpack this definition making 3 basic points.

1) Data is made up of **recognisable** characters.
2) Data is orderly and **sequential**.
3) Data has to be **stored** in some way.

1) Data is made up of Recognisable Characters

The characters that make up the data have to be recognisable. This is because data has to be expressed within the context of a meaningful language. Once a line of data has been written, its individual digits or characters need to make sense to either someone or something, otherwise it is not data. In other words the data has to be,

- recognisable
- readable

…by someone or by something. It does not have to be recognisable and readable to everyone, just to someone or something. This is because there is always a language behind data and that language is made up of meaningful symbols – typically expressed as characters, letters or digits. Each character, letter or digit has to be recognisable within the context of a language. Without a *language context*, via which the symbols can be recognised, there is no data at all! Data does not even begin to exist without the context of language. I could draw unrecognisable squiggles in the sand and those squiggles would **not** be data, unless there was a 'squiggly language' already created beforehand to **interpret** them.

No squiggly language = no squiggly data.

If an archaeologist came across ancient text, etched into stone, then the job of **deciphering the language** to understand the *meaning* of the *symbols*, would be next on the 'to do' list. The archaeologist **would not** *try to invent a language* in order to find out what the symbols meant, the archaeologist would try and understand the language that the *lettering expresses*. This is because,

*…the language comes first, the symbols/lettering **always** come second. The language is the context via which the symbols/lettering is expressed.*

> **Note:** If there is no language, then there is no data. This is most important. We will specifically pick this up in a short while when we look at the evolutionist's attempts at saying

that data/life can arise by accident, by a naturalist means. The humanist will try and create data first (by a random chemical activity) and then the language afterwards by which that data can be understood. This cannot and will never work. That's like trying to write code without a language in place. It's impossible to do. Yet despite this **foundational fact of life**, evolutionists, as we have already seen, insist on talking about simple data first arising from the cosmos by itself and then somehow 'processing itself' and then becoming more complex. Their lack of understanding of the I.T. industry causes them to put things the wrong way round.

2) Data is Orderly and Sequential

The above definition talks about a 'sequential order' to data. This is so that data can be read in some way. That order can be read sideways or diagonally or it can be ordered and read vertically if needs be. It does not matter how the data order is expressed, as long as the order of the data is sequential and orderly. A set of cards, each with a symbol or character on that you throw up into the air and let fall onto the ground in a haphazard manner, is **not** data. The cards will be everywhere and not in a neat line. There will be **no recognisable order** to the characters scattered across the floor from which a **sequence** can be constructed. If there is no sequence to the recognisable characters, then we do not have data. Data has to have order so it can be read.

3) Data has to be Stored in some way

Data has to have at least some measure of temporary stability to it. That is, it has to be at least momentarily holding its shape as a group of orderly characters so that it can be either read by something or by someone. That 'holding of its shape' is what we call '**storage**'. The substance of storage is not the issue, though in the natural world where life is located that 'substance' seems to be the same materials used again and again. Human beings can create and express data through a whole variety of media. Within nature, however, data is expressed via a very narrow medium – specifically within the DNA and RNA strands or the electronic signals of the brain. Outside of these, you'll be pushed to find data expressed in the natural world.

So these three points give us a good starting point for a working definition of data. Data is,

- made up of recognisable characters from a language
- orderly and sequential
- stored in some way

Data can be difficult to understand properly unless it is looked at in a variety of contexts. Once you can see it expressed in different circumstances, however, data becomes a lot easier to understand. Data has commonality in the way in which it is expressed in the natural world and in the way in which it behaves. So whether you see data in the cell of a human or the cell of an animal or the cell of a plant or the cell of a fish or in a single celled bacteria, you will see the same format and behaviour. It always conforms to the above three points. Evolutionists will use this as a poor attempt at suggesting that this is evidence for evolution, rather than evidence for a creator/designer who has used the same basic operating system to run life. They will insist on saying that data and information arose from that natural world by itself and then developed over time, which is why there is commonality in every area of nature. We'll put this idea to bed over the next few pages and chapters by showing that it is not possible for the forces within nature to construct data, develop code and then create the context by which to process that code in order for information to facilitate a job being done.

Data comes from an Intelligent Mind

We've already begun to illustrate that data can't evolve by showing that language comes first and then data afterwards.

Language requires intelligence to exist; intelligence, therefore, has to exist before data does.

As I've already said, humanity can create and express data in a variety of ways by taking readings from observable events within the natural world. Humanity can then record/store that data in a variety of media. In fact, wherever you see information created and expressed by human beings, you see some form of data that is the result of a thinking mind. Information can be printed or imprinted onto almost any substance. I once heard of someone who is meant to have written a signed cheque on the side of a shark (don't know how they processed the cheque in the bank) but wherever you have information imprinted, there you also have data and wherever you have data you have a mind that has created it. From counting and recording fifty cows in a field and expressing that data on a notepad or on a clipboard, to expressing fifty years in the icing of a birthday cake, data can be found expressed by humanity almost anywhere and onto almost anything. Data expressed, however, always comes from a thinking and reasoning mind within the context of language.

Let me complete this section by quoting from an online YouTube video. Here's the address, https://www.youtube.com/watch?v=Oqm0jCIMSgY

Here the film makers talk about the impossibility of the genetic code that makes up DNA coming together as a result of an unguided process. Natural selection and random processes will never produce the hugely complex instruction manual to life. Everything in the code conforms to language, proper sequences of lettering and coding and the rules of coding for an intelligent expression of rules by which life works. Below is a quotation which summarises the main points about the language of DNA.

"...we now know that DNA contains a very specific genetic language. For any string of information to be accurately called a language, it must contain the following elements,

- *an alphabet or a coding system*
- *correct spelling*
- *grammar- a proper arrangement of the words*
- *and then meaning or semantics*
- *and an intended purpose*

When those elements are together in a string of information you have a language. Scientists have now discovered that the genetic code has all of these key elements. The coding regions of DNA have the very same properties as a computer code or a human language."

160

So you can see from the last few pages that even data, the foundation of life, is very complex. Let's develop our understanding of data some more by looking at the computer world, as that is something that is close to us all and something that we can hopefully easily relate to.

Data in the Computer World

Introducing Digital Data

On a computer, data is simply electrical signals stored as '**bits**' and '**bytes**', as they are called. A 'bit' is a storage space on the computer's hard disk that can store an electrical signal that is recorded as either the number 0 or the number 1. It is the smallest piece of data that there is in computing. To help keep the computer world tidy we collect up those tiny 'bits' and organise them into groups (clusters) of **8** 'bits'. Each group of 8 bits is called a 'byte'. So 1 'byte' contains 8 'bits'. If we group just over 1000 bytes together, we get what is called a 'kilobyte'. If we group just over 1,000,000 bytes together,

we get what is called a 'megabyte'

...and most people will be familiar with that phrase, even if they don't actually know what it means.

So the grouping and storage of data in the computer world is done in terms of bits, bytes, kilobytes, megabytes, terabytes etc. Each of these names represents an increasing scale of data storage in the computer world.

When you type on your keyboard, *data is created* by **your activity** as you *press down each keyboard key*, and this data is then stored as **bits**. These bits are then organised and looked after by the computer. As I have said, this is done by storing them in groups as bytes, kilobytes or megabytes. This is so that, as you type your newsletter on your computer and it gets longer and longer, the computer can easily locate all of the data that makes it up and can easily ***present the data as information*** on the screen for you to,

- read
- work on
- or print out

It's a very clever system that has taken a lot of thought and work to put together. You may well be able to remember the amount of criticism that Microsoft went through when it was developing its Windows operating system, getting something so complex and new off the ground takes a lot of effort. The words 'my computer has crashed' were often heard when something went wrong and these bits and bytes were lost and someone had to start their work over again. Computers are a lot more stable now and it's very rare for someone to lose work, if they know what they're doing that is or, in my case, if the electricity supply to the village you live in doesn't suddenly drop off whilst you're in the middle of typing…!

Generating Data via Your Keyboard
A Fictitious Keyboard
I'm not going to go into how a keyboard works, talking about the grid matrix that is behind each keyboard key and how each key depression makes a circuit connection, sending an electrical charge and creating what is called 'bounce' which is then often (depending on the level of sophistication of your keyboard) processed by an inbuilt micro-processor before it is sent off to the computer. I don't want to overload you with unnecessary information. What I want to do is to invent a simplistic fictitious keyboard that will illustrate how the letter 'A' is created on your computer screen each time the letter 'A' key is pressed on your keyboard.

Binary Numbering
I also **do not** want to talk about binary numbering here and how it translates into letters. All I will say is that binary lettering is made up of eight digits set in a pattern like this **000**00000. The first three determine if the letter is upper or lower case.

- if the letter appearing on your computer screen is **lower** case then in the binary code it will begin like this **011**
- if it is **upper** case the binary code will begin like this **010**

162

The last 5 digits of the code determine which letter of the alphabet the letter is. So the letter 'a' is made up of 5 characters *00001* and the capital letter 'A' is **01***00001*. That's all I'll say on the matter.

So I want you to imagine the following.

1) Imagine a fictitious keyboard that has 8 wires running from it to the computer.
2) Each time you press a keyboard key some of those wires will have a signal (a voltage) sent down them and some will not.
3) If there is a signal going down the wire it will mean that the wire carries a number 1.
4) If there is no signal (no voltage) going down the wire then it will mean that the wire carries a 0.
5) Pressing the capital letter 'A' will send a voltage down wires 2 and 8 and no-voltage down the other wires.
6) This enters your computer like this. **01***00001*.
7) The computer is **programmed** to understand that **01***00001* is the letter 'A' and knows how to **translate** these numbers into an 'A' character in your document.
8) So, in your word processing document that you've got open, the computer will display the letter 'A', though on the computer's *hard disk* this letter 'A' is actually stored as **01***00001*.

> **NOTE:** I have added in the **bold** and *italic* text into the numbering to show you wish part of the code is capitalisation and which part is the letter. In reality the code is 01000001.

The process that I've described above is a very simplified one. I've missed out how the data from the keyboard is initially passed around via the computer's motherboard and the CPU unit and other components and programmes that take charge of it, but they are not necessary for the initial point I want to make.

PC Data and its Environment

The point is that data, in the computer world, is an electrical signal which exists as a collection of bits, that is zeros or ones, and these are organised into bytes. These bit signals are **stored** and then **interpreted** by the computer's **language** to represent characters or symbols that have meaning to us. When you open up your word processing package these 1's and 0's are read and **interpreted** by the computer and presented on your screens as characters and symbols in, for example, a newsletter. All this is made possible by a background programme called the computer's 'Operating System'. The operating system is a programme that is itself made up of code; like all computer programmes it is stored as bits and bytes on the computer's hard disk. This code 'runs' as your computer starts up (a little like you and me waking up in the morning where we have to 'come to' from our deep sleep and sometimes our minds can be a little groggy and it takes us a few moments to remember who we are, where we are etc.) So, when the computer is switched on, this operating system programme runs in the background and helps all the other programmes on the computer, like your Word processing programme, to run well and receives its data as you type on your keyboard to create your letter.

It is important to note, therefore, that the data is created by your typing activity and then it is transported, processed, interpreted and then finally stored on your computer. Data is therefore '**moved around**' and made sense of by your PC before finding its final resting place on the computer's hard disk.

Data – Storage and Movement
One more thing to say before we continue to develop our definition of what data is. Data can be stored in different formats. We've just seen how a computer stores data on a hard disk. However, if you were to purchase an abacus, you would also have a data storage and processing device in your hands. The storage may be very temporary, compared with a computer, and the calculations may be nowhere near as complex as that which a computer can perform, but you can still do very good mathematical calculations on an abacus. Data can be represented by the different beads on each bar and the **movement** (processing) of the beads in a sensible manner will **produce** mathematical information, that is, data outputs that are answers to questions.

Data in the Cell
Looking inside the cell, we have seen that DNA is made up of molecules which have four bases on them, adenine (A), thymine (T),

guanine (G) and cytosine (C). These four bases, and **the order in which they are repeated** on the DNA ladder, make up the code to run life within the body of the living creature. This is what is commonly called, 'the genetic code'. The DNA double helix strand (ladder) is the place where the code is stored. Each of the strands of the ladder, whether they are adenine (A), thymine (T), guanine (G) or cytosine (C), are classed as data - which together are collectively called code. So we see that data is part of the foundation stones of life. Data forms the basis for code and for information. Without data we have no ability to make life possible.

This also means that the RNA Messenger platform that is created from the DNA helix (via which a protein is created) is also a string of data. Each base on that platform is a piece of data. Collectively this group of data bases form the template code for a new protein. So we have bases of data in the DNA helix ladder, which is where data resides in the cell, and bases of data on the RNA strand, which is how data is transported in the cell.

> **Note:** When evolutionists talk about 'new information' being developed in nature over time, whereby animals or plants begin to 'look different' and adapt to their environment, this is a misrepresentation of the facts. In fact calling it 'new information' is a *deception* and a *misuse of language*. What they are actually talking about is **not** new information but simply **data expression change**, where the bases on the DNA ladder are changed perhaps from A to T or from G to C etc. so that, within the current limitations of the plant or animal's body parts, a sideways movement takes place. A simple change in the bases in the established code of the plant or creature is not new information. The bases are simply *stands of data* **within established code**.

Tweaking data digits is not new code.

> You will understand this properly after you have read the chapter on information. Data change is common in the natural world, but new information does not happen at all!

Data, by itself, is Useless

Pointless, Useless and without Purpose

Why am I going into all this detail about data? Well, it is not only important for us to understand what data is, how it is expressed and what it does, but we must also see that data has certain characteristics and strong limitations. Understanding the real life limitations of data is very important, as that will keep you from believing the evolutionist's rhetoric about data somehow *evolving* and learning to process itself. So the main limitation that is characteristic of data simply 'being data' is this. That data is, of itself...

*...absolutely **useless**!*

Yes that's right. Data, if left to itself, is one of the most useless things in the universe. Data is as useless as the dust resting on the furniture in your house. Left to its own devices, data does nothing. It sits there, being itself, and nothing more. It is powerless to communicate, powerless to effect change and powerless to change itself or to create, no matter what form that data takes. This is especially so if data is randomly put together, as the evolutionists believe. Here are some examples of data,

Example 1 - Random Data

- 554897837489
- MMYdfd77t$$8
- TPY04555Gggu£333
- 222

You can look at the above list and **recognise** the different characters and symbols that make up each line of data...

...this means that the data above has been written within the context of a known language.

You can recognise letters (upper case and lower case) and you can recognise digits, some in repeating patterns. You can read the names

166

of those characters or symbols from right to left or from left to right. One of the examples above has a mirror property, the 222 example. It can be read from either the left or from the right side and it will say the same thing. However, all of the examples above, of themselves and by themselves, are totally useless. There is **no message** there. There are **no instructions** there. You can leave that data on the page, or on anywhere else in the cosmos in fact, for over a thousand years (or millions of years) and at the end of that time nothing will have happened. It will just sit there, if it hasn't been wiped out by the forces of nature, being itself will have achieved nothing at all! Data is powerless, of itself, to effect change. This is the nature of data.

The above example also has another factor to take into account.

*It is **random** data.*

Randomness will never write sensible code and it will never write code **in the context of a language** to **express intent** for **work** to be done. Random data is useless and always will be – which is why RNA strands or even a single chain of amino acids accidently coming together...

...will do nothing to start life.

There is no meaning in randomness without intelligence. This is why information theory will always trace information, which is made up of data, back to a thinking mind.

> **NOTE:** How do you know what language the data is written in? That's easy. Simply ask the one who wrote the data. ;-)

> **NOTE:** You may not understand the language yourself but the one who wrote data must know what the language is, what the symbols mean, or it is not data.

The amazing thing to say about the above example of random data, however, is that it already **has a level of sophistication** that would **not be there** if you were to argue that the data 'came about' by its own auto-organisational route from within the natural world. As I've already said, all the characters, letters and numbers in the above example are ***recognisable***. They are all written from a language context – which is expressed by a Western computer keyboard which created them. For example, there are no Chinese characters appearing within the above example of data. The data, therefore, already has a language **sophistication** and a language **limitation** imposed upon it. It is sophisticated because each letter or numerical character has an expression of sound behind it that can be phonetically sounded out and a limitation because the same lettering and characters do not express the 'sounds' of the Chinese language.

The data is not data expressed 'in Chinese' it is data expressed 'in English'!

Yet despite this level of sophistication, which you would never find arising out of the natural world via an unguided random process because the natural world cannot,

- come up with a language to talk and communicate through
- produce meaningful data symbols within the context of that same language to express meaning through those symbols
- because the cosmos is dead and cannot think for itself

...despite this level of sophistication, therefore, the above example of data is still totally useless. Even though it is already sophisticated, it cannot do anything and it cannot achieve anything. It is powerless to effect change.

Example 2 General Data
Here's another example of data, but this is non-random data.
681, 568, 795, 848, 614, 592, 620, 1017, 660, 1998

The data above is very specific. It is expressed firstly in what we call the Arabic numeral system, which is the ten digits by which we express and construct number values, 0,1,2,3,4,5,6,7,8,9. This is the most widespread method for calculation in the world today.

Note: Other examples of numerical systems are Roman numerals (used by the Roman Empire) or the Cyrillic numerals (used by the Russian Empire as late as the 18th Century).

The above data, though specific in nature, is still absolutely useless. You can look over the data again and again and not find meaning. The last four digit number in the line of data, 1998, might suggest a year date. You might ask, "Does this number represent a year towards the end of the 20th Century? Is it the year 1998?" The problem would be that there is only one other four digit bit of data in there which is 1017. Now they could all be dates, if the other collections of digits were data representations of dates before the 11th Century. That might open a door for you. You have, however, no way of verifying those thoughts. So in its *current format* the data simply is not useful. It does nothing. It just sits there, being meaningless and achieving nothing. This is the very nature of data. By itself **data is at least three things**. It is,

...useless, **incredibly boring** and without purpose.

Even data that has what looks like pattern within it is useless. If left to its own devices, then it does nothing at all. It **CANNOT SELF-INITATE** change in any way. It has no power to do so. So here's the first conclusion on data to arrive at. Even when data is,

- orderly and sequential
- has recognisable characters within a set language
- is stored in some way

...it is still **useless**,

unless it is **empowered**

from **outside itself**.

Adding Context
So if I were to tell you a little bit more about the data in example 2 that we've just mentioned on the previous page, then we can begin to **empower** the data. So if I told you that that data was about,

- weather
- location
- measurements

Then your mind will begin to look at the data in a new light. If I were then to tell you that it was also about,

- rainfall
- places in southern England
- recordings in millimetres

...then you would be able to see that the data is showing you how much rainfall had fallen. There's still not enough **information** on the page to tell you the place of the rainfall, how long the rain fell for and in what year, but you now know that the 1998 figure can no longer be interpreted as a year date at the end of the 20th Century but it now means that 1,998 millimetres of rainwater fell in a certain part of southern England over a certain time period. The **information** in its current form is incomplete, but you can now begin to understand the data. If you had the rest of the **information** then it may well become useful to you, especially if your job was looking at where in the UK you needed to spend some money on flood defences. Then the data would be empowered and become very useful to you.

> **Note:** I have used the word 'information' in the above paragraph 3 times. This is because I have begun to tell you about the *context* of the data. It is no longer just data. The context empowers it and gives it meaning.

Data Becomes Meaningful on the Move

'Moved' by a Context that gives Meaning

Precision data, that is purposefully assembled, when given context and *put on the move,* (**processed**) is empowered and becomes very interesting and very useful. As soon as precision data is *on the move,* processed for a reason, then it comes alive. That sent code must be in some way either *worked with* or *moved* into the right place for it to be **interpreted** by the **reader of the data**. The data, therefore, has to be written within the context of a set language, so that the data has meaning, and also the interpreter of the data has to speak the same language as the sender or receive a translation of that language that it can understand. Without a common language of expression, the data is not processed. Let's again take the above example of rainfall. Here's the rainfall data again, but this time in full.

Days	Place	Millimetres
125	Birmingham	**681**
108	Cambridge	**568**
115	Eastbourne	**795**
122	Exeter	**848**
116	Ipswich	**614**
110	London	**592**
117	Lowestoft	**620**
155	Newquay	**1017**
116	Oxford	**660**
183	Princetown	**1998**

We have two languages at work in this more complete form of the data.

- Column 3 - the language of millimetres expressed in the Arabic numerical system
- Column 2 - the English language used to express place names where the rain fell
- Column 1 - the title of the column written in English and the data in the column expressed in the Arabic numerical system where we're told for how many days the rain fell.

Column 3, the column in bold, is the same data that we've already looked at a few pages ago. Now we can see it within a better **context**. The highest recording of rainfall is the last one, 1998. So we know that, over a specific period of time 1,998 millimetres of rain fell in a place called Princetown.

You could ask, what is the 'movement' within the data so that it has become empowered and useful? Well, simply that the data has been set within a proper context (communicated by the labelling around it) and that extra context has been...

*...**read by your mind** and so*
***processed** in some way,*
so that you can
***understand**/interpret it.*

This turns useless data into something useful, i.e. information. A processing and an interpretation of the data has taken place in some way by your thinking and reasoning mind. A language has been used by your brain to 'sift through' the data and to 'put it to work' for us so that we are informed. A person with a flood defence budget, based on the data shown, may well be looking towards Princetown, Newquay or Exeter to spend their money.

These initial thoughts/conclusions have been arrived at because,

- 2 languages have been used to read the data
  - English language to read the data labels showing where the rain has fallen
  - Arabic numerical language to read the amount of rainfall in millimetres
- in the context of these languages the data has been read and interpreted

However, there is still not enough **context** to the data to provide enough processing of that data for the fullness of the **information** to be expressed so that the spend of the flood defence money can sensibly take place. For example, do any of those places have a river that has a tendency towards flooding? Do they already have a good land drainage system in place? Have they had floods recently? I need more **contextual data** adding to the current data in order to make an informed choice.

Data Languages, Translations and Interpretations

If the person who had created the rainfall weather data had labelled the column titles in Chinese and used Roman numerals to convey the rainfall measurements, then the data would have remained useless to the budget holder if the budget holder only spoke and read English and struggled to understand Roman numerals. There has to be **a common language** between the data recorder and data reader or it will still remain useless. Let's unpack this some more.

"Do You Speak English mate?"

One of the jokes that the English have about themselves is that we are notoriously bad at learning other people's languages; this is because so many of the people from around the world today speak English as a second language. The result of this is that we are, and have been for a long time in our history, a little lazy in our need to speak anything but English – though we are better than we used to be. So back in both the 19th and the early 20th Centuries a 'traditional 'Englishman', if I may call him that, if he could not be understood by someone from a different culture, would just continue to speak English **more slowly** and in a **louder voice** in order to try and make himself understood. The louder that he spoke and the slower that he spoke, the easier it was (in his mind) for the other person to understand him. It never worked, but for some reason this strange behaviour would happen again and again. Now that we are part of a global community, we all know that language has to be meaningful to the listener as well as the speaker for proper communication to take place. The listener also has to be trained/programmed/educated to understand the language being used. For example, I could walk up to someone and speak gobbledygook and that 'noise of sounds' would be absolutely useless because it's not a real language. There isn't a correct interpretation of the gobbledygook *'noise'*. If I was to go and talk to the average person in Mandarin Chinese (no, I can't speak Mandarin Chinese – though I once could speak a little Russian – but with a Polish accent because my school teacher learnt Russian in Poland) again that wouldn't be a very good communication tool to use because most people that I know don't speak Mandarin Chinese, they would need to have an interpreter who would need to know how to translate the communication and **relay it accurately** in another language. For communication to happen in the world of data, a **common language** has to be spoken and an **interpretation of the data** has to take place.

Back in the Computer World

So too we have to understand that there are computer languages that are used to create the programmes on our computers; these programmes are the *data interpreters* within the computer. Like oral languages today, you can use a different word to mean the same thing, e.g. 'hello' can be said as 'bonjour' in French or 'hola' in Spanish, so too in the computer world. If a different language has been used to create a programme then the code that drives the programme will be different, even if it has the **same effect on the computer screen**. This is why if you create a newsletter on an Apple Mac machine and then bring that same file to a computer that runs the Microsoft operating system, then a translation/interpretation process has to take place on your newsletter file before you can open it, read it and work on it. If that translation/interpretation process does not take place then, at best, all the characters on the screen will either be mixed up or will appear as meaningless gobbledegook; if the file will open up at all that is! This is because the programming environment that runs and interprets the file is profoundly different, even though it looks similar on the screen.

A Sender and a Receiver and a Handshake!

We'll learn very soon that precision data on the move (processed) is actually called 'information' (oops, I've let the cat out of the bag again) but we need to focus for the moment on the fact that the data needs to be *interpreted* within the context of the *language* of the **programmer** by someone who **receives** the information. The common language between **the sender** (the one who sends the letter 'a' data by pressing the 'a' keyboard key) and **the receiver** (the Word processing package who interprets the 1000001 data and processes it, then adds the letter 'a' into your newsletter) is vital. There has to be an intelligent '**handshake**' between the two. This handshake ensures the delivery of the data so that, after being received, the data can be processed and expressed as a job done.

NOTE: In the cell the handshake is when the Ribosome factory reads three RNA bases and selects an amino acid from that reading. The language of the RNA code is read to select a resource, an amino acid. The data has been 'sent' on the RNA strand and it is read and interpreted by the Ribosome factory. Handshake accomplished! This is why this part of the process is called 'translation'.

174

So the handshake in the computer world is when you type the letter 'a' on your keyboard. The numbers 1000001 are sent into the computer and the operating system has to pass that 'number set' to the correct interpreter, which is your Word Processing programme. That 1000001 code is then interpreted by your Word Processing programme and translated into the 'a' that you see on your screen, i.e. your newsletter now displays the letter 'a' within its text.

A **common language** is therefore needed for this task. If more than one language is used, then a transcription/translation '**handshake**' process has to take place. When the letter 'a' appears on your computer screen, that letter 'a' is a translation of 1000001. One language has been translated into another. Once the job has been done, therefore, we see a minimum two stage process at work;

1. A sender of the data (where the data has been collected in some way).
2. A receiver (who will understand and process the data in some way).

*So data has to be sent, read (processed) and interpreted so that it will then **complete a job**, and that interpretation has to be within the context of a meaningful language.*

Let's add another component to this example to explain it a little more. Attached to your computer is often a printer. The printer is a receiver and interpreter (processor) of the data that you send it. If the data sent to the printer is not written in the same language that the printer is expecting, then it will not print out your page of text or image correctly. Both the sender and the receiver have to speak the same language as the data is passed from environment to environment. Clicking the 'print' button will cause the word processing package to then 'talk' to the printer to print out your letter. Once the data is sent the computer loses control of it and it is all down to the printer to read, process and translate the data into an image on the page. If the data is not read and translated, no image will be printed off.

Note: The printer is *crafted with intent* to fulfil an 'intended job' that is sent to it from the computer. The common language prepares the way for the 'talk' to happen between the printer and the computer. The handshake that takes place between them is when the sent data is translated by the printer and converted into 'motion' instructions to determine what the printer's print heads will do on the page to impose the ink onto the paper. The 'ink' that appears on the paper will be a representation of what the data means in the computer world. A handshake has taken place and the 1000001 data can now be seen as the letter 'a' in the physical world on a piece of paper that you can hold in your hands. The printer machine is the answer to the question, "How do I get people to read my newsletter." This is the exactly the same as the work done by a protein – being the answer to a question about solving a problem within the body.

Sometimes the data that is communicated is able to generate an **event** and sometimes the data that is sent off is able to generate an **object**. For example,

- a computer programmed feeding station for animals that provides regular food for them at certain times of the day
- a 3D printer receiving information to create a specifically designed object

This is how data is passed around and becomes useful. Processed data either **means** something or is an instruction **to do** something.

The Five Fundamentals of Data
So there are five basic fundamental things to know about data in order for it to be meaningful *and to become information*. They are that data has to be,

- constructed
- precision accurate
- sent
- received
- processed

Here's the list again but with more details added to it.

- data has to be **constructed** in the context of a **meaningful language**
- data has to be **precision accurate** in its order to corporately mean something
- data has to **move** (either by being **sent** somewhere or **sifted** through)
- data has to be **received** by an **interpreter** (a handshake) who knows how to,
    - 'read the code' within the context of a specific language
    - implement its meaning
- data has to be **processed** (interpreted) to create an **output**
    - an output as a set of instructions to do something
    - an output as a communication about something

A Definition of <u>Useful</u> Data
So let's develop our definition of data a little more. Useful data is,

*A set of stored, recognisable characters or symbols written in a specific language which, by being assembled one after the other in a particular order, corporately conveys a meaningful (code) that can be moved (**processed**) for a specific purpose to ensure a job done.*

Data in the Cell

Stored, Recognised, Read, Prepared, Sent and Processed
So what has all of this got to do with the cell? Well, absolutely everything to be honest. All that we have said about data, its structure and how it is made useful, is replicated in the cell. The data reading handshake is prepared for in the cell in two ways.

First it takes place when the DNA is unzipped and an almost exact copy of the DNA is placed onto the RNA Messenger platform. A slight change is made to the data as it is copied so that the RNA strand is not an exact copy of the DNA, but a change is made in the translation of one of the letters. Secondly the RNA Messenger strand is taken apart, spliced open by enzymes, adjusted and put back together again before being sent off for processing by the ribosome factory. The RNA strand is therefore made 'fit for purpose' so that it can be read properly by the Ribosome factory to enable it to create an accurately assembled protein. The Ribosome factory would not be able to read the RNA strand correctly, and create a proper chain of amino acids from it, if these first two procedures had not previously been carried out.

The final 'handshake' is performed by the ribosome factory as it processes/translates the RNA strand into an amino acid string. This is sooooooooo important! Just as a printer will take the numerous zeros and ones that are sent over to it from the computer and process/translate them so that text and/or an image is printed onto paper, so too the Ribosome factory will read and translate the RNA platform that has been sent over to it from the DNA within the nucleus of the cell and translate that RNA platform into...

...the language of a protein.

It does this by the Ribosome factory sequentially reading every three strands of data on the RNA platform and, as each three strands of data are read, a specific amino acid is selected and then added to the amino acid chain that it is creating. In other words, each three strands of data on the RNA platform is a coded message for the identity of a specific amino acid. Once each coded message has been **read** and **translated**, a resource is selected and added to the building process. This reading and translation of the RNA platform is a direct parallel to the computer world that we have just outlined.

> **NOTE:** Once the amino acid chain is formed and the protein created then the 'intent' within the DNA code is realised as

the protein completes work in the cell that it was fashioned and created for.

NOTE: By the way, you cannot evolve this 'handshake mechanism' via a naturalistic random process. The gradual assembly of random data characters will never be able to create a context **via which a handshake is performed**, especially that which is done within the cell which requires preparation jobs to be performed on the data string first and a translation process to be completed. The final outcome of the process, a working protein, fashioned for its purpose, is totally dependent on other components within the cell 'doing their jobs' first and they only perform these jobs in the light of 'the handshake taking place'. If the full process is not followed through to conclusion then none of the process at any stage of its happening, makes any sense or has any purpose. Only a totally completed process from beginning to end will bring about the desired outcome. This process is where the naturalistic world view completely falls over!

Final Conclusions on Data

Data has to be Recognised, Ordered and Sent

Data is a set of recognisable characters or symbols, put in a specific order, where the order carries meaning. That stored data has to be written in a recognisable language and has to be sent somewhere and received and processed for it to be meaningful. Data is only meaningful, therefore, when it is,

- looked at in the *context* of its environment
- **fits the language** of the environment
- is sent somewhere within the environment
- **is received** by the environment
- is **processed** by the environment

So 1000001 is only meaningful if we understand that it came from,

- pressing the letter 'a' on a keyboard

179

- it has been sent from the keyboard via the motherboard to the computer's brain (called a CPU)
- the CPU then passes on the data to an interpreter
- the data is taken via the interpreter into the Word Processing package and displayed as an 'a' on the screen

Data has to be Precise and Interpreted Correctly

On the American keyboard the '@' symbol and the 'speech marks' symbol are the opposite way round when compared with a UK keyboard. So on an American keyboard pressing the 'shift' keyboard key and the number '2' keyboard key together produces the '@' symbol. On a UK keyboard pressing the same combination of keys produces the 'speech marks' symbol. This is because the keyboard keys are **programmed** the opposite way round. Once you know this, its fine, but if this is not known to you then it can be very frustrating to get an '@' symbol when you're looking for a 'speech marks' symbol. Sending the wrong signal, therefore, gets the wrong result.

Data, therefore, has to be **orderly** and **precise**!

Environment Pre-Construction and Pre-Calibration

For data in the cell to be processed correctly the environment also has to be constructed and calibrated, **fully prepared beforehand**. If this is not the case then there is no data output produced. The context, the environment, *must be fully prepared first*. Until that time, data is and remains useless. The environment and the code have to be together at the same time!

If one of the wires that sends either a 0 or a 1 down it on my keyboard became broken, then I would not be able to send a seven digit code to my PC. I could press that keyboard key as many times as I liked, but the computer environment is programmed to receive 7 digit bits of data not 6. The computer could not then interpret the signal sent and it would be useless. It could not handle '**bad code**' and then slowly evolve to make the code 'less bad' over time!

As I've just said, if the environment is broken, the data is totally and utterly useless.

Both the environment and the data have to be precision correct **at the same time** for information to flow and work.

NOTE: This in the biological world is the fingerprint of the divine on the cosmos. God touches the cosmos to put all these together at once so that they work together right from the start.

I could press my keyboard letter 'a' key as often as I wanted to, over billions of years, but it would not do anything if all of the following were not in place,

- the keyboard's inner wiring was faulty (thus sending an incorrect data signal)
- the cable from the keyboard to the computer was faulty (sending no data signal at all)
- the computer was not switched on (not able to receive a data signal)
- the CPU was faulty (not able to process a data signal)
- the memory within the PC was faulty (not able to load the data signal)
- the motherboard was faulty (unable to pass the data signal)
- the operating system was not loaded (unable to interpret the data signal)
- the Word processing package was not open (not able to receive the data signal)
- the Word processing package was not the 'default window' ready to receive the letter 'a' into it (not able to display the data signal)
- there wasn't any electric current reaching the computer so that it could be switched on (all machinery dead from the start and no data signal is produced)

Again the above list is very simplistic, but it's just there to make the point. Data comes alive by the fact of 'where it is placed' in a **pre-prepared environment** and 'what is looking at/processing it' in order to interpret it; without these things it is rendered useless. It cannot help itself and it cannot self-initiate change within its environment. Here is a most important statement that will render all evolutionists' attempts at making data the driving force for the creation of a living cell.

*It is the environment that **uses data**, NOT data that **shapes and crafts the environment**! The environment is intelligently prepared first, and then the data is placed within it.*

The above statement is probably one of the most profound statements that I will make in this part of the book. **The data itself does not shape/build the environment.** The components within the environment take charge of the data and use it (process it) to effect change **within** the environment. The environment helps itself, via the data. <u>The initiative, therefore, is with the environment, not the data</u>!

*The data is not in charge, **the environment is**.*

This is why evolution cannot happen. Evolutionists try and put data in charge, as in the RNA World Hypothesis. In that theory it is the RNA strand that is in charge and initiating change. This is completely the wrong way round. All that happens in the cell is that a gene is 'switched on'. That switching on of the gene tells the environment that a machine needs making. The resources within the environment and the machines within it then **take charge** of the DNA and create the protein.

The DNA and RNA data are both 'passive' during the whole protein creation process.

They are worked on by other components within the cell. DNA is copied, spliced, reassembled and RNA is read and translated by other objects. The objects within the cell **do the work**, *not the data*. The data just sits there, doing what data normally does, that is 'nothing at all'. Everything around it does the work. This tells us that it is the environment that is in control. The natural world, the cosmos, has no thinking within itself to sensibly prepare an environment in this way.

By-products from chemical reactions or from energy movements in the cosmos will not construct the machinery to facilitate the 'workings on data' that are needed to make life work!

In the RNA World Hypothesis we saw that the RNA did everything. This is why that theory is totally wrong. RNA does nothing; the objects within the environment do everything!

Processed Data Initiates Change
A Snowflake is not Data
You can find some patterns and interesting shapes in the natural world. Pattern, however, is not data. Data can have pattern within it but only in the order in which it is presented and only in the context of language in which the data is written. Data, as we have seen, is based on characters and symbols written in a set language. A snowflake, therefore, though it is beautiful in its form, is not data and it cannot be turned into data. It has nothing to communicate that will create an **output** or a set of instructions that can be processed to change the environment outside of itself. It is just simply a snowflake. It may have a 'wow' factor to it but it will not **'tell'** something else to **'do'** something simply by 'being itself' and by being processed by the weather as it falls through the sky. A snowflake cannot send a signal to effect change outside itself. Snow may be a problem when there is too much of it in one place, but it does not communicate anything outside itself. Picking up snow in a digger and **moving** it off the road, so that cars can run again, does not cause the snow to communicate anything. It is just **unwanted material** that is being moved out of the way, it is a **by-product** of the natural world.

A piece of data, processed code, however, that says, "send off this rocket towards our enemies", will have a devastating effect upon humanity. Pressing the 'red button' to release the code is a most difficult thing. The code 'runs' and via it being processed, then changes the environment beyond itself. This is the reason why we call data 'data' and processed data 'information' (oops, I've let the cat out of the bag again). The environment can work on it and use it to change things, be that the sending off of a rocket or the sending off of a 'print' instruction to a printer to print out a graph or chart from a

183

spreadsheet. Processed data (information) 'says' something to the environment outside itself that is meaningful and causes change.

The environment, however, has to be both working on the data, sending it, and at the same time **expecting** the data, **ready** to receive it and know **how** to process it - or the data is **useless**. When that data is processed within the correct environment it will produce something, whether that is a communication of some kind or a product of some kind. Whatever the final 'output' it will be one that has specifically been,

...crafted for purpose,

...such as a printed newsletter or a signal to say something specific.

We see, therefore, that 'data processed' produces **products**. This is the heart of the protein creation activity within the cell. A protein is a specialised and sophisticated product that is created via coded data being read, copied, prepared for transportation, interpreted and processed in order to create a **specific object** that has **a job to perform** within the set environment.

*The protein is a **specialised** product,*
*not a **by-product**.*

This means that the activities within the cell are **foreign** and **alien** to the natural forces that we see within the cosmos itself. The random and unguided movements of energy within the cosmos can only produce by-products. Fashioned products do not occur naturally within the natural world. From that perspective nature and the natural world are separate! I will dedicate a whole chapter to this towards the end of the book. For now we just need to make the point that by-products are the only thing that the forces within the natural world can create. By-products cannot fashion an environment for the processing of data nor can by-products from chemical reactions write meaningful code. This brings us nicely onto the subject of coding and information.

Chapter 7 – It's Information Jim…

…and completely beyond our intelligence to compute it!

- -
Starting with Code
- -

A Quick Definition of Code

As we've already said, code is carefully assembled data that is *written* **with purpose**. Code, therefore, cannot arise from the natural world as bits of data randomly selected and thrown together via a haphazard and unguided process. Data needs a language to come first, by which to express itself, and it needs to have **a sensible sequential arrangement** so that it can be read.

*Code, however, is the <u>intelligent assembling</u> of that data in a **very specific order** where the data characters <u>together</u> **corporately express purpose** and **intent**, not just character recognition.*

Just like reading a book, where each paragraph of words is made up of letters that together corporately form sentences, so too code has to corporately/purposefully mean something within a set language, otherwise it is not code.

The assembly of that code, therefore, has nothing to do with randomness.

The last thing that code is, is random. In fact there is no such thing as random code. Code can be used to generate random numbers, but those numbers are the products of carefully written code, not the assembly of the code itself – **which is why code CANNOT EVOLVE**!

*Code is one thing – **purposefully** written data characters within the context of the rules of programming for the purpose of producing an intelligent output.*

185

Code is not the casual assembly of data characters or data digits over time, added together via a haphazard and unguided random process. That so called evolutionary 'process' of random character selection via chemical reactions assembling data blocks together will only produce one thing, gobbledygook. Gobbledygook never produced anything of value. Anyone who is a computer programmer knows that code must be expressed as purposeful and exact text/characters that must adhere to the rules of the computer language if the code is to work. Code is written with one **expectation** in mind, that it **will be** processed in some way, by something other than itself, in order to do or to communicate something. Once that processing of the code has been initiated, then the code becomes information within the context of the environment that processes it.

Intent – the Reason for Code

So the first thing to remember from what we have said so far is that code is written **with intent**. Intent doesn't just appear by a random means. **Intent** is the *reason* for the code's existence, for the code to be purposefully written. **Intent** provides the **drive** for the code writing. What is the code meant to do or to achieve 'out there' by the act of the code being processed? What is the **intended** output that the code hopes to **accomplish**? Or to put it another way,

Why is the code here at all?

What is the purpose of the code's existence? Why do we find code in the cosmos? What is the driving force for it to be here? Notice we **are not** asking the question, "Why is data here?" If we were asking that question we would be simply looking at a, "Who did this?" question; that is who wrote the markings that are imprinted onto the cosmos that are set in a sequential order and expressed via certain recognisable characters in a known language? No. When looking at code we're actually asking something completely different; we are asking **why** the code has been written. What is the **intent** of the code writer? **Why has purposeful writing taken place** to create outputs via being processed? Well, the answer simply is this.

***Purpose** and **intent** to produce an output,
expressed in the language of data,
is the reason for code!*

That's code in a nutshell! (Wow, you know I'm really pleased with that definition above – I give myself a pat on the back every time I read that bit of text... sad man that I am.) There is always a reasonable and logical purpose for the code's existence and this can be seen by the **intent** written within it for something to be achieved.

*The code's very existence shows knowledge of what will be done **after it has been processed**.*

The reason for the code is seeing beyond the code itself to the job fulfilled. Behind the code is a knowledge of 'what needs doing out there' and the code finds its purpose once that job has been done.

Code, therefore, comes from an intelligence that wants to accomplish something, not from a random and unguided process causing the assembly of a hotchpotch bunch of data symbols. This, therefore, gives us a clear distinction between data and code. Data is **impossible** to find arising in the natural world. Not only have we seen this in a previous chapter where we understood the odds against amino acids linking together in a correct order to form a single data string that mimics data strings in the cell but also because there has to be a **language** behind that data string that the data is expressed through. Code, however, is the **intelligent assembly of that data**, with **intent** to **create** or **communicate**, and that is a *quantum leap in difficulty* compared with data. Code not only has to be exact, the correct data characters in just the right order in relationship with each other, it also has to '**be creative**' to imagine/create an impact.

1. *Data is a set of recognisable, sequential characters*
2. *Code is a set of carefully assembled data characters, sensibly ordered*
*to **make <u>something imagined</u> actually happen**!*

This is the foundational difference between data and code. In code, something has to be **imagined to happen**.

> Without that imagination seeking to create
> **something that is *not yet* realised**,
> there is no reason for the code in the first place.

So coding is the route by which you can make something imagined, realised.

- -
A Working Definition of Information
- -

A Simple Definition

Now that we've got a working definition of code under our belts, we can go deeper into the subject and unpack it so that we can slowly formulate a working definition of information. This is what all of the previous chapter has been building towards. This is so that we can clearly see that the attempts of secularists (Darwinian thinkers) to suggest that life can arise by chance and by purely naturalistic means is impossible. If you've been reading carefully so far, you'll have noticed that I've already not only defined data and code but I've also been actively talking about information as well, because it is very hard to talk about data and code without straying into the world of information. This is because...

...information is made up from code and data.

Data and code are the building blocks of information – we've already visited this concept when we looked at the examples of the car and the house – where the different parts of the car or the different bricks and mortar that make up the house are components of the house, but not the full life of the home that the building houses. With this in mind, here's our first simplistic definition of information.

*Information **is useful** data (code) that is processed for purpose.*

Many people will say that the above definition is too simple, which it is. Let me briefly unpack it, however. First it is useful data/code. That means that the assembly of the data characters corporately express a language of code that has something to communicate – code always does that. It also has a purpose that is expressed within a contextual meaning. What do I mean by that? Well, simply that there is an environment into which the code is put and then processed in some way. If that explanation still sounds confusing to you then let me give another definition of information, spoken from a slightly different angle, and then I'll unpack it using an example of a telephone exchange.

*Information is coding, made up of precision data, which is processed **within a given context**.*

Information can be seen in two different ways or from two different angles. Information is:

1) Precision Data (code) with **Context** – *it communicates* something.
2) Precision Data (code) that is **Processed** – *it does* something **within** an environment.

It is the **context** and the **processing** that makes data information.

Example: The Telephone Exchange
In order to ground this properly, let me explain the above definition **outside the environment** of the cell so that we have a little more clarity. If I were to type the digits 222 then most people would recognise this as a repeating pattern of the number 2. It **could be** the number 'two hundred and twenty two' or simply the digit 2 in a repeating pattern of three digits, one after the other. This set of numbers 222 does not have any context and therefore has little or no meaning. Even though it has a level of sophistication due to the fact

that it is written in the context of the Arabic numerical system, it is still what we would call useless data, a collection of recognisable characters put together in an assembled order **without any context**. You don't know what 222 means. Is it in fact the number two hundred and twenty two? If so, then is it two hundred and twenty two of what items? Is it two hundred and twenty two cabbages? Is it two hundred and twenty two cars? Without the context, the number is just meaningless data. It is just a set of recognisable characters which do not do or communicate anything. Of itself, 222 is useless.

If you lived in the USA, however, and you came across the set of digits 911, or if you lived in the United Kingdom and came across the digits 999, then you would know that this is the *telephone number* of the emergency services. You recognise this as an *electronic address* that will *connect* your phone to someone when you need help. The **context** that provides **meaning** to the number 911 or 999 is,

- the telephone and its key pad
- the infrastructure behind the phone technology that allows you to '*connect*' with another person
- the emergency services that can be contacted through that phone using the dialled number
- your current need of help

Without the above context, the digits 911 or 999 are simply useless. They are digits of meaningless, unassembled and unconnected characters, which we call data. When those digits are understood for what they can do and are '**entered into**' the right environment, i.e. pressed on a telephone key pad, then those numbers are **processed** and will connect you to a person or service that you need. This is where data **becomes** *information* and **becomes** *useful*.

Question: "How do I get help?" you might ask?
Answer: "Dial 911 or 999," is the reply.

The **answer is the *information*** that you are looking for. The code 911 or 999 is precision data that, once entered into the telephone exchange system, (processed) will connect you to your help.

A Better Definition of Information

Here's a really important and foundational statement about information.

> *It is the **act** of data **moving** and*
> ***being processed** within a **specific** <u>context</u>*
> *that turns coded data into information.*

So when we add a meaningful context to data, when we process it, then it **becomes** information (or perhaps you could say that when it is processed the information is revealed for what it is – but I don't want to complicate things too much so I won't look at it from that angle again in this book).

Example: A Computer Password

Let me put it another way. If I were to write out the following digits,

91022bCR

...then those digits (data) would **not** be meaningful to you. If it has no context, it is just gobbledygook; a non-meaningful combination of jumbled numbers and letters. It is what we have been calling **useless data**. However, if I were to say that...

9102bCR is the password to my computer...

(which it is not I might add!) ...then I would have immediately given you some **information**; giving an identity to the data and telling you how to access my computer. This is because I have **provided a context** to those digits and characters of data. Once you understand the context, it is a password to my PC, the data becomes meaningful and ceases to be data and moves into the realm of being information. This movement is clear because if I were to speak into your ear, "The password to my computer is 91022bCR", then I would have given you some **information** about **how** to access my computer. You could use that information to unlock my PC and see what I've been doing on my computer. Information is **coded data** with **context** (with a context that has to be understood) and allows something to be either communicated or allows something to be **done** in the light of that communication. Data is useless of itself. Code is also useless unless it is understood, picked up and processed in some way. Once the data code is **understood for what it is,** i.e. the purpose for which the code was written**, and processed** in the **correct context**, then we have useful **information** on our hands. Without any understanding of what the code is meant to do and without the processing context, **data and code have no value** or use for anything or anyone. It always needs to be,

- understood for what it is (to have a context)
- to be processed **with purpose**

…in order for coded data to make the transition from just being itself, which is just data digits of useless organised code, to being information. 911 or 999 have to be understood for what they are (help line numbers) and processed within the environment of the telephone exchange, otherwise by themselves and of themselves they are useless strings of data.

So too the password 9102bCR only works because there is an **environment** (a context) that has been <u>created</u> and <u>crafted</u> **for it**. That **environment** has been,

- constructed
- calibrated (fine-tuned)
- so that **precision** data (password) can be
  - entered
  - processed
  - and a **job** be completed (entry into the computer) as a result

So in my example above of a password we need to have the following in place.

- a computer that will store the password on its hard disk
- an operating system to run the computer

- a prompt when first starting up the PC that asks the user to enter a password that it will recognise
- a 'password programme' that 'runs' every time the user enters a password in an attempt to unlock the PC
- a keyboard through which a user can type the password

All of these things (and more) need constructing in the physical realm and then the calibration needs to take place in the programming world to make sure that all of the code that runs the 'please enter your password programme' works correctly. **Partially created code won't work**. This is why in one of the YouTube films referred to earlier, that stated that the early RNA Code was '*bad code*' and that later the code '*stabilised*', well as a computer person I can laugh and laugh and laugh at such a blatantly uninformed statement.

Bad code doesn't work, full stop.

Neither does it work without the correct environment to receive it and process it.

- -
The Environment and the Code
- -

The Perfect Match
If **the environment is not in place at the same time as the code**, the code will not be able to do its job nor will there be any purpose in the code's existence. Evolution cannot look forward in time to a place where the environment is just right for any code, that *is under development,* to be sensibly processed. Evolution has no intelligence of its own. Evolution cannot,

- write **sensible** code with **imagined intent** to do something in the future
- see what the code will need to be in the future in order to get the job fully done once the code has been processed
- carefully construct and calibrate the environment for the purpose of
  - matching the code to the environment
  - using the environment's resources, via the processed code, to get the job done

193

So here is a foundational statement about the impossibility of using evolution as a driver for the creation of life within the cell. It is all to do with being able to '**see**' what something needs to '**become**' when you create it and '**matching**' it to something else.

Evolution cannot look into the future for what...
*the <u>environment</u> **needs to be***
*and what the <u>code</u> **needs to become***
in order to bring them together
to kick-start, sustain and develop life.

So even if by some miracle the data coding may be correct (which is impossible), if the environment cannot properly **understand** and **process** the coded data to be used as the information it was intended to be, it is just useless data – like dialling 999 or 911 on a telephone key pad, only to find that the telephone exchange is broken or is not there in the first place; or even worse, like trying to type a computer password into the telephone exchange. The environment has to be calibrated with the specific resources made available that **the code expects to be available** to use to fulfil its intended job!

*DNA coding **expects there to be amino acids** within the environment for the Ribosome factory to use to create a protein!*

This expectation of amino acid resources tells us there is a mind behind the code that knows what is available 'out there' in other parts of the cell for the code to 'work with' in order to get the job done!

Without this pre-construction and pre-calibration of the environment on my PC, therefore, the password I enter is useless. It only finds its meaning **within the context** of the *working* environment and the resources within that environment that are there to match the code. Then, once the password has been 'entered into the computer' via the *fully working* keyboard, then the *fully working* programme processes the password i.e. it makes sure that the password that the user entered matches the same password that it

194

has listed in its programming list. This 'password matching process' then does a job; it **unlocks** the computer so that the user can access its resources. Job done!

A Mature Definition of Information

So now that we've understood more of the environment and the processes that surrounds information, and how that environment works on data expressed as code to turn it into information, let me re-write the definition of information again that I outlined a few pages ago so that we can have a fuller and much better understanding of what information actually is.

Information in the cell is
precision data,
coded *with* ***intent*** *for work to be done*
which is then ***processed***
via a ***constructed*** *and* ***calibrated*** *environment*
in order to ***create protein machines***
that will ***ensure*** *that the*
work ***imagined*** *is completed.*

That is an excellent working definition of information. If you can get that definition clearly into your head as you read through the next few pages, then you'll understand why information cannot arise from the natural world by itself **without the intervention of the divine**. This is most important because you and I, and all living things, have information at the heart of us. Life is **not** driven by mere useless data that haphazardly come together via a random and unguided process. Random and unguided processes would at very best just create jumbled up bits of data symbols that mean nothing (if the forces of nature could actually even achieve that – which would be a miracle as the natural world would have to invent a language first to express those data digits, otherwise they are not classed as data). However, life is in fact driven and sustained by information and information needs to be written in a precise way within an intelligent context to work!

195

This is why evolutionists are always wrong...

This is why whenever evolutionists try and put together theories on how life started, whether through a string of amino acids coming together or a RNA strand forming by itself, then they are already off to a nonstarter. Not only are the odds against them, that somehow the correct order of amino acids or RNA bases should somehow by chance assemble, but once *miraculously put together* in the correct order they have...

- no **language** to express themselves with
- no **imagined intent** within the code to do something
- no **mechanism** or **context** to work in via a constructed and calibrated environment with resources within the environment made available to the processed code (that the code intends to find available to it) to get its job done

They just float there in the imagined primordial soup without any contextual meaning or any way of processing themselves or any power to process or to fetch resources from their immediate environment to m**ake something from themselves**! It is a fraudulent attempt at making **useless** data do something that it cannot do in order to keep God out of science.

*These attempts at data strings can never **become** information.*

Don't forget that without language these strings of amino acids and/or RNA strands are not actually data!

This is because there isn't any 'context' for the string of amino acids or the RNA strand to work in and because there is no created and crafted resources within the environment to '**take hold**' of the coded data and process it for the purpose of doing something. There is therefore no **mechanism** in the environment by which the amino acid string or RNA strand can be sensibly read and processed! We know, for example, that in the setup of the cell that the DNA is first unzipped and read by a protein and copy made from it. That copy is the resulting RNA Messenger strand which is read by a Ribosome factory which then gathers the amino acids from the environment and assembles them into a meaningful order to make the protein. There are **extra agents**, therefore, that are involved in the assembly line to make the process work. These, extra agents of change, work within the carefully constructed and crafted context of the cell and the body. They are there because the DNA programming, that makes life in the cell work, has been specifically written to **partner with them**. DNA is dependent upon them for the imagined work that is expressed in the DNA code to be fulfilled.

The same agents, however, only exist because they too have been written within the DNA code and are created by the DNA code. So on the one hand these proteins are needed to create proteins and on the other these same proteins (agents of change) must have been created themselves by the very same process. What came first, DNA or the proteins designed to work with it? It is a circular and interdependent process that is not reducible and therefore not buildable via small steps, as the evolutionists would have you believe. It has what I call,

impossible auto assembly!

They all work together at the same time to produce protein products and those products work to keep the internal integrity within the body in order, but their very existence is dependent upon the pre-existence of each other and **a mind that will match them with each other** in the context of code.

Outside Help and Team Work
Let me work this point for just a little longer. The DNA code of life needs processing so that…

the information within it is released…

…to do the job of creating proteins. Proteins are needed to do the jobs within the cell, including keeping the DNA code pure from copy errors. You need processed code (information) to create proteins; you need proteins to look after the code and the rest of the body. The whole environment has been constructed and calibrated for this specific purpose. It is a complete team effort. The whole team needs to be on board. The whole **team** of,

- DNA
- cell structure
- multiple components (organelles, proteins etc.)

...all work together to keep everything working. DNA is a central part of that team but it is as useless outside the cell, as any other data or code would be. It is completely dependent on the infrastructure of the other parts and machines that are in the cell for it to **fulfil its purpose** for **being written**. (This is why DNA is information, not just code). In fact, DNA is written and assembled/designed with the other components in the cell 'in mind' to enable it to work. The components within the cell cannot be here without DNA and DNA doesn't work without fully created and working components to process it and use its code to create and sustain the life of the cell. So here's another conclusion about information.

*Coded Data (DNA) becomes information in the context of **outside help**!*

This interdependent and irreducible process is just one area where the divine touched the cosmos for life to exist. Random amino acid strings or RNA strands don't just process themselves by themselves. It is a fundamental flaw in the thinking of evolutionary theory that goes directly in the face of what information is. Data cannot turn itself in to information.

Data cannot have self-knowledge about itself and construct an environment via which to process itself.

Data does not have a mind of its own to imagine a creative, useful output by itself being processed!

999 or 911 need the outside help of a telephone exchange to become information. There needs to be a mind that programmes the 999 or 911 code in the light of the context of the environment in

which the code will run or in the light of how the code will be processed. So not only do we need the telephone exchange in place, we need the programming that says, 999 or 911 means…

'connect me to the emergency services'.

The same is true in any environment where information is used to create a product that is crafted for purpose, to ensure a job done. It is not the information that creates the product, it is the resources working with the information that creates the product. A 3D printer creates great items, the information tells it what to do, the printer is the resource that **does it**. Without the printer working correctly, the information sent to the printer is useless. That is the bottom line and no amount of meddling with theories and ideas about what you could do with a string of amino acids or a single RNA strand will work.

*Code **needs agents of change** to execute the commands within the code and make the intent within the code **happen in the real world**!*

Without these agents of change the code can do nothing. Imagined RNA strands or a single string of DNA, which are fantasised about by evolutionists when putting together their theories about how life could start from a dead cosmos, will do nothing. They have nothing to partner with. Partnership is central to code working. Code and information are all to do with team work. If this is not so then there is no real world change. Any I.T. programmer will tell you that!

The Physical Structure of the Code
One final point on this matter. All code is conveyed/expressed in some way, in a particular format. The format of the code is often as important as what is written within the code itself. On my PC it is stored as bits and bytes on my hard disk. This storage of digital code enables both the format of the code and the substance of the code to work together to make the PC work. The fact that the code is 'digital' in nature means that the code can be passed around a 'digital environment' and be processed by components that can read and work with digital data! So it's not just what is written within the code that matters, it is the format of the code that is vital too. If I wrote

1000001 in the sand on a beach then I might very well understand that this means the letter 'a' on my computer but the format of the 1000001 cannot be processed by the environment of my computer because the data is expressed in the **wrong substance**.

My PC cannot process sand particles!

The code may be right but it is the substance that the code is expressed in that dictates whether the code is workable within the environment. The data expressed has to be matched **in its substance** and **formatted to the substance** of the **resources/helpers** within the environment. Each, on both sides of the partnership, has to be specialised in their own physical make-up to interact with each other!

The substance of the coding has to match the substance of the agents of help that the data finds itself working and co-operating with.

DNA needs to be in the shape and form that it is in. It has to be made from the correct substance and be the right shape and be 'unzip-able' in its structural format and the right size so that minute molecular machines (proteins) can interact with it, unzip it and read it. Their physical substances that make them what they are in the real world have to match each other. The cable that runs from the computer to the printer has to be the right size and shape. If the connector does not fit at one end of the cable then the physical environment does not match the data flow and nothing, absolutely nothing, will ever get printed. So too in the microbiological world. Each part of the team has to be **physically fashioned** for the purpose of information flow. Every team member, who along the way helps in the process of turning DNA code into a protein, has to be made of,

- the correct substance
- the correct size
- the correct shape

...in order for it to interact properly with the process of code execution and the creation of meaningful products for the body to work. This is another reason why it takes a working/intelligent mind to make information work. The substance of the code and the format of the code have to be matched to the code's helpers, those agents of change that make the code work in the real world. Once again this is where evolutionists fall over because their thinking, their theories are all imaginations in their heads. They haven't even begun to understand the situation because they are biologists, not I.T. people. Information drives biology, not the other way around!

- -
The Contextual Question of Information
- -

Information Speaks Beyond Itself

Here's one last thing to say about information before we move on. I need to ground this properly before we leave the structure of information and go onto the subject of the 'nature' of information. The contextual question of information is that information is not there to **talk about itself**. Information does not point to **itself as if it were an end in itself**. Information speaks about something else; it speaks beyond what it is or what it conveys and *looks to a solution* that can be achieved once a job is done. This is so important. Without this understanding we will never understand what information is and we will always confuse it with data, as all evolutionists do when they try to prove their theory. So, we need to understand that, where there is information...

...there is 'talk' taking place behind the scenes about something...

...often about a job that needs doing for a specific purpose. Information **begins with a question** about that job. Then **an answer is given** and that answer is **specifically expressed** within the data code that makes up the information.

The answer, as I have said, lies beyond the information itself. The information simply conveys the *means to the answer* or talks about *what could be done* for the answer to be made effective. The information itself and how that information is processed is **NOT** the answer. Let's unpack this some more.

201

We've already said that coded data can be processed and when coded data is processed it becomes information; it is processed for a purpose. That purpose speaks of a job to be done. That job achieved is **beyond** the data's initial meaning and **beyond** the *processing mechanism* that processes the data. Here's why.

Example 1 – Police Catching Speed Offenders

So, for example, your local council or police force may be wondering how safe a certain road is. Perhaps members of the public have been complaining that cars are travelling down the road too fast and they and their children are not safe. Your local authorities, therefore, may decide they want to find out if these accusations about speeding drivers misbehaving themselves on a certain road are true or not. They may want to find out the following,

- if there are people speeding on a certain road
- if there are specific repeating behaviours on that road committed by the same individuals
- on what specific days of the week are those people going over the speed limit
- at what specific times are those people going over the speed limit

This is all done for *the purpose* of catching those who are breaking the law and imposing a fine on them in order to get them to change their behaviour. This *change of behaviour* **is the final outcome**, the final **job-done** that needs to be completed.

So the local authorities will have to begin their probing into the problem by firstly seeking to **generate** and **collect data**. They will first stretch two rubber cables across the road. These rubber cables will be tightly fitted to the floor and, as any car wheels run over those cables, a measurement of the car's speed is taken. Through this data collection process the police have the capacity to not only record the speed of any car but also to see on which particular day and at which particular time any car was travelling. After several weeks a good amount of data will have been gathered and that data is then taken away and **collated, analysed**, i.e. **processed**. The processing of that data is what *changes it into information*. That information is often expressed as a graph. That graph would show the police at which points in the day and on which days there were persistent offenders who drove over the speed limit. That information however is **not** the answer to the question. The general public were **not** complaining that the local council and police **didn't know** *when* the speeding was taking place. They wanted a **job done** *in the light* of the problem.

The question is,

> ## *"In the light of the information that shows speeding patterns,*
> ## ***how*** *do we* ***make***
> ## ***this road safer*** *than it is?"*

The answer is, after the data is processed, to look at the information (the graph) and see when the graph indicates that the speed limit is persistently being broken. Then, **in the light of this information**, the police now need to implement action to do a job. That job is to go out, on those days and at those times when we most expect certain people who travel down that road to be breaking the law, and to set up a speed trap. The data gathering process is pre-done in order for that final outcome to happen. The processing of that initial precision data gave the police the information they needed; a graph whereby they could see an overview of the different speed changes on a specific road over a period of time so that they could **be enabled** to catch speed offenders. The gathering of that data and its processing to turn it into information (a graph) was **not the final outcome** of the project. The police did not go about the whole process in order to get the graph, mount it and put it on their office wall and say, "Now we know when people are speeding down this road. Isn't this graph amazing?"

*They are **not there** to <u>celebrate the bar chart</u>!*

The chart is not the purpose of the exercise. The purpose is to...

*...enable the policeman to **catch** the culprits*

...who are making the road unsafe for the pedestrians. The information therefore, the graph or bar chart, **speaks beyond itself**. It speaks of a question that has been asked and an answer that has been given for a job to be done. So wherever we see information...

*...we see **pre-knowledge** of the environment...*

*...and a **solution***

put together within that same environment to...

*...**cause** certain things to **happen**.*

Information therefore...

...always speaks beyond itself to a question asked, a solution given and a job completed.

This is the contextual question of information.

Example 2 – Jobs Completed in the Human Body

Let's bring this analogy back to the human body. So, in the same way, when DNA creates proteins, three questions have been already asked.

1. What problems are there in the human body that need overcoming in order to make the human body work?
2. What needs to be done to tackle those problems, to ensure that the problems are fixed so that the human body works properly?
3. What resources can be utilised from within the environment in order to implement the effectual tackling of those problems that have been identified?

The answer to those questions is normally proteins. Those proteins have pre-set jobs to do within the human body. Those jobs that are done are completely and utterly beyond the original DNA programming itself. A gene, as we have seen, exists as a set of coded data along the string of DNA. It simply speaks of a code via which different amino acids will eventually be, by the processes of transcription and translation, assembled together to form a very complex machine. That however is **not the end of the matter**, nor is it the purpose of the matter. Just saying to yourself, "I am a piece of code that if processed will provide the information to construct a machine," is of itself, a complete nonsense. Just like hanging the graph on the wall of the police station for everyone to simply look at, so too the DNA code is not the point. After the DNA code (the gene) is processed a machine is created. That machine needs to have a purpose. That machine needs to have…

*a **place***

and

*a **role to play***

…within its environment. Just as the police react to the information of the graph and do the job of catching people who are speeding down the road, so too the newly formed protein now has a job to do and a role to fulfil. Without that job to do there is no true information.

*When proteins do their job, then the meaning of the DNA code's existence is **fully realised** and the **questions** that were asked **before the code was written** are finally answered.*

It's the difference between a useful machine that fulfils jobs in the body and one of those crackpot mad inventor devices that are often wheeled on to a stage in front of children in order to provide entertainment; you know one of those devices where all of the wheels go round and the lights shine, smoke comes out of little chimneys and there are bells and music to accompany the most fantastic looking *but totally useless device*. The mad-scientist children's entertainer shows off his amazing device. The children clap their hands with glee at the incredible sight, but no actual useful work is done by the machine to make any difference to life, except to amuse the children. So whenever you see information in the human body, the different sections of DNA that we called genes from which proteins are made, you are **not** looking at random and isolated coding that has somehow come together. The reason why we know this is simply because a question has already been asked and an answer has been provided and the information on the gene is just **part of the answer**. The gene is not the answer itself, it *points* to a solution that is *beyond itself* which has already been figured out by logical and intelligent reasoning. It is essential and critical, therefore, that each gene, each set of precision data, is processed in an exact way in order to produce a very useful and specific tool. That useful tool is also not an end in itself. It is a means to an end, an answer to a question to solve a problem that exists within the human body.

When a protein does its job, then the answer to the question is expressed!

When the answer is expressed in this way, the meaning of the information is fully revealed!

A gene on the DNA ladder exists, therefore, not because it is part of an evolutionary process that made the body but that the maker/designer of the body needed genes to help sustain what was already there!

MOST IMPORTANT
Genes are <u>answers to questions</u> and not <u>drivers of evolutionary change</u>!

This is why, '*It's hard to know what you are seeing if you don't know what you are looking at!*' As they don't know what they're looking at, evolutionists misinterpret genes and give them a role that they do not and cannot fulfil. They are a store of information to sustain and provide answers to the problems of life, not drivers to develop life.

Example 3 – Enzymes
So here's an example. Enzymes are a type of protein. Enzymes perform many types of critical duties within the body and without these duties fulfilled **we could not survive**. They are created with a specific purpose. Their roles can be varied, such as starting off

chemical reactions in the body – some of which would not normally take place at body temperature or take too long to happen in order for them to be useful to our body's wellbeing. Those chemical reactions can, for example, facilitate the breaking down of foods within the body so that our body can feed itself. So a series of questions has been asked such as,

1. What sort of chemical reactions do I need in order to break down this material to make it useful in the body?
2. What could I use as a catalyst can to start off this chemical reaction?
3. What resources do I have at my disposal that I could use to get this solution implemented?

The answers to these questions would be,

1. A protein could be used to do this particular job.
2. I could use a category of protein called an enzyme.
3. I could create the enzyme using amino acids

QUOTE: *"Enzymes help speed up chemical reactions in the human body. They bind to molecules and alter them in specific ways. They are essential for respiration, digesting food, muscle and nerve function, among thousands of other roles."* https://www.medicalnewstoday.com/articles/319704.php
To find out more about enzymes read the article that the link above points to.

In order for the enzyme protein to be created I need a construction process, based on information, about the new machine. So what I have to do, to create an enzyme, is the following,

- understand what chemical reactions need to happen within the body
- understand what a particular enzyme's **shape** needs to be in order for it to do its job
- understand how that enzyme shape is created by folding amino acids
- understand the order in which the amino acids need to be assembled to form the folded shape

207

- understand that the RNA Messenger strand can be used, after being processed by the ribosome factory, as the intermediate tool to select the amino acids in a specific order and to form them into the correct string ready for folding into a protein
- understand the original DNA code that, after being read and copied, will create the RNA Messenger code template

The above is the logical backwards reasoning that has to take place when you work backwards from the solution (the job done by the machine) to how you go about facilitating the solution (the creation of that machine) from the stored code (DNA). This is what information in the cell is actually about. It is purposefully put there with the **intent** for work to be done in **answer to a question**!

A question is asked and an answer provided and DNA information is an expression of that answer.

So the enzyme proteins, having pre-set jobs in the body to fulfil, are the answers to questions. Their activity is the answer. The overall meaning of the work of the proteins is the continued health of the body. That health is written into the DNA coding. What they do in the body is not explicitly shown in the original DNA code. The DNA code does not talk about,

- where the enzymes will be travelling to
- what they will be interacting with
- how enzymes will behave when they interact with other objects in the body

Their activity, however, is *prophetically suggested* by the code – otherwise the code would not be there in the first place. The DNA code does not write the story of, "Once upon a time there was an enzyme that was the catalyst for the speeding up of chemical reactions…" The DNA code facilitates only the information to make the machine. It,

- **assumes** the problem is there
- **assumes** the fulfilment of the problem via the protein

- **assumes** the resources are available for the building of the protein

...otherwise the code to produce the protein would not exist. So the DNA code is **not** there to talk about itself. The DNA code is **part of the answer**. It points to something else, something outside of itself. There is nothing written into the gene which describes what the enzyme will be doing after it has been created, but the code tells you that the problem has been **thought about** and **an answer provided**. This is because information always speaks beyond itself.

This is the contextual question of information.

The graph in the hands of the police, indicating when people are speeding, does not also show pictures of,

- the police using a speed camera
- the police catching the offenders
- the offenders paying their fines
- the offenders changing their behaviour on the roads

Those details are not needed for information to do its job. The graph, however, is prophetic. It shows a purposeful activity undertaken, the gathering, organising and sifting through of precision data to form a graph, so that the police can be informed and get on with their job. If the police do not go out to do a job, the existence of the graph is meaningless. The graph finds the justification for its existence as the police catch the offenders!

*The graph is full of **intent, intent** to do something.*

The graph's existence shows us that a question has been asked, information given in response to that question and that same information is then used as the...

*...foundation **from which actions** are **implemented***

...and the job fulfilled. That, in a nutshell, is the contextual question of information. It is exactly the same with DNA information in the cell! Without the protein doing its job at the end of the process, the DNA code does not make sense at all. The information in the DNA is not there for itself, the information shows that there was pre-knowledge of the problem and pre-knowledge of the solution before the information was created/expressed/processed. The product that is produced, the enzyme protein, is that which **effects change**. It is the enzyme protein, and specifically its activities within the body to fulfil essential jobs for the body's survival, which makes sense of the original DNA information and give us the answers to the questions that have been asked. So a problem within the body has already **been**

- identified
- thought about

The solution to that problem is the enzyme protein. The information in the DNA is therefore the *expression of the answer* that has been given according to the pre-question being asked. When the enzyme does its job, the DNA's existence and purpose is realised. What is its purpose? The health and wellbeing of the body!

Example 4 Computer Login

Let's look at this example *just one more time* (and I promise I won't come back to this again) going back to my computer and wanting to login to it. When I enter my password into my computer and press the 'Enter' key on my keyboard, this initiates a processing procedure. That procedure is the coding that runs the password programme. It looks at the password that I've just entered via the keyboard (precision data) and it asks the initial question,

"Does the data (password) that's just been added via the keyboard match the password that I have listed in my coding?"

If the password entered into the computer matches up with the password listed in the computer code, then the job is done for the computer to be unlocked. That is the **initial** processing that takes place, but that initial processing to unlock the machine is **not the answer to the question** that created the information in the first place. Instead you need to ask a more probing question. That is,

*"What is the **intent** of the computer user*
in entering the password?"

If you answered,

"The computer user entered the password so
that the password programme could check if the
password was correct..."

...then you'd be wrong. No-one sits down at their computer during their normal working day and enters in a password to see if the password programme is working correctly. They enter their password so that they can...

...get at the computer's resources and
__do something else.__

So the act of inputting the password information into the computer, and it being processed, does not convey the **intent** for the reason **why** the password is being entered, i.e. the password being processed does not tell you what the end user wants to do next,

- use a word document
- use an art programme
- use a video creation programme
- check their emails
- go onto social media

The reason why the password (information) is entered and processed is not conveyed within the information itself, but the unlocking of the computer tells us that the user **does intend** to do something after the PC is unlocked. The computer's resources are therefore ready for use. Note, however, that the coding that simply checks the password does not contain a detailed description of **what the end user will do** after the password has been entered. The information that is processed facilitates something that is **beyond itself**. That is part of the contextual question of information. So the unlocking of the computer does something which is beyond the code itself – which is to open up a whole wide variety of resources from which the end user can choose to use. So too in the human body, the processed DNA code unlocks resources for use elsewhere in the body. It opens the door for resources to be moved and made useful, for solutions to be implemented and problems to be solved.

All of this can only be put together by a questioning, reasoning mind.

Now that we've established what information really is and how it works and behaves, it is time to go behind the scenes and to look at the nature of information.

- -
The Nature of Information
- -

Information has no relationship to mass or energy

Have you ever considered that information has no mass? It's something that's so profound that most people totally miss it. Here's a quote from an online video where Philosopher of Science Dr Stephen Meyer, who holds a PHD from Cambridge University and is Director of Discovery Institute, outlines why information has no mass. https://www.youtube.com/watch?v=u20gVY8qyPE

He says,

"One of the things that I do in my classes, to get this idea across to students, is I hold up two computer discs. One is loaded with software, the other one is blank. I ask, "What is the difference in mass between these two computer discs as a result of the difference in the information content that they possess?" Of course the answer is zero, none. There is no difference as a result of the information. That's because information is a massless quantity."

So let me unpack this insight of Dr Stephen Meyer a little more to see why information hasn't any mass – at the same time I'm also going to show that there is absolutely no relationship between energy and information as well. These following five examples will establish

212

that, if information has no mass and no direct relationship with energy, then it cannot arise from the natural world via biological or chemical processes. It is therefore not just the environment but the very essence of information itself that tells us that the forces in the natural world can never, and will never, produce it. Where there is no relationship from the start, there cannot be a relationship established.

Example 1 – Writing in the Sand
If I were to go onto a beach and write with my finger in the sand,

"Hello World,"

...then I would have added information into the sand, or added information onto the beach. By the time I had finished writing in the sand, the sand now has something **extra** engraved within it, or imprinted onto it, which it did not have a few moments before I started writing. The beach now **contains** the words,

"Hello World."

It now has information on/in it because I have imprinted a purposed and planned communication from me to anyone who can process those symbols, that we called 'words', by *reading* them. When those words are processed (read by someone) then a job is done, that is a greeting from me is sent to anyone who can read it.

However the mass of the sand on the beach has not changed in any way.

It is the same mass from the time before I wrote in the sand as to when I finished. All that has happened is that part of the sand has changed shape to express lettering within a specific language, i.e. the English language. I have imposed my thoughts onto the natural world via pattern expressed in the sand. The information is now there for anyone who can read and understand the English language, but there is no extra mass within the sand. So as Stephen Myers said in the interview just quoted,

"…information is a massless quantity."

Now let's look at the same example in relation to energy. Rather than writing with my finger, "Hello World" in the sand I might use a spade. I might dig the lettering deep and wide and by the time I'd finished I might have worked up a good sweat. The words may be more visible from the air or from a distance because they are so much larger and deeper in the sand. I might feel satisfied with a job well done as I'd spent more time and energy doing the work, and moved around a greater measure of the mass of sand on the beach. However, there's still exactly the same amount of information on the beach as when I'd used less energy. It still says, "Hello World", whether I've used a spade or written the letters with my finger. It would take less time and less energy with my finger, but the **same amount** of information is added.

I could use even **more energy** by getting a digger onto the beach and make the lettering of each word trench deep. As I used the digger I could, at the same time, ensure that the sand I shifted is removed from the beach and taken offshore. This would **reduce the mass** on the beach, but we'd still have the *same amount of information*. It would still say, "Hello World", for anyone to read.

I could add more sand back onto the beach, so **increasing the mass**. I could spray it everywhere, and we could **lose information** as this new sand covered up the words that were etched onto the beach. I could add yet more sand to the beach (**increase the mass**) and pile it up in the shape of the words "Hello World" and **gain information**. So I could,

- simply **move** sand around and **add** information
- **take away** sand and keep the **same** amount of information
- **add** more sand and **lose** information
- **add** yet more sand and **gain** information

This tells us that there is no direct relationship, therefore, between information, energy and mass. It is **the way in which I manipulate the sand** that shows the information on the beach, not how much or how little sand there is on it and how much energy is used.

I could then, very gently with the tip of my finger, write in the sand, "Hello world, it is a beautiful day," and I've used **less** energy to add **more** information. This is because there is no direct relationship between energy and information. The important thing is **how** my mind **chooses** to **imprint** the information, not the amount of energy used!

Example 2 – Concrete and Chiselling

Let me illustrate this in another way. If I were to take a block of concrete and I chiselled the words, "Hello World," out of it, then the overall block of concrete would actually **lose** mass, but it would **gain** information. On the floor next to the block of concrete there would be the chips and dust from my chiselling activity (and if you added up the mass of the debris and the mass of the original block of concrete you'd find that the mass was the same as when we first started) but the block itself would have lost mass due to me chiselling pieces out of it. This loss of mass and the moderate energy used in this process, results in the adding of information. This information has been imposed onto the concrete block.

This chiselled lettering (information) that I've just added onto the concrete block could also be lost. Here are two examples.

1. If I put the block of concrete on the top of a hill and left it open to the elements, then the wind and rain would over time erode the face of the concrete, and so **remove** more mass, and the pattern that I'd chiselled into it would fade and the information be **lost**. (As we have said, the forces within the natural world always remove information.)
2. If I sprayed the concrete block with wet concrete I would **add** mass to the block, but the wet concrete would cover over my writing on the block and we would **lose** information.

So I can do the following,

- **remove** mass and **add** information (by chiselling at the concrete block's face)

215

- **remove** mass and **lose** information (via the elements blowing and raining on the block over time to deface my chiselled words)
- **add** mass and **lose** information (as long as the wet concrete is sprayed directly over the top of the writing)

The reasons for this are that the information that is chiselled into the rock is simply **an imprint of a pattern or shape onto physical material that means something to a mind that reads it** (processes it). If the shape of the imprint is disturbed, then the information is lost, even if the amount of physical matter remains the same, increases or decreases.

From the point of view of energy and time, I could spend an hour chiselling the words "Hello World" into the concrete block. I could make those letters nice and deep. It would look very solid and secure and durable. I could then spend **less energy** and **less time** chiselling very lightly on the surface of the block of concrete and I could write several sentences. I would have spent **less energy** and **less time** but added **more information** to the concrete block. If the concrete block was left exposed to the elements then the lettering in both examples would eventually disappear. One would last longer than the other but, in both cases, the imprinting is only temporary. This is because,

...the natural world **cannot hold onto information,** it has only been temporarily imprinted onto it!

The wind and rain would eventually eradicate them both. The natural world cannot hold onto the information (**because information has no mass and does not arise from the natural world**) and the random processes of nature, according to the 2nd law of thermodynamics, would not add to the information in either case, just remove it. The rock does not 'own' the information. The information is simply temporarily imposed upon it, put onto it by an external source where the shapes in the rock symbolise the thoughts of the writer. There is no direct relationship, therefore, between energy, mass and information and the cosmos cannot hold onto the information as if to own it. Its existence is always temporal, even if humanly speaking it remains for a long time.

Example 3 – Paper and Ink

A piece of paper has a set mass. The ink in a pen has a set mass. If I transfer some of the ink in the pen onto the paper and I write, "Hello World," on the piece of paper, then the paper itself, combined with the ink, will now contain information. However, even though there is now **extra information** in the universe, there is **no extra mass** in the universe. All that has happened is that some of the mass from the ink in the pen has been moved to the paper. I have therefore expressed information via the shape of the mass, the pattern that the ink makes on the page. The total mass of the paper plus the ink, however, is the same as it was before I wrote as it was afterwards. The shape of the ink has changed, that's all – just as the shape of the sand on the seashore would change if I were to write the same sentence on the beach or if I were to chip away at a concrete block. In this instance the pattern of the information has been formed and put onto the paper by spreading/imprinting the ink in a certain way.

> **Note:** It is the **pattern** made with the ink by a thinking mind guiding the pen on the page (and the mind that reads that lettering) however, that communicates the information – not the amount of mass of the ink.

If I were to use more energy by **adding more ink** directly onto the paper, spilling it where the words are written, then eventually the lettering pattern would be lost as the ink would become a pool of ink on the paper and, as the lettering and words disappeared, so the information originally written there **would be lost**. As always, however, the total mass of the paper plus the ink remains the same. The extra energy used to spill the ink has done nothing to increase the information, it just takes it away. So it is important to say that,

...*chance actions, such as spillages (or chemical reactions) never create information.*

It takes a mind that uses the ink to apply it to the page in a specific way to add information, as the pattern of the ink represents the processed thoughts of the person who is doing the thinking and the writing.

*It is the **mind** that creates information, not the **raw energy** in the fingers.*

It is the mind that controls the fingers holding the pen that applies the ink in a specific way, not the law of gravity that allows the ink to flow downwards onto the paper. No-one opens up an ink bottle and pours the ink onto the page and expects to get a written essay as a result. The ink itself does not **contain** the information, because information has no mass and **information is not constructed by raw energy**.

If I was to add a lot of energy to the paper by burning it, then the mass of the paper and ink would be transformed but there would be no other outcome except for a loss of information. It does not matter what pattern can be haphazardly formed via the ashes from the paper, the wind and the law of gravity, the information from the mind of the person who originally wrote the message (with **purpose** and **intent**) upon the page, is now gone. Natural processes do not produce information; they simply take it away, which we call a loss of information.

Unguided energy, working on mass, therefore, will do nothing to add information. The amount of energy used is also not important. It is the way in which that energy is used by a mind imprinting its thoughts onto the paper that matters. A little energy expressed through the fingers as they guide the pen can create a lot of information.

Summary of Examples 4 and 5
So that you don't get bored with me repeating myself over and over again I'm going to give a summary of the next two examples. If you wish to read them in detail then go to Appendix C where you can see the examples fully illustrated.

Jelly in a mould
I could get three moulds. Each mould could have different amounts of lettering in it. The same energy is put into heating up the jelly and then the jelly is poured into each mould. The end result

would be that, even though each jelly has the same mass and the same amount of energy has been used to add it to the mould, when the set jelly is tipped out there will be a different amount of information imprinted onto each jelly from the mould.

Sticks Assembled Together

I could use sticks or twigs to form letters. The wood does not contain the information – it does not arise from the wood. The information is contained in the pattern that is imprinted onto the shapes that the wood makes as the sticks are placed in a **spatial relationship with each other**. Disturb the spatial relationship between the twigs/sticks and the information is lost.

> **NOTE:** This is where we're getting a little closer to the bases in DNA and the Messenger RNA platform. The bases there are symbols of information. Pick off the bases and float them around the cell and they lose their meaning. With them aligned together, sitting side by side, they become a code that can be read. The bases themselves are not the information but it is their order together, as symbols read in the light of a specific order, which makes them information, just like data has a specific order.

Pattern Imprinted Produces Information

So, if it is the pattern imprinted on the mass that communicates the information, where does the pattern come from?

The pattern comes from a mind actively imprinting its thoughts onto the object.

This is most profound. Information cannot be reduced to mass or energy because it has no relationship with mass or energy. It has to come from an active mind that chooses the mass and initiates a process that interferes with the mass in order for information to be **expressed**.

Summary about Information, Mass and Energy

So the last five examples of

- lettering on the beach
- letters chiselled into stone
- letters written by a pen onto paper
- jelly in a mould
- assembled sticks

...shows us that information, mass and energy are not related. You can

- **move mass** but still add and or **lose information**
  - a finger adds information to the beach
  - a wave from the tide coming in takes away information from the beach
- **lose mass** but still **add** or **lose information**
  - a hammer and chisel, whilst removing bits of the rock face, adds information to the rock
  - weather erodes the rock face and information is lost
- **add mass** but still **add** or **lose information**
  - the pattern of the ink added to the paper reveals information
  - the spillage of extra ink onto the paper removes the pattern and information is lost
- use **lots of energy** but have **only a little information** by using a digger to shift large amounts of sand to create large letters that say, "Hello World"
- use **little energy** and have **lots of information** by writing in the sand with your finger to create letters that say, "Hello World. It is a beautiful day today. The weather is great and the sun is hot..."

In each example the total mass of the beach, the block of concrete, the paper and the ink, the jelly in the mould or the sticks from the tree has not changed. There are different amounts of energy used as each example event has occurred, yet there is always the same resulting 'Hello World' message pattern but with no mathematical equation to use by which to get that message. There might be an increase in information, but in the physical world there has just been a **movement in the mass** initiated by an intelligent interference, using little or lots of energy, which comes from a thinking mind. So we conclude.

There is no direct relationship between the amount of mass moved or the amount of mass removed and the amount of information displayed.

and

There is no relationship between the amount of energy used and the amount of information displayed.

If information was a part of the physical world, and had any established relationship with it, then it would produce the same results every time **or** there would be a mathematical pattern to predict the relationship. It does not, however. Information is **imprinted onto** the physical world by the intervention of an external mind and that imprinting **is only temporary**, even if, humanly speaking, it is there for a long time. We recognise information because it communicates something to a mind that can either process its meaning (read it) or because it can be processed to ensure a job done. So we can confidently say,

Information cannot arise from raw energy moving the mass in a dead cosmos.

and

Wherever you come across information in the universe, it has been temporarily imprinted there by a source with a mind.

The fact that information can only be temporarily 'imprinted' onto/into the physical world, but it will always over time be lost, gives

221

us some clues as to how amazing information really is. Read the comments of Dr Stephen Meyer below,

https://www.youtube.com/watch?v=u20gVY8qyPE

*"Now if information is not a material entity, then how can any materialistic explanation explain its origin? How can any material cause explain its origin? This is the real fundamental problem that the presence of information in biology has posed. It creates a fundamental challenge to the materialistic evolutionary scenarios because information is a different kind of entity **that matter and energy cannot produce**. In the 19th century we thought that there were two fundamental entities in science, matter and energy. At the beginning of the 21st century we now recognise that there is a third fundamental entity and it is information. It is **not reducible to matter**, is **not reducible to energy**, but it's still a very important thing that is real. We buy it, we sell it, we send it down wires. Now, what do we make of the fact that information is present at the very root of all biological function? That in biology we have matter, we have energy but we also have this third very important entity, information. The biology of the information age, I think, poses a fundamental challenge to any materialistic approach to the origin of life."*

On top of this temporal imprinting we have the fact that DNA is so complicated we still don't properly understand it. 97% of DNA was said, by evolutionists, to be 'dormant' coding that had died with the evolutionary process. This is now recognised as not being true. The other 97% we now find is absolutely critical to turn genes on and off as the foetus (fetus) of any living creature grows and takes shape. The more we look at DNA the more we are amazed by it. Much of it can be read in both directions and even when it is put into 3D shapes it communicates something different all over again. We are in fact therefore saying that the super complexity of DNA, at the heart of all life, tells us that there is indeed a super intelligence behind life. That super intelligence goes by a name that the religion of secular spirituality will not want to own or admit to. Why? Simply because humanism does not want to have 'God' in the picture of life because it is a *God replacement* spirituality. If God takes centre stage again, then we're accountable to him and the spiritual world has a life of its own beyond the spirituality of secularism, which is just, mere, personal

self-initiated *belief*. Here again we see the real clash that is behind science. The astounding and amazing complexity of life and the

- language that is used to express coded data
- environment that is fitted together for the code to work
- contextual question of information
- nature of information

...all point to a non-naturalistic beginning. The natural world does not have 'intent' in it; it just has unguided processes that produce by-products. There is no relationship, therefore, between matter, energy and information and information cannot arise by itself from the natural world. So let me say this one final thing to sum up what we've said so far, which in many different ways I've already said over and over again in the last few pages. There is **no mathematical equation** that says,

raw energy + non-living matter = information

It does not work. Whenever we see information in the material world we see it imprinted there by a thinking mind.

- -
The Personality behind the Code
- -

A 'Mother' but not a 'God'
Life **intends** to do two things,

- preserve itself
- reproduce itself

To do so it has to

- protect the flow of information inside it
- pass on that information to its offspring

These are the two drivers of this **intent**. The DNA programming in all life looks towards these two goals whether that is expressed in a plant, a bee, a cat, a cow, a frog, a shrimp or a human being. This **intent** to live and reproduce also means, to some extent, **self-awareness**. Consciousness and self-awareness, however, still do not explain the level of programming that drives us all. Our intent to live is expressed in our desire/need to eat, drink, sleep etc. At the same time, however, none of us are conscious of the trillions upon trillions upon trillions of microbiological mechanisms that run our bodies and keep the information flowing and intact. They just happen at a programming level without us thinking about them or even being aware of them. Where a living thing is not self-aware, like a bacterium or a plant, then the **intent** to live in all aspects of life has to be totally put into the DNA of the bacteria or the plant cells to **drive that intent forward at a raw programming level** without consciousness. The programming forces the behaviour of the life form to specifically interact with its environment in a **technologically intelligent** way, to take advantage of the raw materials in the natural world that surround it and to turn those raw materials into life sustaining fuel. Photosynthesis, for example, is an amazing technology that is built into plant life. Without it the plant cannot survive. That pre-programming allows the plant to take advantage of the free energy from the sun. A plant does this, not because it is aware of what the sun is or what it is doing in using the sun's energy, but because it is simply programmed to do so. The intelligence needed to make this happen is amazing. This super intelligence, therefore, is clearly revealed by the complexity of the pre-set programming that keeps such life forms, in fact all life forms, alive. DNA coding forces all life forms to follow...

...an intelligent pre-given pattern of behaviour at the microbiological level

...this is expressed in the complexity of the coding that enables life to intelligently sift through the basic resources of the natural world and to use them to sustain itself. This is done without any living creature having to depend on *any intelligence of its own*. All life is intelligently assembled at this microbiological coding level. A super intelligence dictates the super complex process. To get around this you'll often hear secularists using such phrases as,

*"**Nature** has <u>designed</u> it this way so that..."*

or

*"**Mother Nature** has <u>found a way</u> to..."*

Nature is therefore given a *personality* and a *thinking process* to go with it. A secularist will **not** say,

"Well the plant must have thought to itself..."

...and then told us how the plant thinks in order to get itself out of trouble. This 'thinking' is ascribed to 'nature' which is one mental step away from the plant and so the secularists get away with this kind of talk. Personality and intelligence is needed to justify the complexity and so 'Mother Nature' gets the credit rather than a brainless plant. The programming that makes a plant work is amazing, astonishing in fact. A huge amount of intelligence has gone into the coding that makes plant life work. Who's responsible for all of this super work, well it's Mother Nature, that's who.

'Mother Nature' steps into science, therefore, where God is not allowed!

She's the one who does it when we listen to those nature and wildlife programmes made by the different humanistic corporations around the world. It's amazing how the language just moves into 'design' and 'personality' behind the intricate and technological constructions in the plant and animal world. This kind of talk enables us to look at irreducible design and to skip over the impossibility that minute steps, caused by random change happenings, could not possibly cause such integrated and interdependent design.

*Biological technology, where intelligent intent is needed to design and create it, is relegated to 'nature' just **doing her stuff**.*

She has done it, we don't know how, but *she* simply has and isn't it amazing. What a gal!

NOTE: Mother Nature is not there to 'call you to account' for your behaviour in life. This lesser 'deity' only facilitates life and lets you do whatever you want to do. That's why she is permitted into the verbal mix. She's a deity that secular spirituality can truly worship because **she serves them**, not the other way around!

On this matter about 'nature' Lee Strobel says…
https://www.youtube.com/watch?v=u20gVY8qyPE

"Nature by itself can't produce information. It can produce patterns. You know if you're walking down the beach and you see ripples in the sand, what's your conclusion? Well that nature, the waves, were coming up on shore and created this pattern. Nature can produce patterns. No problem. But if you're walking down the beach and you see, "John Loves Mary" in a heart with an arrow through it, you wouldn't conclude that the waves created that. Why? Because that's information with content. Nature doesn't do that. Nature produces pattern, it doesn't produce information with content. Whenever we see written information like that, whether it's in a book, whether it's in a newspaper, whether it's in a computer code, we know that there is intelligence behind it. When we look at DNA and we see these written instructions for the assembly of proteins in our bodies, I believe we are looking at some of the most powerful evidence that there must be intelligence behind life."

Chapter 8 – Data Expression Change

...is not the foundation for new information.

Data Change is NOT New Information!

Data Change Produces Variety

A lot of what I've said previously has also been building up to this chapter in the book. This next section, therefore, is crucial to your understanding of **how** evolution **does not** work. I want to show you one of the key areas that evolutionists get completely wrong and by which they misrepresent reality when they interpret the natural world that is in front of their eyes; the difference between **new** *information* and simple *data* **expression change**. Data change **is not** new information, it is only a movement *within current coding*.

So let's make a most important foundational statement.

> *Information Coding*
> ***forms*** *the body parts.*

and

> *Data within the coding*
> ***expresses*** *those body parts.*

Understanding this is crucial to gaining a proper understanding of what happens in the cell under the influences of DNA mix and mutation. Data change is effective in that it enables a creature to adapt to its environment in a sideways movement but does not interfere with the creature's basic body code, which is the code that defines the creature for being what it is. As we saw in a previous chapter, all evolution does is move sideways. **Data expression change** is responsible for all these movements that we've looked at so far. Data expression change produces different,

- breeds of dogs
- types of cat in the cat family
- types of finches on the Galapagos islands viewed by Darwin
- types of lemur on the island of Madagascar

227

This is the natural result of the reshuffling of pre-programmed coding to produce different kinds of cats, dogs, finches, lemurs, etc. All of them are 'kinds' within a kind – that is within their family group. The **foundational code** that makes the creature what it is, however, **remains the same**. Dogs have,

- four legs
- two ears
- one tail
- have hair to cover their bodies
- pant to cool themselves
- go woof or howl (one breed of dogs has lost information and is now classed as a 'silent breed')
- are pack animals
- etc.

The coded data that *expresses* the **non-foundational coding** in a dog can change so that a dog can have short hair, long hair, short legs, long legs, short nose, long nose etc.

*These adjustments in the data are not new information, just **changes** in the **expression** of the **current coding** without changing the foundational coded information that makes the creature what it is.*

Sideways adjustments happen all of the time. It is the reason for the astonishing variety within the different species as you look at expressions of creatures around the world. A frog in your back garden may vary in size and colour to a frog in the Amazon jungle. They will, however, behave in the same way. They will use their back legs to jump, croak to communicate, produce tadpoles to reproduce and have the same body shape. All of the data expression movements are sideways – even having a poisonous skin is a sideways movement. None of them are half-birds or half something else that they've decided to 'evolve' UPWARDS into. The movements we see in frogs around the world are **adaptation**, not evolution.

NOTE: Never has a cell auto-organised itself into a higher state of organised information simply by copying itself or via copy error or via DNA mix. Information development (newly organised coding added into the DNA to form new body parts) is not happening in the cosmos in front of our eyes today. New body parts require new information, changes in body shape simply requires **data expression** change within the current information that is already in the creature.

A Misrepresentation of Reality

This adaptation that takes place in the environment happens due to the established coded data being **tweaked**, not the foundational code that defines what the creature is being changed. All these sideways movements into what evolutionists call a 'new species' (which theists call a 'new kind within a family group') are all achieved by data expression change. Data expression change takes the code **that is already there** and provides a **sideways** movement within it for the animal that **tweaks the data** to adapt the animal to its environment. **Tweaking** is not new foundational code for new body parts or new animal behaviours or for a new flesh type. **Tweaking** is evidence for adaptation, not evolution. This is very place where evolutionists misrepresent the truth and twist reality.

I remember, after watching numerous online evolutionist videos, noticing a pattern amongst the variety of messages and so called 'evidences' that are often given as proof of evolution. That pattern is simply this. Evidence of **sideways change** is shown to the person watching the video. This sideways change is then called 'evolution' and not adaptation. UPWARDS evolution is then talked about where creatures in the past are meant to have developed from one type of creature into another and then these very same examples of **sideways change**, that have just been shown in the video, are then referenced as **direct evidence** for this **UPWARDS** evolutionary movement. UPWARDS evolution, however, requires new foundational code within the creature, not just data expression change tweaking. This foundational difference is totally overlooked by the evolutionists. Let me give you an example.

Example 1 – Long Hair Short Hair

I once saw a video where the video writers talked about data change. They looked at a bit of DNA code within a dog and said that one single letter change in that data on the DNA strand would cause a short haired dog to have long hair. They hailed this as an example of something small in DNA that affects big change within an animal. The video finished with statements about how small changes like this can make big differences to the creature and it called these changes 'evolution'. It did not call the change from a short haired dog to a long haired dog '**data expression change**' or '**adaptation**' it insisted on calling it 'evolution'. Then, in another video that talked about a supposed UPWARDS movement from frog to bird, the same company who made the videos referenced a justification for this so called UPWARDS movement by talking about the single DNA data change that makes a dog's hair long or short. So basically it said, "Just as a single change in the DNA code leads to long hair in a dog, so **exactly the same process** of DNA change will cause a frog to 'evolve' into a bird. The comparison, however, is a complete nonsense. The first example (short haired dog to long haired dog) is data expression change that happens within the current multi-complex coded information **that is already in the animal**. The second example (movement from frog to bird)...

*...requires a whole new set of **complex foundational coded** information that is **not in the frog** in any way, shape or form.*

This new level of coded information is so complex in nature it can only be written by a super intelligent mind that has the capacity to write a level of programming that is totally beyond our current capabilities amongst humanity. This type of code change does not come about by a **random** and **unguided copy-error process**. No amount of step-by-step random **tweaking** will do that. The code that we see within a bird, which is not in a frog, is purposefully written code that takes into account the following,

230

- the shape of the bird – engineered to be aerodynamic and ready for flight
- the placement of the wings – that is,
  - in a mirror image of each other
  - and correctly attached to the right place on the bird's sides/back
- the structure of the wings
  - the bone structure
  - the flesh structure
- the size of the wings
- the feathers on the wings
  - their size
  - their shape
  - their substance – what they are made of i.e. that which makes them different from frog skin
- the tail feathers
  - their size
  - their shape
  - their substance – what they are made of i.e. that which makes them different from frog skin
- the nervous system that makes the information highway to carry the nerve impulses from the bird's aerodynamic body parts to its brain so that it can use its wings properly
- the multi-trillion cell structures, written into the DNA code, which makes all of the above possible
- etc.

Example 2 – An Elongated Beak

Data expression change, *which we see all around us all the time*, is totally different from new information. So when a bird gets a longer beak because it has, for generations, lived on mud flaps and each generation of bird has mated with other birds that have had long beaks to feed in the mud with, then the beak gets longer. This long beak is not information change, just **data adjustment**.

*It is the **foundational information** that <u>creates</u> the beak;*

*...it is the individual **'data expression change'** that elongates the beak.*

Remember that data is simply single digits within the body of the code. It is the strings of code (made up from data) that corporately mean something within DNA. Changing single bits of data within that code is an adjustment to the current code, not new code. **No new jobs are imagined**, no new technology is created, no new body parts developed, **no fresh questions asked** and **no new answers given**. There is just a **change of expression** in the current coded data that is already there, prewritten for purpose.

Evolution has no Design Intelligence

DNA is still too complex a puzzle for us to fully follow, and we have intelligence. Evolution cannot think in a constructive way. There is nothing in the theory of evolution (no agent of intelligent change) to construct and assemble new and sensible coding that will construct new body parts in the light of biological engineering. Biological engineering has to be precision perfect; just the same as the human engineers have to be perfect in the world of our construction industry which happens all round us on a daily basis. Structural engineers know what the laws of physics determine, giving limitations on what they can build and how the multiple parts can assemble. Only an intelligent mind can put together engineering. Even the most cutting edge parts of the construction industry, those that run from computers that can now work as 3D printers to create single story houses made of cement, have very specific programming procedures to follow.

You would never expect even an A.I. robot to develop, through a process of copy error, their construction programming so that a single story house could 'evolve' other technologies over time. Copy errors within any code would not produce new engineering technology – and that is also true in biological life as no one has ever seen a copy error produce useful new information in a plant or an animal. The reasons why the changes that we do see in the animal and insect kingdom are effective, those adaptations of animals within set environments that will change the shape of a beak for the acquisition of new food sources or the length of hair to keep out the cold, is due to the fact that the coding that runs the DNA programming is so fantastic and

232

sophisticated that it can handle slight alterations without the code falling over.

The designer of the original code allowed for data expression movements within the code so that different generations of animals could change if their environment changed and still maintain the code's foundational integrity. That's the careful programming of a genius, a great artist and designer. The religious agenda of an evolutionist will not allow them to interpret the evidence in that way. They have to interpret those movements in the DNA **code** to be beyond what they can do in order to justify a religious idea that…

*…science will never point to God as there will **always be** a process to justify everything.*

So the data expression change movement within the hereditary mix will facilitate the changing of generations of creatures when their feeding habits alter according to diet change dictated by competition for food or a changing environment. It will not facilitate, however, brand new and sensible precision code being written to work with newly engineered materials in the body for the formation of a new body part(s) with incredible technology attached to them, such as a frog developing a wing set. If such new data could arise then we would see all kinds of random bits of flesh sticking out of the animal and plant kingdoms expressed in all kinds of directions whilst the creature(s) tried to evolve something that worked by random chance and an unguided process! Thankfully this is not the case and the nature of information will not allow it to happen.

This is quite a relief because it keeps the different kinds of plants and animals looking elegant and beautiful.

If evolution did happen and plants and animals were able to generate new information for **experimenting with new potential body parts**, then you can guarantee one thing, nature would continually look…

...downright ugly!

Evolution would have to experiment with new bits and bobs of flesh and other materials growing out of all of the potential new body parts that might or might not evolve properly via a random and unguided process. Random change will always be ugly. The creation we see around us is beautiful – the work of a supreme artist.

- -

Data Expression Change in a Web Page

- -

A Lesson in HTML Code

Let me illustrate this in greater detail by showing how some very simple code creates a basic web page. Let's look at some low level/easy to understand coding, explain how it works, and then let's look at how a **one digit data change**, like the example given that changes the length of hair in a dog, will cause a web page to change from a white background to yellow.

How to create a web page with Code

Here's some data,
#ffffff

It doesn't look very interesting does it? I have already told you that data (of itself) is not information. Data is just data, a string of recognisable characters, letters or numbers within a set language, that are written one after the other. By itself and of itself data does nothing useful. It just sits there and waits to be organised into something meaningful (where all the data characters and digits corporately mean something together), then processed and, if it is not processed, then it is powerless to effect change. So the above example of data, #ffffff, is completely useless.

So to most people #ffffff is not very meaningful and by itself it does nothing. This #ffffff data, however, will be recognisable to anyone who knows a computer language called HTML. HTML is one of the languages that drives the internet and is the code that forms the different web pages that you view when you go online. So when you're viewing each page on your phone or tablet device or PC or

Mac, then every page you view has lines and lines of code that makes it work. Your web browser picks up that page's code, reads it, and then processes that code by displaying a web page based on what that code means. Your web browser translates that code into a nice page putting all the text and images into place in a moment of time. The creation of the page, from the code, is the processing of the code. That reading and processing of the code means that the code is information, not data.

Within the code are bits of precision data that have been specifically set there for processing. Remember our definition of information earlier on?

Information is **precision** data, (coded with intent) **processed** through a **constructed** and **calibrated** environment in order to **ensure** a job done.

Well #ffffff in the HTML language is the processed precision data within the code that determines something on a web page being **coloured with the colour *white***. Whenever a computer sees #ffffff written within some HTML code, then the precision data shouts out to the computer programme that is reading it,

"This is 'white' and you need to put the white colour onto the webpage wherever you see this bit of data!"

That 'white' can be a white background colour or a white bar across the page to separate different parts of the page from each other or even white text on a dark background to make the text stand out.

Let me illustrate and unpack this by teaching you some very basic coding. The text below is written in what we call HTML5 code. The reason why it is called HTML5 is because it is the 5th version of the HTML language where the language has been purposefully written and rewritten over and over again by intelligent human beings to enable it to become more sophisticated and to create better websites. The numbers following at the left side of each line are not part of the code; they are put there by me so that you know which line of code I'm talking about when I explain how it all works. Do not worry if at first you don't understand the code, I'll explain it in a moment. Here it is.

```
1) <html>
2) <head>
3) <title>Hello World Message</title>
4) <style>
5) body {
6)    background-color: #ffffff;
7) }
8) </style>
9) </head>
10)
11) <body>
12) Hello World, it's a beautiful day.
13) </body>
14) </html>
```

All the very basic code above does is to create a web page that displays the message, "Hello World, it's a beautiful day." on the screen. The background colour to the website page is white and on the tab at the top of the browser page are the words, "Hello World Message". Let me explain how the code works.

Explaining the Code

HTML works in what we call 'tags'. A tag is some text that is surrounded by the mathematical symbols that are used to express 'less than' and 'greater than' in a maths equation. So for example,

$$5 < 8$$

reads

$$5 \text{ is } \textit{less than } 8$$

...because the symbol '<' in mathematics means 'less than'.

That same symbol means something different in the HTML language. When used with the greater than symbol '>' it means to

236

begin a new 'tag'. So when you see *<text here>*, in the HTML language these symbols <> surround the text and tells the computer what is happening. So when a computer opens up a file and sees a tag that says <html> then it understands that this means, "Listen up computer, this text that you're about to read from now on is all written in a computer language called HTML and everything you read below this <html> tag is written in HTML code so **use the rules** of the HTML language when you read, interpret and process this code."

So here's the first line of code again and what it means,

1) <html> - this means everything after this tag is written in the HTML language.

The second line of code written like this,

2) <head>

This is also a tag and opens up the very top part of the web page called **the header**. All kinds of code can be put in the header area and it won't be displayed on the page for the website viewer to see. This code is often background information to the web page that you don't want to appear directly on the page but helps you define how the page will work.

The third line of code is written like this,

3) <title>Hello World Message</title>

Here we see another tag called a **title** tag. Notice that at the end of the line we see the same title tag again but it has a forward slash symbol just before the word 'title'. So the opening tag is <title> and the closing tag that tells the computer that we have come to the end of the 'title' code is </title>. In-between these two tags are the words, "Hello World Message". When this web page is viewed you will see at the top of the web page a tab. Having many web pages opened at the same time in a browser window will cause several tabs at the top of the page. You can click on the different tabs as you want to view each page. What this code does,

3) <title>Hello World Message</title>

...is to put the words, "Hello World Message" onto the tab itself. This is so that, if you have several web pages open at the same time you can look at the tabs at the top of the browser window and read them and see which one is the "Hello World" message and can easily click back onto it to see/view the page.

The next section of the code looks like this,

```
4) <style>
5) body {
6)    background-color: #ffffff;
7) }
8) </style>
```

The style tag <style> opens up all kinds of opportunities for the programmer. You can, for example, dictate here what size or style of text to display on your web page, if you want the text centred on the page or aligned from the left or the right etc. So on line 4 we get the <style> tag that tells the computer, "We're about to put some commands in here that will dictate the style of the web page," and then we have on line 8 </style> which is a tag that closes the style section and when the computer sees this it reads, "Ok computer, this is the end of the style commands for this web page."

Lines 5, 6 and 7 are bits of interesting code. Line 5,
```
5) body {
```
tells the computer that we're now talking about commands that affect the main body of the page. The curly bracket tells the computer that a command of some type is about to be given and that it needs to take note of it.

Line 6,
```
6)    background-color: #ffffff;
```
is a command. It tells the computer that the background colour of the web page is #ffffff – and this is the **precision data expression** that we've been talking about in this science section. Line 6 tells the computer, "Hey computer, when you load this web page make sure that you put a white background colour on the page!"

Line 7,

7) }

just has the curly brackets close symbol on it to show that the command has now finished and we've already seen that line 8,

8) </style>

is the closing tag to tell the computer that the style commands are now finished.

Line 9 closes the header part of the webpage.

9) </head>

There isn't any text on line 10 just simply to help the human eye to see the gap between the header and the rest of the web page. The computer doesn't need a gap on this line but programmers put gaps in their code just to help them read it. So the next bit of code appears on line 11. It reads,

11) <body>

This is a tag that opens up what is called the main body area of the web page. The body is the place where all the contents of the web page are displayed. Here appears the text, the images, the videos and clickable buttons etc. that you see when you look at a web page.

Line 12,

12) Hello World, it's a beautiful day.

...contains the message that appears on the web page. It's a simple text message, "Hello World, it's a beautiful day." that sits on the page on a white background. (The white background, as we have seen, has been produced by lines 5,6 and 7.)

Line 13 has the close body tag on it,

13) </body>

and this tells the computer that all the information that is to be displayed on the webpage finishes here.

Line 14,

14) </html>

is the tag that closes the HTML language and tells the computer that this is the end of the code.

Foundation Code and its Internal Integrity

So that is how very basic computer code works. Why have I outlined the above? Simply because it illustrates fantastically the difference between foundation code and data expression changes.

> **NOTE:** Remember that whenever we see information we see that a question has been asked and answered. Information is the answer to the question that has been asked.

So in this instance we see that the question was,

> *"How do I want my 'Hello world, it's a beautiful day," message expressed on the internet?"*

The answer is,

> *"I want it to be written in English on a web page written in the HTML language with a white background."*

To do this we need to **create a context** via which this page can be produced. The web page is a precision made virtual object that is crafted for **intent**, that is, I **intend** to send a greeting message to the world via a web page.

Most of the code that we've looked at in this example is **foundational code** which is there to **set up a context** via which **the code** is processed to create the page.

> **NOTE:** Changes to the **foundational code** will destroy the page completely!

It is important to understand that...

...you cannot evolve the foundational code in a step-by-step process.

Foundational code has to be 'all there' at the same time for the web page to work. Partial code, or bad code, does not work. Even code that is poorly constructed and has 'bugs' in it has a level of sophistication that you would never find from a random and unguided character generation process where symbols and digits were randomly selected and put side by side – as the evolutionists imagine to be the case when the first code is said to have randomly arrived/assembled/developed/evolved. So our web page code example is very exact and very sophisticated in that it all has meaning and purpose. Together it expresses meaning and sets up a context for the page to be created.

That *context* in the code is the following,
- tell the computer we're using the HTML language – **<html>**
- define the header area – **<header>**
    - tell the computer that text will appear in the header title tab – **<title>**
    - tell the computer that the text that will appear in this title area is - **Hello World Message**
    - define the end of the title area **</title>**
    - define the start of the style code **<style>**
    - tell the computer what background colour you want the page to be – **background-color: #ffffff;**
    - define the end of the style area **</style>**
- define the end of the header area – **</header>**
- define the body area – **<body>**
- tell the computer that the text that will appear in this body area is - **Hello World, it's a beautiful day**.
- define the end of the body area – **</body>**
- define the end of the HTML code – **<html>**

So the context for the page to appear is that we have to,

1. Tell the computer what language we're using
2. Tell it that there is a defined header area with,
    a. a title to be displayed in the page's top tab

   b.   page formatting to do, i.e. a white background.
3. Tell the computer that there is a defined body area with a message to go into it.

All of the above must go into the computer code for the web page to be **crafted** to fulfil the **intent** to communicate to the world my greeting.

So here's the code again. Cast your eye over it and you should be able to read it yourself now and know what you're looking at.

```
1) <html>
2) <head>
3) <title>Hello World Message</title>
4) <style>
5) body {
6)    background-color: #ffffff;
7) }
8) </style>
9) </head>
10)
11) <body>
12) Hello World, it's a beautiful day.
13) </body>
14) </html>
```

This foundational code has to write it **with intent**. The programmer has to know what s/he is aiming for, i.e. to imagine what the web page should look like **before** the code is written. Everything also has to obey the rules of HTML in order to display the information correctly.

Example: A Sideways Single Digit Data Expression Change!

Now that I've shown you the foundational code and its context that's needed to create the web page, let's talk about simple **data expression change** that will cause the page to 'adapt sideways', which is the main reason why I'm giving this illustration. Let's look at line 6 again. It says,

```
6)    background-color: #ffffff;
```

If I were to change the lettering of any part of the code 'background-color' then the code would break. That part of the code must have utter, precision integrity. So if I were to change the spelling of color from the American to UK English, and so write 'color' as 'colour' then the code would stop working. We cannot create data expression change with that part of the code. However, '#ffffff' is pure data that is **ready for changing**. As we have already said, data by itself is useless. Once processed, however, #ffffff has a big effect and determines that the web page is white. Let me show you what happens if this code changes, even by one digit. If we changed the 5th 'f' to a '0' it will now read, #ffff0f rather than #ffffff. The result on the web page will be dramatic. It completely changes the background colour of the page! #ffffff is white and #ffff0f is yellow! Changing the 5th 'f' character in the data string from 'f' to '0' brings about a complete change of colour from white to a bright yellow! One data character change and, like a miracle, we have yellow, not white! Wow, we could say, see how this little change in the code makes such a big difference on the web page. **Little changes in the code add up to big changes on the web page**! See how all of that 'white' background has suddenly become 'yellow' and it's such a huge change on the page! The yellow now dominates the page and is so 'in your face' due to it being a bright and dominant colour that the text message now becomes secondary to the colour. We've therefore managed to affect such a huge amount of change via one digit in the code being different! The impression that you can give, therefore, is that something great has happened, just as the humanist video said about one change in the DNA code could change a dog's hair from being long to short. Actually, in reality, nothing much has happened at all. The basic foundational coding that makes the page work is still intact and has not been added to in any way shape or form.

No new coding,
__no new information__
has been added.

All that has happened is that a single digit **within the current code** has been altered, and a **new colour has been expressed via that code being processed**. The change may be dramatic to the human eye, but the change is actually extremely minor. It is a mere **sideways data expression** change. The important thing to note is that...

...no new information has been added to the website!

So this 'dramatic' change from white background to yellow background is ***data expression change*** <u>NOT</u> new information. Data change is a very easy thing to do (and happens all the time in the insect, animal and plant kingdoms).

Example: Adding New Information

The lie of secularism, however, is that the last example given of data expression change (background colour changing from white to yellow) is a true and real representation of new information being added to the web page. If I did want to add new information into the web page, such as adding an image or a video file, then I would need **brand new, totally different code** to achieve that. That code would need to be constructed within the context of the HTML language, it would have to obey its rules, it would have to be accurate and precision written and it would have to have knowledge of the **resources that are available to it** so that the code could **refer to those resources** and **use them** when it is **processed**, i.e. it would have to know the exact name and the exact location of the picture file that I wanted to display on the web page so that, as the code is processed by the computer and the file is read by the web browser, the image can be inserted onto the page. So, if I wanted to add a 'smiley face' image underneath the text that says "Hello World, it's a beautiful day", here's the code that would do just that.

```
<br>
<img src="smileyface.jpg">
```

Without line two being fully in place and the image file called 'smileyface.jpg' also being in the same folder on my computer as the html web page file, there would not be a new image displayed on the web page. The code and the resource have to be there, in full, at the same time to work together for the new expression of information to work. So now the end of the code looks like this,

12) Hello World, it's a beautiful day.
13)
14) <img src="smileyface.jpg">
15) </body>
16) </html>

Let me explain this new code.

 simply means a line break, i.e. go down one line so that, whatever happens next on the web page, takes place one line beneath the message, "Hello World, it's a beautiful day." This makes sure that the image does not sit on the same line as the message and so looks untidy.

The next line of code inserts the image onto the page. Let's look at it. I've highlighted in bold and slightly increased the font size of the bit that I want to talk about.

14) <**img** src="smileyface.jpg"> - well the start of this tag has three letters, 'img' and these stand for the word 'image'.

14) <img **src**="smileyface.jpg"> - The next part of the tag is made up by the letters 'src' and these stand for the word 'source'.

14) <**img src**="smileyface.jpg"> - So the start of the code 'img src' stands for 'image source'. The computer reads this code and understands according to the language rules of html that an image is to be inserted into the web page and that I am about to tell it what the source of that image is, i.e. where that image can be found by the computer and what its name is in order for it to be displayed on the web page.

The next part of the line which I've highlighted in bold,
14) <img src="**smileyface.jpg**"> tells the computer that there is a file called 'smileyface.jpg' and this image file is in the same folder as the file that contains the html code that creates the web page. So the code basically tells the computer browser to insert this smileyface.jpg file into the web page underneath the welcome message.

So, once this new code is added to the html file, the computer will read it, display the text, "Hello World, it's a beautiful day" on the page and then, directly underneath that text, the computer will add an image of a smiley face.

If you are brand new to programming, and the above is a little difficult to follow, then don't worry. The main point I want to make is that this new information is new code; it is **not simple data expression change**. Data expression change is like changing the background colour of the page (or the length of hair on a dog), it is a **tweak** of the code that *is already there*. To add the image I've not had to make a mere couple of data changes to the code *that's already there*. I've had to create brand new code with a knowledge of a particular resource that is available to me, i.e. I've had to know that, stored in the same folder as the web page file that contains the html code, is an image file called smileyface.jpg, and that by using specific code, <img src="smileyface.jpg">, I can insert the image into the page.

> **NOTE:** Also a question of some type has been asked and the code has been written with intent. The question might be, "How can I make my message look friendlier than it currently is?" The answer comes in the form of a friendly smiley face that complements the message. Without the question, the code will not be written.

The Chances of this Code Randomly Appearing

What are the chances of this tiny bit of simple code appearing by a random process? Let's go into the world of fantasy (as evolutionists often do when imagining the past) and say that there was a freak fluctuation of power during a copy and paste process whilst I was working on my PC and that, as I was pasting the code into another file, the power fluctuation almost, but not quite, turned my PC off. This computer error caused not only the pasting of the current code into the new file but also, somehow, added an extra line of text. What is the chance that those extra digits of code would be...

<img src="smileyface.jpg">

...so that the computer could read and process it properly for an image to be added to the web page? Well there are 26 letters in the alphabet and we also have these extra symbols in the code <="."> so that means that there are 32 characters to choose from. What's the chance that these two lines of text,

13)
14) <img src="smileyface.jpg">

...could appear by a random and unguided process?

Well if there are roughly 32 characters available then the chance that the symbol '<' would appear first on this line is one in thirty two. The chance that the second letter is an 'b' is also one in thirty two. So the chance that we could get <b at the start of this code is 32 times 32 which is expressed as 32^2. Each letter that is then added into the line of code has to be exactly correct and is expressed as another '1 in 32 chance' chance. **Get one letter wrong in the data string and the whole line of code fails**. By the time we add up all of the letters we have 32^{30} as the final sum as there are 30 slots to be filled in (including one blank space) and each slot is a 1 in 32 chance of it being correct. The odds of even this very simple string of code being randomly assembled in a correct order is beyond comprehension. My Excel spreadsheet won't calculate it for me. It is not even trillions to one.

Remember, we're not looking at creating random numbers here, like a lottery. A lottery is a cinch to win in comparison. All a lottery is, is a set of random numbers and any randomly picked set of numbers can win, it doesn't matter which order the numbers appear in. All you have to do is to have the same numbers in your list. We're looking at something far, far, far more difficult. We're looking at recreating a precision line of characters that has to be **exactly correct in order to communicate**, with intent for work to be done within a specific language, that there is a resource to put into a web page. If you get just one of the characters in that string of code wrong, then you have to start again. This is because we're not constructing random data that can appear in any order, **we're constructing a purposeful line of code for processing to become information**! In a lottery it doesn't matter which order the numbers come out, just that the numbers finally match. For code to be correct the characters and digits have to be in the **correct sequential order** to communicate something.

*Every character in the line of code **builds towards a corporate meaning** and if one part is wrong, then the meaning of the whole line of code fails.*

If the line of code contained the data #ffffff and instead we got #ffff0f, then that wouldn't matter because that part of the code is **not foundational code** to make the page work; we would simply display the colour yellow rather than white. The code on this line, however, to insert an image...

14) <img src="smileyface.jpg">

...is <u>ALL precision code</u> that cannot be incorrect because it **foundationally sets the context** for the image to be displayed. Just like the <html> tag **foundationally sets the context** for the whole code to follow on, so too this code has to be exactly correct. Coded foundational information is not just expression data. Data, like #ffffff, can be changed and the effects of that change will show up on the web page or in the physical makeup of the creature if it is done in a specific part of the DNA. If the coding that affects **the structure** of the creature goes wrong at the time of hereditary exchange, however, then we call it 'a deformity' and if the cell copying processes within us continually goes wrong we call it 'cancer' (not evolution) and that is something that we have to be actively cured of. Cancer (copy error) does not drive forward change within the body of any creature to create new information for new body parts – and neither does hereditary DNA exchange!

> **NOTE:** We also have to understand that the new line of code to insert the image is not the only miracle that has to take place. We also need the smiley faced image to appear within the same folder as the file that contains the HTML code too. Without this extra resource appearing in the folder, well then there's nothing to insert into the web page. Both the precision code and the smiley faced image have to appear together at the same time. If they do not 'arrive on the scene' together –

then the code is totally useless and without purpose. No-one in their right mind would believe that this could happen, but for some reason we're allowed to believe it about code and resources in the cell!

The Bigger Question

DNA's complexity and HTML's Simplicity

What about the differences between html code and DNA code? Aren't they very different from each other? The answer is 'Yes, of course they are different' but all coding follows the same rules of expression. It is easier to show in html how coding can go wrong as html is very simplistic compared with DNA. If there is an error in the code that defines the tags, for example if during the copying process the top <html> tag got written <htmm> instead, then the whole code would stop working. There would be no web page to display! DNA is more robust than that because the 'copying and pasting' of DNA mix that happens when a sperm meets an egg is hugely complex, beyond our wildest dreams to replicate in the computer world, and it is written by a genius that designed a large amount of information to *shuffle itself* into place. At the same time, however, this code follows the same basic principle that the shuffle has to obey a set of rules to keep the integrity of the limbs and body shape of the creature that is being created. Shuffle processes are just that, a reshuffling of foundational code and data sets within the code that can find new expressions, such as skin colour, hair colour, limb length etc. Offspring will look like their parents, just with **data expression differences** between them. Errors within the code can be handled better by DNA than by html as html falls apart easily, as I have illustrated. However, errors within DNA code are still just that, errors that represent damage to the integrity of the code rather than errors that lead to new technologically intelligent code for the constructing of new body parts. So let me say more accurately that...

...the smallest errors, added together over long periods of time, can lead to the most <u>catastrophic</u> changes!

249

DNA must still maintain its integrity – which is why there are two enzyme proteins on every string of DNA in your body that have the sole job of fixing copy errors in the code. Mutation will never lead to new code; it always attacks the integrity of DNA. This level of knowledge shows clearly how fraudulent evolution theory is. Data change is common, but it is not responsible for the basic components that make a creature what it is. Data change is not new information, just sideways adjustments within the code to re-express an emphasis within the code that is already there. Coding that expresses foundational contexts, such as body parts, is very sophisticated and that type of information cannot come about by random copy error.

Let's also remember that I could have said so much more on this subject, but there is not the space in this book to do so. We could have looked at the fact that evolutionists start with the DNA hereditary exchange mechanism to justify evolution but do not attempt at all to explain how that DNA hereditary exchange mechanism evolved, 'got there' in the first place. DNA hereditary exchange (the meeting of a sperm and an egg) is basically a super computer programme written by a mastermind intelligence. Evolutionists start with it, as if it is sensible to believe that this mechanism just 'got there' by some process of evolution itself, giving the excuse that at a microbiological level a bacteria cell can swallow another bacteria cell and take its DNA into it and think that this is a reasonable example of DNA growth – which it is not.

For some strange reason the leap from that kind of bacteria exchange to saying that the hereditary DNA exchange mechanism just happened, it 'evolved', is accepted without question. Yet they never even begin to give a proper account as to how this amazing DNA hereditary exchange programme moved step-by-step into its current mind-boggling complexity!

It is probably the most complex programme in the universe.

The whole so called 'evolutionary process' is said to be driven by this hereditary exchange along with the copy errors that occur – all taking place within the context of the environment which is subject to the processes of natural selection. So, let's put it in simple terms so that we can look at what evolutionists are asking us to believe in; why they suggest that this hereditary exchange programme evolved, but we'll do this within the context of the computer gaming world.

Example: From 2D Pac Man to Minecraft!

Most people today still know what the computer programme Pac Man is. For those of you who are either much older than me or much younger than me, well Pac Man is a computer game where a yellow circle goes around a maze and eats up white dots. The dots are scattered all around the maze and so the Pac Man has to travel over every part of the maze in order to complete that part of the game. There are other characters, who look a little like simplistically drawn jellyfish and are called 'ghosts' that travel the maze in order to catch the Pac Man before the Pac Man has had the chance to eat all the dots; a simple but very effective game. If you want to know what the game looks like then just go onto the internet and type the words Pac Man into any search engine and you'll see images of it. Simple as it is, there will be a good amount of code behind this game to make it work. Lots of people have written their versions of Pac Man over the years, each looking slightly different, but all of them doing essentially the same job. So let's imagine that something amazing happened. Let's imagine that someone out there wanted to develop an artificially intelligent (A.I.) programme that automatically created variants of the Pac Man programme. Let's say that someone was so clever that they found a way by which a computer could look at two slightly different Pac Man programmes, take half of the programming code from each, and then merge them together in such a way as to form a brand new programme out of the two *without totally destroying* the essentials of the Pac Man programme in the process. Such an A.I. programme would have to be very aware that there are certain bits of the code that **must be kept in place** in order for the game to work. If the code breaks that,

- forms and makes the Pac Man figure move
- forms the maze
- forms and moves the ghosts

...then the game does not work. So whoever writes this new A.I. code that takes two different versions of Pac Man and mergers them into a new game has to know exactly what they're up to. The basic fundamental code that makes it all 'happen' for the end user to still enjoy the game and still interact with the characters has to be intact every time a 'merge' of the codes takes place. You have to know **which bits of code can change** and which bits **must remain the same**. So here are some things that could change.

- the colour and shape of the Pac Man
- the colour and shape of the ghosts
- the colour and shape of the dots
- the colour and shape of the maze
- the route of the maze as long as it remained a maze
- etc.

All of these things are 'non essentials' within the game. Changes like this are just 'data expression change' that would bring about a sideways movement within the game. Each 'child' programme of Pac Man that was produced by a merge between two Pac Man programmes would have a slightly different look to what would be classed as their 'parent' programmes but it would work essentially the same way. The different colours in the game and the different shapes that might appear would be **data expression change**, NOT new information. So you could end up with a tall Pac Man a small Pac Man, a slim Pac Man or a fat Pac Man, a yellow Pac Man, blue Pac Man or even an invisible Pac Man – which would be fun! Sideways data expression changes could happen left, right and centre.

If you added an option in the A.I. programming for random 'copy error' to appear within the code so that a small amount of error could randomly appear within the programme every time a merge of two Pac Man programmes took place, then you could absolutely guarantee one thing as a definite outcome over time. As the merge programme was run again and again and again, in order to give the copy error a chance to have an effect on the game, the outcome would be that the Pac Man programme would eventually do one thing...

...it would stop working!
It would break.

Why? Well that's the nature of **foundational coded** information. The **foundational** coding would degenerate over time unless there was some extra 'living code' inside the programme that did the job of locating and fixing code errors. This code fixing programme would add yet another new level of sophistication to the Pac Man programme.

> **NOTE:** This is why, as I have already said over and over again, that we have two enzymes on each strand of DNA in every cell in our bodies that goes up and down the strand fixing copy errors. This living self-fix activity that lives inside every living creature is a work of extraordinary programming. The activities of these enzymes also shows that a question has been asked about how to keep the integrity of the code and the answer to that question is these enzymes – which have been purposefully written into the genes on the DNA ladder.

There is also one more thing that you would for sure **not expect** from this continual merging of Pac Man programmes. You would certainly not expect this copying and merging A.I. programme of each Pac Man game, along with copy error, to over a long period of time turn the 2D Pac Man game into an online 3D world game, such as Minecraft for example or any other 3D world programme! There is a huge amount of new information needed in a 3D world game compared with the 2D Pac Man game. Evolutionists, however, would have us believe that this is possible via merging the code and copy error over millions of years. This is in effect what they are asking you to believe when you move from a frog to a bird!

Putting it in those terms, people would never ever believe it could happen. If you added error into the mix you would quite rightfully say that eventually your 2D Pac Man game would fail. As more and more errors crept into the code the original programme would die. It would not develop new levels of code to self-transform into something better than itself. **Unguided and random processes do not create new, sophisticated coded information**. The code that runs Minecraft is specifically written with the 'story in mind from the programmer' anticipating what will happen as the 3D game progresses and what information needs to be processed in order to make it happen. It requires intelligence to write a 3D world code and the code needs to be written with intent; multiple questions need to be asked and multiple answers found and all of those answers need to be expressed in the code, that's information! Digital engineering needs to be planned and implemented in order for the final crafted and precision made product to work. So too with a bird. For a bird to fly you need to ask questions such as,

1. What are the laws of aerodynamics?
2. How can I construct a wing structure that obeys the laws of aerodynamics?
3. How do I power and move those wings in order to gain flight?
4. How do feathers help me gain flight and what shape and size do they need to be?
5. What code needs to be specifically written in the DNA in order to construct these new body parts so that they all relate to each other correctly?
6. etc.

In fact there are so many questions that need asking and then answering. Those questions and answers then need to be expressed in the code in great detail and with great accuracy.

None of those 'bird' questions have been asked or answered in the coding that makes up a frog!

So why on earth would you believe that data change in a frog, that creates different types of frogs (but all of them still frogs) would ever end up creating newly written code to 'run a bird' via a random and unguided process called hereditary DNA exchange coupled with copy error and natural selection?

> **NOTE:** Remember that natural selection just performs the job of removing DNA from the data pool as creatures die; it adds nothing to the code.

So with natural selection removing DNA from the gene pool, i.e. it takes out those variants of frog that are easy to eat by a predator, and with copy error not writing new code, all you have is hereditary DNA exchange where the programming itself puts limits on the DNA shuffle so that the foundational coding remains the same and the only room for data movement is within the data expressions of the body parts. This ensures that, at the programming level, there is no **mechanism** for the writing of new code to drive the creature in an UPWARDS evolutionary way. You **only have the opportunity for sideways expression change** in the insect, animal and plant kingdoms. So when an evolutionist says that a frog has turned into a bird, that's just an example of pure blind faith based on the belief that the so called 'evolutionary process' is plausible at the microbiological level. As far as the facts of the matter go, it is a fraudulent statement to make based on a complete lack of understanding of how code and data work in the real world of programming.

A Confined Programming and Information Loss

Information always decreases in the natural world over time and is lost except that, when a copying process takes place, it is temporarily preserved. When this happens the information is **guided and kept safe by a pre-programmed route.** What I mean is that the information that is communicated via the sperm combining with the egg all happens within a controlled environment. The data re-expressed by the DNA shuffle is always subject to the confines of the original processing programme that dictates how the information that makes up the new creature is moved and implemented.

A very, very simple illustration of this would be if you were to open up a new word processing document on your computer and, after typing some text, you were to highlight it, copy it and then paste it into a new document. According to the pre-set programming in your computer the best you could hope for would be an exact copy of the text. You could highlight and copy the same text a hundred billion times and, due to the limits that the intelligent programmer had placed upon the environment, you would still have at best a copy of the original text. If there was a partial power cut, caused by the haphazard interference of the natural world, then you would expect a loss of data due to the fluctuation in the power supply as you were pasting the text into a new document. You would not expect, due to that fluctuation of the power supply, any copy errors to produce a beautiful multi-layered poem of immense complexity that communicates information on a mind boggling scale. No-one believes that that would be possible. No-one would also believe that suddenly, within your word processing document, the text to turn from plain text into a fantastic programming language that the computer could somehow, via a random flux of energy, incorporate into its current programming structure so that it, like the other programmes, run in the background and **provide a new service** to the user. You can't copy and paste text over and over and expect to come up with a music programme or an art package. The computer is just not built to develop in that way. Each part of its environment has **pre-programmed limits**.

So too in the body of every creature, the copying of information within every living thing happens within a clearly defined, crafted and calibrated context. Whenever a cell copies itself or whenever DNA mix takes place, the information that is being duplicated is guided by the duplication process so that, at best, we get a good copy of the original code made, even if there are slight data expression changes in the code. Each time the code is copied then there is just an opportunity for **data loss**, **not data gain**.

*According to the haphazard decay of the natural world, **we are all devolving**, not evolving.*

The reproductive system is actually a way of life escaping extinction, a way of cheating death, not for developing new forms of life. Life is not thriving to evolve on this planet, that's how a humanist wants you to see it according to their religious world view – one that desperately wants to say "There is no God." Life is actually continually fighting to retain its place and the movements we see within the data structures, a copy error here and a copy error there, are simply data spots that add no new technology, no new body parts, no **UPWARDS** evolution, **no new information** to the creature. Information escapes wipe-out by the next generation coming along. It escapes the forces of this natural world which would destroy it and manages to retain its place in the cosmos with every new creature that is born. This nicely takes us onto the next chapter.

Chapter 9 – It's Impossible Jim!

...and the second law of thermodynamics tells us so.

- -
The Second Law of Thermodynamics
- -

A Closed System Increasing in Chaos

The biggest problem that secular science faces is the second law of thermodynamics. Here's an excellent definition of that law taken from Britannica.com -

https://www.britannica.com/science/life#ref1014187

"The second law of thermodynamics states that, in a closed system, no processes will tend to occur that increases the net organization (or decrease the net entropy) of the system. Thus, the universe taken as a whole is **steadily moving toward a state of complete randomness,** *lacking any order, pattern, or beauty."*

Let me translate that quote for anyone without a science background. Our universe is classed as a *closed system*. In simple terms this means that there is nothing else outside our universe that is impacting our universe with energy and so interfering with anything contained within it. Our universe is isolated, just like you would use a thermos flask to isolate hot coffee to keep it hot so that you could drink it later on. In this isolated state, any movements of energy within our universe will not organise the materials contained within the universe into a higher state of being, i.e. it will not make their makeup more complex. The cosmos, and everything in it, is becoming more and more chaotic. It is becoming more random and moving away from any order that can be found within it.

Home Experiment 1

You can prove this yourself with a variety of homemade experiments. For example you can get a piece of string and wind it around your finger so that, if you were to carefully take the string off your finger, you would see a coil shape. The string now has a 'shape' and a 'pattern' to it. All you have to do now is to **add raw energy** to the string by throwing it into the air and, when it lands, it will begin to lose its shape. The more you add energy to the string, by repeatedly throwing it into the air, the more the shape will go till it disappears altogether and becomes a jumbled mess. You can repeat this experiment as often as you like and you will never observe the string landing on the floor in an increased state of complexity. This is a down-to-earth example of the second law of thermodynamics.

Home Experiment 2

Another way of proving this law is to simply make a hot drink, pour it into a mug, and then to put the mug onto a cold surface. Over time the energy within the hot drink and the cold surface will become equally warm (as one impacts the other) and then they will both cool down together as all the heat will be lost to its surroundings and 'room temperature' will once again be the norm. This is called equilibrium – that is where the **balance** of room temperature has been reached again. The universe is cooling down and one day everything will be cold and dead, all life will be wiped out and it will be **as if all that we see around us had never been**. Everything will be equally cold and equally dead. This is the equilibrium that we are all heading towards, despite our planet's current, temporary climate change. The long term forecast for the whole universe is freezing cold!

Equilibrium and Information Loss

This same equilibrium movement also means one thing...

...the total loss of life and the removal of all information from the cosmos!

This is the state of the universe. The humanist creation **story starts off with chaos**, a Big Bang explosion, and then continually **moves towards an even greater chaos** – the cooling down of the universe where all order will be wiped out. So we have chaos (Big Bang) and then a movement to even greater chaos (cold equilibrium) and somehow along the time line of this **continuous movement from chaos to even greater chaos**, evolutionists want us to believe...

...that the chaotic and random movements of raw energy within the cosmos have had the ability to bring about order, complexity and interdependent design...

...via these unguided movements of raw energy – and so breaking the 2nd law of thermodynamics over and over and over and over again! The 2nd law of thermodynamics dictates that chaos only produces more chaos.

Haphazard and unguided forces of the natural world will do nothing but remove information at the heart of life. This is why chemical reactions of any kind of movements within the cosmos cannot create order or complexity or code. All the movements within the cosmos move towards randomness. Information cannot arise from this nor can it survive the impacts of raw energy as the 2nd law of thermodynamics tells us that information will be wiped out by the encounter. This is why the DNA information is carefully housed and protected in a very specific way to keep it safe. Information has been hidden in the cell and surrounded by blockages to the natural world's processes so that the information in the cell cannot be accessed by the outside world. Raw energy will always increase entropy (chaos) the results of which always end in data loss and a falling apart of the inner cell's environment that would take hold of the DNA code and process it. The whole environment package that makes information work within a creature, therefore, is protected via the cell membrane. This membrane is precision made to lock in the environment so that it can work together as a unit and to lock out anything that would interfere with the workings of that environment.

The laws of science tell us that natural processes do not construct, they always deconstruct and move towards equilibrium, which in the world of information is expressed as information loss.

If I wrote on the beach, "Hello World," and then a wave was to come up onto the shore, that random and unguided event would not be beneficial to the information etched in the sand. The wave hitting the sand would not change the text, "Hello World," into any other constructed words that could mean something more than that which I have already written. As those sand particles are moved by the random motion of the waves, the formation of the text on the beach will not become more complex, as if to communicate something more after the event. In fact the wave on the sand would not, and never will, add letters. The sand will move and the pattern will become more chaotic, entropy will naturally increase, information will disappear. This is because, as we have already said, the 2nd law of thermodynamics tells us that everything within the naturalistic world moves towards equilibrium, information wipe out and is therefore called an increase in entropy (disorder or chaos). The natural world will do nothing, therefore, amongst its haphazard processes of chance and random collision, to create, retain or add information over time. This applies to all the forces within the natural world, whether the movements of the waves of the sea or chemical reactions of any kind in any type of environment, which evolutionists try to use to kick-start life without the divine. Random processes coming from the forces of nature do not construct information in any way shape or form.

The raw energies found in the natural world, therefore, being random in nature and moving everything towards a greater loss of order are…

…hostile to life.

This movement is the opposite direction from that which is needed for life to 'evolve'. The whole environment of the universe is continually moving in the wrong direction. So if the natural workings of the forces of nature (or chemical reactions) are subject to a law of science that moves towards equilibrium, randomness and data loss, then the natural world cannot **of itself or by itself**, assemble sensible coded data and then craft or create or calibrate an environment to enable specialised resources in the environment to process that coded data and turn it into information to ensure the creation of molecular machines to get a job done. Neither do these chaotic forces have the ability to **ask questions** and to **problem solve** for life to sustain itself. In short, the forces of the natural world cannot,

- create the assembled data strings into sensible and meaningful code (in the context of a language) with intent to create something

- create the context (environment) via which information is processed to create machines (proteins) that will help sustain life
- ask questions and provide solutions to the many problems that life has to overcome within the context of a hostile environment

All such theories and attempts are self-imagined fantasy theories that tickle the minds of people who will believe anything – except that there is a God. The very laws of science prevent information from coming into the cosmos by itself. The cosmos is on a continual journey into disorder. An unguided chemical reaction, therefore, will never prepare the way for data to arise, to organise itself into code and to provide an environmental context by which that code can be read (and so become information) whereby the reading of that code can cause the selection of specific resources from within the environment in order to build machines that are fashioned and tailored for doing sensible and needed work within the cosmos. This 2nd law of thermodynamics renders all attempts of chemical evolution, no matter how fancy and intricate they sound, as flawed and impossible.

Summary
Non-living matter and non-living processes, including chemical reactions cannot therefore break the 2nd law of thermodynamics and so,

- express **intent** to create or communicate
- **ask questions** about what needs doing in an environment
- create code **as an answer** to those questions
- create and **calibrate** an environment, and create resources within that environment, which will specifically be used to process code
- write code with **pre-knowledge** and **intent** to enable the generation of a precision made molecular machines (proteins) to ensure known jobs done.

The forces of the natural world can only produce by-products, and by-products will not create constructed and calibrated environments. By-products lack structure and are by nature without complexity or

261

shape. Volcanic dust will not house anything. Lava will not craft a stable environment. By-products do not construct in any way. The 2nd law of thermodynamics ensures that this is the case.

Escaping Wipe-out

Copying the Information into another Creature

Reproduction, as we have said, is a way of information escaping the **aging process** as all things living around us are **subject to decay** – that is the 2nd law of thermodynamics. Decay and loss of order continually express themselves in the natural world. It is a clever mind that packages up information to keep those forces away from it and at the same time uses the raw materials of the natural world

- soil, water, sun, etc.
  - that in themselves have no intelligent crafted structure to them
- as fuels to ensure that the bodies that house the information are fed and nourished
  - in order for information to not only live on for a season but to fuel themselves to make a copy of their information (when creatures reproduce)
- and for that information to live on in a young, newly created creature that makes up part of what is called the 'next generation'.

Let's briefly look at this some more.

As we have already demonstrated there are different ways of storing information in the natural world, but it is always a temporary storage. So too the DNA information in the body of any living creature is only temporary. It is merely imprinted information; when a person or creature dies their body decays and all of the information in the DNA rots away. The DNA loses its shape and all that information is lost. As we've already seen, the 2nd law of thermodynamics means that information will be removed from the physical world as the environment increases entropy. All around us we see deterioration from complexity. We see a continual loss of information as species become extinct or as plants and animals continue to reproduce over the generations and copy errors in the code lead to mutations (none of which produce new technology). Along with this we see the weather and/or haphazard events of life work on the surroundings of the physical world to threaten and take away life. Life is continually pounded. For example, I could write in the sand on the seashore, as often as I wanted to, "Hello World." I could do it every single day on the beach. Every time, however, that the waves of the sea came back upon the shore, they would wash away those words. Every time the wind blew across the dry sand, those words would begin to deteriorate. This is the fate of all data/information that is temporarily imprinted into/onto the physical world. It will at some point be wiped out. Reproduction, therefore, is **_not_** *an attempt at...*

...*creating new information,*

but at

...*saving current* *information*

in the natural world. Here's a most important statement.

Reproduction is a **preservation** process, not a generation process!

So, whilst the information that is in the parents will one day be destroyed, reproduction will ensure that the overall information is kept from total decay and loss within the bodies of the children. So life on earth continually comes under fire. It is attacked by copy errors, disease, pollution, the weather and the ageing process. All around us we see an attempt to remove the data that is expressed in life. Attempts at keeping the information, through hereditary exchange (creatures reproducing) may produce variants of current information, but not new information. Evolutionists are deceived when they label 'new species' arising from long term isolated breeding and label it as information evolving within nature. All a new species is, is a family type, expressed in a slightly different way, that has enabled the next generation of that family of creatures to live on for yet another generation of time. That next generation, with their unique mix of their family's DNA code, lives on for another season to keep the essential coded data within them alive in a hostile cosmos.

An Explosion of Imprinted Information

This persistent and continuous movement away from complexity and towards loss of information in the natural world tells us that there was once a time when information (which makes up all life) was massively imprinted onto the natural world from an external source. The Cambrian explosion in the fossil record that we mentioned is an excellent example of this. For everything around us in the natural world to be in a state of loss of information with,

- no new information being created
- no new environments being constructed
- no new mechanisms being created
- no new information technologies being created

...due to the natural world not being able to bring about order by itself, this tells us that a huge information imprinting took place at one time in the past (which theists call 'creation'). It is so complex in its structure and nature that the imprinting had to be done by a super intelligence. Everything around us also now points to the fact that this information imprinting activity has now totally ceased – God rested or ceased from his creation work, (we're told in the Bible) and all we have now is an attempt at the preservation of that which was once imprinted onto the natural world.

The whole thing was invented and created at the same time and there haven't been any reinventions of it and no improvements made to it. There is absolutely no movement in the plant, insect or animal kingdoms to 'make this process better' because it cannot be made better. You cannot redevelop it and 'upgrade' it. There are no **mechanisms** in the natural world to change it and improve it. It cannot happen. All it can do is to seek to **retain its current integrity**. Life is clinging to the surface of this planet and fighting to survive the ageing process and the movements in the natural world. The forces of nature would remove life if it were not protected. If anything...

...life is devolving, not evolving.

It is a fact that we are losing information as a human race. Yes our diet may be getting better and with the invention of computers we are able to do more and more things. We're now able to retain knowledge and access it at will. We are getting technologically more advanced, but within our bodies we are not improving at all. The information within us and in the rest of life on this planet is in a constant fight to survive and maintain its integrity, not to reinvent and advance itself. All of this points to a time of imprinting onto the cosmos by an exterior mind. A onetime only purposeful activity that has come and gone and now we're left with the legacy of that work.

- -
There is so much more to say...
- -

We could have kept this chapter going forever. Sophisticated, mindboggling information is everywhere within living creatures and we could have looked at example upon example of impossible technology.

Butterfly Metamorphosis

The butterfly metamorphosis is an excellent illustration of a non-evolutionary step-by-step process. You cannot evolve the procedure of butterfly metamorphosis. Metamorphosis it too complex to develop stage by stage, it all had to be invented at the same time. This is because the butterfly life cycle requires the caterpillar to completely turn into a liquid whilst within its chrysalis, not many people know this. Once in this liquid state it is only the **pre-programmed** DNA within the creature that tells which bits of the 'goo caterpillar soup' to go off and turn into the body parts that eventually become the butterfly! Each bit of 'goo' forms correctly into what that particular bit of DNA tells it to become and at the same time connects perfectly with other bits of 'goo' that are changing into their own body parts and then it all fits together into one fantastic information highway that allows what once was a 'crawling grub' to take to the air, fly, and find a totally different food source from which to feed itself and then mate to pass its genes on the next generation. Caterpillars do not mate – butterflies do. Both have to be alive together, within the same generation, for the species to continue. No amount of 'happy accidents' will ever produce such an amazing spectacle! Yet this most wonderful and remarkable example of expert coding is still not the apex of '*information in motion*' when we look at the natural world!

DNA Storage

The way in which the information within us is stored is an amazing thing and beyond the scope of being random. If you were to fetch the DNA out of one of your cells and stretched it out from end to end it would be over six feet tall. That may sound surprising. However, if you were to take the entire DNA that is contained within the tens of trillions of cells that make up your body and put them end to end then the distance covered would take you to the sun and back many, many, times over. Don't forget it takes 10 minutes for light to travel from the sun to Earth. This shows us that there is an incredible level of sophistication in the way in which DNA is stored within us, let alone the complexity of the code itself.

The Human Brain

The brain of any creature is incredible. The apex of information, however, is found inside your head. You may not feel particularly intelligent, but the brain that enables your soul to take hold of the steering wheel and *drive your body through this world* is the most magnificent example of stunning engineering and information technology that you'll ever come across. We could look at the brain from many angles, statistics for example. Did you know that your brain processes 400 billion bits of information every second of the day? Without magnificent calibration in your brain, that amount of data flow would drive you and I mad. Our thinking would be so overwhelmed by the impact of these signals that we'd not be able to handle the processing that continually takes place for us to live and move. All the five senses are continually sending signals to the brain. Amazingly we are **only aware of a very small amount of that processing** within our consciousness. We're able to put all of that processing work into the background so that it ticks over without us even knowing that it's happening – which gives us the space to think and reason and to enjoy living. We don't have a continual headache, therefore, of the processing 'noise' going on within us. We're free from all of the hard work that our brains are constantly doing.

The brain's own activity is also amazing. Here's a quote from the website Basic Knowledge 101.
http://www.basicknowledge101.com/subjects/brain.html

"The Brain has 400 miles of Capillaries, 86 Billion Microscopic Neurons in constant Synaptic communication, making 10 quadrillion calculations every second. Each neuron is like a tiny branching tree, whose limbs reach out and touch other neurons making between 5,000 and 10,000 connections with other neurons, that's more than 500 trillion connections performing a dazzling array of complex mental processes every second, geared to generating and regulating our sensations and perceptions, how we reason, how we think, our emotions, our mental images, our attention span, learning, and our memory which is essentially a pattern of connections between neurons."

The more anyone understands the brain, the more it becomes clear that there is information engineering in us that is totally beyond our ability to create and programme or indeed beyond our imagination. It is impossible to create such a masterpiece of engineering, technology and information via an unguided and random process. Raw energy movements within a mindless, dead cosmos cannot build a brain.

Deep Learning
We could then take a look at deep learning, observing how the brain learns and processes information. We could look at the way in which computers and A.I. robots are making use of the same processes to solve complicated problems. Information can be used and processed in the most sophisticated of ways, and the human brain is the apex of that sophistication. This chapter, however, has to come to an end at some point. So here's where I'm going to draw the line and finish this part of it. I've said enough over the last chapters to show that our complexity and our relationship with data and information makes us stand out from the natural world as beings that simply cannot arrive from the cosmos by chance.

Electron Transport Chain
We could look at Electron Transport Chain where protons are pumped

out of the Mitochondria – the powerhouse of the cell. It is an impossible process to evolve. It is not buildable in a step-by-step process. Here's an excellent animation of the process.
https://www.youtube.com/watch?v=rdF3mnyS1p0

Once you understand what's involved, even the idea of us being here by a naturalistic and unguided process is ludicrous. A trillion, trillion years could not do it. The only reason why anyone would want to hold onto an evolutionary theory, when all of the evidence points to a super-intelligence behind life, is to retain a humanistic religious world view.

- -

Products and By-products

- -

Finally we need to talk about the difference between products and by-products, between the forces of the natural world and the activities within *constructed nature, i.e. life*. This topic, and the topic on the difference between the natural world and nature, will bring us to the end of this chapter and complete much of the evidence that's within this book.

A quick definition of Products and By-products
A Product
A product is something that is planned and purposefully made. It is crafted by a processing of raw materials, often using either tools or information or both, in a carefully constructed and calibrated environment.

The product is *crafted for purpose* so that it can **fulfil a job**. This **job fulfilment** role is crucial to understanding what a product is. Even a piece of art fulfils a role, to communicate something to the soul that is looking at it. On the whole, however, a product will have a usage within a certain environment. It will have something to communicate or something to manipulate or it will support a structure of some kind. It always has its **part to play**, whether for the purposes of industrial or domestic work or for entertainment. There is always a purpose to a product.

A product exists because it has been planned before being created.

A By-product

A by-product is something that is the 'result' of an event taking place, such as a volcanic eruption and an ash cloud being spewed out. As long as the event happens in roughly the same way, it will always give the same by-product, i.e. an ash cloud accompanies all volcanic eruptions. The by-product, however, is not purposed, planned or crafted. By-products are the mere result of energy movement such as chemical reactions. They are **not precision crafted** for a defined purpose. The 2nd law of thermodynamics ensures that this will always be the case. Chemical reactions, therefore, will never produce the circumstances whereby crafted products can be made, such as an RNA strand with a sensible code expressed within a known language or an environment that has machines within it that can take hold of data and process it.

Uses for by-products

Often we can get by-products when we are creating a product. An easy example to mention is sawdust. Sawdust appears each time you cut through wood. This by-product can be **made useful** if an **intelligent mind** picks it up and applies it carefully into an environment. So sawdust, if carefully applied within an environment by an intelligent mind,

- will enable a car stuck in the mud to get out of the mud because it gives the wheels grip
- will soak up spillages so that they can be swept away with a broom
- can be crafted into a product like a Firestarter

So by-products can be picked up and used effectively if there is a **process created** by which the by-product can be worked with. Volcanic ash falling on the ground can, after rotting down into the soil, be picked up by a plant's roots and be used to nourish the plant. This, however, is due to the plant already having technology/information built within it to accomplish that task. The volcanic ash will not, however, be a direct cause of information arising out of the cosmos.

There is a huge difference between ash being a fertilizer and ash creating information.

The Natural World and By-Products

The first thing to say is that,

*...the **forces** of the natural world only produce by-products.*

Here are a few examples.

1. Much rain on a hillside can produce a mud slide. Sloppy mud is a by-product of the soil becoming saturated with water. The sliding mud flow is not a precision made or crafted product with intent to fulfil a job.

2. A volcano will emit huge amounts of molten rock onto the surface of the earth. The resulting lava flow is a by-product of the volcano being active. All that the lava is, and all that it does as it reacts with its environment, is a by-product of volcanic activity. There is nothing crafted or purposed in the lava flow.

3. A wave of the sea coming up onto the shoreline produces only by-products. These by-products can be stones and pebbles that are smoothed over time or warn down into sand. There is no 'product' created by this activity. Sometimes wave patterns can be left behind in the sand but these patterns do not contain information, there is no language being used and no products fashioned for purpose by its activity, it is a by-product.

These are the workings of the forces within the natural world; we see them all around us all the time. These forces do not

- **gather** resources for purpose
- create components to be used in a later process
- create 'talk' between components for a purpose
- and they do not bring order out of chaos

Neither do the chemical reactions that take place via heat exchange etc. do any of the above. How do we know, therefore, that life, and specifically the complex DNA in the cell, does not arise from the forces in the natural world? Simply because DNA itself is crafted for purpose (written specifically with precision coding) so that it can actively produce intelligent products, not by-products. The processing of the DNA initiates a process that will create proteins. Each protein is programmed and crafted for purpose. It is there because of the...

...*unnatural* coding / programming

...that we find that DNA is made up of. A protein has a specific job to do. It is created at the end of a production line.

Production Lines and Products

A product is the direct result of a production line. There are always several stages in the creation of a product. Each stage is purposeful within the context of the final product being made.

> **IMPORTANT NOTE:** There are no precision made production lines amongst the forces of the natural world; not in the wind, the rain, fire, lightning or the storm nor within the chemical reactions of any of the movements that are expressed by raw energy in the cosmos!

There are no production lines in chemical reactions where items of resources are intelligently **selected and assembled for purpose**, like the amino acids are at the end of the protein creation process. Production lines are alien/foreign to the forces of the natural world. They do not exist; neither can any patterns of their existence or partial existence be found. No collecting, no assembling, no sorting, no crafting, no finishing. The forces found active around this planet and across the universe do none of these things. The universe is void of order of itself by the nature of the raw energy exchanges that are within it.

This tells us that the coding within DNA is also *foreign to the natural world.*

Pre-Written Predestination
What is even more important to note, however, is that DNA not only

does not follow the pattern of the natural world, it is a complete step away from the natural world. This is because these resources, these amino acids that are selected for purpose, have their identity and pre-assembly **pre-written** before they ever come into being. That is to say that their life and identity (as a collective set of amino acids forming a protein) is **pre-written** *into* the DNA code. How they are assembled, and therefore what they will be, is prophetically written by a coder who,

- knows what needs to be done in the cell
- knows what resources to get in order to produce what need doing
- knows the name of each amino acid – written in DNA language
- knows the place that each amino acid has to take in order for it to play its part in making up the structure of the protein
- knows what pre-assigned jobs that need to be done right across in the body and how the protein can fulfil those jobs

This pre-written behaviour is what we theologically call *predestination*!

The DNA code tells us that certain amino acids are predestined for purpose in the body. They will be selected, according to their properties and their physical makeup, and they will be assembled in a particular way for a purpose. The fullness of what their role (their life) is or will be, therefore, is prewritten before it comes into being. Before it happens, we know by looking at the gene what they will become and what they will do before the event actually happens. This is an astonishing thing to think about. The identity and the purpose of each protein is prewritten in the DNA code.

> **Note:** Let me get overtly religious here for a few moments, something that I've not done for most of this book. The only religious literature that writes in this style of predestination is the Bible, which talks about the life of the Christ in detail in the Old Testament before he is born – talking about who he will be, where he will be born, what his life means and the job

272

that he will accomplish via his death and resurrection. Predestination also spills over into the life of the Church and the calling and role of the Church. This theology of predestination is therefore also viewable in the programming of DNA. The pattern is the same! It's just another way in which the God of the Bible leaves his fingerprints on his creation as a sign of who he is and that he is responsible for that which we're looking at.

Before I jump too far ahead of myself, however, and start writing not my next book but my 'next but one book' which tackles this subject, it is now time to turn our attention specifically to show just how **unnatural** life is, that it does not naturally arise from what is called the 'forces of nature' or the 'natural world'.

The difference between the Natural World & Nature

They are Totally Unconnected
As we have seen, the forces in the natural world do not create products that are crafted and fashioned for purpose. The programming within life, however, does create such products. Proteins – microbiological sophisticated machines that are fit for purpose. So we're going to bring this chapter to its close by asking a very fundamental question which is,

"What is the difference between the natural world and nature?"

Our language in the West continually mixes them both up. It goes from one to the other as if they were the same, in fact they are not. The only reason why they are considered the same is because of the theory of evolution which seeks to link them together, which it still cannot do despite all of our advances in science. It is still not possible to produce life in a science laboratory. We have such sophisticated equipment and can create carefully controlled environments in order to produce the most unnatural and stable conditions, but even then we still can't artificially create life. No such link between the natural world and nature, therefore, has ever been made. Yet the talk of humanistic science continually mixes the forces of the natural world and nature together. Their behaviour, however, is absolutely different from each other. The natural world is dead. It is random and haphazard due to the raw energy that is continually expressed between its components, heat from the sun, heat from the Earth's lava flows from under the Earth's crust, wind that blows across the face of the mountains and seas, rivers that flow and rain that falls.. All these forces of nature are expressions of raw energy amongst the elements. They are all haphazard, dead and lifeless. Nature, however, is highly organised, sophisticated and programmed. Its programming allows it to live off the elements found in the natural world, to take advantage of them, to process them and use them for its own benefit and survival. That is their relationship. Humanists are desperate to forge another relationship between them, that the dead natural world gave rise to nature without any help from the divine. They wish to say that,

> *....life appeared*
> **from the resources** *of the natural world*
> **via the forces** *of the natural world.*

This link will never work, as we have seen over the last chapters. They are totally distinct because the resources of the natural world have been 'messed with' by the divine to imprint the information of life upon the cosmos. Without the divine touching the cosmos in this way, there is no life.

Clarifying the Differences between Nature and the Natural World

What is the criterion set that we can use to bring these distinctions into clear view? How can we expose the difference between the forces and elements that make up the natural world and the life that lives in the midst of those forces – which we call nature? So we need to ask the following questions. How do we strongly distinguish between,

1) A growing plant and a volcano?
2) An animal and the wind or the rain?

In the light of the above, here are just a few extra questions to consider, a guide us in our thinking, as we briefly open up this subject.

Looking at **nature** as something distinct from the forces and elements that make up **the natural world** we have to ask,

1. What determines its behaviour, its movements? Are they,
   a. driven by programming?
   b. or completely random based on energy transfer?
2. Does it **interact** with its environment or simply **impact** the environment?
   a. are its movements **random clashes** of energy where one substance impacts another?
   b. or does it **move/interact with purpose**, e.g. process foods to enable growth?
3. What does each produce? Does it produce
   a. a product?
   b. a by-product?
   c. or both?
4. Does it have purpose?
5. Does it do jobs?
6. Does it reproduce?
7. Does it have self-awareness?
8. Does it need sustaining in any way in order to 'keep its identity'?
9. Is everywhere 'its home' or can it be 'out of place' in such a way as to lose its substance? i.e. a cow in the desert without water is not in its calibrated 'home' and so dies. Wind, however, will 'blow anywhere' where there is air to move whether that be in a desert or over a ploughed field.

Here's a brief answer to those obvious questions.

The Forces and Substances that make up the Natural World
The forces in natural world are expressed through the many energy exchange 'collisions' of earth, air, fire and water. These movements of the wind, the rain, volcanic activity, lightning strike, earthquake, temperature change, etc. all have...

- no programming
- simply impacts the environment by its random movements
- only produces by-products
- moves around via energy influences without any guided purpose
- does not reproduce or perform constructive jobs
- does not need sustaining via 'food'
- has no 'home' via which it retains its identity
- removes information due to the nature of its haphazard movements

The natural world, therefore, is dead. Dead things to not **auto**-organise themselves into life, even if raw energy is added to them. Dead things rot away, lose information, and simply become part of the chaos that the universe is continually moving towards.

The Nature of Nature
Here's a really important statement.

> *Nature is **not natural**. It is once lifeless material that has been **gathered, moulded, crafted** and **constructed** with **purpose**. It has coded information **imprinted** onto it, at its heart, and that information is housed in a **constructed** and **calibrated** environment. Resources have been added to that environment so that they can process the information in order to **initiate change** and so produce **fashioned** and **purpose** built machines to aid in nature's survival.*

Nature is made up of what we call 'living' material. It is living because it,

- has purpose to maintain its complexity and its internal organisation via,
  - locating and taking food into itself to sustain itself

276

- o performing jobs within itself in order to maintain its wellbeing
  - holds data within itself for the fulfilment of those jobs
  - uses processed information to create and craft precision machines
- reproduces itself
  - o is able to copy cells whilst retaining its information
  - o is able to combine a sperm and an egg to form a new 'young' creature where the information is kept safe for another generation
- has self-awareness, at least at the programming level which shows 'what needs to be done' in order for the body of the plant/creature to function

The natural world does not behave like this. The natural world 'removes information', it does not create information or add to it. It is **not a leap** from the natural world to nature. It is not a **process to follow** from the natural world to nature. Just as **computer code** *cannot arise* from the **physical cabling** in a robot, so too life (nature) cannot arise from the dead forces and elements of this planet.

So when we look at nature, what are the behaviours that we see? It is life, **using** non-life, to sustain itself. The patterns of the natural world and the patterns of nature are quite different. That which each 'produces' for example, are totally different.

Nature, for example, produces products that are **not natural** to the *forces of nature* as they are:

- full of information
- crafted with intent
- fashioned and designed with purpose
- there to fulfil a specific job within an environment
- guided by carefully controlled movements of energy when a product is created
- multi-part and multi-dependent in their constructions of machine based outputs
- information processed through specific procedures

- created for the retention of information

The Volcano and the Factory Illustration

To help us look at these things let's use an illustration. What's the difference between a volcano and an industrial steel factory? These environments are totally different. The volcano represents the behaviours of the natural world and the steel factory represents the behaviour of nature, i.e. life.

The Volcano

The first environment, the volcano, is part of the natural world. We get an opening in the earth's crust and lava spews out. Over time, as more volcanic eruptions take place, the volcano becomes a mountain. All it does, however, each time the volcano erupts, is to produce by-products. The gases, the lava, the ash, the movements in the earth, they are all by-products, none of them crafted for purpose, none of them carry **intent** at the heart of the reason for their existence, they're just a chemical result of unguided and random explosive energy.

The Steel Factory

This environment is a made up of a constructed and crafted set of rooms, each with specific and specialised resources within it. The resources either provide spaces for jobs to be done or are directly involved in the processing of materials for jobs to be achieved. All the jobs within the factory are carefully thought through within the context of,

- how the environment works together
- which end products are to be fashioned

There is a sensible, **logical information work flow** that reveals planning and design in the crafting of the products. Like a volcano there is great heat produced within the walls of the factory, but this heat is guided and controlled at every stage of its existence. The factory needs power to make it work and it needs machines to fulfil its 'job list'. This job list can only be fulfilled by those machines following **set procedures** and **rules**. The factory's layout, therefore, and those who work in it, are subject to an imprinted knowledge from a designer who understands how the environment and its resources should work together in the light of the products that need to be fashioned and made. The complex and interdependent processes that we see at work tell us that a designer has constructed and calibrated the environment with **intent** so that a clear information flow around the factory floor enables the creation of precision products and at the same time the life of the factory is maintained in an orderly manner.

You can see clearly the difference between a volcano and a factory. Once this way of seeing the world is in your head then you can never see your lawn in your back garden in the same light ever again. When I sit in my back garden and look at the green grass or look at the plants and the surrounding trees, I see information **imprinted onto** the cosmos. It is an amazing thing called 'life' which is not part of the natural world. It clings to the surface of the natural world, uses the resources of the natural world, and from those resources of sunshine, rain, wind, earth etc. it continually fights to stay alive and to reproduce itself. My back lawn is not natural. It is imprinted material, imposed onto the cosmos via an external mind which we collectively call, 'nature'.

The last thing that 'nature' is, is natural.

Conclusion

You cannot have a sophisticated 'nature' arising from an unsophisticated 'natural world' via unsophisticated random events. They are separate.

*You cannot move from an environment that **only produces by-products** to an environment that uses information and a variety of agents to fashion and craft precision products with purpose.*

That movement cannot be facilitated, organised and assembled via random and unguided processes, especially when those random and unguided processes do nothing but remove information from the cosmos. Nor can you use such an environment to house chemical reactions to generate life. The movement from the natural world to nature, therefore, is impossible!

*Random and unguided processes that remove information cannot be used as the **agents of intelligent change** to construct information or construct the environment that is needed to process information to start and sustain life and get it all working together as a unified unit.*

Life has information at its centre, at its heart, and so life cannot naturally arise from non-life. The forces of that natural world will always prevent this from happening.

Chapter 10 – Making the Unbelievable Appear Believable

A Book Summary

Pulling it all Together

In this short chapter I'm going to summarise all that I've said so far and also pick out of each chapter that I revisit how evolutionists use their arguments and theories **to make the unbelievable appear believable**. Then I'm going to outline in more detail an illustration that I've already been visiting throughout the book.

I remember my dad recently commenting on this subject of the impossibility of evolution. He said,

> *"If it's impossible, then it's impossible.*
> *If it's impossible after one year then it will*
> *still be impossible after a million years."*

What he meant was this. You can't make something possible simply by adding time. Adding time to something simply means that there's been **a longer period of time in which to observe the fact that the impossible can never happen!** Millions of years, however, represent a time scale that cannot be imagined or observed by the human mind. We know what ten years looks like, simply because most people have lived ten years. One hundred years is understandable because we can talk to the older generations about their grandparent's lives. We can trace history through books or through the observation of paintings and other art that depict culture and civilisation for thousands of years. However, getting your head around millions of years is too difficult for the human mind to comprehend. We easily talk about millions of years, the words quickly roll off the tongue in conversation, but to cast your mind over that amount of time so that you can '*see it all*' and '*take it all in*' is impossible. Millions and billions of years become almost fantastical. Through the mystery of such incomprehensible time, evolutionists are able to justify things that you can't quite see or imagine. Within such a huge and incomprehensible timescale, people just accept that things 'happened' because 'deep time' has made it possible. So what humanism is doing, when it is proclaiming its theory that everything evolved over billions of years, is…

…*clothing* the impossible with the **unimaginable**.

It says that the impossible, that is the bringing of order, complexity and interdependent design out of chaos via a random and unguided process, suddenly becomes possible because we *clothe* it in the **unimaginable**, that is of billions of years, and because we can't imagine billions of years, or watch the step-by-step processes of evolutionary change unfold during that time, then somehow, by using the phrases 'small changes' and 'it evolved' or 'it mutated' or 'happy accidents' and adding those phrases to billions of years, then we can somehow believe in the construction of that which is impossible because we clothe it in the unimaginable. Using that combination of 'deep time' (billions of years) and phrases like 'it evolved' or 'it mutated' then something magical or miraculous happens within that timeframe. A half built creature with half formed new limbs is not looked at in fine detail to see if it works or not. Why? Simply because that part of the process is 'lost in the mist of millions or billions of years' and we cannot look at the creature until it **comes out the other side of evolution** showing itself to be the 'fully evolved' creature that it now is. We'll look at this at the end of this chapter where I will outline a couple of final illustrations to pull everything together. Firstly, however, here's an overview of the book so far.

Chapter 1 – Getting Started
Here are the main themes covered by chapter 1.

- Who Owns Science?
- The World View Question
- My Focus
- Two Specific Language Problems
- Mechanism & Evidence
- Where Science & Religion Meet

I started off by asking the question, "Who owns science?" I looked at the fact that so many people have seen science as secular and separate from religion. I stated that the assumptions of many people today is that it is sensible to think that we can be here without God; that the complexities of life that we see all round us within the universe can be explained (and have been sensibly explained) by the many scientific theories that we are all currently familiar with. Secular science is seen by so many people as the only viable theory to explain our existence. I then went on to say that life is multi-complex and interdependent. I cited a quick example of how a baby makes its own blood. For a baby to be kept safe and for it to still make its own blood it needs the following in place,

- a placenta to keep it safe from the mother's blood
- a transthyretin protein that is programmed to fetch and retrieve the haemoglobin which contains iron

I followed this up with talk about how the theories of evolution do not deal with the step-by-step process of how multi-complex organisms came into being. Instead they talk in broad terms, punctuated with general phrases, which enables their theories to stay appealing to the masses.

We then looked at 'world view' and saw that everyone has a religious backdrop to their thinking to help them make sense of life. If your religious convictions are, 'there is no God' then when you come to look at anything in science you'll always have a mind-set that asks this question,

*What are the **natural processes** which have **caused** that which I am currently observing to be in the form that it currently is?*

I stated that his/her mind-set will direct a humanist's reasoning away from the possibility of seeing the work of the divine in the world and will always cause him/her to look for a natural event to be the reason for everything being as it is. It's like wearing a pair of blinkers that keeps a person from seeing a broader perspective. I then illustrated that a theist could look at exactly **the same physical**

evidence and see that this points to God, not to a natural set of processes that stem back to a 'Big Bang' at the start of time and space.

I then outlined that I would be examining the mechanisms that evolutionists lean upon to present their theory to see if they could possibly be viable agents of evolutionary change. I then said that I would be looking at these mechanisms from the specific angle of 'information creation' to see if life really could evolve. I also outlined that there were four specific language problems for me to deal with.

1. The confusion between UPWARDS evolution and sideways change.
2. The confusion between data and information.
3. The confusion between data expression change and new information.
4. Confusion via the misapplication of the word evolution.

I said that we see adaptation all of the time but adaptation is not evidence for UPWARDS evolution. I also said that evolutionists see **data change** as **new information**, which it is not.

I then went on to say that mechanism and evidence drive science, not theory. If the mechanism cannot be proved by the evidence, then the theory is useless – no matter how many **other interesting observations** can be made about the subject. I then said that if there is no mechanism for naturalism then the only alternative is to look for a creator. I made the statement that,

> *It is part of the true calling of science*
> *to **find the divine**,*
> *not to direct our thinking*
> *away from God.*

I posed some questions about life from non-life mechanisms about how auto-organisation is said to have taken place. I then said,

*You cannot put **supposed extra evidence and imaginary ideas** above the mechanism and the practical engineering!*

So if the engineering at the microbiological level does not work, no amount of other interesting ideas, theories or fantasy thinking will justify holding onto the initial theory.

So chapter 1 outlines for us the main reasons why evolutionists make the unbelievable believable.

1) **The perception of the general public is that,**
   - secular thinking is rooted in science but religious thinking is not
   - as God is not necessary, all life can be explained by processes
   - the complexities of life are explainable by multiple theories
   - on the whole the practicalities of those impossible complexities are not fully understood, i.e. people just don't know how impossible it is for the interdependent organisms that make up life to evolve in a step-by-step process
   - language problems – the misrepresentation of sideways adaptation for UPWARDS evolution and the talk about data and information as if they are the same thing, bring about an added layer of confusion to the subject

2) **The results of this thinking is that,**
   - the same evidence that points to God is misinterpreted
   - where those complex organisms are impossible to be evolved into existence, due to their complexity, the humanist gets around this by using general phrases like 'it mutated' etc.
   - the root problem of an un-evolvable organism or process is therefore not exposed and people are not given the opportunity to think about God
   - mechanisms that do not work are misrepresented by language problems that make them sound as if they do work
   - even though a mechanism may **not** work in practice, the world view of the person keeps the theory of evolution in place in their thinking, i.e. as there is 'no God' – then there

has to be a process to explain everything, so we stay with a process based science rather than one that points to the divine

3) **The results of the above is that,**
- evolutionary theory in our general education systems and TV programmes continues to drive science rather than mechanisms that point to God
- the general populace is not free to think clearly on the subject

Chapter 2 – To Evolve or Not To Evolve?

Here are the main themes covered by chapter 2.

- Biogenesis from Many Sources
- The Theory of Evolution – how we got here
- Criticisms of Darwin's Basic Mechanism
- Hindrances to the Mutation Mechanism
- An Example of Evolutionary Propaganda

I began this chapter by saying that many scientists today no longer hold to the theory of evolution – the evolutionary tree of life is rejected. I then said that I would outline the mechanisms for evolutionary theory, which are,

- information, DNA, is at the heart of life and determines our characteristics
- a DNA mix takes place whenever creatures have offspring
- mutations happen within the DNA code
- natural selection takes some creatures out of the environment if they don't fit it as well as others and so the DNA within them fails to get passed on to the next generation
- all of these influences combined together change the DNA and are the drivers for evolutionary change and together they are responsible for all of the variety of life that we see around us in the world today

I then criticised the mechanisms by saying that,

- DNA mix (when creatures breed) will only produce sideways shuffles in the DNA code, not new code for new body parts for UPWARDS evolutionary change
- mutation is better called 'copy error' and copy errors do not write sensible new code for UPWARDS evolutionary change
- natural selection only removes DNA from the gene pool and therefore no new information is written/created for UPWARDS evolutionary change

I then looked at the misuse of the phrase 'new species' whereby evolutionists call a sideways shift within a family group a 'new species'; lions, tigers, cheetahs, jaguars, leopards, within the cat family or Darwin's finches or John Cleese's Lemurs etc. Then evolutionists use exactly the same phrase when talking about a supposed UPWARDS movement whereby it is believed, by faith, that sideways animal shifts have the ability to move a creature UPWARDS into a new creature type – a frog into a bird. The phrase 'new species' is used in exactly the same way in both instances.

One is proved, however, and the other is not! The problem is that the phrases are equally used...

...as if one is as true as the other.

"Look, we have a new species of fish," an evolutionist will say. This movement of a new type of fish appearing through a sideways shift is presented as direct evidence for UPWARDS evolution. This misuse of language is a deception for those listening to the evolutionist's conversation on the subject.

We said that an evolutionist sees this sideways shift (which it calls a new species) as,

- **a new expression**
- of an *ever moving* creature
- *away from its own kind*

whereas in reality it is,

- **a new expression**
- of an *established* creature
- **within its own kind**

and so we see that different family groups are established by family shifts but none of those new family groups represent a break away from the kind of creature that they all are, i.e. cats in the cat family, birds in the bird family etc.

So the unestablished assumption of the evolutionist is that all creatures are 'ever moving' UPWARDS towards a new creature. All the creatures we currently see within their family groups are only temporary in their biological make-up, they are all steadily moving away from that family group towards something new.

> *This is an **unproven assumption** BUT it is **not portrayed** as an assumption – it is spoken about **as if it is a fact**.*

Neither is the correct interpretation, that each family group is in fact an established unmovable biological group, shared within our education system to enable people to think in an alternative way when seeing the world. So this way of seeing the evidence, that sideways movements within a set family group ONLY produces 'different kinds of creatures within their own unmoveable family', is not offered up to the general population as an alternative way of thinking. This is because it would completely undo the theory of evolution.

So people are kept from thinking in a certain direction by a rhetoric that says, "All creatures are moving UPWARDS," (which is totally unproven) rather than the fact of the matter which is, "All creatures are moving sideways." The way in which it does this is to use the phrase, 'new species' interchangeably between the two as if they are the same thing. Sideways shift, therefore, is made to be the same as UPWARDS evolution. One is made out to be as true as the other.

Chapter 3 – Taking the Conversation Elsewhere

Here are the main themes covered by chapter 3.

- Common Ancestry
- The Problem of Homology
- Integrated Technologies & Processes
- The Fossil Record
- Basic Evolutionary Assumptions

The next chapter continued this theme of how humanism makes the unbelievable believable by introducing the statement,

...the conversation is taking place at the wrong level.

By this I meant that the evidence for our supposed link to the animal kingdom moves away from the mechanisms at the microbiological level (where DNA mix, mutation and natural selection fail to give us new information for new body parts) and the conversation now moves to shared technology. So we are looking at life using the lens of the human eye and not the lens of a microscope. We've lost the fine-detailed evidence, **moved away from the mechanisms of actual change** and are now looking 'in the wrong place' for the real evidence that underpins life. As I said near the start of this book, if the mechanisms for change do not work then it doesn't matter how many other 'evidences' are put forward, the theory is false!

Again it is easy to see the religious influence of the secular world view at work. Rather than concluding that shared technologies point to a creator who used the same/similar engineering to put together His creation, we continually hear deductions from the religious assumption that 'there is no God' and therefore **a process is responsible** for putting us together – so 'shared technology' is naturally concluded as evidence for evolution, not deity. Through the active promotion of looking at and interpreting shared technology and shared engineering from this viewpoint, evolutionists can ignore the fact that the real mechanisms for change at the microbiological level do not work and move the conversation to point towards a so called common ancestry.

NOTE: It's a little bit like walking into a room full of different sized robots all of which have their own jobs to do within a specific environment. Each robot will have shared technology and unique technology. An evolutionist would say that these evolved from each other as they have shared components and a shared operating system. A theist would say that, despite that fact that all of these robots have commonality between them, each is the work of a designer who put them together for a purpose and there are no mechanisms to justify the evolutionist's position that one came from another.

I then looked at the similarities of the bones of a frog with those of humanity. In a frog's front limbs are bones called the humerus, the radius and the ulna – just like those in humans. Then I said,

*If one thing came from another then that which had been 'established so far' by this so called evolutionary process would be **retained and built upon** to be made more complex.*

I outlined the problem of ontogenesis. Ontogenesis is the development of an organism from its earliest stage through to maturity. So yes, according to the eye, a human hand and a frog's 'hand' are similar. The problem, however, lies in **the way in which they develop** from their embryonic stage to find their final shape. If we had evolved from each other then...

*...the programming that makes all living creatures **take their form**, as they develop in the womb or change from a tadpole into a frog, would basically follow the **same <u>pattern of execution</u>**.*

I showed how the programming that causes a frog's front toes to appear and the programming that causes a child's fingers to appear in the womb are two totally different things. There is no evolutionary continuation at the microbiological level. This logical conclusion has already been thought about by evolutionists who have spent a good amount of time trying to find evidence to prove continuity, which they still can't find. So the question is, "How did the evolutionists keep us believing that the unbelievable is believable?" Simply through Haeckel's fraudulent drawings that suggested the very opposite of reality. Even though the ontogenesis problem is huge for evolutionists and it is quite conclusive at the microbiological level that one thing did not evolve from the other, the very place where there is a major problem has been turned to their advantage by a blatant lie.

Then I talked about the problem of integrated technologies; their impossible auto assembly and irreducible complexity. I briefly mentioned examples such as the technology of flight for birds and that of sonar, called echolocation, in the dolphin and the metamorphosis undertaken by a butterfly. Half way constructions on all these technologies are an engineering impossibility. Again the way that evolutionists get around this is simply not to go there in their conversations, if they can help it, so as not to draw attention to the flaws in their theories. There is no attempt at showing how a caterpillar evolved metamorphosis, to show how a half evolved process was beneficial to the species.

I outlined the fossil record and the claims for transitional fossils and the Cambrian explosion. I said that despite the fact that real transitional fossils do not exist, along with the fact that the ones that had been heralded in the past as truly transitional have been proved to be false, the idea still persists that there are lots of transitional fossils for us to observe. This is due to the use of sideways adaptation fossils being classed as evidence for UPWARDS change. It is the same lie all over again, just represented this time within the fossil record. Even though the Cambrian explosion talks to us of creation, which it is, the conversation is moved away from this to sideways shift change within a species and the fossil remains of these shifts is again presented as genuine evidence for evolution.

The end of this chapter listed the many **unproven** assumptions that evolutionists make behind their arguments to justify their theory. These assumptions hide the flaws in their thinking. Without the ability to think critically, many people blindly accept them and they therefore go unchallenged.

Chapter 4 – It's Life Jim…

Here are the main themes covered by chapter 4.

- Initial Questions
- The Complexity of the Cell
- The Incredibly Busy Life in the Cell
- The Cell – How it works

I said in this chapter that the DNA that drives life is incredibly complex. Even more complex, however, is the cell's structure. The cell is far more complex than the average person thinks. I posed questions about,

- the placement of the cell's resources within it
- the processing techniques that are established there

…and asked how these intricate mechanisms of life were able to be brought about by random and unguided processes.

I then quoted from various sources showing the complexity of the cell, which compared the cell to a most complicated and interdependent factory/city where there are so many parts, packages and components that you cannot trace and keep track of them. I then said that you cannot have a starting point for this factory's logical assembly, to build it in a step-by-step process from a simple format.

Three billion units of DNA go into the DNA that is found in the average human cell, called a eukaryotic cell. I quoted Michael Behe's work on the bacterial flagellum, which is a multi-part, complex rotary motor machine that exists and works within the cell. It has been labelled the most efficient machine in the universe and only works once nearly 40 separate protein machines are correctly assembled together. We then looked at a phrase that Michael Behe gave to the flagellum which is 'irreducible complexity'. This means that you cannot reduce the complex object that you are looking at without it breaking and becoming pointless. Then I quoted a film saying that Darwin himself admitted that…

*"...if someone identified a biological system that could not have been **constructed in <u>incremental steps</u>** over long periods of time then his theory would be invalid."*

I looked at how the cell works and focussed on the role of proteins. These proteins are fitted for purpose within the cell and play very specific roles according to their shapes which were created by the programming within the DNA. I pointed out that there is a two stage process to turn the DNA code into a protein and that each stage of the process happens within a different room within the cell with specific resources available to it to complete the task. I explained in a little more detail how the processes of transcription and translation work in order to create a protein – all parts of the process being necessary for it to happen correctly so that the original DNA code can be read/processed in order for the protein to be created.

I then made the brief statement that the forces of the natural world do not make products, they make by-products. A product is something that is fashioned for purposeful use – such as a protein; chemical reactions do not create environments for products. I then outlined one more basic question about which came first, DNA or the cell? The cell does not work without DNA and DNA is useless outside of the cell. Both have to appear together, in their highly sophisticated and calibrated state, at the same time.

Chapter 5 – The Theories of Cell Creation
Here are the main themes covered by chapter 5.

- THEORY 1 - A Single Protein Forming by Chance
- THEORY 2 - The RNA World Hypothesis
- Criticisms of the RNA Hypothesis

So how do evolutionists make the unbelievable believable? They have two theories about cell creation; a single protein coming together by chance and the RNA World hypothesis.

I looked at the theory that a single protein could come together by chance and we saw that the odds against even one short protein string coming together are unbelievable. As there are around 20 different types of amino acids to choose from, getting the right order is a 1:20 each time which brings about an unimaginable number of wrong options to choose from. Even if a miracle of science happened then you would only have a single protein and proteins do not build cells.

Then we looked at the RNA World Hypothesis and saw that again most of the phrases used were inaccurate. We were told by the video that RNA can,

- store information
- perform various functions so that the cell is kept alive

Both of these statements are false. It also said that the RNA was self-replicating and via this multiplication process was able to evolve its code to become 'stable' and 'mature'. It puts this down to...

*"...trillions of tiny steps and **happy accidents**."*

Then it added these words about RNA Messenger strands,

*"**Today** they can **slice, dice, catalyse, build, destroy, code, replicate** and **transform**; a remarkable diversity from the simplest of beginnings, a single self-replicating RNA molecule."*

Let's make it clear that 'today' the RNA strand does none of those things. They are all done by proteins which work on the DNA ladder to create the RNA strand and to prepare it for the ribosome factory which then creates the protein. The RNA Messenger strand is a passive object. It is worked upon by the environment around it whilst it just sits there, totally inert and without any self-initiated activity of its own.

We also have the problem that evolutionists think that 'bad code' can be turned into 'good code' over a long period of time and that RNA strands could survive as 'bad code' within the environment and duplicate themselves and, at the same time, refine their bad code. They say that this can be done through that very same duplication process whilst being 'worked upon' by the environment with 'competition' and 'time' being added into the cauldron of life. A little verbal 'stirring' and we are expected to believe this fantasy message that code can become more complex without a person having to write it! Again, the conversation is, therefore, steered away from the fact that the DNA inside the simplest of cells is ridiculously complex and the theory presents a fantasy idea for people to believe in.

So the religious word view of evolutionists is adhered to by saying that time, the environment and reproduction, is responsible for code that is beyond our imagination. It also assigns attributes to the RNA strand that it cannot even begin to do today. All of which is not true.

Chapter 6 – It's Data Jim…
Here are the main themes covered by chapter 6.

- Introducing Data
- A Definition of Data
- Data in the Computer World
- Data, by itself, is Useless
- Data Becomes Meaningful on the Move
- Data in the Cell
- Final Conclusions on Data

I made this very important analogy about the cell,

1. Data acts as **the basis** for life in the cell.
2. Code is the **expression of intent** for life in the cell.
3. Information flow **actively facilitates** the life of the cell.

I looked at data and defined it as "recognisable characters – set in a sequential order." I made the point that if the characters were not recognisable then they were not data. This is because language comes before data. Where there is data there is intelligence. After looking at data in a PC, so that we could understand it more, we looked at data in the cell. Then we made the point that data, by itself and of itself is useless. Data, in order to be made useful, has to be empowered from outside of itself!

Then I said that data is only useful if it is **on the move**, i.e. it is processed in some way. I said that a 'handshake' has to take place between the different objects that are passing the data between them, that is, they have to understand the same language or have to be able to translate the language that the data is written in to another language that can be used by the second handler of the data. I also said that data has to be precise to work and that data is used for making products, not by-products. I then reminded us that the natural forces of nature only make by-products, not products fashioned for purpose.

I also made the point that,

*It is the environment that **uses data**,*
*NOT data that **shapes the environment**!*
The environment is intelligently prepared first,
and then the data is placed within it.

So how do evolutionists go about making the unbelievable believable in the light of the above information? Simply by **not going there** in their conversations. Just break the laws of information theory and hope that no-one notices. Talk about data as if it can be self-replicating and as if it can come out of chemical reactions and pretend that a mind does not have to be behind its existence. Data, to the evolutionist, is a 'play thing' that can be moulded from nothing into usefulness by chance chemical reactions. Nothing could be further from the truth.

To have such a view denies the very definition of what data is. A mind has to create data. It has to be sequential and expressed within a known language. It is also useless, and therefore powerless to effect change, unless it is actively worked on by its environment. The environment has to have the right components within it to 'take hold' of data' and make it useful. Data is passive, not active. It will not self-initiate anything, all of which evolutionists ignore in their theories.

Chapter 7 – It's Information Jim…
Here are the main themes covered by chapter 7.

- Starting with Code
- A Working Definition of Information
- The Environment and the Code
- The Contextual Question of Information
- The Nature of Information
- The Personality Behind the Code

I began this section by defining code.

> *Code is the <u>intelligent assembling</u> of data in a **very specific order** where the data characters <u>together</u> **corporately express purpose** and **intent**.*

I said that code by definition, therefore, could not be random – as the evolutionists say when they talk about code evolving. Randomness also does not work towards a goal with intent for specific work to be done. Every code writer knows that they want to have a **final output** from their coding, they **intend** for something to happen at the end of the processing procedure. So here's another way of looking at code,

> *Purpose* and *intent* to produce an *output*, expressed in the language of data, is the *reason* for code!

If data is impossible to manufacture from the activities of the forces of the natural world then code multiplies that impossibility many times over. Code is the **intelligent assembly of that data**, with **intent** to **create** or **communicate**, and that is a quantum leap in difficulty compared with data. In code,

...something has to be
imagined to happen...

> Without that imagination seeking to create
> **something that is *not yet* realised**,
> there is no reason for the code in the first place.

I outlined that information is one step up from code. I said that,

Information is coding, made up of
precision data, which is processed
within a given context.

It is the processing and the context that makes information what it is. Information is there to communicate something or to do something or both. I then said,

*It is the **act** of data **moving** and*
being processed** within a **specific context
that turns coded data into information.

I gave the examples of the telephone exchange and entering a password into a computer to gain access. The processing of the information ensures that a job is done, whether to communicate something or to get something done. I also said that the environment and the code needed to be in place at the same time for the information to work. I then said that evolution **cannot match these two together**. There is no intelligence in evolution to achieve this. This is yet another layer of difficulty for the evolutionist. This is why evolutionists are always wrong. There needs to be,

- language to express the data
- precision data to write to code
- imagined work to be achieved to give meaning to the code
- an environment that can read the code

- extra agents, within the environment, that aid in the processing of the code
- **an environment that, once the code has been processed, has the resources available to respond to the code's instructions and do the job that the code wants doing**

I then concluded that DNA inside the cell is part of an interdependent and irreducible process that cannot be evolved! I said that, data cannot auto-organise itself into information.

Data cannot have self-knowledge about itself and construct an environment via which to process itself. Data does not have a mind of its own.

I then said that code always speaks beyond itself. Code is the answer to a question. A discussion has taken place about a solution to a problem in order for code to exist. We see that there is pre-knowledge of,

- the environment
- the problem
- the solution

...and the code is the answer. I then said,

*When a protein does its job, then the answer to the question is **expressed**!*

I then looked at the nature of information and said that information has no mass and no relationship to energy. Giving examples of,

- writing in the sand
- concrete and chiselling
- paper and ink
- jelly and moulds
- sticks assembled in a pattern

I illustrated this point over and over again. So as information has no mass or relationship with energy we see that the origins of information can only be something that is,

...*imprinted* onto the cosmos via an external mind.

So, in the light of all of the above, how do evolutionists make the unbelievable appear as believable? How do they get around all the impossible examples that I've just mentioned. Well, simply in two ways.

1) They don't go there in their conversations
2) They talk about 'mother nature' rather than God!

I then said,

Biological technology, where intelligent intent is needed to design and create it, is relegated to 'nature' just '*doing her stuff*'.

She has done it, we don't know how, but *she* simply has and isn't it amazing. What a gal! So we have personality behind the technology that is verbally set into 'someone' who is a 'mother' who will always be on your side and won't lay claim to 'your life' rather than to God to whom we are accountable. Once again a religious world view takes over and robs us of a proper definition of that which we're looking at! The, '**Anything but God Society**' takes its stand and twists the language that we should be using and creates a 'lesser deity' to whom we can look who will give us a reason for why things are as they are. God still does not get a look in.

Chapter 8 – Data Expression Change
Here are the main themes covered by chapter 8.

- Data Expression Change is NOT New Information!
- Data Expression Change in a Web Page
- The Bigger Question

This next section brings together the false labelling that we looked at about sideways shifts being called 'a new species' and the same thing happening again with data expression change being labelled as so-called 'new information'.

I started off by saying that foundational coding forms the body parts of every creature. There is foundational coding in every different type of creature, the cat family for example. All cats will have the same foundational DNA that determines 'cat shape' and 'cat technology'. The sideways shifts within the species are caused by **data expressions** within the coding changing. Data expression change will make the difference between a cat **expressed** as a <u>lion</u> and a cat **expressed** as a <u>leopard</u>. Both are fully cat, both are a different kind of cat. Data expression change has not altered the basic code that gives them cat mannerisms and cat shape. Yet there is enough of a change between them for the expressions of that basic code to show that they are no longer compatible with each other.

> *However, no new information is there that*
> *is not '**cat code**'.*

There is no upwards movement taking place that will change either of them from being a 'cat'.

These sideways movements happen all of the time. So...

> *...these adjustments in the data are*
> *not new information,*
> *just **changes** in the **expression***
> *of the **current coding***
> *without changing the*
> *<u>foundational coded information</u>*
> *that makes the creature what it is.*

Then I said,

This adaptation that takes place in the environment happens due to the established coded data being **tweaked**, not the foundational code that defines what the creature is being **changed**. All of these sideways movements into what evolutionists call a 'new species' (which theists call a 'new kind within a family group') are achieved by data expression change. Data expression change takes the code **that is already there** and provides a **sideways** movement within it for the animal that **tweaks the data** to adapt the animal to its environment. Tweaking is not new foundational code for new body parts or for new animal behaviours or for a new flesh type. Tweaking is evidence for adaptation, not evolution. It is this very place where evolutionists misrepresent the truth and twist reality.

Then I used an example of data expression change by looking at very simple coding that makes a web page. I showed that a small **tweak** in the code could change the background colour of the page from white to yellow. No new information, however, has been added to the code; just a tweak that changes the expression of the page from white to yellow. I then said that mutation will never cause the writing of more complex code. The nature of code is that copy errors will take away the integrity of the code, not add sophistication to it for new body parts. I also said that 'bird questions' have been asked and answered within the coding of the bird, e.g. flight and the laws of aerodynamics.

These questions cannot be answered by sideways shifts within a frog!

I said that the code within us all is devolving and not evolving. Life is fighting to survive and maintain its place and its internal integrity rather than 'advancing itself' to new levels of sophistication.

So, how do evolutionists make the unbelievable appear believable? Simply by stating that data expression change that causes sideways shifts in a creature's DNA is new information. It is a blatant misrepresentation of the facts.

Chapter 9 – It's Impossible Jim!

Here are the main themes covered by chapter 9.

- The Second Law of Thermodynamics
- Escaping Wipe-out
- There is so much more...
- Products and By-products
- Differences between the Natural World & Nature

I began this section by saying that the second law of thermodynamics dictates that everything in our universe is on a continual movement towards randomness, which in the world of information means chaos and data loss. I said that this would eventually lead to,

...the total loss of life and the removal of all information from the cosmos.

I stated that the humanist creation story starts with chaos and moves towards even greater chaos. Therefore the random and unguided movements of raw energy that are within the cosmos do not have the capacity to bring about order or complexity or data or code or interdependent design or construct the contexts for the code to become information. The humanist creation story breaks the laws of science. The universe is therefore naturally hostile to life. I then said that nothing within the universe could of itself and by itself,

- express intent to create or communicate
- ask questions about what needs doing in an environment
- create code as an answer to those questions
- create and calibrate an environment, and create resources within that environment, which will specifically be used to process code
- write code with pre-knowledge and intent to enable the generation of a precision made molecular machines (proteins) to ensure known jobs done.

I said that life is continually escaping wipe-out rather than growing in evolutionary momentum.

Reproduction is a **preservation** process, *not a generation process!*

I said that the only reason why we have life on this planet is that there must have been at one time an explosion of imprinted information, purposefully put here by an extremely intelligent mind who was able to take non-living matter and impose life onto it. I said that this had to be the case. I made the point that nature and the natural world are totally different.

Nature is imprinted life onto the cosmos. The forces of the natural world (the movements of wind, rain, fire, chemical reactions, etc.) are all hostile to information and so are also hostile to the self-generation of life from non-living matter.

I then outlined that nature is,

- driven by programming
- has controlled energy interactions within it that take place with purpose
- produces products that are crafted for the purpose of jobs fulfilled
- has a 'home' in which it finds its purpose
- has internal organisation to maintain its wellbeing to feed, defend and reproduce itself
- has self-awareness at the programming level to enable it to survive within a hostile environment
  - o if life does not 'help itself' to survive on planet earth, the forces of nature will not help it do that
  - o the sun gives light and heat but it does not hand out manuals on photosynthesis

I then said that,

*Nature is **not natural**. It is moulded for purpose by someone outside of itself.*

This is because the natural world is the opposite to all of the above.

*This also dictates that the natural world **cannot** be the driving force **for the origins of life**.*

I gave the examples of the volcano and the steel factory. Both have extreme heat but one is an example of the natural world and the other an example of a constructed and calibrated environment that has been sensibly crafted for the purpose of creating products via a specific information flow. The factory illustration represents nature, not the forces of the natural world. I concluded that you cannot, therefore, have a sophisticated 'nature' arising from an unsophisticated 'natural world'. It does not work. I said that,

*Random and unguided processes that remove information cannot be used as the **agents of intelligent change** to construct information – or construct the environment that is needed to process information to start and sustain life.*

How do evolutionists make the unbelievable appear believable? They confuse the word **nature** with the **natural world** and make them one and the same. They are in fact totally separate.

- -
A Summary of the Summaries
- -

Putting it in a Nutshell
Here's a short outline of everything that we've said so far in this chapter. The secularist camp makes the unbelievable appear believable by suggesting/saying,

- science belongs to secularism
- religious thinking is not scientific
- a process is always responsible for everything
- the complexities of life are explainable by multiple theories

- DNA mix, mutation and natural selection cause evolutionary adaptation
- sideways adaptation shows us that creatures are always on the move away from their family group
- sideways adaptation is responsible for new species which leads to new types of creature
- the creation of new species today is a living example that sideways adaptation is responsible for the evolutionary tree of life
- the common operating system that we see in all living creatures tells us that they evolved from each other
- new information is created whenever we see a new species emerge
- the fossil record shows many sideways adaptations that will/have created new species
- the code that runs life came into being by a combination of chance chemical reactions
- the code of life developed over billions of years by self-replication, copy error and influences from the environment
- the expert code and design that we see around us today is the work of 'mother nature' doing her stuff
- nature (life in all living plants and creatures) comes from the unguided and hostile forces found within natural world
- nature and the natural world are one and the same, one came from the other via natural processes
- past mistakes, such as Haeckel's fraudulent drawings, live on in student handbooks and apart from short articles here and there, evolutionists haven't gone out of their way to overtly point out that these drawing are wrong
- other illustrations, such as the iconic drawings of a line of apes evolving into upright man, are also seen as illustrations based on science rather than the pure imaginations of evolutionary artists who are indulging their fantasies
- missing links are relabelled 'transitional creatures' so that the fact that they are 'missing' is no longer highlighted

So the evolutionist will say:

We see evolution taking place in the plant, insect and animal kingdoms. We see adaptation by creatures within their environments.

This adaptation causes the formation of new species. This *new species process* that we see all around us today was and is responsible for the setting into motion, millions of years ago, of an UPWARDS evolutionary chain of events that led to the formation of all of the creatures that we currently see on our planet. This is true because we can find commonality between body parts of the creatures on the evolutionary ladder and we can see a similar pattern at the microbiological level where all creatures share the same operating system, DNA.

So we see that sideways movements within creatures, as they adapt within the environment, produces new information within the creature which forms new body parts, mannerisms, flesh types and technologies for advanced living. This is traceable back through the fossil record where we can see these sideways movements of change that take place over long periods of time.

So all of life comes from a single cell organism
that evolved itself into everything that
we see around us today.

Here is the above paragraph in a short point format.

- adaptation via DNA mix and mutation creates new information within creatures that will evolve them away from each other
- adaptation will create an UPWARDS evolutionary chain of events for higher technologically developed creatures
- this process is traceable via common body parts, a common operating system that drives life and fossil evidence that shows evolutionary movements

Theists will say, however, that:
It is impossible for us to be here without deity. Here are just five reasons why.

1) Information is the basis for life and information cannot evolve from the cosmos.

307

2) New information is not generated by any of the programming that is within nature.
3) The engineering that makes life possible is not evolvable in a step-by-step process.
4) The forces within the natural world only remove information; they do not and cannot, therefore, create life.
5) Evidence for evolution is better fitted to be interpreted as the work of a designer.

Now I'll unpack those five reasons using a short outline of everything that we've said so far in this chapter that opposes the theory of evolution.

1) **Information is the basis for life. Information cannot evolve from a dead cosmos because...**
- information is made up from data and code and the environment that gives context to the code
  - data is preceded by language and without language there is no data
  - code is precision data that cannot be written by random processes, it requires intelligent assembly
  - code has to contain intent within it for work to be achieved
  - the work has to be imagined in the code before it can be written
  - the work achieved by the code comes as answers to questions that have been asked about the 'needs that need to be met' within the environment
  - the environment to process the code has to be specifically constructed and calibrated so that the information can flow and move the resources to enable the work (described in the code) to be done
- information has no mass but is imprinted onto the cosmos via an external mind
- information has no mathematical relationship with energy and so *movements of raw energy* will not automatically produce information
- information in the cell produces outputs that are fashioned products for purpose and the forces of the natural world only produce by-products

2) **New information is not generated by any of the programming that is within nature.**
- hereditary exchange (DNA mix) will only shuffle the DNA providing data expressions of the original code
- data expression changes will only lead to sideways shifts in the code – which eventually will lead to what evolutionists call a 'new species' but in reality they are just a 'family group expression' that can no longer mate with other family group members
- data expression changes are not new information
- mutations are copy errors in the code and do not represent new sensible code for UPWARDS evolutionary change
- natural selection only removes information from the gene pool and does not create new information
- we know that interbreeding from a limited gene pool leads to deformity due to there not being a large enough variety of DNA information to be mixed
    - this tells us that not having a wide enough gene pool to choose from produces a long term reduced viability for generational living
    - this tells shows us that there needs to be a wide amount of information available for offspring to be healthy down the generational line
    - this tells us that it is impossible to develop greater information from a lesser information base as all of the evidence we can see around us points in the opposite direction
    - this tells us that the massive amount of DNA that can be seen today, scattered across all life, cannot have evolved from one single cell of limited information

3) **The engineering that makes life technologically possible is not evolvable in a step-by-step process.**
- interdependency is at the heart of the creature and plant worlds that inhabit the earth
- each piece of specialised technology is dependent on multiple parts and therefore,
    - each component is useless and pointless by itself

309

- each component only makes sense when it is put correctly together with other components
- the technology does not work unless it is purposefully put together all at the same time
- the technology has irreducible complexity
- using unscientific phrases like 'happy accident's or 'it evolved' or 'it mutated' or 'punctuated evolution' are just cover ups so that the impossible auto assembly of the technology is not looked at properly

4) **The forces within the natural world do not create life because...**

- life has information processes within it that result in technologically products fashioned for purpose
  - the natural world only produces by-products
  - the 2nd law of thermodynamics states that the natural world can only make by-products
  - by-products are without engineering
  - by-products cannot fit together to complete a technological structure
  - by-products do not require mature information processing to be created
  - each movement of raw energy that results from a by-product will remove information
- nature and the natural world are separate
- nature is un-natural, it has been tampered with and had information imprinted onto it in a way in which the forces within the natural world cannot auto-organise because there is no organisation process that can come about from raw energy within the cosmos
- the natural world has no 'self-knowledge' of itself whereas all life has programming within it where the intent within the code shows an understanding of what 'needs doing' within the body of the plant, insect or animal to keep it alive
- the release of energy within life is carefully controlled so that work can be done but the energy movements within the natural world are raw, random and unguided
- the humanist creation story starts off with chaos, a 'Big Bang' explosion and then moves towards greater chaos, the cooling

310

down of the universe guided by the 2nd law of thermodynamics which determines that all structures of order will be lost

- o so we move from chaos to an even greater chaos
- o   this movement ensures that the chaotic and random and unguided movements of raw energy that are expressed within the cosmos cannot bring about the order, complexity and interdependent design that we see around us today that is necessary for life to exist

5) **Evidence for evolution is better fitted to be interpreted as the work of a designer.**

- having a common operating system shows the work of a code writer
- common technology within different creatures shows the work of a designer who used those same technologies over again
- the fossil base only shows the sideways movements that we see today
- the gaps (missing links) on the evolutionary tree of life are there because there is nothing with which to fill them
- insisting that a process is still responsible for all life, in the face of all of the evidence against it, is simply a religious expression of being a part of the '**Anything but God Society**'
- the religious world view of secularists drives their scientific investigation to keep God out of science

These are just five of the many reasons why biological evolution does not take place within our universe. Secular science just skips over the problems with wishy-washy arguments that mean very little in reality except that they serve as an excuse not to accept the fact that evolution is debunked and dead in the water. There is no longer any merit in the theory now that we can see that information drives life and **the last thing that information is, is natural to the cosmos and the movements of raw energy that are within it**.

The question has to be asked, therefore, as to why the word 'evolution' has such great weight within our culture. If there is so much wrong with biological evolution, then why do people still so readily accept it? What is it that causes us to believe the unbelievable? The next section will open up the answers to us.

Keeping it believable by…

Language Misuse – Evolution, Devolution and Change
A Quick Recap on Chapter 1

I have already talked about this in chapter 1 where I outlined how the word 'evolution' is misapplied within our culture. I said that the word 'evolution' or the phrases 'it evolved' or 'it's evolving' are today used left, right and centre to express any kind of change. I said that you will hear talk about the 'evolution' of the car or the 'evolution' of the train or how society has 'evolved' over the millennia or how the computer world and the internet are currently 'evolving' as each decade goes by. I said that everything is described in terms of evolution; the mobile phone industry, the fashion industry, the film industry, the arts, education, our culinary appetites, our appetites for entertainment or what to do in our spare time, our political landscapes and even our physical landscapes – which are subject to continuous change on a daily basis. Some parts of our world culture are subject to rapid 'evolutionary change' due to intense human activity to develop them, for example 3D virtual reality technology and the development of social media. Whilst other parts of our culture are subject to a more gentle and careful 'evolutionary' transformation, such as our recording and re-evaluating of history; still slowly 'evolving' as interpretations of the past are challenged and altered according to fresh evidence being 'dug up' on the subject – whether that *digging* is via archaeology or via systematic book reading. Everything in the world, therefore, is said to 'evolve' in some way.

I said that this continual usage of the phrase gives the word 'evolution' credibility within the culture. We can 'see it happening' all the time. Everything 'evolves' on a day-to-day basis. This is because everything in the world is subject to daily change. At the end of each day everything has 'moved on' a little. Our cars are a day older and not only a day closer to the scrap yard but the designers of that car have had *one more day* to think about the 'next model' – which will one day be produced by the car manufacturer and so replace the current one. Our bodies are a day older and a day closer to wearing out, so society will change as each generation goes by and new relationships and new ways of doing things are formed by each generation of people. At the end of each day our immediate relationships have also 'evolved' in some way, either by getting deeper or becoming fractured and becoming increasingly distant, depending on the interactions or lack of interactions that we've been involved in. So the **fact of evolution** is continually presented to us through the *daily drama* of this continual soap opera called 'life' in which we find ourselves. Our lives are therefore submerged in what is termed as 'evolutionary change'; evolution just happens and we are witnesses to it.

In chapter 1 I said that sometimes the word evolution is correctly applied in our culture. I gave the example that the word 'evolution' is best illustrated in the world of technology, though it extends to other areas of life too, such as human social structures. However, it is important to note that when we look at each example of true evolution in society (true evolution meaning that there is a genuine increase in complexity and sophistication) there is one thing that stands out. That is that...

> ...*all of the **mechanisms** that push forward true evolutionary activity are classed as 'intelligent drivers of change'.*

Have a think about where the word 'evolved' is correctly used in our culture. You'll see that where there is an increase in sophistication and technology there is always intelligence that makes it happen. Without intelligence none of these evolutionary activities would work. These 'intelligent drivers' guide evolutionary development and are the **sole cause** for the increase in complexity. For example the car engine, the steam engine, the jet engine (in fact any type of engine) have all 'evolved' because humans have worked hard at **thinking** about how to develop the technology. There is, therefore, an *intelligent input* into the evolutionary process. It is intelligence that is the **mechanism** that initiates the **driver** for evolutionary change. Where *true evolution* takes place, you will ALWAYS find that *intelligence* is the **mechanism** that drives forward the evolutionary process.

Our problem is, however, that devolution also happens via mechanisms that are 'non-intelligent' drivers of change, such as the erosion of a landscape via the wind and the rain. This devolutionary process is driven forward by mechanisms that are haphazard, that is random and unguided in nature. The wind and the rain will continually erode the landscape without intelligent input.

*However, the word **'evolved'** is still used by many people today to describe those devolutionary changes.*

The word *'evolution'*, therefore, is sometimes misused. The result of which is that,

- a misinterpretation of its activity is placed on that which happens – devolution is actually taking place
- it does not have the correct drivers for change behind it – they are random and unguided

So incorrect inputs and drivers are sometimes added to the usage of the word 'evolution' and when this happens we know that real evolution is not taking place, just some form of either devolutionary change or a **remixing of the same without sophistication gain**. The fact that our culture will talk about the 'evolution' of the car and the 'evolution' of the geographical landscape, as if their evolution is the same, is an example of mixed uses of the concept. One has the correct mechanisms and drivers for change and the other does not. It is nothing short of language misuse. The changing of a landscape via the wind and the rain **is not evolution**. Change may happen but **erosion is not development**. It is the opposite. Nothing gets technically improved by erosion. So the problem is this.

There is intelligent evolution and unintelligent devolution. Both are now labelled as 'evolution' in today's culture.

This is very misleading as this talk is seldom challenged in our culture. The more the word is used, the more credible it is in our thinking. By the time we've heard the word misapplied many times over, anything can 'evolve' – as long as it is changing in some way. However, intelligent evolution that brings about purposeful change where sophistication increases and chaos decreases is the only true use of the word. When this happens there are always calculated inputs and crafted outputs that drive the change.

Methodology Misuse – Machines, Methods, Inputs & Outputs

Wherever true evolutionary processes take place within society you'll always see that they happened where there is a machine or a method. There is also a process that has to take place that determines how the drivers of change impact the evolution of that machine or method. They are,

- intelligently *crafted* **inputs**
- *crafted* **processing** of the inputs
- intelligently *crafted* **outputs**

As we have already illustrated in this book, the forces within the natural world do **not** do this. I'll very briefly revisit this illustration just one last time. A volcano has,

1) A **non**-intelligent input – lava is pushed up through the earth's crust.
   a. The force of the explosive eruption is **NOT crafted or controlled** in any way.
      i. Any energy that can escape by the blast will escape.
      ii. The energy release will be random and haphazard.
      iii. Its input is not controlled or crafted.
2) Non-crafted processing – the lava is **NOT processed** in any way as it passes through the volcano.
   a. During this time when the lava travels up the volcano, before it spurts out into the atmosphere, there is **NO crafted** work being done on the lava.

  b. The heat or the substance of molten rock is **NOT** being worked upon in any way shape or form to...
   i. purposefully change the lava,
   ii. use the lava for another purpose that will intelligently change something else via its heat properties,
   iii. the lava is simply being ejected into the atmosphere.
 3) Non-intelligent output – the ejection of material from the volcano is haphazard. It is all in the form of by-product. The heat, the lava, the smoke and ash are all by-products of the eruption and are scattered here and there according to the chaotic blast that ejects them.

So wherever you see true evolution taking place then there are two things happening.

1) Intelligent mechanisms that are used as drivers for change.
2) Crafted inputs, crafted processing and crafted outputs.

This is the case in every area of life, where the word 'evolution' is correctly used. We can accept this every time we look at the word's usage. We can say, "Yes, the car evolves," and "No, the seashore landscape doesn't actually evolve, it moves towards a dusty and sandy equilibrium which is actually devolution." When we properly examine the situation it becomes clear to us where true evolutionary change actually happens. We see the correct usage and the incorrect usage and we can easily have great clarity on this – except within the area of biology!

The Evolutionary Biological Misfit
Back into Random Mechanisms
In the area of theoretic evolutionary biology we leave behind sensible drivers for UPWARDS change (the examples of the car or jet engine where intelligent **input** is carefully **crafted** into its evolution by qualified engineers) and move back into the haphazard movements of random happenings that are meant to be the mechanisms and drivers of design increase. Mutation, for example, is the same random change that we find in the movements of the wind and the rain that alter the landscape. Mutation has no guiding force behind it, no reasoning

mind. We've already seen that code cannot be developed this way. Randomness will always destroy code, not add to it or increase it in complexity. So the fact that so many evolutionary scientists still use the word 'mutation' in their conversations tells us that they've not even begun to understand the misfit that mutation is in the real world. In the minds of evolutionists, in their theoretical imagined world, mutation has a part to play. In reality, however, mutation cannot even maintain basic code integrity, let alone add sophistication to it.

So what's the problem? Why are we still in the place where hereditary exchange (DNA mix), mutation and natural selection are readily accepted as being able to do the same job as **intelligent drivers** of change that produce the equivalent to,

- **crafted** *inputs*,
- **crafted** *processing* of the inputs
- and **crafted** *outputs*?

How is it that we are to still led to believe that random and unguided movements within the biological world can craft technology at the DNA level and provide sophisticated answers to life? Why is it that evolutionists are still getting away with claims that evolutionary theory can be used to justify...

1) The start of life.
   - The so called first data/code string that is meant to be the beginnings of the DNA information that makes up life.
   - The environment that houses and runs the code.
2) The development of life.
   - The structure of life (the cell's interconnected organelles).
   - The processes within life (the cell's interconnected workings based around DNA and protein creation).
   - The increase in coding complexity creating more and more protein machines which in themselves are answers to problems that enable health in the body of the creature to aid its survival.

As we've already illustrated, right across the pages of this book, neither the start of life nor the development of life can evolve via random and unguided drivers for change. So how is it, therefore, that such an unbelievable thing can still be maintained? The answer comes in the confused mislabelling of what we see in front of us.

The Mislabelling of Intelligent Design within Biology

When we look at the amazing variety of life that we see around us in the world today we are **all in agreement** that this incredible diversity is due to the natural ability of plants, insects and animals to adapt in order for them to fit within their environments. This remarkable ability is due to two drivers of change.

1) DNA mix
2) Natural Selection

These two drivers are the cause of all the different types of family lines within the plant, insect and animal kingdoms. For example, they are the cause of lions, tigers, cheetahs, leopards etc. within the cat family. The reasons for this adaptive ability are simple – an intelligent driver for change that is called hereditary exchange (DNA mix).

Hereditary exchange (DNA mix) is an intelligent driver for change because...

...hereditary exchange (DNA mix)
is intelligent design.

A huge amount of thinking has gone into the sperm and the egg mixing together to form a new creature. It has taken a brilliant mind to create such a programme that will not only shuffle complex DNA, whilst still keeping the integrity of the basic code, but also provide the ability for sideways change so that, if the environment changes, multiple generations of the creature can better survive within it. The whole process screams out, "intelligence" at the top of its voice! So, when we look at the huge variety of different creatures in the world, their existence should be correctly attributed to,

1) **Super Intelligence** – DNA mix
2) **Randomness** – mutation (**almost no effect**)
3) **Randomness** – natural selection

The reason why adaptation happens is because,

...it is supposed to happen.

An intelligent driver (DNA mix) has been invented to 'craft' the change so that a sensible movement can be gained over the course of several generations where the same family type continues to have offspring. DNA mix is the most complex programme in the known universe. In it we have the equivalent of two separate programmes working together, the programme of the egg and the programme of the sperm. Both are independently produced by separate bodies, one male and one female. Yet they both fit and merge perfectly together as their **environments clash** via mating. It is impossible for a human being to write an equivalent programme in the computer world. It is also impossible for unintelligent movements of energy within the cosmos to write such code, no matter how much time you add to the equation!

Evolutionists deny this fact. They just assume, by pure blind faith, that this process of mating (DNA mix) has evolved in some way, though they cannot in any way, shape or form show how a sperm or an egg could

- evolve
- would be useful before it was fully evolved

...or present

- a step-by-step model for their development
- even justify random and unguided movements of energy providing the concept of male or female in the first place

...and so, as usual, the evolutionist just doesn't go there in their general conversations so that its impossibility is hidden behind the silence of absent conversations.

319

The problem that we face, therefore, is that there is great sophistication at the heart of life and even though we see intelligent change within biology through hereditary exchange...

- the creation of the sperm and the egg
- the mixing of the sperm and the egg's DNA to create a perfectly balanced new creature
- sensible sideways kicks that aid adaptation

...evolutionists insist that this amazing technology,

- got here by random and unguided behaviours
- is able to develop the creature UPWARDS

...because the technology of DNA mix is already able to develop the creature sideways **and this is where the confusion lies**. They are taking an intelligent driver for change (DNA mix programming) that causes a certain amount of **intended** change and labelling it as a *'random'* driver for change. Then they insist that this 'random' driver is itself a product of random evolution and that it is capable of doing far more than it can do in reality – if it is assisted by other drivers of random change. So the humanist's model is relabelled like this,

1) **Randomness** – DNA mix
2) **Randomness** – mutation (**can have a good amount of effect**)
3) **Randomness** – natural selection

With the other *drivers for change* **evolutionists insist** that,

1) Hereditary exchange *'initiates'* sensible change
2) Mutation *'sensibly'* adds to the DNA mix process
3) Natural selection *'refines'* the process

The problem we have is that DNA mix **does initiate** change and that natural selection **does refine** those changes. As these two things are totally true it can be difficult to initially see through the deception. We see that this mixture of intelligent design (DNA mix) and unintelligent change (mutation and natural selection) are relabelled and used to justify *unintelligent* **UPWARDS** evolution. As a consequence of this mislabelling and the blurring of the correct meaning of adaptation we are presented with an evolutionary model that justifies life without God. That which should be used to prove deity is again misrepresented to *prove* the very opposite!

Final Illustrations

I thought I'd save the best till last by looking at two illustrations of why evolution theory is false. The first is a lecture based on the evolution eye by Richard Dawkins and the second is a sarcastic look at the idea that a frog can turn into a lizard and then a bird. Let me first of all remind you of a few scientific facts,

- it has **never been observed** whereby a cell has increased in information complexity via the routes of cell duplication, hereditary exchange or mutation
- sideways kicks in DNA are data expression changes that will **re-express current limbs** and internal organs, not new information that will develop new technological body parts
- evolutionists take the conversation to the wrong level, observing the *so called* evidence from the perspective of the naked eye rather than from the perspective of the microbiological world as seen through a microscope, in order to make their theories sound plausible

Therefore, just assuming that as the generations go by that UPWARDS evolutionary change will automatically naturally occur is foundationally wrong. This is the reason why evolutionists will use phrases like, 'happy accidents' or 'punctuated evolution' or 'luck' and other such pseudo-science vocabulary to justify their assumptions and assertions. We'll see more of this in a moment.

With those basic scientific principles in mind, let's outline what I call Mr Dawkins' ***Fantastical Eye Evolution Fantasy*** theory (sounds like something from Roald Dahl doesn't it) and see how he makes all the mistakes that we have outlined in this book so far.

You can watch his lecture at this following address:
https://www.youtube.com/watch?v=Nwew5gHoh3E
Here's a general outline of all that he has to say:

1) Mr Dawkins and his Fantastical Eye Evolution Fantasy!

He starts off by quoting Darwin who said, "To this day the eye makes me shudder." He then cites creationists who argue that the eye has to be fully in place to work. Then he gives an inferred sideways poke at creationist scientists by saying that, "even *serious scientists* have sometimes queried…" if there has been enough time for the eye to evolve.

> **NOTE:** In this last statement, therefore, he infers that creationist scientists are not serious scientists simply because they don't adhere to evolution – conveniently putting to one side the fact that there are many creationist scientists who are far more qualified than he is.

He then cites what he calls an 'ancestor' who has what he describes as a "*simple* sheet of light sensitive cells."

> **NOTE:** I personally can't stand it when an evolutionist uses the word '*simple*' as there is no such thing as *simple* in biology when it is viewed from the perspective of the microbiological world. The DNA code to build any body part, even a so called '*simple sheet of light sensitive cells*', is very complex.

> **NOTE:** He gives no explanation as the **where** or **how** this '*simple*' sheet of the light sensitive cells came from; he just starts off with it **already in place** as if it is scientifically acceptable for it to have just 'evolved' itself into being. This is quite typical of an evolutionist. Start off with technology, without any justification for it, and then launch off from that point with your theory. This is just like those evolutionists who start off with hereditary exchange (DNA mix) and just assume that a sperm and an egg can evolve themselves into existence.

NOTE: For some reason these light sensitive cells in Dawkins' model are still preserved and kept **in good working order** as his imagined evolutionary process matures over time. Logic would tell us, however, that if mutation and DNA mix happen via random and unguided incidents within the DNA code (remember in evolutionary theory there is no code writer who is developing the DNA code in a specific direction) that at some point this amazing bit of light sensitive cell technology would be invaded somehow by these haphazard mutations, which appear at the DNA level, and spoil it. These invasions within the code would eventually break up/destroy those light sensitive cells. Random copy error changes within any code will always bring about disorder and not increased complexity. So even if you did start off with light sensitive cells *that just happened to be* there then if you choose mutation (copy error) as being one of the mechanisms that drives forward evolutionary change within a creature then those light sensitive cells would eventually malfunction.

He then sets up a screen based on completely different physical substances and technology to *represent these light sensitive cells* and films the screen, relaying what happens on the screen onto a TV monitor. He says that the image we can see on the TV monitor **is equivalent** to that which this 'primitive' creature would also 'see' on its sheet of light sensitive cells – which is a bold and presumptuous statement to make. Then he states that this un-named animal, who hardly has an eye, can tell the difference between dark and light.

NOTE: He assumes that these light sensitive cells *mean something* to the programming within his imaginary creature's brain. Don't forget that when we, or any other creature, see something that the picture in our heads makes sense to us because a designer has put into place all of the coding in our DNA to link up our eyes to our brain. It is our brain that interprets the information sent via the light. He assumes too that this *primitive creature* has a developed and fully integrated brain connection to those light sensitive cells – that is, a specifically designed and crafted nerve system that is able to carry those meaningful, converted neural signal messages from those light sensitive cells to its brain. (For this to be achieved it needs to be written in the creature's DNA.) He then also assumes that these messages can be correctly interpreted by the creature's brain in such a way that makes the signals meaningful to it, i.e. it can 'see' and has enough wits about it to understand that it is 'seeing' something and should **respond** to what is 'sees'. Don't forget that with evolution **consciousness has to evolve as well as physicality**! This means that all of the connections to the brain have to somehow be in place for it to sense touch etc. and to know how to interpret them. He also conveniently forgets that the DNA coding behind each of these technologies, the light sensitive cells, the nerve system and the calibrated part of the brain that will interpret the signals, is very complex.

He then talks about light, shadows and predators and continues to talk about these for much of the lecture suggesting that it is the ability to 'see' and 'get away' from *predators* that is the **driving motive for evolutionary change**. This is similar to that which we saw expressed in the John Cleese video we mentioned earlier in the book where 'competition' was cited as being the driving force for evolution, which we saw was not true.

> **NOTE:** At what level of life is he talking about when he is talking about *getting away* from predators? Can this primitive creature recognise *'danger'* as a concept when it hasn't been able to *see* before? Does it have the concept of being alive or of self-awareness or of fear?

He then says, "Now, the next stage in evolution would be to have a shallow cup."

> **NOTE:** He gives no reason for this 'shallow cup' example being the 'next stage' in evolution's **random mutation** development except that **this is what he wants** the evolution to be – because **he wants to see** an eye at the end of his imagined process! If something is by nature random and based on uncontrolled mutation then you have no way of knowing **what will happen next**. The only reason why he puts this very convenient 'next stage' of orderly and fashioned 'shallow cup' technology in place is so that he can make his

self-imagined eye evolution model succeed. To say that this is the *next stage*, **as if it is a logical thing to naturally happen amongst random mutations**, is a misrepresentation of the real world. There is no 'next stage' when something is unguided and random in nature. *All technology within any creature is purposeful because the intelligent coding at the DNA level forces it to be the case – which tells us there is a code writer behind the DNA.* Change driven by unguided copy error, however, will never have a logical 'next stage' to move towards. His language has left reality behind.

NOTE: Remember there is no reason why, at a DNA level, any brilliant new coding should be randomly written via mutation. Mutation (copy error) doesn't write anything new. So Dawkins has no DNA development route for this excellent shallow cup technology to appear, he just assumes it to be the case. Note also that this new randomly created evolutionary shape *conveniently* **retains the hole** in the middle of its shape so that light can *still pass through it* and so shine onto the exact spot that it needs to, the light sensitive screen of cells that the creature has somewhere on its body. The DNA coding to retain this hole in the correct position in the midst of this new shape, so that the light going through it lands in just the right location, is quite exquisite.

Next he introduces the concept of a '*sense of direction*' and continues with his concept of '*predators*'.

NOTE: These concepts of 'direction' and 'predators' are very sophisticated for 'early life' to **get their heads around** and yet he persists with it without any explanation or justification of how 'early life' would ever have these concepts.

He therefore suggests that it is *not just competition* that drives evolution, as we have read about earlier in the book, but it is the need to **get away** from **predators** that *ignites* evolutionary change. Then he changes the technology of the creature by saying that the evolution of the shallow cup would probably have been indented compared with his model, making his model incorrect.

325

NOTE: **NOTE:** So he admits that his model, from which he is going to demonstrate his theory, is now a misrepresentation of what his theory actually says happened in the past.

He points out that as the cup gets bigger the shadow effect increases. Then he says that, with the sphere he is using becoming almost a full globe, except for a small purposeful circle at its front, he can get an almost image of some sort displaying on the screen – the screen remember represents the light sensitive cells. He then shows a smudge of the helper's hand appearing on the screen. Then he adds, "So an animal with an eye like this would be able to see perhaps just a little bit of what kind of predator it was." Then he makes an amazing statement that we have to go to the next, "logical conclusion," which is that of a pin hole.

NOTE: Again, there is no 'logical conclusion' for random and unguided mutation processes. His choice of language here is highly inappropriate. He is using the *language of intelligence*, not the language of random activity. Logic has nothing to do with evolution. Shuffling DNA mix with mutation will not create new sophisticated code for the development of new pieces of technology that either complement or build upon lower technology from the past. All DNA mix does is take that which is already pre-programmed into the creature and move it *sideways*, not UPWARDS. Mutation just gets in the way of new technology.

Then he reminds us that all of this is, "gradual, gradual change",

NOTE: This phrase, "gradual, gradual change" is used as an excuse to try and justify his theory. Gradual means a tiny bit at a time, just like adding a brick at a time to a Lego machine. This phrase, however, does not get around the fact that each 'brick' needs to be **purposefully placed** in the light of the final shape that is being made. Just because something is said to be gradual does not mean that it bypasses the rules of engineering and that randomness does not create technological order. His use of the word 'gradual' simply invited you to believe that this step-by-step blind process must be true – just because it is gradual!

Adding a pinhole now gives his model the technical ability to create a "precise picture of the hand". Then he cites the nautilus mollusc as an example of a creature that has a pin-hole eye. Then he links these nautilus molluscs to ammonites and **imagines** the 'dramas' that they 'witnessed' through their eyes – but then he admits that,

> *"**We can't be sure** they had pin-hole camera eyes,"*

...then adds,

> *"but it seems quite likely."*

NOTE: Here Dawkins is solely using his imagination. There is no scientific hard evidence for what he is saying and so his statement that, "it seems quite likely" is not based on science at all – just his wishful imagination.

NOTE: The nautilus mollusc has a complex brain. It has short and long term memory. Dawkins still hasn't in any way, shape or form described the brain of his original *primitive* creature.

Then he admits that a pin-hole camera is not a very good way to see as it hardly lets any light in. He says,

> "The **answer to this problem** is that ingenious device, the lens."

NOTE: We have been saying over the last few chapters that intelligent coding at the DNA level is there because of a *question that has been asked* in the light of a *known* problem. Coding is the purposeful, imagined answer to a question. The code is put into effect once it is processed and the known available resources released in order to fix the problem. Here Dawkins goes into the language of purposeful coding by admitting that there is an '**answer**' which is only there because there is a '**problem**' to overcome. Problems are not solved by random and unguided processes; they are solved by intelligent minds, especially when that answer is expressed through meaningful and purposeful coding at the DNA level.

Next he poses the question as to why nautilus has not evolved a lens. (The real answer to that is simply that it can't). He sets up an imagined illustration called 'Mount Improbable' whereby he uses the side of a bumpy mountain model (that he has imagined as if it is an accurate representation of reality) to show how evolution gets stuck on a 'little peak'. He says that, "the **rule in evolution** is to just keep on going uphill" and "when the ancestors of nautilus came up the track here," (pointing to a place where there are two possible uphill routes to take) "...and got to this point, that way up hill looked **just as inviting**, so to speak evolutionarily, as that way," – looking at another peak on his model.

> **NOTE:** He has now introduced a 'rule' into evolution. Randomness, however, has no rules. It has no route and it has no methodology, i.e. a continuous movement to build upon the past. So the notion that evolution has a rule to keep going uphill (that is to technologically increase in complexity) is without foundation. Here Dawkins is again putting ideas and concepts onto the theory that are not based on the real world of randomness. Rules are for intelligent guidance. There is no intelligence in random and unguided actions.

> **NOTE:** He uses the word 'inviting'. For something to be 'inviting' there has to be someone to receive the invitation. Evolution is not a person with a personality. It does not have intelligence and it does not have the ability to be enticed or attracted to something in any way.

Then he reminds us that, "Evolution has no foresight; evolution has no way of knowing that if you travel up that way that you're going to end up with a lens." Then he adds, "For the moment this appears to be a perfectly good way to travel because the pin-hole camera at this level of illumination is an effective eye.

NOTE: He talks about evolution as if it is some kind of little child who can't quite see around the corner of life to where it is going but 'likes the look' of a certain route that 'might be nice' to follow. Here again we see a perfect example of the beginnings of a personality language for this 'thing' called evolution. We mentioned this kind of talk earlier in the book where 'mother nature' is given an identity to choose to design things, rather than admit that there is an intelligent God behind it all. So he moves into the language of 'intelligence' but attributes it to evolution and not a creator.

Then he continues by saying, "So I wonder whether perhaps nautilus has got itself trapped on top of this little hillock and is now unable to escape because escaping would mean going downhill, into the valley, and the one thing you **cannot do** on Mount Improbable is **ever go downhill**."

> **NOTE:** The repercussions of this statement are huge. If evolution cannot go downhill then this means that when you are looking at any kind of excellent technology within the body of any living creature that this creature's technology is the result of a completely successful chain of evolutionary events that continually **got it right** every time it moved along its road/line of evolutionary development! This cannot happen at a DNA level. Random and unguided processes, such as copy error mutations, do not have the ability to move coding forward into **continuous** increased complexity without ending up with errors and dead end routes.

Then he tells us to **use our imagination** to see that the ancestors of the squid and octopus didn't go the evolutionary route of the pin-hole but started to evolve a lens instead, just as we ourselves did "at a different time in history."

Then he poses the question as to how the lens might have evolved and again asks us to use our *imagination* and encourages us to think of a "single sheet of **transparent** material."

> **NOTE:** Why is this *imagined sheet* that's in Dawkins' mind a sheet that has the properties of being **transparent**? Remember

Dawkins' words that, "Evolution has no foresight…" and therefore there is **absolutely no reason** why any negative or even neutral cell mutations within the body of any creature **should produce transparent cells** from *parent cells that were not transparent*! An evolutionist will reply, "They're transparent so that the lens can let the light through it, so that an image can be formed on what will eventually be called the retina," but those are the words of someone who **knows what they are aiming at** in *wanting to create an eye*! There is no logical thinking in evolution that comes via random and unguided mutations. So to say that there simply was a sheet of transparent material that was 'just there' which we are encouraged to '*imagine*' into place as part of Mr Dawkins' lecture is totally irrational. Why would, at the DNA level, a set of code suddenly be written by cells duplicating themselves via copy error (mutation) or via hereditary exchange (that only provides a sideways kick in DNA) that would facilitate the making of a new **transparent** substance? When cells replicate they do so to create other cells that **look like the cells** that they have been engineered from. Sideways kicks, even mutations, always do that. A lion's paw, a leopard's paw, a panther's paw, a cheetah's paw and a pussy cat's paw will all be based on the same DNA technology because they represent sideways kicks in the cat family's coding. The cells that make up their paws have parent cells going back to a common ancestor who was still 100% cat. You will not find any cat animal developing transparent paw pads in the future. The DNA code turned on within any creature's body part will express the characteristics of what that body part looks like. The essentials of that code will be **successfully retained** and reproduced over the generations, as the cat family demonstrates. So the act of copying or DNA mixing **will not create transparent code** *where there wasn't transparent code in the first place*. It is illogical, therefore, to say that we must **imagine** that there is a piece of transparent material that *just happens* to conveniently appear in this area of an eye that is supposed to be forming itself. Remember also that this new bit of technology *just happens* to appear **in the right place** and **in the right shape** for it to be effective as the eye continues to 'evolve'; all done by pure chance. What an incredibly fortunate accident! Wow!

Dawkins then cites the fact that nautilus has sea water going straight into its eye and that a single transparent sheet would **serve the purpose** of protecting the eye. He then makes the excuse that they can't use this single sheet of transparent material, to squeeze it into a lens shape, but instead he's going to use a set of **humanly professionally crafted opticians' lenses** to *illustrate the evolution of the lens*. Then, using these humanly crafted lenses he gets, quite predictably, better and better images. He then says that animals having lenses *like these humanly crafted lenses* would have a better view of the world.

Next he says that we now have, "a gradual pathway, all the way up mount improbable from no eye to an eye."

> **NOTE:** In fact we don't have this at all. Just an imagined fairy-tale that has deliberately taken place in the imagination of Mr Dawkins. He hasn't proved anything by his demonstration, just that you can humanly craft a pinhole camera and get an image by shining a light in a specific direction through the hole. He has shown that if you then place *precision made human lenses* in front of the light source you can create a clearer image. He **chooses to impose** this human activity back onto the animal kingdom and **chooses to believe** it happened via randomness. There is, in fact, no correlation between the two. There is not a shred of biological or fossil evidence to suggest a semi-blind creature evolved its way to sight in this way. Neither has he even begun to say how the DNA conveniently wrote new fantastic and sophisticated code for this to happen. All this proves is that he has a *'fantastical'* **imagination**!

Then he poses the 'time' question asking if there has been enough time for evolution to happen. He cites a Swedish scientist, Dan Neilson, who put together a computer model that outlined what they've just illustrated except he did it in small steps. Each one of these steps is an assumed 1% successful mutation in **the right technological direction**. His computer simulation model shows this gradual evolution, measuring sight efficiency along the way, and shows the change from flat retina to ending with a full eye.

NOTE: We will look at this so called *'computer model'* in more detail later.

He then says that Neilson's *results* are the same as their *results* that they've just established in the lecture.

> **NOTE:** There are no 'results' in his lecture. Dawkins hasn't done any scientific investigation during his talk. He's not done any measuring or gathering of data or made any real-life observations at the microbiological level. He's just talked from his humanly constructed models and from his imagination. So to say that they have the same 'results' is meaningless. There are no results from his activities to compare with Dan Neilson's so called 'results' - which in effect is nothing more than a pre-programmed computer simulation.

He then adds that, "There is a smooth progression up Mount Improbable for the eye."

> **NOTE:** There's nothing smooth about randomness. The nature of random mutation and new technology is that smoothness does not exist. Technological increase is only 'made smooth' by thinking minds who think around the subject and actively create and assemble the different parts of the new machine in order for it all to fit together. Without intelligence, there is nothing smooth about technological development; in fact without intelligence there is no technological development at all!

He then outlines that Neilson estimated, via more detailed **assumptions** that were based on 'quantities' which, "geneticists out in the field can measure and have measured." After these conservative *quantities*, which slowed down real evolutionary change, were put into the computer model, Neilson's computer model showed that it would only take 250 thousand generations for the evolution of the eye to happen; as there is a new generation each year that would make in total 250 thousand years.

He then concludes, "So there really was no need for Darwin to shudder. Half an eye is better than no eye." He adds, "...the evolution of the eye is so **quick** and **easy** that it must have happened many, many times over. Eyes can evolve **at the drop of a hat**..." He says this because he then admits that in the animal kingdom there are lots of eyes that, "work on completely different principles" which tells him that they have, "**evolved quite independently** of each other." He then gives examples of many different types of creatures with different eyes, saying that they all **evolved separately**, (that they did not come from each other up an evolutionary ladder but arose independently) and presents this fact that they cannot evolve from each other as evidence for evolution.

He then reminds us that each evolutionary step is, "a small piece of *random* **luck**" and that each step is, "not particularly impressive." He makes sure that it is not labelled as impressive as **otherwise it would be a miracle** (which really is him scoring an own goal as his statement is *a poke in the eye* for those secular scientists who adhere to what is called punctuated evolution).

He then says that as a result of his lecture we have a **true explanation** as the, "whole point of evolution is that it gets us up 'Mount Improbable' *without miracles*," – which basically translates into the phrase, 'We can evolve multi-complex life, little by little, without the interventions of the divine because we don't want God in science.'

Extra Critique of Dawkins' Eye Evolution Theory

I've already been criticising this lecture as I outlined it but I'll add a few more thoughts here so that I can expand on what I've said so far.

A) He is religiously driven.

In this lecture we see that he is religiously driven by his atheism. He will only ask the questions of 'how?' things came about and never 'who?' His statement at the end of his lecture that we don't want miracles in science is a decision that he has religiously made whereby he does not want God meddling with the cosmos in any way in order for us to be here. This drives the way in which he reasons and theorises about our origins.

B) The Computer Programme

The computer programme that he mentions, created by the Swedish scientist Dan Neilson, upon which he intellectually leans for much of his lecture, is a sham. Dawkins' audience doesn't automatically see this. This is because back in the days when this lecture was made computers were still a mysterious thing and so you could make up scenarios about someone 'writing a programme' and a sense of awe amongst the audience would naturally arise. Today, however, so many people write apps or other types of software that just saying that someone *wrote a programme* without going into the details of the pre-programmed parameters that the programmer used, showing how the software is set up to work, is no longer acceptable. Today's audience naturally asks extra questions before they accept the validity of the findings of any computer programme. So when you listen to what Dawkins describes about this software programme it is clear that the programming behind Neilson's software is bogus in two ways.

1) It assumes that evolution is true.
   a. It is set up for evolution to technologically succeed. The pre-set values entered into the computer programme determine that there is a 1% **success** rate with the passing of each new generation.
   b. It also assumes that the 1% success rate is moving the creature in the correct evolutionary direction, i.e. the

latest evolutionary change technically builds correctly on top of the last evolutionary 'blob of flesh' that randomly appeared within the creature's parent generation.

Both of these false assumptions mean that the programme **will succeed** in creating a sensible new technology. Here are some more objections to this assumption.

c. No-one has ever viewed and recorded an UPWARDS evolutionary movement of any amount (let alone 1%) within the cell at the DNA level that would bring about new, successful technology. Cells dividing themselves or DNA mix produce, at best, the same technology from which they came.

d. 1% change doesn't sound like very much physically, but at a microbiological level it is huge. The amount of new DNA that 1% represents **is not just a few lines** of code!

e. Any amount of new code, let along 1% of new code, is not possible. Random digit changing and the mixing of DNA via hereditary exchange and mutation will never produce a 1% increase in technological advance within a creature.

2) It is a programme that does not calculate anything **in reality**. There is nothing random about the programme that will cause it to fail. It is just a simulation model that simply declares evolution to be true and creates what the programmer wants to see happening.

So the computer programme is prewritten with bias right at its heart. As I said a few moments ago, it is a sham; a simulation, written by an evolutionist, to simply show what the person imagines in their mind. There is nothing scientific about this computer programme nor is it based in any way on genuine data readings that represent reality. Dawkins uses it throughout his lecture as if the 'data' it produces is actually true! He does this even though he admits that Dan Neilson only 'tries' to answer the question of evolution. He also makes the assertion that 1% is a tiny amount of change and that this amount of change is labelled as 'conservative'. His statement is completely false and based only on the wishful thinking.

C) The Time Estimated for Evolution to Succeed

As we have already seen, the 1% success rate that Neilson's computer simulation suggests for the evolution of the eye is bogus. As this is the case, his estimation that it would only take 250,000 years for the full evolution of the eye to complete is also bogus. Dawkins suggests that the reason why we can't find fossils showing evolutionary change is because it happens so quickly. He says that, just like trying to use the hour hand on a clock to record minutes, it is also impossible to find such a small amount of fossils that would be available over that 250,000 year process – as normally we only find fossils that show change over millions of years. However, understanding that the time scale is woefully wrong, and taking into account that so many different creatures developed sight independently of each other, there still should be lots of fossils out there showing eye development if it had actually happened that way.

D) The Properties of a Lens

The lens has no healing properties of its own. If it had evolved from other materials around it then, like the rest of the human body, it would have the capacity to self-heal – just like the skin on your arm or leg. This tells us that the lens is specifically designed by a non-evolutionary route. This tells us that a designer, choosing to use a different substance to create the lens from that which makes up the rest of the eye, had to write intricate programming at the DNA level which would select just the right materials whilst the creature was in its embryonic state, that is right at the heart of the creature's initial development! The eye is not a matter of one 'blob of flesh' mutating from another 'blob of flesh'. It is precision coding that has been carefully thought through as the DNA code drives forward the development of the creature via the genes switching themselves on and off as the creature initially grows.

E) Independent Evolutionary Eye Technology

Dawkins completes his lecture by saying, "...the evolution of the eye is so quick and easy that it must have happened many, many times over. Eyes can evolve at the drop of a hat, and in fact if we look around at the animal kingdom there are lots of different kinds of eyes dotted around..." Then he follows this up by showing the different creatures with different levels of eye technology in them. This ridiculous slide show is just like my alien that I introduced in chapter 3 that had the idea that transport machines evolved from each other. Having had time to think about his theory since his initial discussions with his friend, my alien's slide show illustrates that a unicycle, a scooter, a tricycle, a child's buggy, a go-cart, a bicycle, a motorbike, a car, an off-road jeep and a racing car all evolved separately from each other! "All of these evolved independently of each other," the alien says. "This is because evolution happens at a 1% rate for every generation and it happens at the drop of a hat!" That's how ridiculous Dawkins' arguments are.

*To suggest that 'eyes' for every advanced creature on this planet are **a natural product of the universe**, if the universe is left to its own random and unguided devices, is unbelievable.*

So it is the most incredible thing that he can suggest that 'eyes' will naturally be evolved by 'every creature' around this planet independently of each other, yet they are all based on similar, if not the same, technology! However, the fact that he admits that there is no evolutionary link between them goes against all the reasons for justifying evolution in the first place. The theory of evolution assumes that everything is meant to have developed over billions of years, slowly adding from creature to creature over many, many generations, and that the reason why it took so long was that the odds against it happening in the first place are so great. We have to have billions of years for all of the **wrong random and unguided processes** to take place as well as the minority of the self-imagined technological 'happy accidents' to have taken place too (which they can't but evolutionists need to have something to cling on to). So to admit that the eyes of so many creatures are not linked by an evolutionary process is an amazing admission. It makes evolution that much more impossible than it already is. It tells us that each of these creatures was designed at a DNA programming level. It tells us that there is a creator behind the amazing variety of life and that this designer wanted his creation to have sight and so he used similar, but not linked, technologies to enable this to happen. Dawkins' lecture is an example of pure, blind faith in his theory because to have any activity of deity would cause us to, in his own words, "no longer have a true explanation. The whole point of evolution is that it gets us up 'Mount Improbable' without miracles."

F) The Role of Luck

The most incredible statement of his whole lecture, however, comes at the end where he says, "...each step is a small piece of **random luck**." So he finishes off his talk with this incredibly pseudo-scientific conclusion that everything that has sight around us has evolved into its sophisticated state via the scientific route of, '**random luck**'! Unbelievable! This **random *luck***, we're told, happens again and again as each small bit of ***luck*** comes together and joins to the next bit of evolutionary ***luck***. It all happens gradually. A little ***luck*** here and a little ***luck*** there. None of each of the ***lucky*** bits of ***luck*** is in itself too ***lucky***. They're just **a bit *lucky*** as too much ***luck*** making too much progress in one go would be a miracle and we're not allowed to have miracles in science, just a little ***luck*** that builds upon more ***luck*** and more ***luck*** and more ***luck***. By the time we've got all of the ***luck*** into all of the creatures right across this planet, that have been so ***lucky*** as to evolve fantastic eyes for themselves, then we have examples of random ***luck*** everywhere. "We're so ***lucky***!" they should sing out. This communal song should be so loud that it should drown out the dawn chorus that the birds chirp out each morning. This song is the all unifying anthem that unites the animal and insect kingdoms and the amazing technologies that run them! "***Lucky, lucky, lucky***, they should sing. Personally I think it's a pity that Kylie Minogue hadn't evolved herself in to existence millions of years ago as she could have led all the eye developing creatures in her unforgettable 1987 song...

> I should be so ***lucky***,
> ***Lucky***, ***lucky***, ***lucky***,
> I should be so ***lucky*** in love.

Change the word 'love' in the lyrics above for the word 'evolution' and we're all singing together on the same hymn sheet – oh, err, perhaps I shouldn't have said the word *hymn* as that sounds religious and not scientific!

Conclusion on Dawkins' Fantastical Eye Evolution Fantasy

Mr Dawkins, in this lecture, does exactly the same thing that my imagined 'alien' did back in chapter 3. If you remember in the illustration called "An Alien Conversation! The Fossil Record – Unicycles, Bikes, Trikes, Cars and Motorbikes." I outlined a scenario whereby an alien visited our planet after a terrible war and began to find bikes, trikes, scooters, motorbikes, cars, etc. I then said:

If after finding all these things the alien said, "Oh look, here is the simplest one, the unicycle, here's the next simplest which is the scooter, then there's the bicycle, then the tricycle, then the go-cart, then the little buggy, then the motorbike, then the car and then finally the racing car. Look at the evolutionary process that has gone from the simple one wheeled item to the two, to the three, to the four, to the different types of four, to the different engines and up to the super racing car. Look how this species has evolved!

*You would know, however, that each one of those items was created separately by someone with a mind, who created different levels of technology according to how each one **fits into the environment** according to its **place in life**. The unicycle for entertainment, the bicycle for easy short distance travelling around, a tricycle for a very young child to learn on, a scooter for fun, a motorbike for the biker who wants to dodge traffic queues, a car for the average person to use to get to work and back and the racing car for the extreme minority who will enter the racing arena. All these have different purposes, different reasons why people use them.*

Then I introduced a second alien who criticised the first alien's evolutionary theory and after an argument the second alien finished the conversation by saying:

"And you're just using your imagination to imagine that they evolved one from another," said the second alien. "The notion that they evolved is all in your head. All you're doing is picking out different levels of sophisticated technology and choosing to believe that a simpler one evolved into another one. The religious blind belief is all on your part, not mine."

This is what Mr Dawkins has done. He has imagined that each of these eye technologies that are found across multiple creatures has evolved, rather than being specifically created by a deity designer who has specifically **made each one fit for its own purpose**. He has taken

God's simpler designs (which at a DNA level are still very complex) and has *imagined* that they are examples of starting points for an evolutionary process. There is nothing, however, of scientific substance in any of his assertions. So my summary conclusion on Mr Dawkins' attempt at showing how the eye can evolve is a very simple one. It is all a load of codswallop! (That's polite slang for rubbish). His whole lecture is self-imagined without a shred of real microbiological evidence to support his theory. In my opinion his lecture is, in fact, an insult to the scientific method and is a typical example of how the evolutionist lives is his/her imagination rather than in reality.

2) The Frog / Bird Illustration!

I'm going to revisit an illustration that will bring together the main points of the last few chapters. We're going to look at how to change a frog into a bird. To do this we need to ask some 'bird questions' such as,

1) How do we turn a hopping frog into a flying bird?
2) What are the laws of aerodynamics?
3) How do those laws,
   a. Impact wing shape?
   b. Impact wing movement?
   c. Impact the nervous system to drive the flying machinery?
   d. Impact feather design?
   e. Impact tail feather balance?
   f. Impact body shape?
   g. Impact body weight?
4) How do we move from frog behaviour to bird behaviour?
   a. Frog croaks to bird song.
   b. Hibernation to migration.
   c. Laying jelly eggs with tadpoles in to laying eggs in a hard shell with a breathing sack in it.
   d. From lily pads to carefully constructed and crafted nests.
5) How do we change skeletal structure?
6) How do we change the flesh of the creature?
7) How do we turn scales into feathers and keep them useful during the time of their development?

8) How do we cause the feet of the frog to turn into the claws of a bird?
9) How do we move from cold blooded to warm blooded and still maintain sensible body temperature whilst the change is taking place?
10) How do we trigger all of these processes within the DNA when **frog behaviours** _do not lean towards_ **bird behaviour** in their daily living?

So the above are **just some** of the 'bird questions' that need to be asked in order for the new information to be created and established within the frog to turn it into a lizard and then a bird. The information change is massively complex and will be beyond the programming capacity of any human being. Then there is the problem of getting it all working along the way **whilst it is still in development**! That's just as big a problem, if not a bigger problem, than the final destination. We all get frustrated when we are on a motorway to find that 'improvements' are being made to the road system and therefore we're forced to drive more slowly than normal. The traffic, however, has to flow (life has to go on) whilst the extra new work is being implemented. So,

1) How will the frog-bird look at each step of the way down its evolutionary process?
2) How will it keep itself working as a viable creature within its environment as each part develops and temporarily stops working or is no longer fitted for purpose?
3) What happens when this process is only half developed and doesn't function anymore due to the nature of programming getting broken when being randomly re-written?

The secularist won't go into any details of how this impossible evolutionary process actually looks at any stage of its partial development, especially when it comes to engineering and interdependent design (whoever heard of a half-formed wing and half-formed tail feathers being useful to a creature as it supposedly turned from a frog into a bird) so we won't show up the stupidity of our thinking by attempting to artistically draw these multiple, millions, billions and trillions of small changes that are meant to add up, over long periods of time, to sophisticated and multi-complex, interdependent change – all expressed in intelligent, high-level, cutting-edge and refined new coding in the DNA that conforms to the laws of aerodynamics. These changes are equivalent to amazing technological jumps. They only work as a unit once each of the parts, those multiple complex and interdependent components, are finally fully assembled and put in place, relating to each other perfectly and in proper balance with each other. No-one suspended the laws of aerodynamics in order for this so called UPWARDS evolution to happen, no one suddenly made copy errors in DNA useful in order for this thing called UPWARDS evolution, this technological miracle, to take place.

The humanist, however, would have us believe that all of the above is possible, even when it breaks the laws of science and engineering. Even though humanity has made itself look completely ridiculous in its attempts to learn to how fly (men jumping off piers with wings strapped to their backs etc.) we're told that somehow the animal kingdom can look just as ridiculous for millions of years and still win the day – getting the technology right without any intelligent planning, guidance and help. Just let the creative handiwork of DNA exchange and 'copy error' and 'time' (lots and lots and lots and lots and lots and lots of copy error and lots and lots and lots and lots and lots of time) do their 'stuff' and all will be well in the end. Throw time into the pot and that great cauldron of evolutionary brewed stew will make it all work. Let's just throw billions of years into that mentally imagined casserole of multiple theories and mixed ideas, stir it all round, and try to say that somehow it happened because we can just use the word 'evolved' or the word 'mutated', and those words will cover over a multitude of sins. That is, they will cover over a multitude of misrepresentations of reality and the impossible breakings of many scientific laws to make the impossible possible. We'll look at the handiwork of a deity designer, who used similar technologies in His creation, and say that this is evidence for evolution; interpreting the evidence in that way allows us to turn 'frog code' into 'bird code' without any viable mechanism to do so. Perverting the interpretation of the evidence like this will allow our fantasy theory to justify completely changing an animal and its behaviours and simply put it down to DNA mix and unguided copy error and the pressures of the environment. None of which have the right **mechanisms** within them to effect UPWARDS technological change.

It becomes believable because the hazy cloud of billions of years covers the event and within that hazy cloud it all somehow happens – even though we can't describe in any kind of detail. Then, out of the cloud, comes a bird. A frog went into the cloud, millions of years passed by, and out of it comes a bird. It's a little like watching a black and white science fiction film from the early 20th Century. Something goes into the box of the mad scientist and then the lights flash and the steam billows and then out of it comes, something completely different. You don't know exactly how, it just came out at the other end. We've added gas and lightning and other 'substances' and then this miraculous UPWARDS evolutionary change has taken place. There has been a complete rewriting of the creature at the cellular level, without the mechanisms to achieve this, and now a new level of sophisticated code within the DNA exists that intricately describes, in a sensible language, the reordering of the millions and billions and trillions of cells that make up the new body parts. Also in the DNA are the new instructions to create the new proteins to look after these new body parts and also a new information highway, a nerve system, from those new parts to the brain so that the brain can take charge of them. Amazing change has occurred. But how has it happened? Well it's the box, the gas, the lightning and the flashing colours in the cloud that makes it all believable. We accept it in the context of the science fiction film genre and the storyline continues with the mad professor having to live with his new creation, which in those kinds of film normally means that the new creature eventually turns bad and eats the scientist for tea!

> **Note:** Ok, take a **DEEP BREATH** because I'm going to write the whole of the next paragraph in **one long sentence** just to get over what you're being asked to believe.

So, via this haphazard set of events we will not only completely change the flesh of the creature from reptile to bird, not only turn it from cold blooded to warm but we'll also construct wings and the bone framework that makes the wings work and the flapping mechanism and get two wings symmetrical evolved, not just one wing at a time, get the wings balanced with each other as a complete and exact mirror image with exactly the same random mutations happening on each wing, in the correct shape and size in comparison with the rest of the body and then we'll get the correct positioning of the wings on the frog's sides and back and we'll streamline the body and we'll change the shape of the head and we'll create a tail with correct feathering on it and create landing gear, slimming down the back legs to be long and stick-like in width, and add feet with claws and we'll hollow out the bones to make the bird light for flight and we'll turn skin into feathers to catch the air (and we'll not even begin to go into the changes that need to take place in the brain and the nervous system to enable all this to happen) and all of this is done by completely rewriting the DNA coding at the microbiological level in order for these new body parts to be designed, developed, and put on one side, laid down as dormant, for millions of years sometimes (because they don't work by themselves until the all the pieces of the technology are finally assembled) and we'll do all of this rewriting of the code via hereditary exchange and 'copy error' – where somehow the remixing of 'frog code' (which will always produce a frog) along with random and unguided data errors in the current code, (which would normally make the code unworkable and produce cancer) will all come together and form not only small data changes but a rewriting of the DNA information and add **brand new information** (from the data error changes that would normally corrupt the code) so that the final new goal of a brand new working DNA programme that dictates how the new body parts are assembled, one to the other to make up the new creature, where precision coding is processed and this new refined information enables the construction of these new body parts and gets them calibrated and effectively working, all works smoothly and beautifully together in harmony and at the same time creates new behaviours within the creature, that has no resemblance to the creature kind it has left behind, and all this is done with **imagined intent** because without **intent** you cannot express new information because information means that you are aware of your environment – even though the evolutionist still insists that the WHOLE PROCESS is driven by chance, random and unguided events!

Phew! If you got through all of that
without taking a breath...
...then it's a miracle,
and so is changing a frog to a bird!

Then, after millions of years, we'll wait and look for the moment when the froggy-bird finally hops and flaps those mostly formed wings that it has been retaining and trying and failing to use for millions of years. Will this generation of froggy-bird finally manage it? Are the bones light enough this time? Are the feathers developed enough this time? Have we caught the direction of the wind this time? If we jump off this rock will we survive this time? Did we remember to quickly mate before we jump in order to preserve our DNA for the next generation? Oh well, here we go, let's jump. Yes! We're up and off and into the air! We're flying! Oops. The tail feathers and bottom shape of the frog are not the correct length for us to sustain flight. Oh well. Let's wait a few more million years before we can develop that technology. Just let's mate and mate and mate again and flap our wings and wiggle our bottoms so that this movement in our bodies can initiate a serious DNA change in that part of the body. The more we wiggle in that part of the body the more that last bit of DNA change will 'wake up and get busy rewriting the code'. Let's force it to happen by a concentration of copy errors. Let's remember that we need to mutate the frogs bottom (and only its bottom) in a certain direction so that the tail feathers can be put into the correct place to stabilise flight and at the same time let's just **cross our fingers and hope** that these unguided copy error processes, these unpredictable and uncontrollable random activities (that can work in and pop out of any part of the bird's body at any time because there's nothing to guide copy error in what it does) doesn't cause us to evolve a none useful body part by mistake that will hinder our desire to fly, like a mutation on the bird's beak or wing which might be useful to help fend off predators but would add weight in the wrong place to stop flight from happening. The newly evolved part may help us survive by fending off competitors for food, but the imbalance of new weight on the beak at the front or on the wing at the side would not stabilise that delicate balance needed for flight to happen. That would certainly stop it from learning to get off the ground! Keep your fingers crossed and we'll evolve a great rear with excellently designed tail feathers to balance things out rather than by mistake developing, for example, a small rhino horn that may protect us from our enemies but at the same time will make the head or wing too heavy and stop us from getting into the air.

Would someone please speak to the DNA in the frog about that and tell the copy errors to give us a break and to construct something useful over this next million years, because the frogs are getting a bit tired of waiting? Their **intent** is to fly, because without **intent** there is no true new information. All of the immense information change within the frog is purposed towards technological change of the most sophisticated kind. It's like watching a group of dedicated mechanics turning a car frame into a mini helicopter. The frame is bashed, warped, shaped with purpose. The internals are rearranged. The electronics completely rewired. The fuel system changed. New technology added where there was none before. Then, finally, after the dedicated mechanics have worked with **intent**, they have evolved the car frame into a helicopter. Every part of the change had purpose because they had pre-knowledge of what the helicopter would look like at the end. The fuel flow, the body shape, the electronic signals, the new landing gear and the chopper blades and all the gearing that moves them were created and assembled with **intent**. It is that **intent** that drives the change because pre-knowledge of what the machine will be after the corporate number of changes has been made is already in place. That's how you make a car fly, corporate change that all works together. That's also how you make a frog fly, massive corporate change from newly developed and completely interdependent technology, sensibly developed and constructed with great purpose to fulfil the final imagined goal! Interdependent technology only works that way.

Simple mutations do not have intent. So believing that these unguided changes can produce anything of **NEW** UPWARDS technological value is based on total and utter blind faith. On this subject of unguided mutations I remember recently watching a TV programme where the speaker opened up a humanist science book and began to rip out of the book all of the pages that had unproven scientific humanistic statements of 'faith' in them rather than scientific fact. It was amazing how many faith statements there were in it. Page after page was ripped out and then dropped to the floor. He then, however, showed the part of the book where humanists gave an example of mutations. They showed a four winged fruit fly. The words added around the image on the page were something like, "Here's an example of mutation. This mutation is not a beneficial one." They also showed a cow that had a fifth leg coming out of its back. It was an example of information gone wrong. The comment that the speaker made was simply this.

> *Why didn't they give an example*
> *of a positive mutation? Simply because they*
> *don't have an example to show you.*

All mutations are non-beneficial (changing eyes from the colour brown to blue is **not** an example of **beneficial change**). They are truly copy errors and nothing more. Copy errors that make individual changes to data (not information) do not build new technology. We've already said that we have a word for copy error when mutation truly gets off the ground in a living organism. It's called cancer. New technology requires a thinking mind to build and design. An insect that looks more like a leaf over time is not new technology; it is simply data change, not new information injection. New technology, where multiple new parts work together to form UPWARDS technological change, requires a thinking mind to create those multiple parts and to put them to the test to see if they work. If the results are promising, then those items are specifically **put on one side**, to retain them, in order for them to be used later on at the final assembly period where **all** of the parts, those finely created and crafted components, will come together, work together, to fulfil the final goal, that is of a machine that **interconnects**, works with **talking and complementary components** (each of which by themselves and of themselves are useless) and through those many components talking and relating to each other, something technologically amazing is enabled. The 'talk' that takes place *between the components*, on what would be classed as 'complex technology' even for a human to create, will be based on new DNA coding. To understand this is essential in order to maintain a proper perspective.

Computer code, for such things as A.I. robots, has to be written **not only** with the new individual body part in mind, but how the body part will function in the light of the rest of the body. The programming is sophisticated and finely tuned to ensure that motion and balances are retained and the specific job that has been defined for that body part is fulfilled. The coding will have pre-knowledge of what the body part is for, so that it can function properly. This pre-knowledge is important and shows the **intent** of the new information that **guides** the new technology to its place of fulfilment *in the light of the rest of the body.*

*The froggy-bird **intends** to fly,*
that is its aim
over millions of years
expressed in tiny changes
coupled with 'happy accidents' that
help the technology 'jump' along its way.

The problem is evolution has no intelligence to drive it, just sideways 'kicks' that come from copy error and DNA mix where natural selection will remove not so well fitting specimens from the environment.

A bird, a bee, a wasp, a butterfly and a bat, however, are able to fly in most incredible ways! Their code for flight is exquisite. Their technologies are amazing. How do sideways copy error 'kicks' in code expressions create new sensible code for new technology via an unguided process of copy errors? A humanist will religiously tell us, according to their blind faith (where they take a leap in the dark and choose to believe that which they cannot explain, sketch or draw) that this unproven UPWARDS EVOLUTION is not the sign of a creator who designed everything and planned and developed and assembled each component in its amazing complexity and who wrote the code to complement it.

It's actually a sign of something far simpler and quite different. It is quite literally...

*...a **miracle** of science!*

SECTION 3

Final Arguments &
Spiritual Truth

Escaping the secularist's excuses for our existence.
The real truth behind life.

***Explosions** do not create,*
construct or calibrate.
*They always **damage**,*
***deconstruct** and **destroy**.*

Our complex existence, therefore,
cannot be accounted for
*by the **random movements***
*of **destructive raw energy***
that we see in the universe today.

Chapters 11-12

- multiple arguments on the fine-tuned calibration of the universe
- dealing with the secularist's arguments
- the underlying spiritual truths that underpin and define living within the confines of the scientific facts of life

Chapter 11 – Bang Goes The Theory!

It's Religion that Drives Us

I need to put in one more set of essential evidence to go into this book. It is an essential chapter that cannot be missed out. It is all to do with why the whole cosmos is **specifically calibrated for life to exist** on this planet. The reason for this, like all of the other chapters in this book, is purely religious. If God is the creator of the heavens and the Earth then you are living on **His** *turf*, you are in **His** *house* or hanging out in **His** *back yard*. If you find yourself a tenant living on someone else's land then you'll also know that it is the land owner who makes the rules. The basic spiritual orientation of humanity is towards self-rule. This self-sufficient orientation that we find within ourselves is viewed very differently by humanism and Christianity. Humanism exclusively labels it as 'normal' and Christianity exclusively labels it as 'fallenness' and 'a continuous expression of our disconnectivity from the divine'. This religious bias that we all continually carry within us (that is a bias either against God or an orientation towards God) is the driving force for science. We unwittingly carry it with us wherever we go and in whatever we do.

This bias is probably expressed more in the science of the origins of the universe than in any other field of study. Our 'creation story' sets the scene for all other religious concepts by which we all live. Start off with God and you not only have to live with God throughout this life but you also have to end with God too, a face to face encounter where you give an account of the life you have lived to someone who is greater than you. So the essential thinking expressed in this next chapter is all about answering the question,

"Are you accountable to God?"

...but the science we will explore in this chapter is whether or not the universe has its current shape and form by chance or by design.

People engaged in this science will insist that they are neutral when 'looking at the evidence' but this claim to neutrality is a denial of our spiritual state. This is the reason why I have to write this chapter. If I again can stand on the shoulders of qualified and experienced scientists and summarise their findings to show that we live in a **finely tuned** universe that cannot be here by accident but one that reveals *design* on an unimaginable scale, then we can establish that we're here by the will and the handiwork of a *designer*. This, as I've already said, changes everything. So I'm now going to outline just some of the main arguments to show that the universe has been highly calibrated by a designer and not assembled by chance. I will, however, keep this chapter as short as possible so that we can move towards finishing this book.

A Clash of Creation Stories
For a long, long time the evolutionist's creation story was called **Steady State Theory**. It was laughable to the humanist that the universe could have a beginning. It was also laughable to the humanist that the Bible not only said, "**In the beginning** God created..." but that the Bible also said that, "...God *created* the heavens and the earth." (Genesis 1:1). The word *created* there literally means...

...to create out of *nothing*.

So there were two things that the humanists mocked.

- there was a beginning
- that all things were created by God out of nothing.

This was seen by secular science as evidence that 'religion' is not based on reality, that Genesis is just a story, and that religion is not in the same league as science. Science is said to be based on fact and religion is said to be based on belief. Nothing could be further from the truth.

> **NOTE:** Every other word for created in the Bible means to create out of something that is already there except for Psalm 51 where David says,

"Create in me a pure heart oh God..."
Psalm 51:10

which matches up with Paul's statement in the New Testament that those who are 'in Christ' are,

"... a new creation..." 2 Corinthians 5:17

So it has been a point of hilarity to the humanist for many years that the Bible affirmed these two basic points,

- there was a **beginning** to the universe
- the universe was created out of **nothing**

However, science did eventually discover the truth that there was a beginning to the universe and the secular science community had to switch over from a universe that was eternally existent to one that started.

> **NOTE:** There are, however, plenty of humanist scientists out there, however, who still believe that the universe is eternal, just in a different way than originally thought. This is expressed, for example, through the bounce theory where the universe expands and then collapses in on itself back to singularity and then explodes out again.

However, most scientists today believe that the universe had a beginning and not only that but that the universe also started from nothing. How amazing. No apology was given to the Christian community for past criticism of the Bible, just a humanistic celebration that *they* had discovered something, as if it was the first time that it had been said.

The Bible, however, goes one step further than the humanist by beginning to describe what that 'nothing' is made from. What the Bible means by something being created out of nothing and what the humanist means by something being created out of nothing may not be the same thing. It is the New Testament that gives us the extra information on this where it says,

> *"...the universe was formed at God's command, so that what is seen was not made out of what was visible."*
> Hebrews 11:3.

So here the Bible says that everything that we see in the universe around us came out of that which, in its original form, cannot be seen. There are two things that need to be taken into account here when we try to understand this statement.

1. You cannot see God's voice, his command.
2. You cannot see that which *he took via the power of his voice* and put into place – from which the universe and the substance of the cosmos were brought into being.

The science and maths that God invented/used in order for Him to bring the universe into being is most probably beyond our understanding. All we're told is that the process that God used was not viewable in its beginnings – and that which is not viewable, to humanity, appears as 'nothing'. This statement is one step further along than the humanist who still cannot account for something randomly appearing out of nothing and then growing, via an unguided random explosion, into immeasurable complexity and order all by itself.

Humanism might catch up with the Bible again at some point. We now know, for example, that information is at the heart of life and information is made up of coded data. Data only exists in the context of **language** and the Bible has told us for millennia that the vehicle God used for creation was **his voice**.

When someone speaks, information (language) is imparted.

This is not a 'happy accident', as the evolutionist would term it, it is a deliberate repeating statement throughout the Bible that as God speaks, so he creates. **Information** and **sound**, therefore, are at the

353

heart of all organisational processes that we see in the universe, amongst both living and non-living material (and if string theory is ever proven to be true that will again back up this statement because string theory is based on the idea of tiny **vibrating** strings and that vibrating will create a sound). The command and sound of God's voice is the engine for the **creation** and **calibration** that is needed to facilitate and sustain life within the cosmos.

The Agents of Creation
We are soon going to look at the above mentioned calibration of the universe, but first I want to make a comparison between the agents of creation, one agent expressed in Christianity and the other in humanism.

The Christian Creation Story
Here are the Christian agents of creation.

> *'You are worthy, our Lord and God, to receive glory and honour and power, for you created all things, and by your will they were created and have their being. Revelation 4:11*

and

> *In the beginning was the Word, and the Word was with God, and the Word was God. He was with God in the beginning. Through him all things were made; without him nothing was made that has been made. John 1:1*

and

> *When you send your Spirit, they are created, and you renew the face of the Earth. Psalm 104:30*

Without going into too much of a theological discussion the Bible makes it clear that all three persons of the trinity were involved in the

354

creation. The *Father* **willed** it, the *Son* **spoke** it and the *Spirit* **implemented** it.

The Bible makes it clear that it is a triune person, therefore, who is behind the universe; the thinking mind of God the Father is specifically the place where it all starts. It is a mind that thought through all of the setup from the quadruple layered calibration of the universe to the microbiological engines and machines that would make up and sustain life. An intelligent mind planned it and purposed it and made it happen; a super intelligence beyond anything that we could imagine. This fits very nicely, in fact now that we have looked at all of the evidence so far, it fits perfectly. By the time we've finished this section you'll understand why.

Then we're told that sound initiated and carried the momentum of creation; not just a noise but a purposeful voice that crafted things into place. Before any humanist scientists scoffs at this notion let me point you in the direction of a genuine scientific discipline, that is still in its infancy – from which we still have much to learn and which may hold all kinds of keys to future knowledge and understanding of the formation of the universe. It is the science of what is called 'Cymatics'.

NOTE: There are some weird cults and other dodgy religious movements in the world today that base some of their thinking on Cymatics. Just because this is the case, it does not mean that Cymatics in itself is wrong – it just means that the idea has been used by other people. The basic science of Cymatics, however, is fundamentally true; just as it is fundamentally true that a magnet has *lines of force* to attract metal objects. Star Wars uses 'the force' in a weirdly religious way but this does not make the true science about magnets taboo!

Cymatics is all about the organisational properties of sound. Here is an excellent silent video to show how non-living matter can be organised into shapes by sound.
https://www.youtube.com/watch?v=wvJAgrUBF4w

It is important to understand, however, that there isn't any data or coded information created by Cymatics, which is **why it will never be able to explain the code at the heart of life** (DNA) but it does show how sound will organise matter into shapes. This science, still in its

355

early stages of development, demonstrates that God using the sound of his voice to create and shape the universe is not alien to the science world. We still have no idea how much 'sound' played in influencing the formation of the universe. The Bible, however, says that sound was central to it all.

> **NOTE:** Language comes before data. Without language we cannot have data, code or information. The fact that God speaks creation into existence, therefore, provides the language base for life. This is not a coincidence. It is just another point of reference to show how fantastic the Biblical account of creation is.

So the Bible says that everything is created by the voice of God and the presence of the person of God the Holy Spirit. As the Bible says,

> *"...and the Spirit of God hovered over the waters." Genesis 1:2*

The Bible goes on to tell us therefore, that all things have come into being via the specific activity of God. The **intent** for creation was 'in God' and the imagined output of what creation would look like was 'in God". He could see what he wanted to create and, via **intent** and **imagined output**, calibrated the universe (and put together the code at the microbiological level of life) to make it all work. The language of God formed the data and the code that expressed the engine of life to be established and at the same time God organised a quadruple calibration of the cosmos that would set up the environment by which life could be sustained; all done via the imagined will of God the Father, the power of the voice of God the Son and the presence of God the Holy Spirit.

The Humanist Creation Story
Let me briefly outline the current humanist creation story. I've written this *slightly sarcastically*, but that is so that I can make the point that there are still a *huge number* of scientific 'unknowns' in this story which can never be verified – just as there is in the Bible which doesn't tell us **how** God did it, as that's not the point of Genesis and the other Biblical texts. The Genesis account is there to tell you

who did it and **who** *you are* in the light of **who** did it. So its communication thrust comes from a totally different angle. The humanist creation story, however, is meant to be a **scientific step-by-step how** story, but it is very, very far from being coherent in any shape or form whatsoever (which is the opposite impression you'll get from our TV screens) hence my sarcasm to emphasise this point.

Here it is from 'Big Bang' to life on Earth.

Once upon the beginning of time, 'nothing' exploded. When that same 'nothing' exploded, something came into being. That something became everything, the universe and all that is in it. Through the 'nothing explosion' therefore, all things came into existence and have their being. Without nothing exploding, there would be nothing at all. The 'everything' that now exists, came into being by the exploding of nothing. In this 'nothing', which is now everything, was light and heat and energy and matter which, through the explosion of nothing, formed the finely tuned calibration of everything. All materials, all life, all machines, all products, all data, all data highways, the exchange of information and the interdependency of processes that cause all things to exist and hold together, these were all exploded into existence by nothing aided by nothing but found their existence and formation through the passing of much time and aided by chance and unguided bumps from casual dead matter. Without nothing, we would not be here. From nothing and by the aid of nothing we live and move and have our being in this multi-complex thing called life. We owe everything to 'nothing' (and therefore we owe nothing to no one) because it is 'nothing' that gave us life.

When put in these terms it is clear to see how much work there is to do. Humanists will tell you that there is so much more to say than that which I've outlined. String theory and inflation theory, for example, are used together to present the idea of the multiverse, but that also opens up a huge can of extra-long and slippery worms.

1) What is this multiverse creator device?
2) What is its substance?
3) What came before the multiverse creator?
4) Did the multiverse creator emerge from something?

5) Was there anything there before the multiverse creator and if so did that appear from nothing?
6) By what power did it evolve itself into existence?
7) If it did evolve, from what did it evolve itself into being?
8) Can a multiverse creator come from nothing?
9) Who/what switched the multiverse creator machine on?
10) What powers the multiverse?
11) What keeps the multiverse going?
12) Where did it get the energy from to create even a single universe?
13) Where does it live?
14) Is there something outside of the multiverse creator?
15) etc.

It is all a vicious circle of arguments which still ends up with **'nothing'** first of all and **then something** *coming into being* from **nothing** and then unimaginable complexity arising from chaos via a set of unguided and random processes.

After all of the above questions about causality have been asked, you then have to continue the questions by asking,

16) What is this multiverse made up of?
17) How did the multiverse making machine come together?
18) Why would it evolve in the first place?
19) What did the multiverse maker look like when it was only partly evolved?
20) What calibrated it so that it created universes correctly?
21) What does the multiverse making machine live inside?
22) Is there anything outside of the multiverse creator?
23) Where does it get all of the energy and matter from to create a new universe?
24) How does it eject universes in such a way as to ensure that they don't bash into one another from the very start?
25) Why would a multiverse creator exist in the first place?

All of these latter questions would be a delight for humanists to look into, though impossible to solve. However, they would not be lacking in imagination, enthusiasm, energy or motivation to produce theory upon theory upon theory to imagine and reimagine what could have been in order for us to be here by chance, no matter how great the odds or how fantastic the imaginations. In the humanist world if you can imagine it, you can believe it – and that makes it ok. The main point, however, that you can see expressed right across the list of questions that I have outlined above, is...

...how do you get something from nothing...

...and what was the **agent(s)** that caused its being and development? Only God is an 'uncaused first cause', as so many theistic scientists and philosophers have pointed out; a timeless and eternal being who has no beginning or end and who decided to create and calibrate this amazing cosmos we see around us today in all its fine-tuned complexity. Humanism has no answer to the causality of everything, so it just keeps quiet about it and doesn't let the conversation go there too often.

Before we get bogged down in this, however, let's look at the calibration of the universe. The biggest problem that humanists have is that the universe has been made 'fit for purpose' and that purpose is for the huge and immense lifeless cosmos to host life on **this planet**. Making sure that the universe is fit for purpose, however, is an indescribably huge job. It is not a matter of just turning a few dials to tweak the cosmos for life to be sustained. The complexity and the intricacy of that fine-tuning shows the workings of a super intelligence that can only be ascribed to God.

The First Level Calibration

The Background Numbers to Life
Wikipedia (yes I've been looking at Wikipedia) quotes Steven Hawking in this way,

*"The laws of science, as we know them at present, contain many fundamental numbers, like the size of the electric charge of the electron and the ratio of the masses of the proton and the electron. ... The remarkable fact is that the values of these numbers seem to have been very **finely adjusted** to make possible the development of life."*

359

Stephen Hawking, 1988. A Brief History of Time, Bantam Books, ISBN 0-553-05340-X, p. 7, 125.

> **NOTE:** The God of the Bible and the 'god' that Stephen Hawking imagines are two different things. Understand that Steven Hawking sees God only in terms of being "a god of the gaps" in science. He assumes that the only reason to believe in 'God' is due to not knowing how things work. Once you understand how something behaves in the universe then you no longer need God. This is again due to a secular background religious conviction that everything is here due to a process. If you want to understand why this 'god of the gaps' concept is wrong can I suggest that you refer to the work of Professor John Lennox. Here's a link to one of his YouTube videos that very effectively puts to bed this idea and says that science points to God rather than takes away any notion that we can be here without God,
> https://www.youtube.com/watch?v=eOr5SM1f0pw

The more that science looks at the universe the greater the puzzle is as to how we got here and how it is all seemingly set up for our survival. We may not be the physical centre of the universe but we seem to be the biological centre of the universe and the universe seems to be purposefully constructed for our benefit.

Even dark energy poses a problem for humanists. Those who say it's there and can be found only open up another door to a corridor of difficult things to walk through. Here again is a quote from Leonard Susskind, (who does not believe in a fine-tuned universe) cited again on Wikipedia,
https://en.wikipedia.org/wiki/Fine-tuned_Universe
...about dark energy and its implications on the cosmological constant. He concedes,

*"The great mystery is not why there is dark energy. The great mystery is **why there is so little of it** [10^{-122}]... The fact that we are just on **the knife edge of existence**, [that] if dark energy were very much bigger we wouldn't be here, that's the mystery. A slightly larger quantity of dark energy, or a slightly larger value of the cosmological*

constant would have caused space to expand rapidly enough that galaxies would not form."

Ananthaswamy, Anil. "Is the Universe Fine-Tuned for Life?" Public Broadcasting Service (PBS).

Even though there are so many humanists out there who do not want God in science, their words and descriptions about the delicately balanced set of fine-tuned numbers that hold the universe together and make life possible, not only unwittingly reveal of the depth of the problem but keep on leaking out and pointing to a 'fine-tuning designer' who is behind it all. For the humanist, it has caused them to rework the language they use to describe what we see in the universe in such a way so that they can keep God out of the picture, which we'll look at soon.

The Constants & Quantities of the Universe
The information below is taken from the YouTube video
https://www.youtube.com/watch?v=EE76nwimuT0

Higgs Vacuum Expectation Value 246.2Gev
Mass of Up, Down Strange Quark 2.4 MeV. 4.8 Me
Mass of the electron, neutrinos (sum) 0.511 MeV, 0.32 eV
Electromagnetism coupling constant 0.00729
Strong nuclear force coupling constant 0.1187
Cosmological Constant $(2.3 \times 10^{-3}$ eV$)^4$
Scalar fluctuation amplitude Q 2×10^{-5}
Baryon dark matter mass per photon 0.57 eV. 3 eV
Entropy of the Universe 4×10^{81} J/K
Number of spacetime dimensions 3 (space) + 1 (time)

These listed numbers may be strange statements made up of mind boggling words and characters to the average person (which they are to me also) but they are deeply meaningful to any physicist or astrophysicist. The YouTube video referenced above starts off in the following way,

"From galaxies and stars down to atoms and subatomic particles the very structure of our universe is determined by these numbers. These are the fundamental constants and quantities of the universe. Scientists have come to the shocking realisation that each of these

*numbers has been carefully dialled to an astonishingly precise value. A value that falls within an exceedingly narrow life permitting range. If **any one of these numbers** were altered by even a hair's breadth, no physical interactive life of any kind could exist anywhere. There'd be no stars, no life, no planets, no chemistry."*

The video then goes on to talk about gravity and says that the force of gravity is determined by the gravitational constant. The Gravitational Constant is 6.67408 × 10-11 m3 kg-1 s-2 and the equation that determines the force of gravity is $F=G \frac{m1m2}{r2}$.

We're then told that if this constant varied by just 1 in 10^{60} parts, none of us would exist. 10^{60} is a number of this length, 1,000,000,000,000,000,000,000,000,000,000,000,000,000,000,000,000,000,000,000,000. It is a number too big for the human brain to get its thinking around. The video explains the enormity of this number by saying that we have 10^{14} number of cells within our bodies. 10^{60}, however, is a much, much bigger number than 10^{14}, in fact 10^{15} is a much bigger number than 10^{14}, so 10^{60} is a quantum leap in size. We know that there are sixty seconds on a clock face that determine one minute's worth of time. We can see each second go by as the second hand 'ticks' from one notch on the clock face to the next. The film goes on to talk about expressing this 10^{60} number on a dial, like a clock face. So, imagine that the 60 notches around the edge of the clock face were changed from 60 notches (that is 60 seconds that together make up one minute of time) to represent the force of gravity which is 10^{60} instead - which is, 1,000,000,000,000,000,000,000,000,000,000,000,000,000,000,000,000,000,000,000,000 notches. Then you zoomed in sooooo much that you could actually see the different notches that ran around the edges of the clock (just like you can when you're watching a second hand go around a clock face) and you watched the gravitational constant move by **just one** of those notches. If you saw the gravitational force move by just one notch then life in the whole of the universe **could not exist**. That's how finely tuned the universe is! So a single movement on the scale of 10^{60} would mean none of us would be here at all!

The film goes on to say,

"If the gravitational constant had been out of tune by just one of these infinitesimally small increments, the universe would have either expanded and thinned out so rapidly that no stars could form and no life could exist or it would have collapsed back on itself with the same result. No stars, no planets and no life."

It's an amazing thing to discover. This, from the very start, is a poke in the eye to anyone who suggests that a big, **random** and **unguided** 'BANG' just started things off by **accident** and for some reason that the gravitational force from that 'BANG' just happened to be *just right* in order for everything else to fall into place. BANG and all of the numbers in the universe that make all of the fine tuning for life to exist were just *'there'* by some word that we call *'chance'*.

The problem for humanists, however, as we've already said, is that this force of gravity does not just stand by itself. The YouTube video I referenced gave us ten numbers as examples at the start of the film and it informed us that there are many more than those mentioned. The video goes on to give more information about other fine-tuned examples and then quotes from various scientists, some of them humanist and pro-evolution, about the fine tuning behind universe.

Here's one that it quotes from Fred Hoyle.
"A common sense interpretation of the facts suggests that a super intellect monkeyed with physics... and that there are no blind forces worth speaking about in nature. The numbers one calculates from the facts seem to me so overwhelming as to put this conclusion almost beyond question." Fred Hoyle

Here's another link to a short YouTube video on the fine tuning of the universe. https://www.youtube.com/watch?v=I37dj9cbgUE
Again this video starts off by saying,

"Scientists once thought that whatever the initial conditions of the universe might have been, given enough time and a little luck, eventually intelligent lifeforms like ourselves would evolve. But instead during the last 50 years or so scientists have discovered, to their surprise, that the existence of intelligent life in this universe depends upon a complex and delicate balance of initial conditions given in the 'Big Bang' itself. In fact it appears that the universe has been

incredibly fine-tuned for the existence of intelligent life from the very moment of its inception. And this fine tuning is beyond comprehension in its delicacy."

The video gives examples of more fine tuning numbers and then quotes Roger Penrose of Oxford University. It says,

"Roger Penrose of Oxford University has estimated that the odds of the initial low entropy state of the early universe obtaining by chance alone is one chance out of 10 to the power of 10 to the power of 123 $10^{10(123)}$; a number which is so incomprehensible that to call it astronomical would be a wild understatement."

Then the video adds,

*"The examples of fine tuning are so **diverse** and so **numerous** that they are unlikely to disappear with any future advance of physics. The fine tuning is here to stay and requires some sort of explanation of its existence."*

Finally the same video quotes Robert Jastrow and says,

"Robert Jastrow, who was the head of NASA's Goddard Institute for space studies, has said that this is the most powerful evidence for the existence of God ever to have come out of science."

So it is beyond question that the basic setup of the universe is extraordinary and demands looking at. This is the first level calibration of the universe; the background numbers that together make life possible.

- -
The Second Level Calibration
- -

I'm going to begin this section by making reference to this video, https://www.youtube.com/watch?v=IMbEVv3IsGY
Here Hugh Ross outlines the second level calibration of the universe. He starts off by saying,

*"Earth has been hung in **precisely** the **right location** to receive all of the elements that are essential for life."*

He unpacks this statement by saying how unlikely it is for life to exist anywhere else in our galaxy due to the fact that there is not only the need for the *just right elements* to have been formed from dead stars…

> **NOTE:** *Carbon*, for example, is a *just right element*. It is essential for life. It forms nearly one fifth of the human body. Carbon is formed when a star goes supernova, i.e. it dies.
>
> Here's a quote from https://www.sciencelearn.org.nz/resources/1727-how-elements-are-formed
>
> *"When a star's core runs out of hydrogen, the star begins to die out. The dying star expands into a red giant, and this now begins to **manufacture carbon atoms** by fusing helium atoms."*

…but that the planet itself has to be carefully placed at a certain distance from the centre of the galaxy itself. If the planet is too close to the centre of the galaxy then the gravitational forces would be too strong for life and if it were too far away from the centre of the galaxy then…

"…the stellar population becomes too sparse for planet building. The heavy elements generated by super novae and white dwarf binaries are too few and far between, not enough building material to make planets."

Hugh Ross goes on to say that there is a thin circular band in our galaxy, a minimum distance from the centre of the galaxy, where our solar system **has to reside** in order for life to exist. That band sits delicately in-between the centre of the galaxy and the outer edge of the galaxy, far enough away from both for life to exist. Our solar system is, therefore, set in just the right place. Outside of that designated space, life cannot exist on planet Earth.

The Third Level Calibration

The same video then goes on to talk about the solar system and how things are set up 'just right' for life to be kept safe. It talks about Jupiter and how it is positioned as a comet shield for Earth. It is positioned 'just so' so that it deflects comets and asteroids and sometimes takes the hit for us. Without it being there, life on Earth would have be wiped out long ago. He goes on to say,

"Any planets capable of sustaining life needs a just right sized Jupiter standing guard to shield them from life ending asteroids and comet impacts."

He also states that the size of Jupiter and its distance from Earth to do its job of being a planet shield has also been carefully calculated. If Jupiter was bigger or closer to us then its gravitational pull would affect our orbit around the sun. Not only that but the other gas planets, Saturn, Uranus and Neptune, that sit in-between us and Jupiter, play the same role of protectors. He says,

"To get the best protection from these hits from comets and asteroids, Jupiter must be the biggest Saturn must be the next biggest and you want smaller gas giants behind it. You need all four in their special orbits."

*For **all** these planets to have an almost circular orbit **on the same horizontal plain** as the Earth is unique. This pattern of protection has **not been observed** anywhere else in the viewable universe. It is again an example of a calibration within our solar system.*

All other objects in the universe that orbit a larger planet, sun or star do not orbit **on the same horizontal plain**. That is, they may well orbit the object together, but at different heights of orbit. What makes our solar system unique is that all of the planets are on the same horizontal plain, the outer gas planets shielding the Earth from meteors. Random 'Big Bang' explosions, or other movements of energy that are the knock-on results of the 'Big Bang', can't achieve that type of sophisticated alignment. Our solar system has been calibrated for life to exist on this planet.

> **NOTE:** I will look at what is called the '**Nebular Theory**' at the end of this chapter which suggests a reason for this horizontal plain line-up.

Hugh Ross finishes off this video by talking about the mean motion resonances that each planet gives off. He says that the mean motion resonances of the larger gas planets would disrupt Earth's orbit but, again, the smaller rock planets that sit between them and the Earth break up these resonances so that we are kept safe. So he says,

"Literally every planet in our solar system plays a crucial role in making advanced life possible here on Earth."

- -
The Fourth Level Calibration
- -

The fourth level of calibration is focussed on the conditions that are on and around the Earth itself. The two most famous of these are,

- the Earth's distance from the sun
- the Earth's electromagnetic field

Most of us know that the life on this planet is due to the Earth being just the right distance from the sun. The sun is the main source of life for this planet. I don't need to tell you the obvious that it provides light and heat. These are basic to life. The situation is, however, not quite as simple as that. The fact is that there is no such thing as a 'just right' distance from the sun. This is because the sun produces a by-product that is very harmful to life on Earth, the solar wind. The sun's solar wind would accomplish two things if it was allowed to impact our planet,

- a destruction of the ozone layer
- a removal of Earth's atmosphere

367

...and it doesn't take a genius to look at those two items and to know that the result of solar wind would mean an end to life on this planet. All of the water would evaporate and we would become as dry as Mars. The solution to this problem is quite specific, the answer lies at the centre of Earth. As you know our planet's core is a very hot place. This central area is vital for life to exist. If our planet's core happened to be different from what it is, life could not be sustained. We have an inner core and an outer core. The outer core is molten. Having a molten outer core produces an electromagnetic field around the planet. That electromagnetic field protects us, shields us, from the sun's activity; the unwanted ultraviolet radiation that is sporadically ejected from the surface of the sun and impacts our planet in the form of solar wind storms.

So on the one hand we have an energy source to keep us alive, the sun gives light and heat, but on the other hand that very same source of energy that sustains life is such an expression of raw power, and so close to us, that the by-products of its activities would take life away. Intervention has to be made on our behalf so that the by-products can be dealt with whilst still maintaining the benefits of being so close to the energy source. It's a little like being in a cold snow storm that is so biting cold it would freeze you to death in moments and at the same time standing next to an all-consuming fire. Step away from the fire and you die, stand too close to the fire and you burn. There is no 'just right place' to prevent death from taking place. Therefore, you have to choose one. The solution is to choose to stand close to the fire but at the same time to have some sort of 'heat protection' so that you will not burn. That's the equivalent to that which we have in our relationship with the sun.

Here's a link to a 2 minute video that outlines how the electromagnetic field works and keeps us safe, https://www.youtube.com/watch?v=URN-XyZD2vQ

More Attuned Circumstances
It's not just this one setup, however, that is essential to form the delicate balance of life on planet Earth. There are multiple finely tuned circumstances that all need to come together at the same time. One of the best websites to see this in condensed form is at the following address:

http://coldcasechristianity.com/2015/four-ways-the-earth-is-fine-tuned-for-life/

Here J. Warner Wallace points out 4 essential conditions for life on earth. Here's a summary of what he says,

1) The Earth's distance from the sun, its tilt and its rotational speed.
    a. The correct distance enables the water cycle to work.
    b. A change in the tilt would not allow climate.
    c. The speed of our rotation keeps us from becoming too hot or too cold for life to exist.
2) Earth's atmospheric conditions determined by gravity.
    a. If gravity were stronger we would have an overdose of methane and ammonia.
    b. If gravity were weaker we would not have enough water.
    c. With the right amount of gravity we can have, *"a finely calibrated ratio of oxygen to nitrogen—just enough carbon dioxide and adequate water vapour levels to promote advanced life,"*
3) The thickness of our planet's crust to ensure the right quantity of oxygen and its seismic activity allows nutrient recycling and stable carbon dioxide release.
4) Our planet having an orbiting moon that stabilises Earth's orbit and rotation.

There is again so much more to be said on the delicate balances we find where life is expressed on this planet. So we see from this quadruple calibration of the universe that we have,

- the wider numbers that determine the shape and size of the universe and how it behaves so that life can exist
- the placement of our solar system within the galaxy
- the positioning of the planets within our solar system to keep life safe on Earth
- the structure of our planet, and its direct relationship with the sun and moon, that allows and sustains life according to the resources that are contained on the earth and within its atmosphere

369

So the big question is, "How did it all get like this?" This 'setup' has to be explained. It is yet another example of the many fires that I mentioned earlier, breaking out in the humanist's camp.

> **NOTE:** There are many more levels of calibration of the universe than those which I have outlined; I've just chosen four as a good number to illustrate the situation. For example, we could look at the shape of the universe or other shapes within the cosmos etc. as another level of calibration to consider. There are so many different things to study when looking at what is necessary for life to exist on this planet. The more we know the more we understand that life is dependent on multiple, multiple conditions being 'just right' before it can inhabit a hostile universe.

- -
The Four Arguments
- -

As I watch more and more videos on this subject it seems that there are four arguments that seek to account for this incredible calibration.

1) The universe has to be set up this way – the laws of nature dictate this is the case.
2) It is pure chance, it has just happened this way.
3) The multiverse – there are loads of universes out there and we just happen to be in one that works.
4) A designer put it together – direct evidence for God.

I'll spend a few moments looking at each of these statements, but you already know that I will be arguing for option 4 as the only viable reason for us being alive in the universe on this planet. As I said earlier on, humanists are trying to look at each of the evidences for fine-tuning as if each were isolated incidents, not connected with each other. Put them all together, however, and we see an amazing multifaceted witness that the divine is behind life.

1) The Universe has to be set up this way

The biggest problem with this stance is that the laws of nature do not dictate such things as the cosmological constant. The cosmological constant is expressed within the universe but there is no underlying reason, based on the laws of nature, for it to be what it is; it is not directly determined by anything else. It has no root causality from any laws in the universe that would justify it for what it is. The cosmological constant value could have been easily set at a different option than it currently is. So too with all of the other variants within the universe, **there is no underlying reason** for them to be as they are, but they are what they are in order for life to exist. That's the problem staring humanists in the face. No reason for it, yet it is as it is.

2) It is Pure Chance

I don't need to say very much on this section because most humanists today will not put this down to just 'chance'. Let me briefly quote from Michael Shermer (who is not a theist) on this where he says in an online interview,
https://www.youtube.com/watch?v=aazsDCqbCoo

Interviewer: *"Michael you've written that the fine-tuning of the universe is the best argument for a theological perspective. Why did you say that?"*

Michael Shermer: *"Well if I was a theist, which I once was, I would make that argument because the **natural explanation** for the fine-tuning is **not all that great**..."*

The statement made by Michael Shermer that the "**natural** explanation for the fine tuning of the universe", which we call 'chance', is "**not all that great**" is a traditional humanistic _understatement_. It is often put this way because it is a genuine admission. However, the humanist will not want that admission to highlight the problem too much. You don't want to create too many waves by your admission, so just stay calm and gently mention the problem, but don't highlight it too much. The understatement saying that the naturalist reason for us being here, *"is not all that great..."* keeps the **alarming evidence** from shouting out too loudly. A humanist will not say that the natural explanation is a,

> ### *"...a way out and total impossibility..."*

or

> ### *"...complete blind faith in the face of the obvious, which is the facing of unbelievable odds beyond our imagination – so much so that any sane person who had any understanding of the subject would say it is impossible for us to be here by chance."*

These sorts of statements are not made by humanists. Gentle and quiet admissions are far better and don't bring our attention to the alarming problem that is in our midst. So let me quickly add to Michael Shermer's statement. He says that the natural explanation is *not all that great,*" I would say that the natural explanation is "totally unworkable" which is a far more accurate representation of the facts.

3) The Multiverse

Agnostic or atheistic scientists, like Michael Shermer or Paul Davies, seem to have opted for the multiverse as the solution to this problem. The idea for multiverse, as I've already hinted at, is based on string theory and inflation theory. Strangely enough Michael Shermer, in the online interview I've quoted above, says about the multiverse that, *"I think it's a reasonable theory, **just as good as the theological answer**, to say that there are multiple bubble universes..."*

Then he adds,
*"If you have enough of these bubble universes, somebody is bound to **win the lottery** and become us..."*

Then he adds,
"Granted there is no empirical evidence for these other bubble universes..."

He then gives the example of how our understanding of the universe has grown over the centuries and uses that to **justify** accepting the bubble universe, the multiverse theory, as a coherent alternative to God.

The interviewer (also not a theist) then says,

"But where we have come in the last few decades is looking at some of these fundamental constants of nature and seeing an extraordinarily tight range required for, not just one, but maybe a half dozen or more of these including the cosmological constant which controls the speed of the expansion of the universe which some say has to be accurate to 60 decimal places, you know 9 decimal places is a billion and 18 decimal places is a billion, billion and they are at 60! What are you going to do with that?"

To which Michael Shermer responds,

"Okay what do you do with that? Well you say okay there must be a God that designed it that way or you say there are multiple bubble universes and if there's enough of them, one of them is bound to be at that parameter or you say, 'Beats me, I don't know.'"

I personally find it amazing that Michael Shermer decides that the *multiple bubble universe* argument is **as good as** *the theological argument* when he admits in the same interview that there is **no empirical evidence** for it. His justification for this is by making reference to our changing world view throughout history as we learnt from generation to generation more about the universe. However, he fails to mention that the reason why the human race has changed its ideas on the size of the universe etc. is all due to the fact that we can...

...see, observe and measure

...that which is constantly around us. We did not change our views on the size of the universe via our imaginations of what we thought might be 'out there'. The history of changing scientific thought has been driven first by observation and then by measurement and mathematical equation. What we see in front of our eyes right now is a set of amazing **known** calibrated numbers that determine the shape and behaviour of the universe and everything in it. To justify it being there on the basis of pure imagination without any empirical evidence for it, to say it is all here as a result of a multiverse, (**and to say that**

373

this theory is as good as the theological one) is pure, unbridled humanistic bias, part of the rhetoric that comes from belonging to the '**Anything but God Society**'. The bubble universe is still complete and utter fantasy in the minds of scientists. Then he adds the phrase,

"If you have enough of these bubble universes, somebody is bound to ***win the lottery*** *and become us…"*

Again, this is an amazing statement. We see lotteries all-round the globe where people win money. Most people who play these lotteries will never ever win them because the odds are too great. However, in comparison to the odds that the cosmological constant ***alone*** would be what it is so that life could exist, winning a human lottery is a cinch! So when you look at his statement that if there were enough universes out there, then one of them has to get the conditions correct (just like in a lottery win), you have to ask,

Just how many universes do you expect to have on your hands in order to make it sensible to believe that one of them, unaided by the divine, could ***get it correct*** *by accident and produce life?*

Not only do you have to have all the background numbers to the universe correct (and even getting one of those correct, as we have said, is a number beyond our imagination) but you also have to have the initial low entropy state at the start of the universe correct too which we've said Roger Penrose of Oxford University has estimated the odds to be $10^{10^{(123)}}$ and then we have the odds of the placement of the solar system within the galaxy, the placement of the planets within that solar system (along with their orbit around a certain sized sun) and then the makeup of those planets from either rock or gas and then the tilt and speed of the Earth and its need of a moon and the thickness of the Earth's crust and its need for a molten centre outer core for an electromagnetic field to act as a shield and then just the right amount of resources on the planet, water, carbon, oxygen etc. along with a sustained atmosphere and water cycle and then the odds in the microbiological world of amino acids randomly coming tougher without purpose and staying together to somehow, without any guidance, auto-organise themselves to form a single protein that somehow forms itself into an amazing 'simple cell' (which is impossible as there is no such thing as a simple cell) that has DNA at its centre which is more complex than we can ever imagine because the code just self-assembled that way...

> **NOTE:** Remember as well we said that even creating code is not like a lottery win. Code has to have every digit within its precision data setup in the **exact right order**. With a lottery you just have to match the numbers no matter which order the numbers are called. Code is a quantum leap away from that. It has to be written within the context of a language, it has to express intent and it has to have each character within that code expressed **in the right order**. In the case of the cell, this order within the code determines the order of the amino acids so that they would 'fold correctly' based on their shape interacting with each other and so forming the correct final shape that gives the newly made protein its identity and abilities to work within the body! So a 'lottery win' doesn't even begin to explain the problem properly!

I could go on and on and on, unpacking the multiple complexity of the situation. Then, in the light of all of this, Michael Shermer tells us that it's like '*winning the lottery*' if a universe gets it right! Is he wanting there to be a trillion, trillion, trillion, trillion, trillion, trillion, trillion, trillion universes out there (and trillions times more) in order to justify his lottery statement? Right in front of our eyes, however, we see a fine-tuned universe for life that has a fine-tuned calibration that extends from the massive size of the universe right down to the microbiological level and the '**Anything but God Society**' still puts it down to a **lottery win**! How inaccurate is that. That statement is a complete misrepresentation of reality and forms part of the mass mis-information that is fed into the Western mind-set.

Let me quote from a YouTube interview with agnostic Paul Davies where he talks briefly about the motivation for the multiverse theory. Don't forget that Paul Davies is a pro-evolutionist figure. https://www.youtube.com/watch?v=HWuC6jh1r0Q

*"Part of the motivation for introducing the multi-verse explanation for the biological fine tuning of the universe was **to finally get rid of**

God because the explanation that the universe is so fit for life **because God made it** that way just appeared **an anathema** to many scientists,"

What an incredibly **honest** statement and it shows the **true anti-God bias** that exists within the scientific community. The reason for moving to multiverse for so many was not 'the need for multiverse theory itself' because science has naturally pointed us in that direction (because of the direct evidence that we see before our very eyes) but the movement towards multiverse for so many is because of the need to...

...keep God out of science.

I would personally add to that statement that if the universe had not been so fine tuned for life and so did not point towards the divine, we would not have the multiverse theory amongst scientists today!

Paul Davies goes on to say,

"Now I think that Darwin did a great job in the eliminating the need for God in designing the species..."

...this is something that we've spent lots of time on in previous chapters showing that Darwin was totally wrong. He then goes on to say,

*"...but I would certainly say that the universe appears as if it's got a meaning or a purpose. A better word I have is that the universe seems to be **about something**. Indeed you can't be a scientist unless you suppose that there is **a coherent scheme of things** and that when we do our science, when we get to the next layer of reality, we sort of uncover what's coming next we expect to find **order** and **rationality**, we don't expect it all to fall apart, if we go to the next level. So science is **predicated on this act of faith** that there is a **coherent** scheme of things and that the universe isn't just some sort of arbitrary hodgepodge of odds and ends, its hanging together. So it's about something.... it does seem to make sense and most physicists, even the most strongly atheistic physicists, expect it to **make sense** to them. As*

an ***act of faith*** they believe that it's **intelligible** and beautiful furthermore but it's not just, "Oh yes, that's what this is, it has such and such mass, and that force does such and such". They expect to have an **underlying theory** where it's that wonderful sense of, "Ah now I see how it all falls into place... the more we do science, the more we learn about the **wonders** of the universe we're in, the more convinced I am that it's **about something**, there is **a scheme of things**, there is ultimately some sort of **meaning** to it all."

Paul Davies still looks to the multiverse to provide the answers and does not seem to want to let God in to that part of the conversation that says, "This is the reason why we are here," but at least he is being very honest in his statements, far more honest than so many humanists I've encountered in books or on film. The Bible, however, has something very specific to say when all of the overwhelming evidence is before humanity and humanists still choose to think in a different direction because it is, as Paul Davies said in the last video *"an anathema to many scientists"* to let God into science. The Bible says this,

> *"For although they knew God, they neither glorified him as God nor gave thanks to him, but their thinking became futile and their foolish hearts were darkened. Although they claimed to be wise, they became fools... They exchanged the truth about God for a lie,"*
> *Romans 1:21-22,25*

A Designer put it Together
I like the work of J. Warner Wallace on this topic where he looks at what he calls *Cold-Case Christianity*. He spent his career on the police force as a homicide detective. He knows what it is to turn up at a potential crime scene and to examine the evidence to see if someone has committed a crime or whether or not the dead person has just died. He outlines in his book, "God's Crime Scene' how he learnt to look at the evidence. As a new member of the team, being 15 years the junior to the others, he found it a steep learning curve when he first joined homicide. He remembers turning up at a crime scene where a gentleman was dead inside his house, though no-one had gone into the house. It looked like suicide, and he himself would have

come to that conclusion, until the experienced team leader arrived and turned over all of their initial ideas by systematically examining all of the minute clues and evidences that were at the scene of the crime. The culprit was eventually caught and the crime solved. So the question always asked was,

Has someone 'off scene' caused
what we now see 'on scene'?

In other words, has that which we now see in front of our eyes been caused by some accident or has someone who is now 'off scene' i.e. not here anymore, been the cause of that which we're looking at? Can we find evidence to prove that someone else **was here** and **did things** to **cause** what we're now seeing?

The question could be put round the other way to ask, "Is there enough evidence inside the location, where the dead person is, to show that the person died of natural causes or even of suicide?" If the answer was 'yes' then case closed. If the answer was 'no' then you know, **by deductive logic**, that someone else who is currently 'outside' the crime scene (they have left the crime scene and are no longer viewable) is party to the crime. Is there enough evidence to show that they **were once there** at the crime scene? Does the evidence tell us, by deductive logic, that **someone needs pursuing** as the culprit of the crime? To establish that this is true,

...he had to look at evidences in the present to see if
*they proved an **activity by an extra unseen person in***
***the past**, even if that person could not be currently*
seen in the present at the crime scene.

Bringing his skills as a detective to the problem of the highly ordered universe, he sets out to use the same principles and shows how the universe has been **meddled** with by someone who is now 'off scene' i.e. from outside the universe in order for it to end up in the state that it currently is in, i.e. ready to sustain life. Here's a link to one of his online teaching videos where he outlines his approach to

discovering truth and how we establish truth in the natural world when we look at the universe,
https://www.youtube.com/watch?v=aT-Rdplb9A4&t=2s

This is exactly what we're doing when we look at the calibration of the universe and the fact that information is at the heart of all life. We're seeing that someone is responsible for us being here because the cosmos has been **tampered with** for life to exist. Deductive logic paves the way for seeing the impossibility of the universe auto-organising itself into existence and into its current level of calibration and for life to come from non-life, flying in the face of the 2nd law of thermodynamics, and creating data, code, information and the context by which to process that information for life to exist. So, in the light of all of this, we can now see **where** God touched the cosmos, even if we don't fully understand **how** he did it. This touching of the cosmos is expressed in two ways, which we have already been looking at in detail. They are,

- a cosmos setup for life
  - calibrated background numbers
  - planetary spatial complexity
  - our planet moulded and shaped for life
- information at the heart of life
  - a cellular environment made ready for information processing
  - DNA coding with intent for work to be done, placed at the heart of the cell

Both of these point to **intervention** rather than auto-organisation, simply because auto-organisation is not only highly unlikely, it is in fact impossible.

- -
The Secularist's Response
- -

A Verbal Get Around
The response of humanists to the fine tuning of the universe has been interesting. They have chosen to use words very carefully in a variety of ways in order to 'keep God out' of the conversation and to

make suggestions in their general talk that provide a 'natural solution' to the problem.

Phrase 1 – Our Type of Life
Evolutionists now commonly use the phrase,

"Our type of life..."

...when talking about our place within the universe. This phrase is repeated by person upon person in their talks, discussions and lectures as if it is quite normal to think that **there are or will be** 'other forms of life' out there (based on the utterly misplaced conviction that we are truly here by accident ourselves). The repetitive use of this phrase gives it a measure of weight in the science community that it should not have at all – there is NO evidence for life anywhere else in the universe. However, this type of language is persistently used in order to back up the secularist's religious world view, a little like philosophers or theologians who come up with a concept and then quote each other using that phrase in their written works and the more it gets repeated, the more it is accepted as 'true' even though it is just an idea. Such and such said it first and then so and so repeated it and then it was quoted and quoted again until it becomes part of the family of the fabric of the general background talk. Once in place, something that is totally unproven becomes acceptable, like the phrase, 'it evolved' where no foundational empirical evidence is given, just the phrase used. Because the phrase is accepted, then that opens the door for the unproven description of what happened to be accepted. Let me give you an example of this from Wikipedia that quotes the physicist Victor Stenger.

https://en.wikipedia.org/wiki/Fine-tuned_Universe
*"Physicist Victor Stenger objected to the fine-tuning, and especially to theist use of fine-tuning arguments. His numerous criticisms included what he called "the wholly **unwarranted assumption** that only **carbon-based life** is possible." In turn, the astrophysicist Luke Barnes has criticised much of Stenger's work."*

So it's amazing that Wikipedia quotes Victor Stenger as saying that it is an "...*unwarranted assumption that only carbon-based life is possible.*" The fact of the matter is that

- there is no evidence whatsoever for life anywhere else
- the theory that life can come from non-life by accident and then auto-organise itself into its current state of mind-boggling complexity is, in the light of the difference between data, code and information, incoherent and unworkable

Yet despite this, we have such strong words from humanists who insist that the fundamentalist style of language that says 'our type of life' is still acceptable within the field of science. The assumption behind the phrase is that...

*...we can **clearly see** that there is **clear evidence** that there **will be** other types of life out there.*

That is what is inferred by the statement. Nothing could be further from the truth. It is an example of blatant wishful thinking that comes from an anti-theistic religious world view commitment. There is no foundational empirical evidence for this stance. It is a wilful choice of humanists to express this kind of thinking which demonstrates a willingness to fly in the face of the facts.

Phrase 2 – From Design to Purpose or Meaning
Physicists, such as Paul Davies, have not liked the way in which Christians have quoted him in the past when he has used the word, 'design' to describe the order within the universe. He says,
https://www.youtube.com/watch?v=HWuC6jh1r0Q

"*...sometimes I used to use that word 'design' but I'm very scared of doing that these days.*"

However, he and so many other scientists **have** used the word 'design' in the past. What is the reason for this? Well simply because this is the **best word** to use to describe the most incredible wonderful set up that we see around us.

> *To not use the word 'design' is to deny the reality of things.*

Wanting to use the word 'purpose' or the phrase 'has meaning' doesn't convey the reality of the universe's complexity. We see all around us, from whatever level of life we're looking at, multiple layers of carefully constructed and calibrated contexts that *all work together* for life to exist. It is, however, the '**Anything but God Society**' that persistently works against seeing life as it truly is. It tries to fit this calibration into another box that is not labelled with God's name; the box does not fit the shape of the evidence nor can it contain the evidence, it just serves to hide the evidence and relabels it something which it is not. Within any other field of life we would call this type of hiding the facts as 'a cover-up'.

Phrase 3 – A Misrepresentation of Odds

In order to justify the impossible secularists have taken to once again misrepresenting the facts when looking at possibility and chance. I remember coming across one pro-evolutionary humanistic argument about 'amazing odds that actually happen'. The argument went something like this,

1) You and I can see stars in the sky.
2) A light particle travels millions of light years from the star across the galaxy to where you are.
3) That light particle enters your eye so that you can see the star.
4) What are the odds that that particular light particle will be the one to enter your eye so that you can see the star?
5) This shows us that events do happen against amazing odds.

It only takes a few moments of looking at this logic to see its flaws. When you look up into the night sky you **have to see** the stars that are there. This is because,

1) Every star is emitting a huge number of particles of light; so many that we don't have the mathematical language to express the number.
2) Those particles of light **travel together** across space.
3) When you look up at the night sky your eye receives a small measure of those light particles so that you can see the star shining in space.
4) You **have to see the star**, however, because there are so many light particles coming from it in mass together that every time you look in that direction, you will **always see the star**.
5) Those travelling particles of light are not doing anything else but travelling and 'being themselves'. We're not looking at 'odds for them evolving' into something else and making a new technology! There is no development in the light particle, just loads and loads of them, collectively travelling together, to enable you to see the star.

This is the point to make. There are so many light particles being emitted by each star that when you look up at the night sky you will always see the stars on a cloudless, clear night.

Let me put it another way. If I were to stand on the sea shore and let the waves move over my feet then I am guaranteed to get my feet wet. Saying, what's the odds that a certain 'drop' of water will be the one to hit my toe out of all of the other 'drops of water' that are in the ocean is a nonsense. The issue is that the ocean is full of drops of water, a number beyond counting, and there are so many of them that if I were to put my feet on the edge of the beach where the sea meets the sand, my feet will be gua**ranteed to encounter the water** and get wet. There are so many droplets in the ocean all working together as 'one' unit of water that I cannot help but get wet. The droplets all work together to form the wave on the beach. Also the droplets of water that make up the wave are not 'evolving' in some way into something else, something that requires information to be at its heart. The water droplets, within the wave, are simply on the move. There is no real comparison between this and evolving life.

So when we look at the cosmological constant we're saying that the odds against it being correct are **one chance** in 10^{60}. Notice the words, 'one chance' that I've just used. When our universe came into existence were saying that there was **one chance** in this number, 1,000,000,000,000,000,000,000,000,000,000,000,000,000,000,000,00 0,000,000,000,000 for the cosmological constant to be correct. We're not saying that suddenly there were a trillion times a trillion times a trillion times a trillion times a trillion universes suddenly coming into being and each one a random 10^{60} chance of the cosmological constant being correct and somehow there were so many universes being given birth out there, from some unknown source of incredible power exploding them all into being, that one of them just had to get the cosmological constant correct! We're talking about 1 universe coming into being and the multiple odds against that one universe having the many and varied conditions that are needed for life to exist and all being in place together at the same time. All of those conditions for life are just as problematic as the cosmological constant and each one is so unlikely that setting up a scenario where even one of them could happen is almost beyond our imagination. Don't forget that after getting all of the impossible background numbers correct, we need to have the second and third and fourth levels of calibration of the universe to take into account as well. Then we have to look at the impossibility of life coming from none life with information at its centre along with a calibrated environment to process the information effectively.

> **NOTE:** On this point too, remember that when we looked at the odds of even a small string of amino acids coming together by chance in the correct order we saw that the odds against this were astounding. We also have to remember that this was also a 'one off' chance scenario as well. The background to this scenario is not that lightning hit a primordial soup trillions upon trillions upon trillions upon trillions of times etc. and that out of that immeasurable number of lightning hits just one of them happened to form a string of amino acids (that then somehow turned itself into a protein and then somehow turned itself into a cell – which is impossible). That many lightning strikes would be seen as stupid, even if we were to fill the oceans with the correct materials and suspended the 2nd law of thermodynamics to give the best opportunity for it to happen, it would still be impossible.

So trying to make a comparison between 1 light particle entering your eye from a star and any of the other impossible 'events' of evolution happening is a false comparison. Your eye **will see** the star out there because there are *so many light particles* all travelling together from the star. It is not a 'one off' chance scenario. It is **not** a one-to-many scenario. It is the very opposite. It is a many-to-one scenario. There are **many** light particles, a number beyond counting, coming from the star and bombarding your **one** eye. This guarantees that the star will be seen, just as there are so **many** drops of water in the ocean that your **one** toe will be guaranteed to get wet when you stand on the sea shore. Again this kind of backwards thinking by evolutionists just confuses the matter and perverts the facts. It clouds people's reasoning to try to get them to believe the impossible.

So, changing an argument that is based upon

one-to-many

(one universe coming into being with many odds against its calibration) and using scenarios that are based upon

many-to-one,

(many light particles coming into one eye) is just another way that evolutionists try and confuse the matter to get their theories accepted. This is the reason why you now hear some humanists talking about an '**infinite number**' of universes 'out there' (each in its own bubble) and we're living in the one that **just happens to be** correct. As I said earlier, humanists will imagine anything to maintain their membership of the 'Anything but God Society'. They will use their imagination at every step in their thinking in order to get away from thinking about God.

The Bottom Line
Once all of this has been said, however, it is still important to remember that explosions, 'Big Bangs' that are meant to start the universe,

- *never create,*
- *never calibrate,*
- always *cause chaos, deconstruct* and *destroy*

You cannot bring about **information** via an explosion or by movements of energy that trace back to an explosion. This is the bottom line as far as life is concerned. It is not just a matter of seeing that life is not possible without this fine-tuning that we've outlined. It is seeing that *impossible* **fine-tuning** that works in conjunction with the presence of *impossible* **information** (that is set at the heart of all life) means that we cannot be here by accident or by any other route than a divine person who has carefully thought it all through. Just as the fine tuning of the environment is absolutely impossible, so also it is impossible for life to arise from non-living matter by itself. There is no route for either to happen by a naturalistic means. The fact is that the universe/galaxy/solar system/Earth is indeed **fine-tuned** and **information**, *of the most complex kind*, has been imprinted onto the cosmos (housed in a specialist environment) in order for life to be expressed and sustained.

In spite of this, humanists will still try and tell us that a chance explosion created order, data (coded with intent), the context for data flow, data processing (information exchanged and read for the intent of jobs fulfilled), interdependent design, miniature molecular machines fashioned and fit for purpose, all via the resulting processes of energy exchanges which are random and unguided in nature and all of it expressed in the context of a quadruple layered calibration of the universe. It is like life living on a knife edge where the universe is fashioned to uniquely allow life to exist. So, if you can believe that a random explosion in a junk yard, followed by a tornado rushing through it, will cause a self-assembly of a most complex and technically advanced robot with,

- fashioned body parts fit for purpose
- powered by random bits of junk coming together to form a self-fuelling system that is able to take raw materials into itself and to transform them into energy to keep it going
- an internal programming code that self-assembles and is so complex it not only 'talks' to each of those body parts

but sends quadrillions of sensible messages every second around the robot's A.I. body to help it move, feed and maintain itself

- also creates A.I. consciousness (something we've not yet achieved with all of our efforts) so that the robot can reason for itself

...if you can believe that an explosion and/or a tornado can create such a thing, then you can believe we're here by chance too – though personally I think that an A.I. robot coming together by chance after an explosion and a tornado in a junk yard is a cinch compared with us getting to where we are today. We are so technologically advanced; we're an absolute **miracle** of technology!

Brian Cox and his attempt at Complexity from Chaos

I want to finish this chapter by briefly looking at what's called the 'Nebular Theory'. This theory states that the phenomenon which is called the 'Conservation of Angular Momentum' is responsible for us being here. The Conservation of Angular Momentum talks about the properties of a spinning object, how its spin is constant until acted upon by external torque and spins faster when extra matter is taken into its core. https://www.youtube.com/watch?v=PwE3eiREYA4

Brain Cox first broadcast his series the, "Wonders of the Solar System" in 2010. In it he outlines the "Nebular Theory' that tries to tell us it is possible to bring order out of chaos. Here are some quotes from his episode that's called, 'Order out of Chaos'.

"The story of the solar system is the story of the creation of order out of chaos."

"I want to explain how that order emerged from the chaos of space,"

*"We'll witness the fundamental forces that control the universe... and see how those forces were unleashed to create the **beautifully ordered** solar system we live in."*

"But what makes the wonders of the solar system even more astonishing is that it all started as nothing more than a chaotic cloud of gas and dust. And it was from that cloud that everything in the solar

*system formed. All this order – the **sun**, the rotating **planets, me** –*
coalesced from a collapsing cloud of dust."

It all sounds very grand – especially when you see the photo images of
space, the video simulation graphics and the complementary music
which are deployed as an accompaniment to the running
commentary. Wow, what an awesome spectacle for the human eye.
Then he goes on to say,

"The whole solar system is full of rhythms. Each planet orbits the
sun at its own distinctive tempo... The solar system is driven by these
rhythms so regular that the whole thing could be run by clockwork. It
__seems extraordinary__ that such a __well-ordered system__ could have
come into being __spontaneously__, but it is in fact a great example of the
__beauty__ and __symmetry__ that lies __at the heart__ of the universe."

Then he adds,

"Everything that we know and see around us as formed from a
nebula – a giant cloud of gas and dust... It's thought that a supernova,
the explosive death of a nearby star, sent shockwaves through the
nebula. This caused a clump to form in the heart of the cloud. Because
it was more dense, its gravitational pull was stronger and it started to
pull in more and more gas. Soon the whole cloud was collapsing, and
crucially, it began to spin. It's a feature of all things that spin that, if
they contract, they must also rotate faster. It's a universal principle
called the conservation of angular momentum."

He then compares this force to the formation of tornadoes that we
see on our planet today.

"The awesome spinning power of tornadoes has __incredibly__
__destructive effects__, but it's this same phenomenon that is responsible
for creating the stability of the solar system, because it was the
conservation of angular momentum that stopped the early solar
system collapsing completely. While gravity caused the nebula to
contract, its conserved spin gave rise to a force that balanced the
inward pull of gravity and allowed a __stable disc to form__. When the sun
ignited, it lit up this spinning disc and within the disc, the planets
formed, all orbiting the sun in their regular, clockwork, patterns. In

*just a few hundred million years the cloud has collapsed to form a star system, our solar system, the sun surrounded by planets, and the journey from **chaos into order** had begun.*"

Then he looks at Saturn's rings, which are made up from small clumps of material, all ordered together in orbit around the planet.

"*Saturn's rings are undoubtedly beautiful and when you see those magnificent pictures of Cassini, it's almost **impossible to imagine** that that level of intricacy and beauty and symmetry could have emerged **spontaneously**, but emerge spontaneously it did.*"

Then he adds,

"*Saturn's rings were initially studied because of their beauty, but understanding their formation and evolution has led to a deep understanding of how form and beauty and order can emerge from violence and chaos. And that understanding can be spread across the entire solar system and remember that **you** and **me** are part of the solar system. **You** and **me** are ordered structures formed from the chaos of the primordial dust cloud 4.5 billion years ago, and that is one of the wonders of the solar system.*"

A Criticism of the Theory

No-one knows if this is actually true or not, but it's the best thing that the humanists have got. I'm not going to go into a long criticism of the theory, as there's no need to. I'll make a few minor points first and then get onto the main point that I want to make.

Minor Point
1) Other Orbit Examples

We see lots of celestial bodies orbiting each other right across the universe. If this 'Nebular Theory' was a standard process then we'd see horizontal alignments of this type repeated over and over again. The fact is, we don't see this exact pattern repeated.

On this subject Hugh Ross says, in order for us to get the best protection from hits from asteroids,

*"These four gas giants, Jupiter, Saturn, Uranus and Neptune travel in unique, almost circular, orbit on a horizontal plane around the Sun. **This stands in stark contrast to gas giants so far discovered outside our solar system** which either orbit too close to their stars or have elliptical and an or **non-horizontal orbits**. Even a **slight deviation** from their appointed paths would be catastrophic for life on Earth."*
https://www.youtube.com/watch?v=IMbEVv3IsGY
17min 40 seconds onwards

Minor Point
2) TYC 8241 2652 1

One of the most recent problems that science has is the events surrounding TYC 8241 2652 1. If you're a geek you'll know what TYC 8241 2652 1 is and why it's important. TYC 8241 2652 1 is a star that had a dust field around it. Not just a small amount of dust but much more than that which currently surrounds and makes up the rings around Saturn. It was first discovered to have this debris in 1983. In 2008 the star was observed again and no significant change had taken place. In 2010, just two years later, to everyone's utter amazement, all of the dust had disappeared. It seems like an impossible event. Impossible that,

- the dust debris should disappear
- that it should disappear in the time scale of just two years

Here's a quote from 'Nature'
https://www.nature.com/articles/nature11210
"The formation of Earth-like planets through collisional accumulation of rocky objects within a disk has mainly been explored in theoretical and computational work in which post-collision ejecta evolution typically is ignored, although recent work has considered the fate of such material. Here we report observations of a young, Sun-like star (TYC 8241 2652 1) where infrared flux from post-collisional ejecta has decreased drastically, by a factor of about 30, over a period of less than two years. The star seems to have gone from hosting substantial quantities of dusty ejecta, in a region analogous to where the rocky planets orbit in the Solar System, to retaining at most a meagre amount of cooler dust. Such a phase of rapid ejecta evolution has not been previously predicted or observed, and no currently available physical model satisfactorily explains the observations."

On this matter sci-news.com, quoting Dr Carl Melis, a postdoctoral scholar at the University of California in San Diego, and Prof Benjamin Zuckerman of the University of California in Los Angeles, in an article located at http://www.sci-news.com/astronomy/article00449.html says,

"It's like the classic magician's trick — now you see it, now you don't... Only in this case, we're talking about enough dust to fill an inner solar system, and it really is gone!"

Talking about the amount of dust the article says,

"This is even more shocking because the dusty disc of rocky debris was bigger and much more massive than Saturn's rings. The disc around this star, if it were in our Solar system, would have extended from the Sun halfway out to Earth, near the orbit of Mercury."

The article said it was *"perplexing"* and *"we don't have a satisfactory explanation to address what happened around this star."*

The dust's disappearance seems independent of the star. Then the article adds,

"Nothing like this has ever been seen in the many hundreds of stars that astronomers have studied for dust rings... This disappearance is remarkably fast, even on a human time scale, much less an astronomical scale."

The problem is that this disappearance of the dust could be interpreted as going totally against the 'Nebular Theory'.

Minor Point
3) Venus' rotation
All scientists will be familiar with this point, that Venus is spinning in the wrong direction, the opposite to the other planets in our solar system – though Uranus is also an exception, but for a different reason. The planet Venus' clockwise rotation is normally explained away by either suggesting that,

a. The gravitational influence of the sun brought its spin to a stop and then it began to spin the other way, but this is unlikely.
b. Another large body in space impacted it to cause it to rotate the other way – though the problem with this idea is that the planet would most probably also be orbiting at an angle and there is no evidence on the surface of the planet to suggest such a large impact.

So this remains a mystery.

"Big deal!" I hear some evolutionary scientists sarcastically say. Well yes, it may be that there is a simple explanation for this. But if you add up all three of these minor points together then they cause enough of a 'wobble' between them to suggest that we may well be missing something in our understanding of how the solar system formed. The above points, however, are not the main objections that I want to make on this matter – I just thought I'd get them out of the way first!

Main Criticism
However, having said all of that, even if this theory was ever proved to be partially or fully true, none of it is actually the point. I want to pick up on just some select words from Brian Cox's commentary that are totally illogical, either because –

- they do not fit the intellection flow from event A to B to C (I'll explain what I mean by this in a few paragraphs time)
- he is mixing different types of 'order'

Here they are.

First he talks about a *"beautifully **ordered** solar system."*

Next he says, *"All this order – the **sun**, the rotating **planets, me** – coalesced from a collapsing cloud of dust."*

Then he says, *"In just a few hundred million years the cloud has collapsed to form a star system, our solar system, the sun surrounded by planets, and the journey from **chaos into order** had begun."*

Then he adds, "*It **seems extraordinary** that such a **well-ordered system** could have come into being **spontaneously**, but it is in fact a great example of the **beauty** and **symmetry** that lies **at the heart** of the universe.*"

Then he says, "*...it's almost **impossible to imagine** that that level of intricacy and beauty and symmetry could have emerged **spontaneously**, but emerge spontaneously it did.*"

Finally he says, "*...and remember that **you** and **me** are part of the solar system. **You** and **me** are ordered structures formed from the chaos of the primordial dust cloud.*"

His assumption is that '**all levels of order**' that we see in the world and the solar system, in fact the universe, come from this same 'Conservation of Angular Momentum' principle.

> **NOTE:** He puts 'you' and 'me' naturally into the equation alongside the formation of the planets by saying "*All this order – the **sun**, the rotating **planets**, me – coalesced from a collapsing cloud of dust...*" and "*You and **me** are ordered structures formed from the chaos of the primordial dust cloud.*"

So the problem is that he automatically talks about planetary organisation and, in the same breath, puts '**me**' and '**you**' into the equation – as if they are the *same thing*. This whole book has been dealing with that very subject, to show that the raw energies within the cosmos can only produce **by-products** and life is a product!

Everything that he has said about how the planets were formed and the so called **order** that *naturally came into place* for life to exist, assumes that the 'Conservation of Angular Momentum' can be responsible for making it all! That we all just, "*...coalesced from a collapsing cloud of dust.*" What he says here is incredibly unscientific. His use of language is appalling. What he should have said, to be properly in line with evolutionary theory, is that the solar system coalesced into shape and, after a certain amount of order was created, then (talking at the microbiological scale) **life appeared** on the Earth which then fashioned the atmosphere by adding oxygen to it which then paved the way for the rest of life to evolve!

> **NOTE:** We will look at the implications of this last idea of life *having to appear* **to pave the way** for the rest of evolution to work in just a few pages time.

So, just to give Brian Cox a helping hand, in reality he assumes that the 'Conservation of Angular Momentum' started it all off and then _one thing led to another_ and finally life emerged - and this evolutionary process can all be **traced back** to this vortex principle.

We will look at this idea that everything naturally flows from one thing to the next, planet formation to human formation, in a few moments. First let me put down some foundational thoughts about the word '**order**'. This is because not all order is the same – something that Brian Cox *conveniently misses out*!

*He calls the world a place of astonishing beauty and complexity but he **does not make a distinction** between the **spatial complexity** of the physical cosmos and the **precision order complexity** of DNA code (life)!*

Types of Order
There are different types of order. Here are just some examples listed below, set in the order of increasing complexity, from the simple to the mega complex.

1) **General Order** – I could put a pile of elastic bands on my desk, near by a pile of paperclips, near by a pile of drawing pins so that I had *easy spatial access* to those resources.
2) **Specific Spatial Order** – I could arrange a set of screwdrivers from smallest to largest and set them *equally apart* from each other for *easy recognition* and *access*.
3) **Calculated Order** – I could *measure* out some ingredients, *carefully mix* them together, *bake* them at *a specific temperature* for a *set amount* of *time* and then *carefully apply*

the last bits of ingredients so that we have a *perfectly iced* and *perfectly baked, beautifully looking* and *tasting* cake!

4) **Precision Order** – I could *write a piece of computer code* that will allow me to *create an app* so that I can *turn* my mobile phone *into* an alarm clock so that at a *pre-set time*, down to a specific second during the day, a *noise is created* for the purpose to *fulfil the job* of waking me up.

Specific Spatial Order is much more complex than **General Order**. Having said that, the last two examples of **Calculated Order** and **Precision Order** are complete quantum leaps away not just from the first two concepts but also from each other too! This is because the latter two types of order...

> *...specifically use tools to **change one thing into something else** for a specific purpose...*

...and

> *...are **cleverly thought out** by applying the **calculated processes** that achieve the **desired** final outcome.*

However, the last order, **Precision Order**, is...

> *...based upon and dependent upon **information** existing and **being processed** to **make it work**.*

It is information that makes the alarm on the mobile phone work. Information has no mass. The cake baking process, that represents the **Calculated Order**, has physical tools that ensure the job is done (yes used by the skilled hands of a human being – but I'm just looking at the process that makes it happen). The code that runs the app is totally different. This is imagined output that comes from the language of data, specifically applied as massless code which is then able to interact within its constructed and calibrated environment, the phone and its operating system, and so to set the alarm off!

> *The fact is that you **need Precision Order** to make life happen. Information is at the heart of all life and without it being **imprinted onto the cosmos**, life cannot even start!*

The issue, therefore, is that there is **no neat line of development** from the vortex to assemble the planets of the solar system to the creation and establishment of life.

The 'Conservation of Angular Momentum' does not contain within it the ability to create something beyond General Order!

The only thing you could possibly expect from a vortex creating a solar system is, at best, the level called 'General order' where things are separated from each other and can be seen to have **their own identity** as separate planets in orbit – like the pile of elastic bands are seen as separate from the pile of paperclips on my desk. All of the other types of order are a quantum leap away from being achieved; even the **Specific Spatial Order** is not achievable. You need **Specific Order** and **Calculated Order** for the following to happen – because there are certain things that a vortex does not auto-determine and has no control over – which are,

1) The size of the Sun.
2) The size of the Earth.
3) The distance of the Earth from the Sun.
4) Earth's angle of rotation, its pro-grade tilt, that is absolutely necessary for life to exist.
5) The electromagnetic field.
6) The thickness of the Earth's crust.
7) The exact combination of the elements on Earth.
8) The exact presence of a moon to provide stability.
9) etc.

On top of that you need **Precision Order** for information to be imprinted onto the cosmos to make life work!

His great mistake is that he applies a general principle, the 'Conservation of Angular Momentum' and makes it do something that it cannot even begin to do. He makes it sound plausible by not **focussing on the whole process** but just views it all from a macro scale – there is no microbiology going on in this programme! So his statement that, "*the **sun**, the rotating **planets, me** – coalesced from a collapsing cloud of dust...*" is a complete nonsense.

All of this is not explained by the theory. This level of exact **'Specific Spatial Order'** that is found at the planetary level is not justified by Nebular theory, let alone the **Precision Order** of information and its surroundings to process it. There is no mathematical equation to be added to the 'Conservation of Angular Momentum' process that would vindicate such a thing happening whereby the Earth is the exact size, distance from the sun etc., unless we're going to go back to Richard Dawkins' 'luck' again. Then the 'luck factor' is back to play its impossible role – which we also call a 'happy accident' – which is just an excuse for the 'we can't explain this but we don't want God' reasoning that infests the world of science.

So, even if we see beyond Mr Cox's verbal error, we can clearly see that...

> *...life will not **'appear'** into any environment because **information** does not **'appear'** anywhere by itself.*

So when I've said throughout this book that,

> *It is not possible to bring about order, complexity, interdependent design and **purposeful coding** out of chaos via **random** and **unguided** processes...*

397

...it is true. Looking at the four levels of order makes this clear.

Life Just Appearing

Evolutionists are also completely reliant on the notion of life just **appearing** after a vortex crafted the planets. Life has to **appear** by itself and has to '**jump**' in its complexity for everything else to evolve. Here are some quotes from a BBC website about what's called the 'Great Oxidation Event'.

http://www.bbc.co.uk/earth/story/20150701-the-origin-of-the-air-we-breathe

*"Up until 2.4 billion years ago, there was no oxygen in the air. It took something big to change that – perhaps the biggest **evolutionary leap** of all."*

"This "Great Oxidation Event" was one of the most important things to ever happen on this planet. Without it, there could never have been any animals that breathe oxygen: no insects, no fish, and certainly no humans."

*"...**simple** life-forms are the prime suspects for the Great Oxidation Event. One group in particular stands out: cyanobacteria. Today, these microscopic organisms sometimes form bright blue-green layers on ponds and oceans. Their ancestors **invented a trick** that has since spread like wildlife. They evolved a way to take energy from sunlight, and use it to make sugars out of water and carbon dioxide. This is called photosynthesis..."*

*"...in the longer term, it allowed a whole new kind of life to evolve. Oxygen is a reactive gas – that's why it starts fires – so when some organisms **figured out** how to harness it, they suddenly had access to a major new source of energy."*

I don't want to get into a long, long discussion on why the BBC article is not correct, I want to finish this book! First let me just again say that the phrase "**simple** life forms" has no place in science – as we've already pointed out, the DNA in the most basic cell is incredibly complex. However, did you also notice the other words that I highlighted into bold text? Somehow this so called *primitive lifeform* is able to '**invent a trick**' and '**figured out** how to harness it' – what a way of expressing such a complex process as photosynthesis! Once again we see the language of the ridiculous used as an excuse for a massive technological leap to take place in biology. The impossible to be labelled as a 'trick'! A trick is something that someone just 'might perform' after a little practice. It does not even begin to communicate the immense complexity of photosynthesis. Calling it a 'trick' gives a completely false impression for what it really is.

I shan't say anything else on this subject. It is so clear cut. A vortex will not create the intricate setup of the Earth's size, its distance from the sun, its level of tilt, etc. and all of the other things required for life. Also life does not just appear into an environment. These two principles tell us that the 'Nebular Theory' – even if partially true, is completely unable to describe how we came into being. Saying, "*the sun, the rotating **planets**, **me** – coalesced from a collapsing cloud of dust...*" is more than inaccurate, it's completely wrong.

I'll stay with Brian Cox and his 'Wonders of the Solar System' series for just a few more moments. In the next episode called 'The Thin Blue Line' he looks at the atmosphere around the Earth and makes the following statements,

"*In this film I want to explain how to laws of physics that created our unique atmosphere are the same laws that created many diverse and different atmospheres across the solar system. When **perfectly balanced**, a world as familiar and beautiful as the Earth can evolve beneath the clouds. But the **slightest changes** can lead to alien and violent worlds.*"

He then adds,

Our Earth is, "*an oasis of calm amidst the **violence** of the solar system. And all that separates us from what's out there is a **thin, flimsy envelope** of gas – our atmosphere. And it's thanks to this 'thin blue line' that we have the air that we breathe, the water that we drink and the landscape that surrounds us.*"

Next he calls this 'thin blue line, "*So **fragile** and so **tenuous**.*"

Then the final statements that I want to quote are,

*"There are places out there in the solar system whose atmospheres have the same ingredients as our own but when the formula is even **slightly remixed** it leads to worlds that couldn't be more different."*

"The thin blue line makes the Earth the wonderfully diverse place it is. It acts as a soothing blanket, that traps the warmth of the sun, yet protects us from the harshness of its radiation."

*"There are **so many ways** for planets to **lose** their atmospheres that it **feels like a miracle** that we've still got ours."*

His commentary is punctuated with words that are unfortunate for evolutionists. You can see them jump off the page! The fact of the matter is that life cannot get here by **General Order**; it is too precise on all levels. So much can still 'go wrong' if everything is not **exactly** in place, which he concedes regularly throughout the film. Let me say this clearly. When you take into account the complexity of life and the multi-multi-layered levels of complexity that it requires to make it all work, it does not just 'feel like a miracle' that even one of these factors is in place, as Brian Cox suggests.

The fact is, it **is a miracle** that we are here.

It is a work that is so fine-tuned and tremendous that it can only be truly described as not just being 'beautiful' but as 'divine' – where the word 'divine' means something that is heavenly, marvellous, exquisite, delightful, awesome and overwhelmingly breath-taking. This is because the creation we see around us today can only come from the divine – it is a *God-given gift* to humanity!

> **NOTE:** Just as an extra note, a planet being formed by a vortex is a **by-product**, not a **product**. It is only when information is imprinted onto the surface of planet that Earth is turned into a *crafted* machine. General Organisation, which might possibly come about via a vortex, only produces by-products and by-products do not form energy movements that are basis for the creation of life!

NOTE: So, one of the big questions that arises from this fact that life is so complex is,

- Why is this beautiful and majestic world such a difficult place for us to live in?
- Why would such a wonderful and intelligent creator allow hardship and evil to co-exist with us?

To go deeper into that subject you'll have to read my other books in this series – which I should be writing in 2020.

Our solar system is an intelligent setup. When Brian Cox says, "...*it's almost **impossible to imagine** that that level of intricacy and beauty and symmetry could have emerged **spontaneously,** he's almost right. It's not, however, a scenario that's '**almost** impossible to image' once you know the facts.

It is indeed **totally impossible to imagine...**

... once you understand the different types of complexity, beyond **General Order**, that it takes to setup the solar system and the universe for life to exist.

The reason why we see such a carefully constructed solar system to enable life to survive and flourish on planet Earth, where **Spatial**, **Calculated** and **Precision Order** are applied at every possible level, is simply because we truly live in nothing short of a deity driven universe!

Chapter 12 – A Mini Sermon on Truth

Meaning & Meaninglessness

Opening Comments

This chapter completes this book and also serves as an introduction to some of the main themes of my next book(s). You'll get a flavour here of some of that which I'll say in my next book – 'Escaping the Secular Box' which will demonstrate that secular spirituality is a religion and how that religion expresses itself and falls short of its own message. I'll also be showing you how to stand up to the rhetoric of secularists who continually speak to preach to us about being 'inclusive' and then misrepresent the words 'equality' and 'respect' in order to maintain their call for conversion.

Atheism is Meaningless – Theism gives us Meaning

Have you noticed that we don't fit ideologically and philosophically into the humanist world view? We constantly live as if life was meaningful. We constantly live with drive and purpose to take hold of life and live it well. Our lives are lived as if there is a reason for us being here in and amongst the numerous daily activities we find ourselves engaged in. Our joys are expressions of pleasure and our tears are there because we behave *as if life matters* and things that 'should be right' are not right or not as we expect them to be. In fact our tears speak to us more about the meaning of life than our laugher does. Tears tell us that 'something is wrong' and that life *should be* '**better than it is**' in some way. We had lived up to that moment with expectations for something better and our tears are about the pain of either a sense of loss or injustice or a longing that is not fulfilled. All of these things that we continually carry with us throughout our days are reminders that we live as if life *was really meaningful* in some way.

However, if we're just an accident from a dead cosmos then there is no ultimate purpose to our existence – which kicks against the feelings that we daily experience. This purposeless ultimate reality, however, is the logical fact of the matter. The humanist creation story tells us that we are just an accident. A 'Big Bang' happened and then we arrived here by a sequence of unguided and random events over a long period of time. Our existence was neither,

- planned
- purposed
- designed
- or desired

We just came into existence without any ultimate meaning to us being alive. Life had no planned beginning, no purposed living and no meaningful final outcome. We just temporarily 'are' and then we die and 'are not' anymore. We are here and then we are gone. Nothing more. Very few people who live the humanist lifestyle face the fact that under the banner of humanism life is ultimately empty. The universe is cooling down. The 2nd law of thermodynamics tells us that, once the cosmos is totally cool, all life, all information, all data, will be lost. There will be no trace of the life that once was. It will totally vanish. It will be as if life and all the history that we have made over the millennia...

...had never existed in the first place.

This is how futile the humanist world view is. There will be no-one to remember us. All of our pains, sufferings, joys, successes, hopes, dreams, desires, political movements, historical moments etc. will all be forgotten and lost forever. There will be no eternal humanity, not even echoes of the sounds that we once made on this planet. When all is said and done and life is gone and the cosmos is cold, then everything that we have worked for and towards as a human race will all come to nothing. The long term meaning of life, in humanism, is that it is ultimately pointless. As King Solomon says in the Bible (once he had lost his relationship with God and chased after his own fantasies and his wealth – making money his 'god' and his gift of 'wisdom' his reason for living) he says at the end of it all,

> Meaningless! Meaningless!" says the
> Teacher. "Utterly meaningless! Everything is
> meaningless." Ecclesiastes 1:2

and

> *"Yet when I surveyed all that my hands had done and what I had toiled to achieve, everything was meaningless, a chasing after the wind; nothing was gained under the sun."*
> *Ecclesiastes 2:11*

Solomon truly looks life in the face and examines the meaning of it all within its temporal state. He calls life *'meaningless'* over thirty times in the book of Ecclesiastes. He says this because,

> *"...nothing was gained under the sun."*
> *Ecclesiastes 2:11*

You cannot hold onto anything

Solomon sees that you cannot hold onto anything in this life. You cannot ultimately possess anything, even your own life. All of it is temporal and it will slip through your fingers. No amount of grasping at it will enable you or I to keep it. As we often say about a rich person, when they die, they can't take their wealth with them; they leave it all behind, every penny. Solomon dedicated his life to work (great projects), study (much learning), pleasure (drinking and womanising) and at the end of it all he was *weary* because he understood that none of that which he had enjoyed would last. He would eventually die and everything he had worked for was to be given to those coming after him and his temporary pleasures and sense of achievement would be gone and lost forever. He desperately wanted to 'hold onto something' that he could say was eternally 'his' in order to give long lasting meaning to life. Yes, time continually goes by and this temporal life and all of its activities will one day come to an abrupt end – not only for the individual when they die but also for the whole human race once the universe has cooled down and the cosmos is completely dead.

The problem of Time

Our problem is that we are temporary creatures who are stuck in time. 'Time' is our biggest conundrum. It is both our friend and our greatest enemy. It enables and allows us to temporarily taste the 'good things' of this world and at the same time continually marches us along the road of life to where we will ultimately lose all of those very same good things that we have enjoyed and endured. Time takes us through life, enables us to live it, taste it, express ourselves within it and then finally time hands us over to death and we are gone. Time is unrelenting. Time is unstoppable. Time simply walks us through each day. It has a grasp on us and it will not let go. Time does not listen to our pleas for more of it nor for it to slow down. It is deaf to a bribe to escape its influence and emotionless when we come to the end of it. We can enjoy its company or resent its passing, but there is one thing to be sure of, time will never stop. You and I will always have to face tomorrow, unless today is our last day. Tomorrow will always come into our today. Time dictates this to be so.

Defining Time

Here are two good definitions of time that both work together to give us a rounded understanding of what it is. Time is:

Living in the 'here and now'...

and

The ever present passing of 'now'.

The Here and Now

We continually live **in** the 'here and now' – that is in the *moment in time* where we find ourselves simply existing. We call this state of continually being alive 'consciousness'. We are 'awake' and can sense that we are alive and that we continually express ourselves in this thing that we call the 'here and now' that is within a 'moment in time'. We are continually expressed within this 'moment'. This is difficult to understand until you see it in the context of time continually passing by.

The Ever Present Passing of Now

Have you also noticed that this 'moment in time' that we find ourselves continually expressed within is not only taking us into our future but also continually moving into the past? What do I mean by that? Well, here's a very simple experiment to illustrate this fact. Click your fingers. That's it, just click your fingers. That 'click' that you've just done has now, in *a moment of time*, instantly become part of human history. The 'moment' of clicking your fingers is a 'moment expressed in time' that has come and gone and instantly been assigned to the past. It doesn't matter how many times you click your fingers, as soon as it is done the moment has gone and it is assigned to your past, to the history of the world. The event has a 'date/time stamp' attached to it. At 8:10am on 08/06/2019 Tim Waters clicked his fingers in-between typing the words of this book. It is something that happened and, once it has happened, it has come and gone and is now lost forever. Why? Simply because you can't hold onto the 'here and now'. Time is the *ever present passing of now*. You can't suspend time and make it stop. You can't *seize the moment* and live in it forever. We are changing, aging, every ticking second that we're alive. Each 'tick' in time is an expression of the 'here and now' that we live within. 'Now' is the 'moment' that we find ourselves conscious within. We live in this 'now' but we can't keep it or hold onto it. It is continually passing through our fingers and into history. The 'here and now' that we live in is continually becoming the past.

A Comet Illustration

It is like a comet rushing through space that continually leaves a trail of dust behind it. The dust shows where the comet was 'a moment in time ago' but it is no longer there as that 'now moment' has passed and gone and now the comet is somewhere else from where it was a moment ago. That is what it is to live 'in time' and to be trapped 'in time'. We're locked into the 'here and now' of history and we can't get away from it! Yes this 'now' that we live in is continually being assigned to history. It is as if we're walking along a timeline into the future and we can't stop the walk. Every step touches the moment of life and brings the immediate future into our lived experience, brings the future into the 'here and now' and then as the immediate next step is taken the 'now' that we experienced is left behind us, gone into the halls of history as we continually walk towards our tomorrow. You can look back through history and see the 'walk' that you have walked through time, just as you can see the trail of dust left behind a comet, but you cannot go back there. Neither can you pause the moment in which we live. It is here, it is gone, it is the past and the future is continually meeting us in the 'now' that we live. This is what it is to live in time.

Eternity and being Temporal

Understanding Eternity

"Who wants to live forever," Freddie Mercury once sang? Well everyone actually. This is why Solomon says that God has put,

> *"...eternity in the human heart."*
> *Ecclesiastes 3:11*

Eternity is a strange thing for us to understand. We live with desires for it within us and yet we are temporal creatures living in the here and now. We do have a desire to stay forever young, however, not to age and not to die. What did the singer and actress Cher say in an interview once she reached the age of 50? She said that being fifty, 'Sucks' and that she had never felt old till hitting her fifties. Very few people are as honest about life in this way. I remember briefly bumping into a lady who was on a Saga holiday. As we passed each other and shared a few polite, friendly words she just said, "I wish I was young again." My heart went out to her. Just a few months before that conversation took place the pastor of my Church had said in a sermon, "I would not be any other age." He wasn't a young man either. The lady from Saga holidays saw life slipping through her fingers. The pastor of my Church has a deep friendship with a timeless God, with whom he would spend all eternity. To go back in time and 'gain youth again' would mean that he would lose the depth of the relationship he had with the eternal God. This 'friendship with God' is the only thing that you can eternally gain in this life and 'youth' is no substitute for it. Walking with God is what it truly is to 'live forever'!

Living forever is probably the best concept that we can imagine to express our desire for eternity. Eternity, however, is something that we will never fully understand until we are 'face to face' with God. Everything we know and see and relate to in this universe has a beginning, middle and an end. A chair starts out as a tree. It is cut down and crafted into a chair. It spends its years being 'sat upon' to fulfil its purpose and then, once it is worn out, it is thrown away, burned on the fire and its ashes are put back into the soil for the next tree or plant to grow.

407

- beginning – tree
- middle – chair
- end - ashes

This pattern is our continual reference point and everything in this universe, including us, follows this pattern.

> **NOTE:** This is why humanists in their arguments against God try and pull God **into time** to ask, 'Who created God?' – as if they're actually asking something sensible. It is a complete misunderstanding of the eternal. You cannot pull an eternal spiritual being into the physical temporal.

Understanding God is Eternal

This is one reason why we will never be able to fully understand God. God is eternal. The Bible says about God that he is 'from eternity'.

> *"Your throne was established long ago; you are from all eternity." Psalm 93:2*

All we have ever known and all we have reference for is being creatures that are locked 'in time' and therefore to be defined by the concepts of 'beginning', 'middle' and 'end'. God is different. He has no beginning or end. God just 'is'. He is the eternal 'I am' as he revealed himself to Moses.

> *"God said to Moses, "I am who I am. This is what you are to say to the Israelites: 'I am has sent me to you.'"" Exodus 3:14*

The phrase 'I am' talks of God being **eternally present** in the 'here and now' without the constraints of time. **Time does not define who God is** – as it does us. He was before time and the creator of time and space. This is why we have the statement,

> *"In the beginning God created..." Genesis 1:1*

For us the beginning begins when God starts to create – yet before the beginning God already existed as this ever present 'I am'. Time, as we know it, only exists in three dimensional space and God created it all. He **was** there 'at the beginning' of all things. Yet he is before the beginning of time. This is why in the book written by John in the New Testament he talks of how God spoke through his Word into the cosmos to bring it all into being and that this 'Word' is described as being in the **past tense** when *the beginning is about to start.*

> *"In the beginning **was** the Word, and the Word **was** with God, and the Word **was** God."*
> *John1:1*

The word '**was**' is continually used to describe God's status at what we call 'the beginning' of time and space. God is spirit and he is 'from' eternity. The physical realm has a beginning. The spiritual realm does not. We will never understand this in this current world history that we are now living in. God also says of himself in the last book of the Bible,

> *"'I am the Alpha and the Omega,' says the Lord God, 'who is, and who was, and who is to come, the Almighty.'" Revelation 1:8*

God **was** there at the beginning; he **is** with us now and God **will always be** there in the future that is **to come**. God is timeless. It is something that we have no reference points for understanding properly.

God Offers Eternity to Humanity
This is why Jesus would talk about us being able to have 'eternal life' and having eternal wealth, i.e. treasure stored up in heaven. The very things that Solomon had lost and said he could not take a hold of, due to his walking away from God, are the very things that Jesus promises to humanity.

> *"I am the resurrection and the life. He who believes in me will live, even though he dies."*
> *John 11:25*

and

> *"...I will raise him up at the last day."*
> *John 6:40b*

and

> *"...store up for yourselves treasures in heaven..." Matthew 6:20*

and

> *"I tell you, use worldly wealth to gain friends for yourselves, so that when it is gone, you will be welcomed into eternal dwellings."*
> *Luke 16:9*

The Bible says that death is our last enemy and that God has specifically through the death and resurrection of his Christ enabled us to finally escape this temporal trap in time that we all face. Everything that Jesus promises us is based on eternity. Everything he says is for an eternal life, eternal living. This is the hope that theism (Christianity) offers. In God's eternal presence nothing is ever lost.

This is why theism has ultimate meaning for our lives and atheism does not.

God is eternal and by sharing in his life we can have eternity too. It is by faith that we walk through this life, living in the scientific reality that we can't be here without deity and that historically deity has come down from heaven to live with us, walk with us, be with us and make a way for us back to God. This is something that humanism can never ever offer. With secular spirituality you choose to believe whatever you want to believe (because there's no substance to the spiritual world except human belief) and in the light of that personal self-initiated belief you live, you die and then that's it. There is nothing of eternal value in saying that we are an accident of the cosmos. There is everything of eternal value in saying that God has prepared a place for all of those who will love and accept him.

> *"And if I go and prepare a place for you, I will also come back and take you to be with me that you also may be where I am." John 14:3*

Anyone who has hope in God hopes for the eternal and not the temporal. The main contradiction of humanism is that its followers too, have one hope for themselves, to live within the confines of **eternal values** as they live out their lives here on Earth.

Summary so far...

So as a human race we live as if life is completely meaningful. We live as if life matters in some way. We have courts within our society because we want 'justice to be done' when we feel deeply that an injustice has happened to someone or some people. We speak out for what is right. We talk about 'love' as if it is something more than the passing on of your genes before you die. We talk about 'honour' and 'forgiveness' and 'mercy' as if these things are real. Yet at the same time we're told by humanists that we live in a temporal environment where we are just an accident of the cosmos. We were neither planned, purposed, designed or desired. There is no ultimate meaning to life and these 'eternal values' that we unwittingly carry with us contradict what it is to come from a random accident. We live with this contradiction of the eternal and the temporal. We are creatures locked into time, only here for a short period, and then we are gone. We are temporal and **yet we want to be eternal**. We want forever youth and to live out of values that do not represent ultimate meaninglessness.

So the true philosophy of the humanist creation story is not good enough for us. Humanists want loyalty, justice, friendship, love, forgiveness etc. Eternal values that only come from deity make life liveable and give everyone something true to live for. Assigning value to life because it is 'rare' doesn't even begin to cut to the heart of the subject. Atheism doesn't even begin to fulfil the deep desires that are written and scrawled over the walls of the inner chambers of our hearts. We constantly live with and for eternal values! We are,

- a people set within the confines of time who want to be timeless.
- a people who want to say that the only ultimate truth is that, "There is no ultimate truth" (and by saying so preach that we live in a temporal environment) and at the same time want the eternal truths of love, justice, hope etc. to live by
- a people who are a living contradiction of values and a clash of origins, the temporal versus the eternal.

This leads us on to the next part of this chapter which is all about understanding the 'eternal' and contrasting it with the temporal.

- -

Eternal Values

- -

The Main Contradiction within Humanism

One of the main contradictions in life for humanists is that

> ...*atheists want to live with **eternal values** in a **temporal environment**.*

Humanism borrows from theism for the basis of its moral code. It takes the eternal values that can only be found in God and firmly puts them with secular humanity. It removes meaninglessness from within its own ranks and marches out under the banners of 'truth' and 'love' and 'justice' and 'honour' and 'forgiveness' etc. None of these things can be evolved from a dead cosmos. Temporal living means just that. It means that everything is temporary and nothing is eternally true. There are no reference points for truth or anything else. Life has no meaning within a temporal structure and humanists borrow a theistic moral code to make life worthwhile. Let's unpack this a little more.

If we're an accident from a dead cosmos then there are no eternal values for us to live by. Eternal values are such things as love, justice, forgiveness and mercy. They come from theism, not atheism. The only concept that you can actually logically deduce from a dead cosmos (if you choose to believe that life miraculously came about by chance) is that...

...life is rare.

If life is rare then you can **choose** to **ascribe** *value to life* – BUT you are...

*...not **obliged** to do so!*

There is no logical obligation to say that life is valuable, just because it is rare. However, you can choose to ascribe value to it. The choice is yours. Others may choose to do the same but you can't force them to follow this pattern. If there is no God behind the universe then there is no eternal purpose to anything. So apart from the concept of rarity, there is no other way of logically 'adding value' to life. Others may protest and say, "But I encounter 'love' and have a deep sense of 'justice' within me." Yes, those feelings that you have may feel very real, and they are real, but they point to the fact that deity is the source behind the universe not a random 'Big Bang'. Your feelings of eternal values within you are evidence for God not evidence for a dead cosmos randomly coming alive. From a logical philosophical position those feelings cannot come from the humanist's creation story.

The Consequences of a Non-Eternal Outlook

If we are just an accident and nothing more, then this environment is temporal in nature and therefore everything within it is up for grabs. The only ultimate truth is that...

...there is no ultimate truth.

This is the foundational bottom line for anyone saying that we're here just because we're here. Theism says that deity is the ultimate truth, that truth is found 'in God' and not humanity. Secular spirituality says that truth is found in the physical cosmos, that which we can measure and observe within the physical universe. Spiritual truth, 'divine law' does not exist. It is simply the beliefs of humanity over the years that resides amongst a variety of religious beliefs. Ultimate truth is found in physicality not spirituality. A dead cosmos has no moral code attached to it from which we can evolve the codes we have here today. A dead cosmos has no obligation, not even to the next generation of life. If we were not purposed or planned, designed

413

or desired, then with the open ended non-descript meaning to life being unanswerable, life becomes just choices without obligation. One thing is for sure, there is no obligation to accept anything and the so called high moral ground that we have in Western culture is again a miscommunication of reality.

This opens the door for anything to be possible over time for a culture run by humanism. Each generation decides what the moral code will be and the general consensus rules – a very dangerous place to be! However, love, justice, forgiveness etc. are eternal values found only in deity. As I've said, the contradiction within humanism is that it borrows from theism to give meaning to life and uses those eternal values for its own ends, *claiming to have a high moral ground* from which to speak to the rest of humanity.

A Proper Balance of Thought!
There are no logical reasons for eternal values. The fact is, however, we can't get away from eternal values and we can't get away from the "What is the meaning of life?" question that dogs every generation. Purpose is at the heart of our daily living. The eternal values of love, justice, peace etc. and the concepts of 'right' and 'wrong' and 'good' and 'evil' continually stay with us. None of these can be evolved ideologically from a dead cosmos. Our very inner spiritual make-up tells us that there is an eternal God.

- -
God's Final Plan
- -

The Answer is Found 'In God'
We're here because of the divine. As God began all creation, then there is nothing physical that is RESPONSIBLE for the beginning of the beginning. As it is the Spirit of God who began the beginning, then the final knowledge of how we all got here is most possibly beyond our reach. If that is the fact of the matter, then true scientific knowledge is out of the hands of the humanist. How the spiritual **initiated** and 'touched the cosmos into being' is beyond the testing of humanity, beyond the scope of science. The *movement* for the creation of the universe is only found *in God*. The initiative for it all happening, that is the 'push' that initiates time, space and physical matter, all comes

from God. Whatever that 'push' was, that caused three dimensional space and time and matter to exist, it is God's 'push' and begins in the spiritual, not the physical. There is no initial *movement* to be found in the physical world to bring itself into being and you can't put the spiritual world into a physical test tube to do tests upon it.

The humanists will continue to look and look and theorise and fantasise and, at the same time due to their religious bias, will be asking the wrong question of 'how?' rather than 'who?' The humanists will insist that it is **they** who are doing 'true science' because all that they do moves towards a model of testing their theories in the physical realm for validity. "Without the physical test, it is not true science!" they will say. Their attempts at ultimate truth, however, will only end in futility. This is because it is not the physical realm that is the ultimate place of truth. Humanists miss the spiritual realm, where the eternal God dwells and you cannot pull the divine into the physical world in order to 'do tests' on God, to validate God by the physical rules of the universe. You cannot put God into a test tube. You cannot use that which is created to validate the creator. It is a fallacy to insist that the physical world contains total truth. Truth is not contained in or by that which is created. Like an immaculate vase put on display for all to see and admire, all we get as we observe the masterpiece are the fingerprints of the master artist who created it and an example of the master's handiwork. If you believe the vase self-assembled and look at the vase from only that perspective, then you're off on the **wrong** foot from the start. To ask, "Is there a potter?" would be a more accurate question, not, "How did this vase self-assemble?" – because we *already don't believe in a potter.*

Today we understand just how amazing life is, and it gets more and more complex the more we learn. The universe is an amazing and astounding place, full of precision, order, complexity and interdependent design. The potter has moulded the clay into his beautiful vase and placed it on display for everyone and anyone to look at. It is not the vase that is the truth, it just witnesses to the skill and handiwork of the one who made it, just as at night time we see the moon in all her glory. Beautiful as she is, she is not the source of life and light for the Earth. She simply reflects the glory of another (the sun) who has temporarily gone out of sight; so too when we look at the universe. We see the glory of another who is currently out of sight but whom the Bible says we will all see 'face to face'.

> *For now we see only a reflection as in a mirror; then we shall see face to face.*
> *1 Corinthians 13:12*

The truth about life is contained within the substance of the creator; the 'being' who is God. It is the person who created all things in whom truth is found. Finding out the **intent** within heart and mind of the maker, who chose 'to make' the vase with a purpose, is where the truth resides. Why is the vase here? Who was it made for? Is it a gift? To whom does it belong? Truth, therefore, is contained within two things,

- the **substance** of the creator
- the **heart/mind** (intent) of the creator

What is God's substance? Well, the most influential person in the history of the human race will tell you that,

> *"God* **is spirit**, *and those who worship him must worship in the Spirit and in truth."*
> *John 4:24*

The primary substance of the creator is spirit, not physical. So if God is spirit then all primary truth is spiritual and the physical is only true in that it witnesses to the spiritual. When we look at the physical we see an ordered and incredibly complex creation. We see an immaculate and delicate balance of maths and science to stabilise and hold in tension everything based on a super intelligence that is so way beyond our own that it can only be described as deity. The question needs to be asked as to why? Why a physical creation when God is spirit? Well, it's not just the splendour of it all, in order to point back to the creator. The answer is more complex than that and requires a good measure of **theology** – *which I shall unpack in another book*. One of the basic facts is, however, that God needed a physical world in which to initially house humanity because he knew that evil would follow his good creation. The heart and mind/intent of the creator, therefore, is to **win us back** after God has given humanity two things,

- free will
- a right to rule this planet

This is the real reason why we humans are above the animal kingdom and stand apart from them. It is not that we have evolved that way, it is because we've been given free will by the divine. That free will enables true relationship with God, but it also opens the door for rebellion, for humanity to seek independence from God's character and goodness as the measuring line for humanity's moral conduct and to seek to be self-determined moral beings instead. It opens the door to us being,

> *"...like God, knowing good and evil,"*
> *Genesis 3:5*

...but at the same time as finding out that we are now 'like God' knowing good and evil, we also find out that we are **not** 'like God', that is...

...not always having the capacity to think and do what is morally good and right and true all the time.

This is the mess that humanity currently finds itself in. Having God-given authority to rule but not godly character or wisdom to know how to implement the rule he has given over to us. We are, therefore, forever living with the contradiction of an eternal high morality, that cannot trace its routes back to the mere physical realm, and at the same time not being able to live up to those eternal moral standards as they are too high and beyond us.

We constantly trip over ourselves.

The stamp mark of the original image of God is still there, but the fractured creatures that we now are, that are the result of our disconnectivity from the divine (which we are born with) continually works against us.

The Real Purpose of the Cosmos

God is a God of justice, however, and will not move away from it. He is what we call 'holy', and that holiness is a total giving over to what is good and right and true. Wherever there is evil, he is obliged to be its judge. As the wages of wrong doing (sin) is death, God needed a physical realm within which to house his creation, one that is able to **facilitate death.** By so doing he could make a way for us to escape after corruption had come into God's creation – which all along he knew would happen. The spiritual realm cannot facilitate this type of death. So this amazing physical world is created in all its glory for a single purpose. That purpose is based on pre-knowledge of what would happen due to our being given free will and God's plan to **rescue us** from its consequences. This world is now tainted and subject to what the Bible calls 'frustration' and 'decay'...

> *"For the creation was subjected to frustration, not by its own choice, but by the will of the one who subjected it,"* Romans 8:20

...due to our turning our backs on God, just as he knew we would. It is only then, after the corruption had taken place, that God could...

...enter the cosmos himself

...and take the punishment himself, the cross of Jesus Christ, for our offence against him. That is **the purpose of a physical world**; it *facilitates God's judgement* against what he calls *sin*. It allows God to deal with our current condition *on our behalf*. That is the huge advantage of the physical cosmos. It allows God's justice courts to be satisfied through the death of an innocent one, Jesus Christ, on our behalf to pay the fine, the penalty, and so make peace between us and a holy God again.

As the most famous verse in the Bible says,

> *For God so loved the world that he gave his one and only Son that whosoever believes in him shall not perish but have eternal life.*
> *John 3:16*

This perfectly executed plan that God hides in and amongst the pages of the Old Testament, speaking of the coming Christ and his work to be achieved, also tells us that amongst all the great troubles that we have on Earth throughout human history, that God actually knows what he's doing – even when we can't see it. He knows the beginning from the end, the Alpha and the Omega, and there are two verses in the Bible that I absolutely love. They are,

> *"No eye has seen, no ear has heard and no mind has conceived what God has prepared for those who love him." 1 Corinthians 2:9*

and

> *"He will wipe away every tear from their eyes. There will be no more death or mourning or crying or pain..." Revelation 21:4*

Eternity is central to the promises of God for humanity. Eternity is something we find in our hearts all the time, eternal longings to live forever and eternal values to accompany us through life. The stamp mark of what it was to be originally made in the image of God still accompanies us, even if that image in is now marred and broken.

If the World were a Car
If the world were a car, then humanism has tried to find out,

- what the car bodywork is made of
- what the tyres are made of
- what the car seats are made of
- what the different components of the engine are made of
- how the engine works
- etc.

Humanism is so focussed on the car, however, and is so convinced that the car has auto-organised itself into its current existence, that it denies a car maker and a car driver. The complete failure of humanism is that it does not know in any way shape or form,

- **who** is driving the car
- **where** the car is going

As a result its claims about the car's existence, the purpose of the car and the destiny of the car are all inaccurate. The repercussions of this in our society are a people who do not know who they truly are, what they're here for and where they are going. A complete misidentify is imposed upon the minds of those who live in Western culture who honestly believe that their existence is a temporal accident, that their lives are their own to do with as they please and that spirituality begins and ends with humanity. The so called science of humanism produces an anti-theistic religion that ignores the fingerprints of the divine that are stamped all over the fabric of the cosmos. It sows misinformation into the culture and reaps a people without understanding and without insight into the awesome journey that is laid out before humanity – to know the divine. It not only misses the point about the universe, that all things point back to a creator, but that the only true meaning of life itself is that we are invited to know this creator who is behind the universe, behind all things.

This is why the Bible itself says,

> *"The heavens declare the glory of God;*
> *the skies proclaim the work of his hands."*
> *Psalm 19:1*

and why Jesus prays to his Father in heaven and says,

> *"This is eternal life: that they might know*
> *you the only true God and Jesus Christ whom*
> *you have sent." John 17:3*

and why the Westminster Catechism says,

*"The chief end of man is to glorify God and
enjoy him forever."*

John completes his book in the New Testament by making this final
observation,

> *"But these things are written that you may
> believe that Jesus is the Christ, the Son of God,
> and that by believing you may have life in his
> name." John 20:31*

That, in a nutshell, is the meaning of life. To know God, love God,
share his love with each other and obey his call to repent and turn to
him in the time of his favour. To glorify him by accepting what he has
done within this physical cosmos that not only speaks to us of the
immensely intelligent creator who put everything together, but to see
that this physical cosmos which has the capacity to house death has
actually brought about God's greatest work – the death of his Son on
our behalf.

The title of this book is,

"God's Magnum Opus?"

So the title poses a question asking,

"Is this God's greatest work?"

Well we've seen that the creation of this universe and that of life in
all of its irreducible complexity is a 'great work'. It is something that is
beyond our imaginations to get our heads around. A calibration of the
widest space (the universe) and a calibration of one of the smallest
spaces (the microbiological life within the cell) in order for life to exist
in such a way that is beyond our ability to comprehend in its
complexity. It truly is a great and awesome work. We have not,
however, touched upon God's greatest work, his real 'magnum opus'
until now. That God would so love us that he would die in our place to
deal with our sin. That he would enter the cosmos himself and pass

through death and rise again on the other side. That he would endure the hatred of humanity and win us over by his love.

This truly is God's magnum opus, his greatest work!

This 'greatest work' that God has done for us is made effective in our lives as we receive it by faith! Without faith, the Bible says, it is impossible to please God. Faith, however, is not blind belief. It is trusting in God who has revealed himself both in the complexity of the cosmos and by entering the cosmos and sharing human history. Faith is to believe what God has said he has done for us. To receive his work into our lives by saying, "Thank you..." It is the most profound thing that a human being can do. It is not to understand all of the humanistic '**how**' questions as to **how** we got here. It is something far more profound. It is to turn away from self-living (repent) and to turn towards God. It is receiving the person (Jesus Christ) and his work that he has done on our behalf; an invitation for him to enter your life by the presence of God the Holy Spirit. This is all done by faith. This greatest work will connect you back with the God who is behind life, behind the universe. Through his creation and through Jesus he has made himself known.

A Prayer of Faith

"Heavenly Father, I thank you for sending your Son, Jesus Christ, into the world to show us who you are. I thank you that you have made your peace with me by Jesus' death – whereby his blood being shed on a cross has paid the price for all of my mistakes including the breaking of God's moral law. By faith I accept your work on my behalf. I turn to you and yield my life to you. I invite Christ into my life. Forgive me for all that is past and give to me the new life that you promise by the indwelling presence of your Holy Spirit. Amen."

- -

Thank you for reading this book, I hope it has enabled you to think clearly on a difficult subject. Keep an eye out for other books being written in this, 'Apologetics not Apologies' series which will *hopefully* be published in late 2019-2020.

Please remember to leave a review of his book if the retailer from whom you purchased it has an online facility to do so.

- -

Appendix A

- -
World View & the Scientific Method
- -

The World View Question
For example, an atheist will have asked at least two basic questions,

1) How did everything get here via an auto-organised route?
2) In the light of how everything got here, who am I?

Notice it is the assumption of question 1 that we are auto-organised into existence, not put here by deity. It is the questions that drive us. These questions set the scene for living, for our thinking and our reasoning, for our looking and for our conclusions after looking. They drive the way we think and provide the backdrop and purpose for what we are looking for. They frame life and what it is to be alive!

In my second book in this series I will outline five foundational questions that everyone unwittingly asks and answers in order to make sense of life. These answers highly influence us when we choose to engage in the scientific process on the origins of the universe. It is the pre-eminence of religion that tells us which questions to ask, what to look for, and so it defines for us (dictates to us) how we go about the subject and how to make conclusions that support the religious world view that we carry. Let me explain.

Examining the Questions

Here again are the two questions that an atheist will ask but this time with the answers attached to them.

1) How did everything get here?
    a. Well, it all got here because the whole cosmos is an unguided accident, a 'Big Bang'.
2) In the light of how everything got here, who am I?
    a. I am a creature that has just appeared by a random process.
    b. I was not planned, purposed, desired or designed...
    c. I can be whatever I want to be, life is open ended.

Notice that the first question that the atheist will ask is based on a single word and that is the word 'how'. How did everything get here? It is a question that is solely focussed on the examination of processes. This is because,

Processes are the only reason why I am here, nothing more and nothing less.

The religious world view of secular spirituality is that physical matter, the cosmos, is pre-eminent. A big 'BANG' and space, time, matter, energy were all suddenly here in an instant. We have a process at the beginning (a Big Bang) we have processes that follow (a calibration of the universe and an evolutionary set of events) and we have processes that we can now observe (generational life, living in the cosmos) which the humanist will watch and measure for the sole reason of verifying the religious world view that,

- the cosmos just appeared – an accident
- physical matter is pre-eminent
- we all come from the cosmos
- we're all here by accident

This mental pre-set choice that says,

"I am just the product of a process..."

...dictates to us that the word 'how' has to be used **as the starting point** for the first question. We ask 'how' because the only focus of the questioning is to find and understand a process of naturalistic evolutionary development from A to B to C to D. The only thing the atheist is interested in is gaining an understanding of this process because s/he only has this idea as a framework for thinking in his/her mind. This sets the scene for all other questions and routes of enquiry to follow. Question 2, 'Who am I?' is only asked in the light of question 1. Question 1 assumes that a process is responsible for me being here, not a person who is the creator of all things. The answer to question 2 'Who am I?' therefore is already carrying a religious bias – the cosmos being pre-eminent, not a divine being. The result of atheistic science, therefore, is a religious life lived from the foundational assumption that I too, like the cosmos, was not designed, desired, planned or purposed and I can live this life as if it were my own because there is 'nothing to look back to' from my origins that might call me to account. The cosmos is cold and disinterested in my behaviour, so I can do what I want because science tells me I'm just the result of a process. Why am I just the result of a process? Simply because the question asked by the scientists is, "What is the process by which we got here?"

So once you are convinced that you are here by random chance then your mind is set on what you're looking for when you continually go back to question 1 to find out more information about your origins. The whole drive of your investigation will be to simply find more clarity on the assertion that you are just an accident. All the science done by you will reinforce this 'I'm an accident' religious world view. So when you use the so called 'neutral scientific method' to find out more about the origins of the universe, the framework of 'I am an accident' will form the basis, the boundaries and the limitations of your thinking and reasoning. When you look at the evidence you will say,

"Because I am an accident of chance, an accident of the cosmos, and because I am a random creature that has just appeared here that has gained consciousness, which has arisen somehow without any divine cause behind it, let me then look at all the evidence contained in the mechanisms of the universe (and I will pre-label those mechanisms as random and unplanned accidents without the divine behind them) and I will observe them and interpret their activity in the cosmos in such a way as to justify my religious world view that we are all here by an accident of chance and we all got here by a random process."

So, when an atheist looks into these things his/her question will always be,

> *"By what process did we get here?"*

and

> *"By what random process did we achieve our current status?"*

The question will never be,

> *"If I can't find a sensible process to justify our existence, then was the cosmos multi-assembled by the hand of the divine and can we see evidence for a designer rather than an explosion?"*

An atheist will, therefore, only interpret the evidence before us as being part of a non-God natural process. This pre-labelling of the mechanisms as non-God and naturalistic will also give a religious language to use to describe and interpret what we're all looking at. This language will be consistent in accordance with the scientist's religious world view. The religious world view, therefore, forms the bias to help you interpret what you're looking at and provides a religious vocabulary, to express it. That non-theistic vocabulary will fence an atheist in. It will put limitations on his/her thinking and reasoning and s/he will unwittingly find themselves confined by it. From that confined space, you will get and express your answers to the questions that caused you to engage in the scientific process.

An atheist, therefore, will not use the word 'creation' when talking about the cosmos, that is in giving the cosmos a single name that sums it up in terms of having a creator. An atheist will not use the phrase, "When we look at all of creation then..." as this language does not point back to the religious world view that all life is an accident. To use the word 'creation' like this is the language of a theist, not that of an atheist. An atheist will use the word 'nature' when talking about the natural world as if 'nature' has a personality and a mind of her own. "Nature has done this," or "Nature has done that." According to this way of expressing things, anything in the cosmos can have a personality, except a divine being.

A theist (someone who says there is a God) will have asked at least three questions before they investigate – with some sub-questions contained within them.

1. Who made everything?
    a. Who is this God who made everything?
    b. What is this God's name?
    c. What has this God said?
    d. What is this God's character?
    e. etc.
2. How did this God create everything?
    a. Can we find the mechanisms that God used?
    b. Did God start something and then leave a 'knock on effect' for things to come into being or is life so intricate that everything that fits together has to be put together by him?
3. Who am I in the light of this amazing God and this amazing creation?

Notice the focus of the first question is 'who' and not 'how'. You are therefore not someone who finds their identity and true purpose by looking at a random 'process' but you are a person who finds their identity and true purpose by relating to another person who is greater than you and who made you. This religious agenda completely changes your outlook and totally changes the driving question that causes you to engage in the scientific method. It also changes how you look at the evidence and what you are looking for in that evidence.

The reason for looking into the cosmos is not only to find out 'how God did it' but a theist will also look for...

...the 'moment of creation', which is where the fingerprint of God is left on the cosmos itself.

This fingerprint is expressed in such phrases as,

"All of these different components of life have to come together at the same time or it doesn't work, as they have irreducible complexity."

There is no step-by-step process available here for the assembly of this living organism. The quick multi-assembly of this organism is the only logical, sensible and reasonable conclusion to come to as we are simply 'seeing the results of the divine in action' when we pose the question 'What happened in the past to cause this 'thing' to come into being?' We are simply looking at a time when God was actively engaged in his speedy creative activity; when God touched and moulded the cosmos in moments of time and things changed from lifeless forms into life with information imprinted onto the cosmos at the centre of the lifeform to sustain it.

Creationists will go as far as they can to understand how the divine created things but they will also be happy to say, "You know, we may well be able to discover how God did lots of things, but if we can't discover them all (because God's maths and science are way beyond ours) or we can't find out about the moment when the divine touched the cosmos to create something, then that doesn't matter. Valid living, and therefore valid science, is in knowing God first and foremost, not in discovering 'how' he did things. We love finding out 'how' he did it, but if that full and final knowledge is out of our reach, then we're content to say, "God himself knows how he did it." We'll keep looking until we one day see God face to face, but if this is as far as we can go in this current world history, then so be it. Knowing him is enough." This is full and valid living and valid science to the theist.

The religious world view of secular spirituality will seek to say that the above scientific conclusions are pseudo-science. Secularists say that the only true science that is done is when something is measureable and repeatable. If you cannot test God 'doing his thing' then saying 'God did it' is not classed as true science. This rejection of 'God created this irreducible complex organism' as true science is only based, however, on the secularist's bias, their religious world view that insists that everything is knowable because there was no God there to do it because we are just here by a haphazard set of processes. Humanism says that we are the centre of the universe...

...because we are the only known conscious minds in the universe, unless other minds have arisen from the cosmos in the same way as our minds have.

Since humanity is the centre of everything, valid living is defined by us testing everything ourselves and our definition of valid science directly follows on from our definition of valid living. If we can't get our hands on it and experiment with it, manipulate it, control it, measure it, weigh it, stretch it, put it in acid, etc. then we're not living true. A humanist will say that ALL KNOWLEDGE is available because life is only made up of the physical world. There is no super intelligence behind the universe and therefore valid living is only when we put all things underneath the feet of humanity by understanding the processes that surround us. We can find out what brought things into being, what formed their current state and why they behave as they do.

Humanists will attack theistic science because it looks for God behind things. It says, "It's not valid science to say, 'God did it' or 'this is how God did it' or to say, 'this multi-complex design has to come together all at the same time to work and so we're looking here at the handiwork of God' and 'this complexity shows us where God touched the cosmos' because you can't test that final conclusion to be true because you can't get a hold of God and force him to do it again in front of you so you can observe him for yourself. You can't get your hands on God and ask him to explain himself, that is to make him explain or demonstrate **how** he did it!"

Humanism insists that it took a long time for everything to auto-organise itself into its current existence because humanism looks at the universe as it is now and then translates it backwards towards a beginning. But the theist will argue that the universe, as it is now, is not how it was whilst God was actively creating it. God is not creating anything right now. His activity within the universe to create cannot be seen or measured.

So the huge mistake that humanists make is to say,

1. "What movements do we see in the universe **right now**?"
2. "How can we trace **those current movements** backwards in order for us to understand how this universe self-constructed itself?"

Theists will say to humanists that these questions that lead to the formation of their scientific theories are completely wrong as those questions start off on the wrong foot. The wrong question causes you to look for the wrong answer. God's creative activity cannot be seen in the cosmos today because he's not doing it right now. This is why we cannot see any new information being created in the universe, only data expression change!

So Humanistic science is just as religious as the science performed by a theist. This is because the religious questions that are used to drive its enquiry come from its religious world view. As humanism is a God-replacement religion, it will actively look for a reason for any process that takes place in the cosmos in the context of only being a random accident and 'without God'. It seeks to reinterpret the evidence within that light. Gravity is here not because the divine has put it here so that we could all survive but because it came about by a random process. Yes, it is very useful and essential for life, but it is still here by an accident of the cosmos. How gravity got here by a random process therefore, is always the question, never who created gravity for the purpose of sustaining life. Humanism religiously does not want science to point towards God. It will never ask the question, "How does that which I can see before me point towards a creator?" That line of enquiry is religiously 'shut down' and prevented from happening as it is religiously labelled as 'non-scientific'. The religious questions of the secular world view, those things that tell what 'true living is', will tell us that true living, true science, is only about processes because it is the processes of the physical world that are pre-eminent in the universe, not deity. That, in a nutshell...

...is pure religion!

So the secularist will come up with all kinds of theories from within the human imagination in order to come to conclusions that don't have God in them. As I've said, it's part of being a member of the...

'Anything but God Society.'

So strong is this conviction that you'll hear all kinds of 'strong conclusions' in the language of the humanist about the past and these things will be spoken of as if they were almost fact, or assumed as fact in the way the person talks. This again clouds the issue and prevents us from having a proper conversation on the subject. Humanism does not want God in the picture, and this religious conviction, therefore, brings a huge bias to the table when scientific discussion is undertaken and the scientific process referred to as evidence for their interpretations of the results. So when you are watching a great nature programme put out by the BBC and the narrator begins to talk about how something 'evolved' or that we are, as Brian Cox once said, "The cosmos made conscious," then what you are looking at and listening to is a humanistic fundamentalist rhetoric that reveals a religious agenda. That agenda is there to seek to highlight, prove and reinforce the religious world view of us all being here without the aid of deity.

There will be some movement amongst this population of film-makers who may say, "I honestly don't know if there is a God or not and I'm setting out to make films about nature, not to overtly promote humanism" but even that agnostic honesty and open statement of 'not-knowing' if God exists will provide a context for the film and it will still have a religious message. All messages on our origins are religiously driven, whether presented in the world of science, the world of the arts or the humanities. Religion drives life and it drives the questions we ask to help us understand life. In response to those questions we then just choose which discipline to pick up and use; science, art, maths, literature etc. to present those pre-set religious convictions to our audiences.

- - - - - - - - - - - - - - - - -

Appendix B

Criticisms of the RNA World Hypothesis

RNA is said to 'Perform Various Tasks'

Remember that the role of the new RNA platform is simply that of a messenger that passes on a **temporary code** to a factory and it is the Ribosome factory that does the reading and creating. A single RNA strand is powerless and useless to 'do' anything. Of itself and by itself the RNA Messenger is just useless data on a platform. It has **no mechanism** to process its own bases. The RNA platform is passed through the Ribosome factory and it is the Ribosome factory that assembles the amino acids and so creates a protein. The RNA platform does nothing, except allow itself to be read by the Ribosome factory. So when the film says that the RNA string, "performs various functions so that the cell is kept alive," well that statement is complete fantasy. An RNA platform cannot do anything at all but just be itself. It has no mechanism to do any work in the cell and perform any actions of its own. That part of the film is a blatant abuse of scientific knowledge, a twist on reality by saying something that is not true. The RNA Messenger platform has limited functions right now as we observe its activity in the cell. Why would it, in the past, have 'super abilities' that it now does not currently have? Well, the answer is simple. Evolutionists want it to have super abilities because they are **imagining a process** by which we are all here because they are imagining a world put here without deity. So the RNA strand became temporarily 'super human' in the past – doing all kinds of things it cannot do now in order to mentally justify not interpreting the irreducible complexity we see in the cell right now as the fingerprints of the divine.

The film then chooses to talk about a 'self-replicating' RNA strand. So, would you please tell me how this single RNA 'strand' could develop the ability to **self-replicate**? It is a nonsense statement without any scientific foundation. Of itself and by itself it is just a platform with bases on it, just some dead data floating in the water.

*The RNA strand again has **no mechanism** or **energy** to **perform** any kind of **self-replicating**.*

DNA is replicated by a protein, RNA polymerase, unzipping it. The protein that unzips the DNA code knows how to interact with the DNA code in order to create a new RNA code. It has been created and fashioned for purpose. It is a purpose built machine to do that very job. There is nothing purpose built about a single RNA strand that could cause it to 'replicate itself' in any way, shape of form, it is simply one tool amongst many that has a limited job to do as part of an information replication process that uses information to create a microbiological machine, a protein. Again, of itself and by itself it can do nothing but float around in the pool of liquid; that primordial soup that the evolutionist imagines was conveniently once there to facilitate some miraculous starting of life by a haphazard and unguided process.

The next thing that the film states is that there are suddenly lots of them. Lots of RNA strands, all 'swimming together' and moving around. All of them now have sensible code and ever developing code. The code is getting better and better over time because it is 'evolving'. There's that word again, 'evolving'. Evolutionists use it whenever they need to, so that they don't have to describe the **mechanism** or the **process** by which they say that something changed. It 'evolved' or it 'mutated' they say, and they don't say **how** or **in what way**. A whole host of questions appear that have not been answered. You could ask,

- why does the code develop?
- why does it continue to develop?
- how does the code develop?
  - it has no way of processing itself, copying itself
  - it has no way a selecting resources from its environment
  - so what is the mechanism by which new blocks of code are added that mean something sensible, along with the rest of the code, for its survival?
- how is it that sensible and precision written code developed on the RNA strand and not just gobbledegook?

433

- what makes randomly added data onto the end of a line of data sensible and meaningful code?
- code is not data, so what causes random data to become sensible code?
- code has to be processed so,
    - how does the RNA strand 'read itself' – because without reading itself then the code is not processed?
    - if the code is not processed it has no purpose, code exists to be processed because code is **deliberately written** *with intent* to do/achieve something
    - who taught an RNA strand to deliberately write something with intent for work to be achieved?

The answer to these questions by evolutionists is to look at the current 'data change' that is happening in the DNA code today and to use that as a basis for **reimagining it** as an example of code writing. This again is a misinterpretation of the facts. Data change is not new code, it is simply a variant within established code. But data change does not enable new limbs to form – that requires new sensible, complex code written with intent and purpose that takes into account biological engineering so that those new body parts can function properly in the real world. That type and level of code writing has never, ever been observed in the natural world. Data change is not new information, just data expression change within the context of current, complex code. So all the evolutionist is doing is looking at current activity and reimagining that activity so that it facilitates something magnificent in the past, new code writing, which the RNA Messenger strand cannot do.

Simple data change is labelled 'new information' by the evolutionist and then that incorrect labelling of the data change activity, which we continually see before our eyes, is used as a pointer to justify an reimagining of the past whereby that same data change process becomes a complex code writing process.

It is a classic case of 'moving the goalposts to suit yourself'. Add billions of years along with these multiple tiny changes, which are not mapped out in detail because the tiny changes don't work whilst the code is 'under development' and, by adding 'time' into the equation, everything gets fixed. Time will fix it and make it all correct. You can't imagine billions of years (in fact you can't imagine millions of years, it is beyond our comprehension) so somehow, in the midst of the mysterious and unimaginable passage of huge time, that which is impossible somehow becomes possible. So when evolutionists talk about billions of years in order for something to happen, something that is not possible, this is what they are doing. They are,

...clothing the impossible with the unimaginable.

When you clothe the **impossible** (RNA strands developing their own sensible code without any mechanism or intelligence driving that code development) with the **unimaginable** (millions of years), then anything in your imagination can be believed. The 'cloud of millions of years' covers over the RNA code and somehow, in the mystery that's there, when the cloud eventually moves, there is RNA turned into DNA! By faith we believe that it came into being because somehow it can happen when we let enough time pass by. There is no mechanism for the change, nothing to keep the RNA strand from falling apart, dissolving or rotting away, no 'food' to give the RNA strand energy from which to duplicate itself etc. So on the back of those statements, here's another set of questions.

1. What is the RNA strand's food/energy source?
2. How did the RNA strand 'feed itself' to give itself the energy to reproduce itself?
3. What is its mouth through which food/energy would enter the strand?
4. How was that food/energy broken down so that it could feed itself?
5. If it were chemical reactions (not food) that supplied the energy for reproduction and data growth then what started those chemical reactions off?
6. What controlled those chemical reactions so that they were useful in the RNA strand's growth and development?
7. How were those chemical reactions purposed in order to
   - generate new sensible code?
   - or to aid in a reproductive process?

Once you look at all of this you begin to see what a fantasy land the evolutionists are living in.

> **NOTE:** The **biggest problem** is, however, that bad code or inaccurate *code does not work*. Any computer programmer knows that. So to even talk about 'evolving code' is ridiculous.

In the next part of the film these RNA strands are suddenly given a new name. They are now called 'proto-lifeforms' and they now 'blossom' – which is the same sort of phrase that you would use for something that is alive, plant life, mature plant life that is. The word blossom has the idea of flourishing. Plants that flourish in the natural world, however, do so because they are purposefully programmed to flourish within certain conditions. They have mature and excellent precision written code that defines for the plant how it should use the environment to survive. The programming within the plant shows knowledge of the natural world outside of the plant. That programming gives them the ability to receive from their environment. They have the sun to warm and power them, they also have plenty of water and good soil nutrients. All of these are used by the plant in a most sophisticated way – where their inner programming is set to capture, change and use these raw materials to nourish and grow. For the film makers to add the word 'blossom' to what is now called 'proto-life' is completely unscientific. There is no path for development, no way of 'feeding itself' no mechanism for it to read itself and become something greater than itself. Suddenly we're in the midst of life that is now 'blossoming' because **millions of years** have passed by and the RNA strand is still safe and sound, floating around, perhaps a little bored with its slow development or its continual lack of self-awareness, but it's still there, somehow alive and growing and feeding itself. Most things erode away with age, even rocks do that, but somehow this RNA strand is made of such strong stuff that it's still there after millions of years...

Next we have the idea that these RNA strands can make proteins. We're told that these proteins are 'strong' proteins that can do complex biological processes. It's amazing how this rhetoric flows.

436

Suddenly, out of nowhere, we have the existence of proteins. Somehow this RNA strand has been able to read itself, grab a hold of amino acids from its environment, process them without the aid of a Ribosome factory, and make proteins. Not just any proteins by the way, but **strong ones** able to perform '**complex**' biological **processes**. Can you also tell me please the answers to the following?

- what enabled the RNA strand to create a protein?
- how did it read itself?
- how did it grab hold of amino acids from its environment to create proteins when it **currently** does not have that ability?
  - did it develop hands to do this?
  - if so, how did it develop those hands?
  - why did it lose those 'hands' later on so that they are not there today?
- why did it begin to assemble amino acids in the first place?
- what powered the RNA strand so that it created movement to process itself?
- how did it get the coding correct so that a correct amino acid was formed?
- why would the amino acid be considered as 'correct' since there is no cell for it to work in and no specific job for it to do?
- what was the purposes of the first protein?
- what makes a protein strong as opposed to a weak one?
- have you ever seen a weak protein?
- who taught the protein to do processes?
- who taught the protein to do multiple processes?
- how did the protein learn to do complex processes?
- what are these 'complex' biological processes?
  - what are they there for and in which context are they performed?
  - which part of the environment are they for?
- has the cell begun to develop itself?
- which bits came first and why were they retained so that they had immediate use when they were part formed?
- how were those parts of the cell renewed once they wore out with age?

- has the cell now begun to develop specialist organelles, if so then how?
    - what purpose did those organelles initially have before all of the processes within the cell were developed?
    - what purpose did those organelles have when they were half-developed and not in their final form?
- how has the RNA strand begun to 'understand its own environment' so that it knows to create a protein in order to help this part of the cell or that part of the cell function?
    - are you telling me that the RNA strand has developed consciousness?
    - does it know what to do as far as 'complex' biological processes are concerned and where that process needs applying in the cell?
    - who taught it that these things needed doing or how did it 'see' that these processes needed doing?
- how are these RNA strands thinking for themselves and reacting to what is called competition?
    - are RNA strands competitive?
    - is it part of their nature to be competitive and so they think they have to develop in some way to compete and survive?
    - since when did they get 'knowledge' of other RNA strands that are in their same location and so compete for food/space/identity etc.?

The next thing that the video tells us is that RNA becomes DNA and that it is now 'stable' – which means that it wasn't stable beforehand but somehow managed to work and survive over millions of years in a hostile environment where the natural forces within nature remove information. Then we're told that, once the DNA is in place, life is able to be more complex with trillions of more 'little steps' and what it now calls 'happy accidents'. This phrase, 'happy accidents' is just another way of saying punctuated evolution, where there are said to be technological jumps in the technology of the creature, i.e. we suddenly get the assembly of multi-interdependent components that come together and work together all at the same time. It is impossible to make them happen via a step-by-step process so, rather than say

438

that a process of development is impossible and therefore deny evolution (and let God into science) we make an excuse and call it a 'happy accident'. This highly religious statement is made because the religious world view of the evolutionist is that physical matter is pre-eminent and that the spiritual world has no substance of its own. So rather than saying, "All of these things have to come together at the same time for it to work and we are seeing the handiwork of a creator," instead they insist that we're NOT seeing where God touched the cosmos and altered it for life to exist; the evolutionist will say that the components are assembled by a set of 'happy accidents' – because we are not looking for God, we're looking for **a process only** by which to interpret that which we see in front of our noses. Again the trillions of tiny changes and the components of the 'happy accidents' are not identified or defined (because they don't work and are not possible to achieve as a viable way forward to account for the assembly of the biomolecular machines) and so the rhetoric does not deal with that part of science at all, that is with the **how, what** and **why** it all worked and came together. It clothes the false reality with a rhetoric called a set of 'happy accidents' and, because all it happed over millions/billions of years, we can somehow believe it!

- - - - - - - - - - - - - - - - -

Appendix C

- -
Nature of Information – Examples 4 & 5
- -

Example 4 – Jelly
I have three jelly moulds.

- mould number 1 has **some text** etched into it
- mould number 2 has **more text** etched into it
- mould number 3 has **no text** etched into it

I could **use energy** to heat some jelly so that it becomes a liquid and then pour that liquid into mould 1 with text etched in it. I have **added** information because when the jelly leaves the mould I can then see the text. I could then use **more energy**, reheat the same jelly, so that it became a liquid again and pour it into mould 2; this has more text etched into the mould's surface. Once the jelly had set and was taken out of the mould 2, I could see **even more information** in the jelly. I could then use more energy to heat up the jelly for a third time and pour it into mould 3, a mould with no text engraved into it. I could then empty the jelly out of mould 3 and all of the text will have disappeared, a **loss** of information. Yet the mass of the jelly has not changed. As the experiment progressed I will have used up more and more **accumulated energy** as the jelly is repeatedly turned into a liquid through a heating process. By the time I have completed three 'heatings' of jelly, and taken note of the amount of information that the jelly had imprinted upon it after each stage, I would see that there is no relationship between mass, energy and the differing amounts of information expressed in the jelly. Here's the same information put into a mathematical format.

- 1ˢᵗ heating of jelly + mould 1 = **some** text
- 2ⁿᵈ heating of jelly + mould 2 = **more** text
- 3ʳᵈ heating of jelly + mould 3 = **no** text

So we have the following as each jelly comes out of its mould,

- a little energy and information added
- more energy and more information added
- even more energy and a total loss of information

Each time I use more energy to reshape the jelly, the amount of information changes – but it is not proportionate to the energy used. A steady increase in energy throughout the experiment ends up with no information at all, despite a steady increase in information for the majority of the times that the jelly was left to set and then removed from its mould.

So we see a **continual increase** in energy used but a **fluctuation** in information.

Throughout the experiment, however, the mass remains the same.

The results would completely change, however, if I chose to repeat the experiment and chose to use the jelly moulds in a different order.

At each stage in the process the same amount of energy is used and at the end the total energy used would also be the same, but a different amount of information is displayed. It is **my mind** that creates the information by choosing which mould to use. There is no direct relationship, therefore, between energy and information. The mass of the jelly, as always, remains the same throughout the experiment. It is the same mass at the beginning as it is at the end – unless of course you're someone like me who enjoys eating jelly, then perhaps the mass will change, but not as a direct result of the experiment!

Example 5 – Sticks

If I were to take a series of large sticks and bind them together I can form the words, "Hello World". The **wood itself** does not contain the information. It is the shape that they make **together** that conveys meaning. As soon as the shape falls apart, the information is lost. There is still the same mass, but no imprinted pattern. I could make the words out of large sticks, using lots of energy, or I could use small twigs, using little energy. The same amount of information, however, would still be there. There is, therefore, no relationship between mass, energy and information. It is how the mind that is constructing the information chooses to imprint it that matters.

What is important in this last illustration, however, is that the wood itself becomes the symbol of the information, like the jelly. As the twigs are rested on each other they form a letter and lettering pattern." Disturb the pattern of wood, however, and the information goes. The assembly of the sticks is that which contains the meaning, not the sticks themselves.

NOTE: This is where we're getting a little closer to the bases in DNA and the Messenger RNA platform. The bases there are symbols of information. Pick off the bases and float them around the cell and they lose their meaning. With them aligned together, sitting side by side, they become a code that can be read. The bases themselves are **not the information** but it is their order together, as symbols read in the light of a specific order, which makes them information, just like data has a specific order.

- - - - - - - - - - - - - - - -

Appendix D

Further Reading

Can Science Explain Everything? – *John Lennox*
Cold-Case Christianity – *J. Warner Wallace*
Darwin's Black Box – *Michael Behe*
Does God Believe in Atheists – John Blanchard
Signature in the Cell – *Stephen C. Meyer*
The Natural Sciences Know Nothing of Evolution –
A.E. Wilder-Smith

Further Research

Answers in Genesis – https://answersingenesis.org
Cold Case Christianity – https://coldcasechristianity.com
Discovery Institute – www.discovery.org
Stephen Meyer – www.stephencmeyer.org
The God Domain – www.thegoddomain.com

Author Tim Waters Web Links

Author website – www.authortimwaters.co.uk
Apologetics website – www.apologeticsnotapologies.com
Tim Waters Books – www.timwatersbooks.com

Printed in Poland
by Amazon Fulfillment
Poland Sp. z o.o., Wrocław

555007R00270